Matriarch of Conspiracy

Matriarch of Conspiracy

Ruth von Kleist
1867-1945
The Second Edition

JANE PEJSA

KENWOOD PUBLISHING
Minneapolis

Library of Congress Catalog Card Number 90-92033
International Standard Book Number 0-9612776-9-6

Designed by Susan Bishop
Edited and Composed by Barbara Field
Printed by Geehan Graphics, Inc.

Kenwood Publishing
2120 Kenwood Parkway
Minneapolis, Minnesota 55405-2326
Phone: (612) 374-3337
Fax: (612) 374-5383

Cataloging-in-Publication Data
Pejsa, Jane, 1929–
    Matriarch of Conspiracy; Ruth v. Kleist, 1867–1945.
    Includes bibliography, index.
    1. Kleist-Retzow, Ruth von, 1867–1945. 2. Hitler, Adolf,
1889–1945—Assassination attempt, 1944 (July 20). 3. Anti-Nazi
movement—Germany—History. I. Title.
DD256.3 .P359   1991   943.085 .P359   LC90-92033

*This book is dedicated
to men and women in every age and place
who have acted to uphold decency and honor
amid indecency and dishonor,
and especially to those who, in so doing, have perished.*

CONTENTS

CONTENTS

IV. The Good Soldier
1912-1930

V. Grandmother Ruth
1931-1938

VI. The Pastor's Friend
1939-1943

VII. The Last Matriarch
1944-1945

CONTENTS

ILLUSTRATIONS

ILLUSTRATIONS

FOREWORD

By Klemens von Klemperer
Professor Emeritus, Smith College

Professor Klemperer is the recognized authority on the German anti-Nazi conspiracy and author of several books pertaining to the subject, including *German Resistance Against Hitler,* Oxford University Press.

The German sociologist Max Weber wrote that it is "dangerous" for an "economically sinking class" to hold political power in its hands.

Jane Pejsa's book projects the story of Ruth von Kleist, a deeply religious and conservative matriarch, against the background of her class, the Prussian Junkers, an essentially precapitalist and preindustrial squirarchy. The main pillars of Imperial Germany, they showed, even after the emergence of capitalism and German industrialization, an astonishing capacity for survival. Then came the revolution of November 1918, after which they maintained much of their hold on society without, as a whole, lending their support to the new Republic. And then came the Nazi "revolution" of January 1933, which brought the country promises of "people's community" *(Volksgemeinschaft)* and national glory and found the Junker class divided in its counsels, some duped by the Nazi temptations, others firmly opposed to the brown "plebeian" mob.

From the very beginning, Ruth von Kleist never wavered in her rejection of the so-called Third Reich. While an ingrained Prusso-German patriot, she saw through the basically anti-Christian thrust of the Nazis, and she clearly set the tone among the large circle of her family and friends. She herself became a resolute patron of the Confessing Church, which within German Protestantism was threatened by the incursion of the Nazis into the Church affairs. The younger members of her family, together with two young clergymen whom she had befriended, Dietrich Bonhoeffer and Eberhard Bethge, became deeply involved in the Resistance against National Socialism which culminated in the abortive plot against Adolf Hitler of 20 July 1944.

To call this group prodemocratic, as one says these days, would be mistaken. Most of them were distinctly conservative. But they had, all of them, an unerring sense of what was right and wrong. In extremis they, whose class by objective standards seemed on its way out, rose above self-interest and marshalled their courage to stand up against manifest evil to the point of martyrdom.

Mrs. Pejsa's book, based largely on family papers and personal interviews, has masterfully chronicled a late chapter of Junker history and has, with considerable empathy and understanding, recorded the everyday existence of a Junker clan, along with the values . She has set a monument to an extraordinary matron of an extraordinary class in an extraordinary time.

PREFACE TO THE
SECOND EDITION

Seven years have passed since *Matriarch of Conspiracy* was first published. In the meantime, the tale has found a receptive audience on both sides of the Atlantic and most recently also in Japan. The original Kenwood Publishing edition is sold out and the Pilgrim Press soft-cover edition is out of print.

Yet the public's interest in twentieth-century history, especially World War II, seems ever to increase, even as we prepare to enter the next millennium. The martyrdom of Dietrich Bonhoeffer continues to engage the minds of thoughtful men and women across the globe. The names of other Germans out of that handful who conspired to bring down the Nazis are still present but fading. The monstrosity of the Holocaust remains an ever-present challenge to all who wrestle with issues of human dignity in an increasingly diverse society. Oddly enough, the lives of Ruth von Kleist, her family, and her circle find their historical significance precisely in this juxtaposition of Good and Evil.

Thus, after careful consideration, we made the decision to publish in soft cover this second edition of *Matriarch of Conspiracy*. The decision gave us the opportunity to add historical details missing in the first edition and to update the Epilogue. This second edition documents the immense changes that have taken place on the ancient Kleist lands since the fall of Communism in Poland. May the reader be inspired to visit these lands, a bastion of Dietrich Bonhoeffer's decade-long fight against the Nazis and the final resting place of his friend Ruth von Kleist.

Minneapolis   Jane Pejsa

ACKNOWLEDGMENTS

Without a generous grant from the Bush Foundation of St. Paul, I could not have undertaken, let alone completed, the extensive research and writing that culminated in this tale out of a time long past. I also am indebted to Margot Siegel of Minneapolis and Phebe Hanson of St. Paul, each of whom wrote appraisals of my work that helped motivate the Bush Foundation to award me the grant.

This account of Ruth von Kleist's life and family is constructed mainly out of anecdotes gleaned from interviews with those who survived and from the scattered papers of those who are gone. For this material I am indebted to nine of Ruth's grandchildren, namely: Konstantin von Kleist-Retzow, Countess Ruth de Pourtales (née Kleist-Retzow), Heinrich von Kleist-Retzow, the late Ruth Roberta Ripke-Heckscher (née Stahlberg), the late Alexander Stahlberg, Luitgarde von Schlabrendorff (née Bismarck), Spes Pompe (née Bismarck), Ruth Alice von Bismarck (née Wedemeyer), and Hans von Wedemeyer.

Only time and distance prevented me from meeting with Ruth von Kleist's other grandchildren. They no doubt would have been just as helpful.

I also feel a deep sense of gratitude to Count Friedrich Carl von Zedlitz and Trützschler, the godson and only surviving nephew of Ruth von Kleist.

I gratefully acknowledge the contributions of several other people whose lives intersected the life of Ruth von Kleist, specifically: Eberhard Bethge and Renate Bethge (née Schleicher) of Wachtberg-Villiprott, Germany; Reinhild von Kleist-Schmenzin Hausherr of Bern, Switzerland, daughter of Ruth's martyred nephew Ewald; Werner and Dita Koch of Emlichheim, Germany; and Wolf Dieter Zimmermann of Berlin.

It was my privilege to be acquainted with two premier historians specializing in nineteenth- and twentieth-century German history, each of whom was kind enough to spend time with me: the late Professor Harold C. Deutsch of the University of Minnesota and Professor Otto Pflanze of the University of Indiana. I hasten to add that neither of these eminent professors was in any way responsible for what I have written in the nature of historical detail or interpretation.

My geographical perspective was molded by personal visits to the places that Ruth von Kleist once called home—Klein Krössin, Kieckow and Grossenborau, all of which are now in Poland. I am deeply grateful to our relative, Franciszek Polcyn of Oborniki, Poland, who guided us through these lovely lands.

A number of letters are described or quoted in the course of this story. Many of these were obtained from the Bundesarchiv of the Federal Republic of Germany. I acknowledge with appreciation the important contribution of Edith Mueller of Minneapolis, who carefully transcribed these and other letters from the German script to the Latin script, enabling me to read all of this source material in the original German.

The bulk of the published source materials used in my research and cited in the bibliography are from the excellent Wilson Library collection at the University of Minnesota. In addition both the Minneapolis Public Library and the Luther Seminary Library in St. Paul yielded rare and useful materials.

I further acknowledge with great appreciation the editing contributions of Barbara Field of Minneapolis, who applied her finely hewn skills to this entire manuscript, paragraph by paragraph.

Finally, I am pleased to acknowledge that without the constant support of my husband Arthur Pejsa I would never have completed this formidable undertaking. It was also he who first critiqued and edited each of the seven chapters that tell the story of this Prussian matriarch.

My thanks to all of those named above and to Professor Klemens von Klemperer, who has graciously contributed the Foreword to this second edition.

Matriarch of Conspiracy

PROLOGUE

In the year 1155, Friedrich Barbarossa of Hohenstaufen was crowned king of the Germans in the ancient city of Aachen. Three years later in Rome, this king was crowned kaiser—Holy Roman Emperor. In earlier centuries the Holy Roman Empire had covered most of Europe, but in Barbarossa's time the exalted title held little value. It was acknowledged mainly by the handful of German princes and dukes who made up his Hohenstaufen kingdom.

Still, Barbarossa's broad vision and his boundless physical energy breathed such life into the German consciousness that his name became legend. He strengthened the bonds among the quarreling German principalities. He organized military expeditions into Polish and Bohemian lands and into places as far away as Asia Minor. He even rearranged the city-states on the Italian peninsula to suit his own purposes. He made peace and war with two successive popes at Rome, and in so doing, he was excommunicated not once, but twice.

Few of these adventures resulted in permanent conquest and some of them ended in disaster. On one campaign in Italy, for instance, Barbarossa lost his entire army to the plague. Yet afterward he was remembered only for his victories.

Over the centuries, especially in times when the fortunes of the German people waned, the legend of Friedrich Barbarossa persisted. He was said to dwell in a cavern under the Thuringian mountains, preparing to rise again one day and lead the German people to greatness.

During his lifetime, Barbarossa had many loyal followers—vassals, knights and common soldiers who fought his battles and sometimes died under his banner. The most loyal of them all was said to have been the vassal Zedlitz, who demonstrated his fidelity to Barbarossa during the king's Polish campaign. At the height of battle, when Barbarossa's royal cape was impaled on an

1

enemy spike, Zedlitz rode to the king's side and slashed the garment with his sword, saving Barbarossa's life. Centuries later the deed was commemorated in a German epic poem that concludes with the lines:

> When men still speak of Brave and True,
> The name of Zedlitz stands thereto.

This loyal Zedlitz was well rewarded for his faithfulness and courage. Not only did he receive Barbarossa's blessing, he was also granted a substantial parcel of land on the eastern border of Thuringia, a German outpost facing the Kingdom of Bohemia. On this spot he built a mighty fortress castle that bore his name, Zedelic. The fortress Zedelic would serve to defend German territory long after both Barbarossa and his loyal vassal Zedlitz were dead.

A hundred years after Barbarossa, in the spring of 1241, the reigning Polish monarch, Henryk the Pious of Piast, sent out an urgent call to arms, a call that transcended all tribal, cultural and ducal interests: The infidel had invaded Silesia!

In this time of the Hohenstaufen and Piast kings, the term *infidel* meant the Tatars, a diverse group of nomadic peoples who for centuries had roamed the Eurasian continent from Mongolia in the east to the Russian Ukraine in the west. The language they spoke was something akin to Turkish, and in the thirteenth century these people had been touched by neither Christianity nor Islam.

Silesia was a remote ducal possession in the outer reaches of the Polish kingdom bounded by the Tatra mountains on the south and by the Neisse River on the west. The Oder River flowed north and west diagonally through the region on its way to the Baltic Sea. The land was rich in forests and fertile fields, and it was also rumored to possess untold mineral treasures underground. No wonder Silesia— *Slansk—Schlesien*—was simultaneously coveted by the Tatars as well as the European rulers.

From south and west, Germanic knights rode east to the Oder River to stem the heathen invasion. Severely encumbered by their heavy coats of armor, they crossed the Neisse River and traversed treacherous swamps and endless forests to join Henryk's knights of Piast. These Polish knights, equally encumbered by their heavy armor, traveled south across more familiar swamps and forests and crossed the Oder from the east.

On the first clear morning in April, these combined armies met the invading Tatars on the wet plains of Silesia. Following practiced maneuvers, carefully regulated as befitted these men of chivalry, armored knights rode forward in close formation, their swords drawn. Foot soldiers trailed after them, wielding their long, awkward spears, all in a sea of mud. The enemy lines were pierced again and again, but always at great cost. Horses and men slipped and fell into the quagmire, and the bodies of the wounded and dying soon outnumbered those still fighting. Again and again the armies regrouped under their respective banners, closed the gaps created by the fallen horses and men, and charged. In the end, order and discipline, the practiced virtues of these god-fearing armies, carried the day.

Among the German banners carried into battle that day were the flags of the knights of Castle Zedelic. They were led by a descendant of Barbarossa's most loyal vassal Zedlitz and supported by soldiers from the Zedelic village on the eastern border of Thuringia. These weary knights and soldiers of Zedlitz buried their dead and crossed the Neisse west to their castle and village.

In the centuries that followed this historic defeat of the Tatars, control of these Silesian lands passed to the king of Bohemia and eventually, through carefully arranged marriages, to the Habsburg dynasty in Austria.

By the eighteenth century, the Hohenstaufen dynasty of Barbarossa and his descendants had long since disappeared. Taking its place as the energetic force among the northern German dukes and princes was the House of Hohenzollern. These were the rulers of Brandenburg, later to become the kings in Prussia, and their royal stronghold was the city of Berlin.

In April 1741, exactly five hundred years after victory over the Tatars, the armies of the Prussian king, Friedrich the Great, seized all of the lands between the Oder and the Neisse rivers belonging to the reigning Habsburg monarch, Empress Maria Theresa. Seven years and many battles later, Austria and Prussia signed an uneasy peace. Maria Theresa kept her throne, but Friedrich kept Silesia. The empress is said to have lamented: "He has taken my lovely garden from me."

The peace lasted less than a decade, and when war broke out again, it took on the dimensions of a world conflict, involving all of the great powers of Europe and territories as distant as North America and India. It came to be known as the Seven Years' War, for like its predecessor, it lasted seven years. When it was over, the Prussian king had Silesia firmly in his grasp.

The land was now inhabited by descendants of the Zedlitzes from Zedelic, who served the king just as their ancestors had centuries earlier. Among these descendants were Ernestine and Gottlieb von Trützschler, distant cousins married to each other. In the year 1800, Ernestine gave birth to their first child, Karl Eduard, at the ancestral Trützschler castle in Thuringia.

The time was just after the French Revolution, with all its cruelties and failed promises. Napoleon Bonaparte had seized power in France and immediately embarked on military adventures in places as close to Prussia as Austria and Russia and as far away as Egypt. By the time Karl Eduard was five years old, Napoleon had reached his zenith in military prowess, defeating the combined armies of Austria and Russia at the Battle of Austerlitz. Flushed with success, he now took on Prussia. The Trützschler castle came under siege and Karl Eduard was sent away to safety with his mother, to the castle Schwentnig in Silesia, home of the boy's great uncle, the Baron von Zedlitz.

A few years later, the old baron died and Schwentnig passed into the possession of Karl Eduard's father, Gottlieb von Trützschler. Gottlieb petitioned the Prussian king for permission to combine the names Zedlitz and Trützschler into a single name that could be carried by him and by all who would come after him. The king not only granted the petition, but elevated Gottlieb to a count. A new entry was inscribed in the register of Prussian aristocracy—Gottlieb, count of Zedlitz and Trützschler. Forever after, the family coat of arms would display the red and white sword buckle of the Zedlitz clan with the black- and yellow-clad soldiers of Trützschler.

Karl Eduard, the second count of Zedlitz and Trützschler, was the first of his family to attend a university, the Friedrich-Wilhelm[1] University in Berlin. There he met and married the Baroness Ulrike of Vernezobre de Laurieux, a striking beauty of French Huguenot descent. In due time, six children were born to this marriage. The last son, Robert, arrived in 1837 at the Schwentnig castle. Soon after his birth Ulrike became ill with tuberculosis and died.

Karl Eduard was eventually appointed to an administrative post in Breslau, the capital of Silesia. There, at age thirteen, Robert entered the gymnasium. The Schwentnig castle had become a country house, a place where the count and his family retreated only on festival and holiday occasions. For Robert, it was a time of restlessness and distraction; he had no interest in the academic courses of the gymnasium, nor in the camaraderie of the other students.

The year was 1853, and throughout Prussia—not to mention the other German states—the twin ideals of nationalism and modern liberalism were taking hold. In fact, they were threatening existing institutions on every front. In the cities, workers were creating organizations to alleviate the exploitation that accompanied the industrial revolution, and for the first time these workers were joined by intellectuals and tradesmen in a common quest for universal suffrage. The historic Prussian institutions, which for centuries had rested on three distinct but interdependent classes, were slowly being undermined.

The French Revolution and the decade of Napoleon's triumphs had a two-edged impact on these developments. His reforms in the conduct of government and the military impressed those who saw the need for reform in Prussia. His humiliation of Prussia stirred Germans of all political persuasions and social classes. A new concept was emerging—a liberating nationalism that should find its expression in a federation of German states.

It was a concept that Robert at age sixteen found immensely attractive. Thus without completing the final gymnasium years, he abandoned his academic education and became a cadet in Prussia's Sixth Armored Cavalry[2] Regiment of Brandenburg. At nineteen, he was commissioned a second lieutenant in the Prussian officer corps and assigned to the most coveted regiment in all of Prussia—the Garde du Corps of the king.

Eventually he was sent by the king to France to study the organization and training methods by which the French had built the premier military organization in Europe. In Paris he first met

Otto von Bismarck, the Prussian ambassador to France who decades later would dominate the politics of Germany and in fact of all Europe. Through his friendship with Bismarck, Robert was introduced into French society; thus began his love affair with the French culture and his own maternal French heritage. Robert was fascinated by the quality of life among the landed gentry, and he began to dream of acquiring his own estate in Silesia, where he would imitate the cultivated atmosphere of his mother's homeland while earning an agricultural livelihood.

Foremost in Robert's dreams was the prospect of marriage, for he was in love with Agnes von Rohr of Dannenwalde. The Rohrs were an old aristocratic family from Brandenburg, Prussia, and they stood much closer to the king than did any of the Zedlitzes. In Robert's mind, Agnes was born to be mistress of some great landholding. For him, a career in the Prussian military was fast losing its allure.

As the second son of Karl Eduard, Robert would never inherit Schwentnig, although it was the only real home he had ever known. Nevertheless, he wrote to his father of his hopes and of his dreams, and Karl Eduard quietly made the appropriate inquiries.

As soon as his military assignment in France was completed, Robert went directly to Schwentnig, traveling by train through Franconia and Thuringia, across lands that his warrior ancestors had traversed on foot and on horseback, into the land of Silesia and as far as the Oder River, to the Schwentnig castle. Karl Eduard made this son welcome and presented him with a proposition. He had just purchased one of the most beautiful landholdings in all of Silesia—the forty-five-hundred-acre estate of Grossenborau.[3] He intended to hand it over as a wedding gift for Robert, to manage and eventually to inherit, provided the son agreed never to sell or to divide the estate and never to mortgage the land. The proposition was accepted without reservation.

Thus Robert's days as a bachelor soldier were about to come to an end. Presumably a predictable future as paterfamilias and Prussian landowner lay ahead for him. In nineteenth-century Europe, however, presumptions were no longer enough.

I

THE COUNTESS OF GROSSENBORAU

1867-1886

"Conti Ruth"

Early in the morning on a cold February day, church bells rouse the villagers at Grossenborau and bring most of them to the gate of the manor house courtyard, where the housekeeper stands with a broad smile on her face. It is the third such occasion since Robert and Agnes, the count and countess of Zedlitz and Trützschler, first arrived at Grossenborau as bride and groom. At the time, the proud villagers viewed the new master and mistress with a mixture of hope and fear—hope that the new owner of this ancient estate might initiate reforms to rescue the ailing agricultural enterprise and fear that he might force the Protestant Lutheran brand of Christianity on this staunchly Catholic community. Since then their hopes have been fulfilled and their fears have been allayed. Grossenborau still has its Catholic priest, and under Count Robert's supervision the old half-timbered church has been renovated and refurbished.

The church stands so near the manor house, separated only by the modest churchyard, that the housekeeper has no chance of being heard above the din of the church bells. But the villagers have patience—a trait developed through centuries of feudalism on these ancient lands. They know the priest will quiet the bells only when the crowd has attained the numbers he deems sufficient.

As the bells finally fall silent and the villagers likewise, the housekeeper raises her voice with a confidence equal to her superior position in the household hierarchy. It is her privilege

to announce the birth of a girl, plump and healthy, to the master
and mistress of Grossenborau. She is to be named Ruth. A
murmur of surprise rustles through the gathering—Ruth, of biblical origin; how unlike the Silesian aristocracy to choose a name
from the Old Testament! Nevertheless, a small cheer rises from
the crowd; then the men return to their chores and the women
scurry to their homes. Little work will get done on this day, for
the birth will be celebrated in one way or another by everyone in
the village.

One month after her birth, this youngest countess of Zedlitz
and Trützschler is made ready by a nurse for her christening in
the family chapel. In the families of both Robert and Agnes,
christenings, weddings and funerals are not just occasions of religious significance. They are also opportunities for strengthening
the threads that knit their families and indeed an entire class of
people together.

From Schwentnig, from Dannenwalde, from Frankenstein,
from Altenburg and Frauenhain—from the great estates of
Silesia, Thuringia and Brandenburg—the aunts and the uncles,
the cousins, and the godparents arrive at the nearest railroad
station, Freystadt, and are fetched by the coachman in the
Grossenborau landau. Robert personally makes the carriage trip
twice, first to greet the Dannenwalde visitors, Agnes's parents,
and to assure them as to the good health of their daughter, then
to greet his own father, Karl Eduard, from Schwentnig.

The old count is hardly into the carriage when he inquires as
to the child's name. "Ruth," the son replies; Karl Eduard is
incredulous. That name has never existed in their family—how
can it happen now? The son is firm and kindly toward the father.
"Father, you must read again the Old Testament story of the
Moabite woman Ruth. It is the story of our people also—
'Faithful onto death.'" The father falls silent. Perhaps he finds
agreement, or perhaps he merely reminds himself that it is not
his place to interfere.

The pastor from Freystadt has come with his wife by wagon to
officiate on this day of christening. For most pastors in Prussia, a
christening among the aristocracy is a day truly heaven sent.
Unlike the Catholic priests, who are often the second sons of the
Polish and Austrian nobility, most pastors of Protestant Prussia

have their origins in the towns and cities of the provinces. They
are often the sons of shopkeepers and of ill-paid teachers. To
become a pastor is a step upward. To be pastor in a church of the
landed nobility is to live in rural isolation and to lead a Spartan
life. Thus the Christian occasions that prompt these gatherings
of the aristocracy become Cinderella interludes in the lives of a
village pastor and his wife. Clearly this is the case with the pastor
of Freystadt.

Every fireplace in the great house has a fire burning today, and
the largest fire of all is burning in the great festival hall. The hall
has been draped in the black and gold colors of the Zedlitz clan,
a kind of tribute to the old count, Karl Eduard, which will probably cause him to forget any objection he had to his granddaughter's name.

Besides the pastor, the family members, and the godparents
gathered in the festival hall, there is another guest, somewhat
unexpected, known personally to some and by reputation to all.
He is Otto von Bismarck, the prime minister of Prussia. Hearing
that Bismarck was to be in Silesia on a state visit just before the
christening date, Robert extended this old friend an invitation,
and he accepted.

Otto von Bismarck stands closer to Prussia's King Wilhelm I
than any other man. He is his foremost advisor on domestic
affairs, and in foreign policy he is creating out of Prussia a power
that rivals both the Austrian Habsburg Empire and Napoleon
III's France. Within the Zedlitz and Trützschler circles, mention
of the Bismarck name makes the heart beat faster. His presence
at the christening of little Ruth lends great significance to an
occasion that is already filled with meaning.

At last the count and countess enter the hall, hand in hand
with their other two children, Robert, who will always be known
as Rob, and Lisa. Behind them are the godfather and the godmother, in whose arms the infant Ruth lies peacefully sleeping.
She is but a tiny bundle, trailing a long christening gown that has
previously been worn and trailed by at least ten other infants in
three generations. The entire gathering gracefully makes room
as the little procession passes through into the family chapel.

Bible in hand, the pastor begins the ceremony with an invocation prayer, followed by a reading from the New Testament.

Commitments are made by the parents and then by the godparents. The pastor dips his hand into the bowl of water and places it on the forehead of the child. "I baptize thee Ruth . . . in the name of the Father, the Son and the Holy Spirit." The ritual concludes with a benediction, and only then does Ruth begin to cry. A nursemaid leads the two older children from the chapel. The baby is handed over to her mother, and she becomes quiet again.

One by one the guests pass by, extending a hand, an embrace, or a kiss according to each relationship. The prime minister, somewhat a stranger to the immediate family, nevertheless chooses not to be outdone. He raises the hand of little Ruth from the folds of her gown and places a kiss upon it. Surprise and happiness light the faces of the proud parents and grandparents. This particular christening day is indeed different from all the others.

When Ruth is old enough to understand, she will be told of this remarkable incident. She will treasure the knowledge that she was kissed by the great Otto von Bismarck. She will also believe that this kiss endowed her with heightened political insight, and as later events will bear out, this may indeed have been the case.

Two years after this festive christening day, there is another christening, this time of Marie Agnes, who will always be known as Anni; then two years later, still another, of Stefan; and finally, two years later, the christening of Ehrengard. Altogether, six children are born to the count and countess, each one in the master bedroom overlooking the garden of the great manor house. Just one will live to see the death of Grossenborau.

Life for each child begins in the nursery, a towerlike room overlooking the garden, under the care of a French nursemaid. Here only French is spoken. Later the nursery evolves into a schoolroom, and a tutor comes to live at Grossenborau. He sleeps in one of the rooms facing the courtyard, joins in the morning and evening devotions, and takes meals with the family at the long banquet table. The sunny tower room becomes the place where the children study grammar and arithmetic and learn about Friedrich Barbarossa, the defeat of the Tatars, and Prussia's own Friedrich the Great.

The young Countess Ruth

Ruth develops into a thoughtful, somewhat headstrong, yet always endearing child. She spends hours alone with her dolls, playing in the family landau that is stored in the stables across the courtyard. The coachman gladly interrupts his work to adjust the hood forward or backward, according to "Conti Ruth's" command. It all depends on whether she is playing the Frog Prince or Sleeping Beauty. Often Ruth brings the coachman flowers or evergreen branches from the garden. Unbeknown to him, she has assigned him character roles in her fairy tale charades.

In this way, Ruth acts out her fantasies, dreaming that one day a handsome Prince Charming will come along and carry her away to a castle somewhere in the vast lands of Prussia. It never occurs to her that she is already the fairy princess.

"A Thousand Times Yes"

1870. The armies of King Wilhelm have dealt the French armies a humiliating defeat. In Prussia, this event will forever after be known as the Victory at Sedan and the fall of Napoleon III, the last French emperor.

1871. On January 18, at the Palace of Versailles outside of Paris, Prussia's King Wilhelm is proclaimed German Kaiser Wilhelm I. His empire is the second German Reich in history, the first having been created in the fifteenth century. It is dominated by Prussia, but it also includes all of the southern and western German principalities. It is the first modern German nation-state; in addition large areas of its territory are inhabited by Slavic, French and Scandinavian peoples. The empire is also distinguished by what it does not include—specifically, the German parts of the Austro-Hungarian Empire. The dream of a modern Holy Roman Empire of the German nations is dead, but the spirit of Friedrich Barbarossa is once again alive and well! Amazingly, the king has been a reluctant partner in the formation of this empire. He is apprehensive about taking on the role of kaiser for all of Germany, but finds it impossible to say no to Otto von Bismarck, his prime minister—now chancellor of this vast German Reich. The new empire is Bismarck's own creation,

The German Reich, 1871-1914

1 Grossenborau
2 Wartenberg
3 Pätzig
4 Schmenzin
5 Klein Krössin
  and Kieckow
6 Lasbeck and
  Kniephof
7 Finkenwalde

and it has brought him to the pinnacle of his career. He has also brought about an elected German Parliament, but with severely limited powers. And he has made the office of chancellor responsible to the kaiser alone.

This bold move by Bismarck has both its supporters and its detractors. Among the supporters of his creation are the intelligentsia, the middle classes, the industrial workers, the independent farmers and even the villagers in faraway places like Silesia and Pomerania. They carry the spirit of nationalism in their hearts and believe that, inevitably, a national state must lead to economic progress and a more egalitarian society. On the other hand, the move alienates the majority of the Prussian landowning aristocracy, precisely those conservatives who originally brought Bismarck to power. They are still the beneficiaries of the remnants of a feudal society, hence they fear the consequences of a modern German nation.

1881. Robert, the count of Zedlitz and Trützschler, is perhaps the most influential landowner in all of Silesia. His own estate, Grossenborau, is a model agricultural enterprise particularly renowned for the modern flood control methods he has implemented. He is a member of the Silesian Economic Development Board, and through this organization, he has introduced his innovative flood control techniques into all of Silesia. As a result, the high-water conditions that formerly posed a continual threat to life and property in the river valleys are now effectively controlled. Robert has also been a leader in the all-German organization of landowners. At the recent Berlin Congress, he succeeded in persuading the participants to think beyond their partisan political interests and to focus their efforts on their common agricultural concerns. His success in overcoming partisan interests has not gone unnoticed by his old friend, the chancellor; in fact Count Robert is one of the few of his own kind on whom Bismarck can rely.

It should come as no surprise, then, that in the summer of 1881, Bismarck arranges to have Robert appointed governor[4] in Silesia. The appointment comes down in the name of the king, not the kaiser, for in Prussia Kaiser Wilhelm still reigns as king.

Among the Silesian landowners, Robert's appointment is cause for much rejoicing. One of their own, not some stranger from Brandenburg or Pomerania, has been selected to rule over them.

At Grossenborau, the appointment is greeted with a mixture of joy and trepidation. In the village, a mood of uncertainty prevails, for the count's presence in daily affairs has generally been a blessing; but there is also shared pride in such an unexpected appointment by the kaiser. The family emotions range from tremendous excitement to genuine sadness. The father's appointment will mean a move to the governor's residence in the city of Oppeln, a palace of sorts with its elegantly furnished living and office quarters.

For Ruth, the thought of moving portends the end of her carefree childhood. There has already been a change. Brother Rob,

The manor house at Grossenborau

to whom she gave her trust in so many ways, left home a year ago to study at a military academy, and now he is a member of the Lichterfelde Cadet Corps, preparing for a career in the military. His occasional visits are dominated by long talks with Father in the library, alone behind closed doors. In Ruth's eyes, Rob has become a man while she is still a child. Is that what happens to all children who leave Grossenborau? Ruth suspects that it is.

What Ruth does not know is that at these meetings with Father, Rob is pleading to be allowed to abandon the military and in fact to abandon a way of life that has characterized the Zedlitz and Trützschler families for seven hundred years—he wants to go to America to become a *self-made* man. Father cannot comprehend this unthinkable desire; he is overcome by sadness and self-recrimination, believing that he has utterly failed in his paternal role. Rob will renounce his dream, for after all, he is a Zedlitz—faithful unto death!

1882: APRIL. The entire family has just returned to Oppeln from Lichterfelde. There, among blooming lilacs and spirea, Rob was commissioned lieutenant in Prussia's First Garde Infantry Regiment. Ruth is filled with such pride for this brother; she claims she could feast her eyes on his uniform forever without even blinking.

Five Zedlitz children are seated at the banquet table in the governor's residence, two on one side and three on the other. Count Robert is seated at one end of the table, and Countess Agnes at the other. Ruth sits to the left of her father. The table prayers have been said and the children are silently eating their soup. Father is speaking, to no one in particular or perhaps to all of them: "Today I met the son of old Kleist; he has just passed his university law exams and he will apprentice in our office."

These few words burst upon Ruth's consciousness in a sudden and peculiar manner. She is convinced that they are meant for her, although she cannot fathom their significance. Old Kleist? She has no idea who he is, but the words file themselves away in her head, awaiting some further revelation. Ruth keeps her silence and continues to eat.

A few days later, she passes the silver card tray on the sideboard in the reception room. The tray is piled high with the calling cards that are always left in pairs, one for the count and one for the countess. There on the top lie two identical cards engraved with the words, "Jürgen von Kleist-Retzow,* Candidate in Law." Kleist—the name is already in Ruth's consciousness.

Weeks later, on a lovely summer evening, Father takes Ruth alone to an outdoor band concert outside Oppeln in the military compound. The reason he gives for the outing is that Ruth, who is diligently learning to play the piano, will especially enjoy the concert. Ruth is seated next to Father in the governor's box as he greets those who pass by. Suddenly he turns to her, and pointing to a young man in the distance, says, "That young man is Kleist's son." The count turns his attention once more to the greeters, but Ruth's eyes remain fixed on the tall, slender man, so handsome with his dark eyes and mustache, and so striking in the earnestness of his expression. No introductions are made, nor does the young man come by to pay his respects to Father. But Ruth knows as well as she knows her own name that this man, Kleist's son, is watching her as intently as she is watching him.

---

*The family name Kleist-Retzow applies to the descendants of Christian von Kleist and Charlotte von Retzow of Kieckow in Pomerania. In this narrative, these descendants will generally be referred to as the Kleists of Kieckow.

In the fall, for the first time in their lives Ruth and Anni are sent away to school. Actually it is not far away—only to a deaconess convent in a nearby town where they will be prepared for confirmation. Childhood fantasies are soon replaced with biblical passages and catechism paragraphs, all to be memorized for examination at confirmation time.

DECEMBER. It happens again in Oppeln! It is Christmas Eve; Ruth and Anni are home from school and Rob is home on leave. After supper, the threesome—Ruth, Anni and Rob—leave the governor's residence for the walk to church. It is snowing lightly. Just outside the residence, Rob is greeted by a man who appears to have been waiting at the corner. Rob introduces the man to his sisters as "my friend, Herr von Kleist, the finest reserve officer in our regiment." Ruth is struck speechless as Rob continues: "So you are also on your way to church!" And Kleist replies as if to apologize: "Yes. I know it's not usual with our generation, but it is the custom in my family and the way I was brought up." Ruth takes to her heart these first words spoken by Kleist's son in her presence. She hears nothing else that is said, though the two young men continue to chat as they walk to church together.

The day after Christmas, Father and Mother, Rob, Ruth and Anni are invited to dinner at the castle of Turawa, which lies just outside Oppeln. This Christmas party is Ruth's first truly grown-up party. Once again *he* is among the guests, and now it begins to make sense to Ruth—the offhand remark at the family dinner table, the calling cards in the tray, two pairs of eyes meeting at the band concert, and the "chance" encounter on the way to church. This is how it is done in Prussia; Ruth is not quite sixteen years old, but she observes and now she understands.

1883. Back at school, all thoughts of the law clerk in Father's office are totally obliterated. Ruth is diligently studying the Luther catechism and trying to learn a mountain of Bible passages, along with their meanings. She earnestly wants to be prepared for the pastor's interrogation in May, taking to heart the religious significance of her confirmation. She also knows from her home life, and from tradition, the further significance of the event—her emergence from childhood into the adult world. The thought is both fearful and joyful, and as May approaches, Ruth finds it difficult to suppress her romantic adolescent fantasies. Her childhood vision of Prince Charming has faded into the image of Jürgen von Kleist.

NOVEMBER. It is the beginning of the ball season in Oppeln—that well-orchestrated series of parties through which daughters of the upper classes step into adulthood. This is the first season for Ruth. At home, the name of Herr von Kleist is no longer mentioned. Ruth believes he has left the city, for Father once mentioned that he was to be apprenticed to a Landrat* in Brandenburg. Ruth vows to purge this Kleist from her heart; it is clear that this longing of hers brings only grief.

Today Ruth is standing patiently before a mirror while the seamstress pins her dress. She has tied her long hair into a bun on top of her head, thinking Mother might permit her to wear it that way to the first winter ball. One of the privileges of Ruth's new adult status is permission to admire herself occasionally in a looking glass, something that was prohibited during childhood at Grossenborau. She studies her grownup hairdo and the lines of the new dress on her figure. She imagines how wide the skirt will flow when she is waltzing double-quick time with the unknown young men she will meet in the ballrooms of Oppeln. This curiosity is enough to generate a bit of enthusiasm for the winter ahead. There is a practical streak in Ruth that says, "Life must go on."

The first ball of the season takes place at the home of Father's chief advisor, who is the father of two eligible daughters and two sons. Each son is a newly commissioned officer in the military, and both are home on leave. Their presence is the ostensible occasion for the party. The guests are the daughters and sons of the Silesian officeholders, along with their parents. On this festive night, their residence is a blaze of candlelight. One after another, carriages and coaches pull up to the entrance of the elegant town house, disgorging ladies and gentlemen in formal dress.

The excitement begins before dinner, over punch in the library. There the young men ask the young women for a place

---

*The supervisor of a Prussian district corresponding to an American county.

on their dance cards, those brightly colored folded papers that hang from their wrists by satin ribbons. Ruth's card is full except for two dances. She congratulates herself that she has not done too badly, then chastises herself for such vanity. Why is she always beset with these inner struggles when the others seem so light-hearted and joyful?

The formal dinner is highly structured—a prayer by the host, the first course, the standing toast to the kaiser and king and to his representative, the governor, Robert, count of Zedlitz and Trützschler, and finally a toast to all of the lovely ladies.

After dinner, the guests promenade to the ballroom, Ruth walking on the arm of the young Dornberg lieutenant. Suddenly the realization that *he* is there strikes like a bolt of lightning! For the rest of the evening, her emotions alternate between delight and torment. Jürgen von Kleist has come all the way from Berlin for the ball, arriving too late for dinner. (In Ruth's heart he is already *Jürgen.*) He asks Ruth if there is still a place on her dance card; of course there is, and he signs for the cotillion and then moves on. It is clear to Ruth that among all the eligible bache-lors, he is the most sought after by the mothers as well as the daughters. It is a torture to witness!

For the rest of the season, Lisa and Ruth, the two Zedlitz countesses, go from ball to ball in the grand homes of Oppeln and the even grander manor houses of the nearby estates. Jürgen is always present, for he is now living in Oppeln and once again working in Father's office. That fact alone raises hope in Ruth's heart. Jürgen always signs early for a cotillion, but for all his kind and gentle ways, he makes no commitment and appears to display the same kind and gentle ways with each one of his dancing partners. Although Ruth dances with many young men and her dance card is always full, her head and her heart think only of Jürgen von Kleist.

1884: APRIL. Ruth's last time with Jürgen before they all go away for the summer is a Sunday excursion into the country in a caravan of open wagons. The men from the governor's office ride in the lead wagon, their families in the caravan of vehicles behind. Jürgen is sitting with Father up front, and Ruth is riding in the last wagon. On the straightaway road the lead wagon is totally obscured from her vision, but when the caravan rounds a bend, Ruth can catch a glimpse of Jürgen's red silk scarf waving in the wind. For a moment she retreats into her fantasies, envisioning Prince Charming on his horse, a long silk scarf trailing behind as he races to her side.

NOVEMBER. Ruth is almost eighteen years old and preparing for the new ball season in Oppeln. Her hair is bobbed and the high collar on her ball gown has disappeared entirely. Together, the hair and gown are her statement that she is now of independent spirit and has every intention of presenting herself to the young men on her own terms. At each of the first two balls, she emerges as the acknowledged belle of the evening. Mother and Father are not blind to this bold development in their daughter; on the contrary, they are alarmed, but it is left for Rob, the brother whom Ruth idolizes, to counsel her before she brings embarrassment to herself or to the family.

Home on Christmas leave, Rob invites Ruth to the library of the governor's residence. Carefully closing the doors behind them, he asks her to sit down, then positions his own chair facing her. With her two hands held tightly in his own, Rob speaks in a tone to which Ruth is unaccustomed. He warns her not to allow her head to be turned by flattery and reminds her that women who are known as coquettes or "playgirls" are soon scorned by the very men who flatter them with their attentions. He assures her that these men rarely choose such women for their wives and then he asks, "You do wish to marry, do you not?"

All this scolding is too much for Ruth. She throws herself into her brother's arms and weeps inconsolably. All of her deep unhappiness and desperation over Jürgen von Kleist pours out in a torrent, along with the admission that her behavior is just an awkward attempt to rebuild the self-esteem so damaged by his inattention. All she really wanted was Jürgen, and now it seems that her heart's desire will be denied her!

Tears are dried and a commitment is made between sister and brother. The conversation will never be mentioned again, neither by Rob nor by Ruth. Yet Rob's words will remain forever engraved on Ruth's soul and they will bind her to this dearly beloved brother, even through the terrible estrangement that later separates him from most of the Zedlitz and Trützschler family.

1885. In late winter, Father brings to the dinner table a sealed letter he has just received. The return address reads Kieckow and the postmark, Belgard. Slitting the envelope with a table knife, he unfolds the letter and reads aloud to the gathered family:

> Honorable Count, Right Honorable Herr Governor:
> Allow me to inform you . . .

The letter is from Jürgen von Kleist, informing Father that he has passed his bar examination and therefore takes the opportunity to thank Father for the help and training he received during his months in the governor's office at Oppeln.

The letter makes no reference whatsoever to the governor's daughter. Father even turns it over, as if to look for something more; perhaps he too is surprised at what it does not contain, but he says nothing. Ruth's spirits, raised so high for a moment, now sink to new depths.

Two months later, Father receives a black-rimmed letter—the return address, Kieckow in Pomerania. It is from the young Herr von Kleist, who announces the death of his mother and informs the count that he has been called up for six weeks' reserve officer duty; he hopes to visit Oppeln when this is finished. This time Father chooses not to share the letter with the family, perhaps wishing to spare his daughter any false hopes regarding this long-absent suitor.

Ruth begins to consider seriously her options in life; there are but three. To be a court lady, a kind of lady in waiting to the queen, who helps with the palace entertainments and is privy to all of the gossip in the royal court. Ruth judges this to be an abominable future of which she wants no part at all. To be principal of a boarding school, or perhaps to be a deaconess sister. She thinks back on the pleasant year when she studied at the convent, but to spend her life there—no, that is definitely not for her. What is left? To marry! A very genteel and aristocratic widower in the family circle, the father of a small child, has of late paid sincere and gentle attentions to Ruth, but so far she has quietly and politely, but firmly, rejected them. She wonders whether God means her to take over this motherless child, and her heart and head are in turmoil. Then she begins to question her inner motivation—is it selfishness that rules her spirit, or is it simply an abiding faith in true love? She chooses to believe the latter. Surely God cannot expect one to go so against one's own heart!

OCTOBER. Father is in Oppeln; Rob, the soldier, is somewhere in Italy; Lisa, Ruth and Anni have been at Grossenborau with Mother since summer, as she and Father have decided to skip the Oppeln ball season this year. Stefan and Ehrengard, normally away at school, are home on holiday. Father is expected in the evening, and it will be much like childhood times, having the entire family, with the exception of Rob, together for a few days.

It is still forenoon, and Ruth is setting the long dining table for late breakfast. Arranging the cups and saucers, she nonchalantly stops at her mother's place to examine the morning mail. She spies an open envelope with a letter from Father partially visible. No doubt Mother has read it earlier. Contrary to her upbringing but driven by her curiosity, Ruth pulls the letter out, and with it comes another envelope, still sealed, addressed in handwriting that unmistakably is Jürgen's. On it are the words, "Countess Ruth von Zedlitz and Trützschler." Ruth seizes the envelope, replaces Father's letter in the outside envelope at Mother's place, abandons the cups and saucers, and races through the hall to the library. She hears her name being called but does not look back and closes the doors behind her. Throwing herself into Father's chair, she tears open the envelope and unfolds the missive. This time there must be no false hope, no disappointment. Ruth pleads silently with the writer to take pity on her poor heart, and then begins to read:

> Gracious Countess: Ever since I have had the honor and
> the joy of knowing you, I have experienced a deep love,
> which only grows stronger through our long separation.
> Will you trust me for your entire life?

Years later Ruth will believe that at this moment she saw God. Burying her head in her hands, she can hardly control herself. He wants me for his wife, he wants me for his wife!

Mother has followed Ruth to the library and now quietly opens one of the great doors. She embraces her daughter and sits beside her to read aloud the other two letters that have arrived— the first from Father to Mother and the second from Father to Ruth. Father insists that Ruth consider the gravity of the commitment she is asked to make before giving any reply to Herr von Kleist's proposal, but Ruth is impatient and listens only reluctantly. To this long-awaited question, the wondrous gift that has finally come to her so totally unexpectedly, there is only one possible response: "Yes, yes, a thousand times yes!"

Father has asked Ruth for an immediate reply. In the event it is positive, Jürgen will come with him from Oppeln this very evening. The code words, to be sent by telegram, are: "Yes, come." Ruth rushes from the house down to the village post office to instruct the postmaster, who will cable the message.

That evening, Ruth paces the floor alone in the unlighted room that looks out to the main entrance of the house. A carriage halts at the steps and Father and Jürgen step out. She can barely hear their voices as Mother welcomes them into the house. A short time later, Ruth hears footsteps directly above the sitting room and surmises that Jürgen has reached the guest room where he will sleep—just as in her wildest dreams. She dares not light the oil lamps for fear of breaking the magic spell. Finally she hears the footfalls that tell her Jürgen is on the staircase. Quickly she lights two lamps, and the glow they cast on the walls and drapes increases the magic of her expectations. An unseen hand opens the door, and suddenly Jürgen steps into the room, closing the door behind him. Without uttering a word, he takes Ruth into his arms—for the first time ever—and he holds her still, almost without breathing.

In later years, when Jürgen's body lies beneath the Kieckow sod, Ruth will come to believe that this divinely ordered meeting will be reenacted in heaven. She will maintain that Jesus may have said one cannot marry God in heaven, but he said nothing to preclude the reuniting of those who loved divinely in this world.

Jürgen's first words to Ruth are, "May I now say 'Du' (the intimate thou)?" Such permission is hardly necessary, for her dear Herr von Kleist holds her in his arms and caresses her without ceasing. And for the first time, Ruth is permitted to whisper the name that has been singing in her heart for more than three years—*Jürgen.*

"Whither Thou Goest"

1886. It would be logical for the wedding to take place in spring, allowing plenty of time for the customary visits to various branches of the two families. Indeed between Ruth and Jürgen almost half of the Prussian aristocracy is intertwined in their family trees. In keeping with this tradition, Mother has suggested devoting the entire winter to the preparation of Ruth's wardrobe and the acquisition of those items that belong to a bride's dowry; then in early spring, a kind of grand tour through Prussia so that Jürgen and Ruth might together visit all of these family groups. The trip would be followed by a June wedding at Grossenborau.

Ruth has vigorously protested against the plan: "Not after waiting these three long years! No, dear Mother, we must not be asked to wait any longer." Ruth's intuition has warned her that each day's postponement means significant time lost in her life with Jürgen. And so it will later prove to be. Jürgen shares this impatience; for three years he struggled mightily with himself to preserve the appropriate distance from his intended bride until he could promise her a sufficient means of support. Were he to do it over, he would never have maintained his silence so long. With such persuasive arguments, the couple obtains parental consent on both sides to bypass the customary engagement period and plan for an early wedding.

The selected date, February 4, coincides with Ruth's nineteenth birthday. The wedding is to take place in Oppeln since Father's responsibilities keep him there in the winter months. It turns out that this early date is also fortuitous for both Father and Rob.

First of all, Father has intervened in Rob's military career. He knows that the military does not suit his son, and in the back of Father's mind is still the fear that Rob might one day emigrate to America. To stave off this eventuality, he has arranged with the foreign office in Berlin to have Rob reassigned to the German embassy in Rome. It will be a new direction in his career, beginning shortly after the fourth of February.

A new and unexpected opportunity has emerged in Father's public service career as well. Since October, he has twice been called to Berlin by Chancellor Bismarck, who is in the midst of a political crisis. It seems that, so far as government is concerned, there is a yearly crisis in Berlin, if not more often. One suspects that these crises are engineered by the chancellor himself as they seem to arise whenever his coalition in Parliament is on the point of dissolving. The most recent crisis has to do with the province of Posen in Prussia, a province that was part of the kingdom of Poland before the three great powers—Prussia, Austria and Russia—partitioned that country decades earlier. There have always been problems of one sort or another in Posen, where the Poles cling to their ancient national identity. Prussians like the Zedlitzes and the Kleists do not understand why the Poles resist the perceived benefits of the German language and culture that Prussia has bestowed on them. And now Bismarck is fueling the fire. In a time of domestic political turmoil and a weakening of his own position as chancellor, he has found it expedient to reactivate an ancient German dream— to populate the rich Polish agricultural regions with Germans.

A new Resettlement Commission has been created, and the German government intends to encourage German farmers from the west to resettle in the Polish areas of Prussia. In fact, the government has announced it will subsidize German purchases of land currently owned by Poles. Families like the Zedlitzes and the Kleists view this latest Bismarck policy as a protective measure to create a bulwark against Polish influences on Germany's eastern frontier. Landless German peasants in the west see the opportunity as a dream fulfilled; the Poles, peasants and landowners alike, consider it a stab at the heart of their heritage and an outright theft of the Polish soil to which this heritage is tied. In fact, the implementation of this policy will turn out to be a breakthrough in uniting the Poles under a national banner that transcends the ancient class divisions.

Bismarck has asked his old friend Robert, count of Zedlitz and Trützschler, to become the first president of this controversial Resettlement Commission. Robert has declined the appointment with a caveat: The presidency of the commission should be given to the governor-general of Posen in order that the tasks of the commission may be administered more humanely. He, Robert, will accept both appointments, if the chancellor so chooses.

Bismarck has so chosen, and Father has just returned from Berlin with his new dual appointments. He of course will give up his office as governor in Silesia, and the family will leave Oppeln right after the wedding, to move north to the Polish city of Posen.

FEBRUARY 4. Although this is Ruth's wedding day, breakfast is a traditional family birthday celebration, and it will remain riveted in her memory as the last celebration of her maidenhood. All of the Grossenborau family is present, plus Jürgen, Jürgen's father Hans Hugo, his sister Elisabeth, and his brother Hans Anton.

During the celebration, Hans Hugo von Kleist takes the opportunity to deliver his own sermon to the bride and groom. He reminds Ruth and Jürgen that life will bring vicissitudes—if not from within the marriage, for certain from without. This life will not be without its tears, he warns, but he exhorts the young couple above all else to put their trust in God.

At midday, the marriage festival begins. Outside the residence, there is mild confusion, involving horses, carriages, drivers, and stablemen. Most of the carriages will remain at the residence through the wedding and banquet; thus both the stables and servants' dining area are taxed to the fullest. The guests, who number seventy, gather in the reception room on the main floor. Known as the Red Hall, this room is customarily used for receiving Father's official visitors. Otto von Bismarck has met with Count Robert in this room a number of times, and even Kaiser Wilhelm once called on Father here. It is treated with great respect.

The decor of the room is distinctive and memorable—elegant red wall coverings, red-velvet upholstered chairs and full-height, double-paneled doors of stained oak, which normally stand closed. Today a servant stands at attention behind each of the doors, prepared to open and close them as each guest enters, and Father and Mother stand inside, extending their hands in welcome to each friend or relative. Mother wears an empire-style white dress sewn at home from a picture of the latest Berlin fashion; she looks every bit the countess that she is. Father is dressed in formal wear, his chest covered with the medals of his past service to the king and kaiser. There can be no doubt that he is in charge of this day's program. He has the uncanny knack of seeing to the smallest detail while appearing to give his undivided attention to each and every guest. In fact, it is the count who determines that all the guests are finally accounted for so that the ceremonies can begin; then he disappears from the room. Presently Jürgen enters the Red Hall and walks straight to the countess, ignoring all others. As he embraces her and turns with her to face the closed doors, there is quiet approval on the faces of everyone present.

For the first time, both double doors are opened, each by a servant. The old butler from Grossenborau, wearing the count's castoff evening jacket, takes his position at the left door. Among all of the servants, he has been selected for this honor in recognition of his long and faithful service to the master of Grossenborau. Ruth enters on Father's arm and walks with him directly to Jürgen. Looking the bridegroom straight in the eye, Father speaks the words that in effect surrender the bride to him. If the bride should contemplate these words too carefully, she might demur from the bargain. But Ruth, like every bride before her, sees them only as part of an ancient Silesian tradition. The moment is so moving that a deep silence settles over the gathering. To break the spell, Father takes the arm of the countess and, in his hospitable way, beckons all to follow him by forming a line behind the bride and groom. The procession moves upstairs to a meeting room ordinarily used for gatherings at which the kaiser is present, either personally or more often through his representative.

This modest-sized room is perhaps the most elegant meeting area in all of eastern Germany's provincial capitals. It does not compare to similar rooms in Bavaria, but then Prussia does not pretend to equal southern Germany when it comes to baroque elegance. On this day, though, the room has been transformed into a wedding chapel and is decorated as never before. Black and yellow ribbons—the Trützschler colors—hang from the chandelier and wall sconces. The large table has been removed, but every other surface as well as each corner of the room is banked with hothouse flowers. The entire arrangement has been done to the count's own specifications, and until this moment he has allowed no one to view his creation. He has even sent for the altar piece from the Grossenborau family chapel so that there might be a visible symbol of the family's roots and traditions. The somber mood in the Red Hall below is replaced by the reverent, yet joyous, spirit present in this mass of color and scented blossoms.

The bridal couple is standing before the altar, facing one Herr Geisler,[5] a member of the evangelical church council in Silesia. This clergyman is attired in elaborate and colorful robes, which Ruth finds jarring and in fact foreign to her religious upbringing. She would have much preferred to face the pastor from Freystadt, but she has deferred to Father's wishes. This is the first time Ruth has experienced annoyance with ecclesiastical organizations, but it will not be the last!

Herr Geisler begins the service with the marriage text selected by Father, who knows well his daughter's mind. It is taken from the Old Testament:

> Whither thou goest, I will go;
> And where thou lodgest, I will lodge;
> Thy people shall be my people
> And thy God my God;
> Where thou diest, will I die,
> And there will I be buried.

The clergyman continues with a long and very forgettable sermon on the religious significance of marriage. Ruth has trouble keeping her attention fixed on this stranger and is relieved when the homily ends. She comforts herself that God, not the clergyman, has in truth united her with Jürgen, who places the wedding ring on the third finger of her right hand. The ring has been molded from two gold coins—ancient ducats issued in the name of Jürgen's forebears. It is indeed a *Kleist* ring! Herr Geisler pronounces the couple man and wife, then concludes with the benediction.

Ruth von Kleist is no longer a countess. As if to give added emphasis to this significant change in her status, Father orders Jürgen to lead his bride from the left side to the right side.

Jürgen complies. The action symbolizes taking possession of the bride by the bridegroom. This too is an old Silesian custom.

Once again in procession—the count and countess leading and the bridal pair immediately behind them—the entire company moves to the great reception hall, dominated by a banquet table lavishly set for the bridal dinner. Seventy places are set, and each is designated by a place card. A servant at each end holds a chair, one for Ruth and one for Mother. On both sides of the table, the gentlemen see to it that each lady is properly seated before taking their places. As everyone looks to the count for guidance, he bows his head for the prayer, as is done before every family meal. Ruth bows her head in gratitude—that Father, not Herr Geisler, speaks to God at her wedding meal.

There is the clatter of dishes, and as the soup course is served, the count strikes his spoon to his glass to gain the attention of his guests. They rise in unison for the predictable toast, the one that has preceded all other toasts for generations of good Prussians—to the well-being of Wilhelm, the Prussian king and German kaiser.

For the next two hours the great hall is filled with the clinking sounds of eating and drinking, both in moderation, and with the more boisterous sounds of laughter and joviality passing from one end of the table to the other. Late in the meal, the count raises his glass in a farewell toast to his daughter, "the sunshine of our lives." Father's voice breaks at these words and he is forced to conclude abruptly. At the far end of the table, Ruth is likewise overcome with emotion. She would like to rush into Father's embrace one last time, but of course does not.

Ruth's father-in-law Hans Hugo von Kleist immediately breeches the silence with an expression of his respect, and indeed love, for the count and countess and his absolute joy over the uniting of two such old and faithful clans as the Zedlitzes and the Kleists. He expounds on the blessedness of this marriage in terms of the future for these ancient Prussian lands, then con- cludes with an allusion to the German nation, a lighthearted ref- erence, but a cutting edge. Everyone present understands Father Kleist's irreverent juxtaposition of Prussia and Germany. Hans Hugo von Kleist, the oldest friend and bachelor roommate of

Otto von Bismarck, does not share the chancellor's view of a modern German nation-state.

By late afternoon, Ruth and Jürgen are ready to begin their wedding journey. The carriage from Grossenborau, its brass gleaming, awaits them at the door. The coachman is in his seat, and the old family servant, holding open the door, bids Ruth farewell: "Madam, may God's blessings be upon you." How strange it sounds to be called *Madam*! Not even at Grossenborau will she ever again be "Conti Ruth."

II

THE LANDRAT'S WIFE

1886-1897

A Visit to Kieckow

FEBRUARY. The wedding journey commences at the railroad station in Oppeln. By express train Ruth and Jürgen travel to Breslau, then on to Leipzig, and finally to Father Kleist's flat in Berlin, where Ruth confronts her new role as sister-in-law to Jürgen's siblings, Elisabeth and Hans Anton. She senses a certain reserve on their part and puzzles as to the reason. It is the first disappointment in her young marriage, and it dampens the joy that has buoyed her spirit since her wedding day.

With Father Kleist, Ruth's initial respect has rapidly evolved into a deepening affection. She is surprised at herself, for her father-in-law possesses neither the flexibility nor the optimism that so endear her to her own father. This father-in-law is a conservative among conservatives and a man for whom the future bodes more ill than good, be it in politics, in religion, or even in family relationships.

Forty years ago Father Kleist and Otto von Bismarck shared a sleeping room at a modest boardinghouse in Berlin. Both were aristocrats and members of the Prussian House of Lords. Bismarck had just married Hans Hugo's niece Johanna von Puttkamer, and in that instant Hans Hugo became "Uncle Hans" to his friend and contemporary. It was a time when Bismarck stood against the liberal and nationalistic sentiments that were engulfing Prussia, along with other German-speaking lands, and in fact most of Europe; Hans Hugo stood with him. It was also a time when Bismarck's religious beliefs were somewhat in question; hence Hans Hugo sought to influence his friend through daily prayer and counseling in their shared living quarters.

31

Between these two landowners from Pomerania there was indeed a common heritage and a common mindset. It went so far that Bismarck not only advised his bachelor uncle in the choice of a bride—Charlotte, the countess of Stolberg and Wernigerode—but also intervened when Hans Hugo delayed his marriage proposal until after Charlotte had entered a Protestant convent.

Over the decades Otto von Bismarck has become less and less a Prussian, let alone a Pomeranian, but more and more a fierce proponent of the expanding German Reich, that nation-state created by him. A superb politician, he has turned enemies into allies and friends into antagonists, all to suit his political needs.

Nowadays there is a weariness in Father Kleist's countenance that even the happiest moments cannot overcome. Ruth suspects this sadness is rooted in politics, for everyone knows that Otto von Bismarck has publicly declared Hans Hugo von Kleist and others like him to be "enemies of the Reich."[6]

Ruth's suspicions, however, are only partly correct. These days Father Kleist thinks more and more about the future of his home and lands in Pomerania. During sleepless nights, he ponders how to present his estates, Kieckow and Klein Krössin, to his younger married son without causing pain to his other two children, both unmarried. In the Prussian aristocracy one is inclined to think ahead to the generations that have not yet been born.

When the Berlin sojourn is concluded, Ruth and Jürgen board the train once more, this time with the expectation of more time for each other. The final segment of the journey will take them to Köslin in Pomerania, where Jürgen has accepted his first full post in the king's bureaucracy. They travel north and east from Berlin, across the Oder River toward the Baltic Sea, moving slowly from town to town. There are no express trains here, for the lands are still empty—a clear reminder that Pomerania is not Silesia. The region is not at all like the countryside around Grossenborau, with its villages of neat homes, the red tile roofs and well-kept gardens. Alone, Ruth might be tempted to turn around and go home. But with Jürgen at her side, she would gladly go to the desert, and Pomerania is by no means a desert!

The day on which Ruth and Jürgen arrive by train at Köslin is cold and without sun, and the city is blanketed with snow. Apart

Ruth and Jürgen von Kleist, on their wedding journey

from its wintry covering, the scene can only be described as one of drab monotony. Even the home to which Jürgen takes his bride is outwardly dreary by any standard—an apartment upstairs from a small shop. The rooms that Ruth and Jürgen will occupy are reached by ascending a dark staircase to the second floor of the bleak stone building. But if Ruth has any qualms as to what awaits her at the top of the stairs, they are quickly dispelled. Jürgen throws open the door, and as Ruth enters the apartment, there before her stands a childhood playmate from the village of Grossenborau, in a starched maid's uniform. Joyously Ruth embraces the young woman, forgetting for the moment that the mistress and the servant must always maintain some distance.

Ruth casts her eyes about the freshly painted and polished apartment that is now to be her home. Like all of the six rooms, the entry room has been furnished by Jürgen especially for his bride—sparsely, to be sure, but with bits and pieces from Kieckow. Like a tour guide at a mountain resort, he announces self-importantly that this is the "Berlin" room, a combination dining-sitting room typical of the large stone apartment flats that are the mode in Germany's capital city. There is a large old buffet with leaded glass doors, and behind them Ruth notices a set of crystal goblets sparkling in the light from the wall sconces. They are among her wedding gifts, all shipped ahead. It is clear that the maid has been industrious during her first days in Pomerania.

Taking Ruth by the arm, Jürgen leads her to the miniature study with its writing desk, which is meant for her alone, then on to a sunny salon where they will take afternoon tea. Returning to the Berlin room, he guides her through half-opened double doors to the inevitably darker gentlemen's parlor, with its large ashtrays and cigar cabinet, and finally to the bedroom, with its great double bed and giant closet cupboard. With the words, "This is *our* room," Jürgen takes his bride into his arms.

On her first Sunday in Köslin, Ruth prepares herself for the long-awaited visit to Kieckow. In spite of fresh snow and cold weather, Jürgen has sent a message to the estate requesting that the Kieckow coachman bring a carriage to Köslin for his bride's first visit to her eventual home. It is a thirty-six-kilometer journey so the carriage must leave the estate in darkness. Hours later the horses and carriage stand ready at the gate of the flat in Köslin as the young couple descends the stairs, Ruth bundled in fur hat, coat and muff—gifts from Father to protect her in this cold northern land. Soon the carriage is off to the south, the horses prancing lively in the cold morning air, the newlyweds wrapped together beneath a warm fur robe.

A journey from Köslin to Kieckow takes the traveler by way of Belgard, the ancient center of the Kleist homeland. Clearly Jürgen feels at home now. He begins to ramble on about his family origins and the ancient ties that still prevail. He speaks of Conrad Klest, the first Kleist, who arrived here in the thirteenth century when the entire region was part of the Polish kingdom of Mazovia. This Klest was of Slavic origin, though he dwelled in the German Hohenstaufen kingdom not far from Friedrich Barbarossa's Thuringian forest.

Jürgen continues his recitation as the carriage enters the bustling city of Belgard, seat of the district government. In the sixteenth century, one or another branch of the Kleist family controlled virtually all of the land in the district. By the eighteenth century, these lands had been further divided; yet the villages and the estates of Muttrin, Villnow, Tychow, Schmenzin, Kieckow and Krössin all carried the Kleist name. If one included the female descendants of the early Belgard Klests, one could easily assume that all of the district landowners were related in one way or another to that early Slavic immigrant, Conrad Klest.

From Belgard on, the ride becomes smoother and the view more inviting. Jürgen continues his reminiscences. Grandfather Hans Jürgen von Kleist owned three of the Belgard estates— Kieckow, Klein Krössin and Gross Tychow, altogether eight thousand acres. He was indeed the largest landowner when the king appointed him Landrat, or supervisor, of the Belgard District. Grandfather immediately set about constructing stone highways connecting all of the estates in the district to each other and to the railroad station at Belgard. And he ordered the planting of trees on each side of the new highways—linden and beech and elm—as protection against the winter winds that rolled down from the Baltic Sea.

Hans Jürgen's roads and trees clearly distinguish this part of the land from all other parts. Fifty years of pounding by horses' hooves have barely dented the surface of the sturdy road. And the trees! After half a century, even with leafless branches, Grandfather's linden trees form a sheltering arch over the Kieckow carriage.

Twenty-four kilometers beyond Belgard, the castle of Gross Tychow rises from the landscape; it is now home to Jürgen's second-cousins, the count and countess of Kleist-Retzow. At one time this castle was home to Grandfather Hans Jürgen; later, after the death of two successive wives, he moved with his five children to Kieckow. There he married for a third time—the widow Auguste von Borcke—Jürgen's grandmother. Hans Hugo—Father Kleist—was the only child born at Kieckow. Hence he was heir to this estate and to the adjacent Klein Krössin. Like his father before him, Hans Hugo was eventually appointed Landrat of the Belgard District. Unlike Hans Jürgen, Hans Hugo ascended rapidly in the Prussian bureaucracy and became an influential force in Prussian politics. Jürgen betrays his disappointment that Kieckow and Klein Krössin have both suffered in recent decades. He has observed that the landowner's absence over long periods usually signals neglect of the estate economy and always a deterioration in the village morale. These observations, however, Jürgen is not ready to share with his bride.

Three kilometers directly south of Gross Tychow the carriage makes a brief halt at the crossroad, then a ninety-degree turn to the left and into a village, still on the well-built road, which at this point is lined with maple trees. A dozen modest wooden huts are scattered to the left, all with thatched roofs, and there is a barn and a granary on the incline to the north. Jürgen points to a larger cottage beyond, of half-timbered stucco, the home of the bailiff. This is the village of Klein Krössin. Ruth's heart sinks as she compares this village of the Kleists to the village of Grossenborau, but she bites her tongue, for she would never knowingly hurt her gentle-hearted husband.

As the carriage passes through the village, a child and a man, hat in hand, wave at them, and Jürgen promptly returns the greeting. Ruth takes note of their broad smiles, reassuring herself that life here cannot be as bad as it first appeared. It is becoming increasingly difficult for the driver to restrain the horses from a gallop, for they are almost home—just three kilometers more, all on lands belonging to Jürgen's father. The first buildings of Kieckow now come into sight—the chicken house, a granary, and a shed to the left, then the first village houses on the right; and in the distance a cluster of brick barns, but without the impressive distillery that normally towers over and dominates every estate. There has never been, nor will there ever be, a distillery on these Kleist lands.

But where is the manor house? Soon that too emerges, as the carriage turns left from the road and starts up a frozen path, bordered on each side by a leafless overgrown hedge. Jürgen tightens his hold on Ruth and points to the bare bushes with his other hand: "In spring, these will be covered with lilacs—just you wait and see, my love." Clearly he has sensed the disappointment of his bride.

The carriage arrives in the open courtyard of the Kieckow manor house, a single-story edifice rising above its stone foundation. The rambling structure is finished entirely in stucco and covered with an artfully designed roof of red tile, including little rolling coves over each of the attic windows in the servants' quarters. To Ruth's eye, this roof is the most joyful surprise of the day—Jürgen never told her that Kieckow would have the loveliest roof she had ever seen. Below the roof are all the family rooms, with pairs of tall, paned windows positioned symmetrically on either side of the center hall.

The carriage rolls up the gently inclined ramp to the entrance stoop and comes to a sudden halt before a glassed-in entry portico. The coachman jumps from his seat, but too late, for Jürgen has already stepped out, ready to take Ruth's hand. As she throws off the carriage robe and joins Jürgen on the stoop, the glass doors are opened by an invisible hand. The couple enters to be greeted by the housekeeper and overseer of the manor house, with a ready smile, a curtsy and a firm handshake.

In recent years, this woman has been alone in the house much of the time since Hans Hugo is in Berlin for long periods. He lives there with Hans Anton, frail from childhood, and Elisabeth, on whom he depends mightily. Father Kleist is now seventy-one years old, and those who live at Kieckow wish him home again. The village and the agricultural enterprises have all suffered greatly from his extended absences. No lessee or hired manager can substitute for the presence of a caring master and mistress.

Ruth crosses the covered portico through the massive wooden doors that lead to the entry hall of Kieckow. Inside everything seems familiar to her despite the fact she has never been so far north before. As in every manor house she has known, there are heavy velvet drapes, closed in winter against the bitter cold. And just as at home, there is a sitting room, the walls of which support portraits of early kings and those loyal vassals from whom the landowner is descended.

Tea is on the table, but Ruth is not yet ready to sit down; she must first learn who are the other "inhabitants" of this room. Of course, first and foremost there is the great Friedrich, now dead for exactly one hundred years but well and alive in every Prussian heart. Flanking him on either side are General von Borcke and General von Kleist, both ancestors of Jürgen.

On the opposite wall are Hans Jürgen, thrice married, and his last wife Auguste, the grandmother whom Jürgen remembers with fondness. Ruth reflects that the past and the present merge so smoothly when one grows up in an old manor house. Finally there are the newly framed portraits of Father Kleist—Hans Hugo—and Mother Kleist, the former Countess Charlotte; around her neck hangs a gold chain from which is suspended an immense black cross rimmed in gold, with a giant amethyst stone at its center. Ruth inquires whether such a cross really exists, or whether the artist took liberties with the portrait. Jürgen assures her that his mother always wore such a cross on Sundays and during Lent as long as he could remember. The cross had been a gift to Jürgen's grandfather, Count Stolberg, from the late Prussian king; after the old count's death, the cross was passed on to his daughter Charlotte, Jürgen's mother. Over the years, the cross took on mystical powers in the eyes of the Kieckow villagers, for whenever his mother visited the sick or the dying, it hung from her neck over her traditional dark gown. In the family it is still called the Stolberg cross, and at present it belongs to Jürgen's sister Elisabeth. (What Jürgen does not know is that in the village it is referred to as the magic cross, and villagers of all ages wonder who will wear it after Elisabeth.)

Beneath Charlotte's portrait stands a vase of birch branches, with buds just opening, obviously placed there by the housekeeper. Kieckow is still in mourning at the loss of the late mistress who wore the magic cross.

Ruth and Jürgen finally sit down to tea and sandwiches, then an assortment of cakes, both fruit and dry, as custom has demanded as long as anyone can remember. Jürgen insists that there be no dallying, for he intends to show his wife every single room of his childhood home before dark. Besides the entry hall and library sitting room, there are the family rooms and the great banquet hall, which leads to a glass-roofed terrace behind. Ruth vows that she will spend much time on the terrace, for it faces the forest of Kieckow and is well-protected, even on rainy days. As a child, her father once told her that one gains wisdom and strength from the forest; this thought continues to inspire her.

But the clammy cold and the gray monotony of this February afternoon continue to press on the visitor. She wants to make alterations, tear away a drape here, open a door there, rearrange this piece of furniture, take away that one. But Ruth knows she must refrain, for she is not the mistress of Kieckow. Until Father Kleist reaches some long-term decision, the mistress is Elisabeth, who has cared for her father and brother ever since her mother's death. Here stands Elisabeth's house. Ruth recalls the coolness she experienced on first meeting her sister-in-law, and why not? To be raised as a landowner's daughter and then never to be the mistress of a landowner's estate would be a bitter pill for any woman to swallow. Perhaps it also explains why the Protestant convents of Prussia are filled with women from the aristocracy.

As Ruth muses about Elisabeth's position and recalls her own adolescent years, the coachman suddenly appears. He must interrupt the tour, for it is already dusk and the carriage is waiting at the front door to take them to the church. There representatives from the village have been standing outside for over an hour, hoping to greet the new Madam von Kleist.

The carriage retraces its course down the lilac-hedged path, left onto the stone road, through the center of the village, past a frozen pond and to the church. Standing in the cold and dressed for Sunday are the three estate bailiffs, two for Kieckow and one for Klein Krössin, the elected spokesmen from each village, and

the village teacher. Jürgen introduces each of the men in their
proper order. Clearly he knows that all are taking stock of this
very young woman, who they presume will be the next mistress of
the Kieckow manor house.

After the delegation is dismissed, Ruth and Jürgen, alone
together, descend the four stone steps that lead to a crypt
beneath the church. Inside a lamp is burning; in the dim light,
Ruth can see an altar at the far end of the low room, and in front
of it, a coffin. Ruth is shocked at first, for Jürgen has not told her
of this, but he is quick to explain that here lie the remains of his
mother. It has been almost a year since her death; Ruth thinks
back to Grossenborau and Schwentnig—never have the dead
gone unburied in her Silesian homeland, except during the
depth of winter! Perhaps it is different in this northern land. In
truth, though, Pomerania is not so different from Silesia. It is
only that Father Kleist has not yet found himself capable of
ordering the final burial of his wife. For a moment, Ruth and
Jürgen sit on the bench before the altar and place their hands
together on Mother Kleist's coffin while Jürgen recites a familiar
psalm. Strangely, it is one of thanksgiving.

Jürgen leads Ruth back out of the crypt and up the steps; a few
paces farther on, they enter the modest church built by Father
and Mother Kleist. The pastor, who is waiting in front of the
altar, has come down from Gross Tychow, for Kieckow is a
mission church without its own pastor. Pointing to the hard stone
floor, Jürgen begins to tell of the most memorable service ever to
take place in this tiny sanctuary. It was in 1878, after an attempt
on the life of Kaiser Wilhelm, and as soon as the news of this
event reached Kieckow, Father Kleist called everyone in the
village to the church and ordered them to kneel while he, on his
knees, offered a mea culpa on behalf of the entire community.
He confessed to the grievous sin of omission that had been committed by an entire people, himself included, who had failed to
give the kaiser its unquestioning devotion. He concluded with a
petition still talked of in the village: "Heavenly Father, we who
are bowed down before You here in the dust beseech You to
strike us with Your hand, blow upon blow!" Such is the juxtaposition of God and king in this land of the Kleists.

With the pastor, Ruth and Jürgen walk to the altar to view the large, carved cross that hangs above it—an exact copy of the famed Achenbach cross created for the crypt of the Charlottenburg castle near Berlin. Ruth is profoundly moved by this artistic symbol of her deep religious beliefs; it will comfort her untold times in her life; and it will survive the final debacle.

Later that night, after the long ride back to Köslin, Ruth lies in her bed and reviews the events of the day. All in all, Kieckow was a disappointment, nothing like the great estates of Silesia. "Jürgen," she asks aloud, "where are the Pomeranian castles?" Half asleep, Jürgen replies: "My love, our forefathers lived in mud cottages; Pomerania has always been a barren land. But you will learn to love it; now just go to sleep."

And of course it will one day be as Jürgen predicts.

The King is Dead

1886: APRIL. It is spring in Pomerania, although the snow has barely disappeared from the fields. For the second time in her life Ruth is traveling to Kieckow, this time for an entire week, to spend Easter with Jürgen's family.

Father Kleist has returned to Kieckow from Berlin, and with him, Elisabeth and Hans Anton. Whatever the political problems in the capital city, Hans Hugo intends to spend this Holy Week in his country house. The state of the house reflects the family's absence, and for days a cadre of people from the village has been working to put the interior and the courtyard in order. It is especially important this year since Jürgen, the heir to Kieckow, has come for Easter with his wife.

How much happier a place Kieckow is in spring. Not that there is much in bloom beyond the early spring crocuses; but the promise is there, reflected in the tender green that cloaks the pastures and the trees. Ruth begins to develop a fondness for her future home.

Father Kleist is in complete control as in earlier times, and he has revived the twice-daily Kieckow religious devotions. In the morning and in the evening, he gathers all of the servants and his family in the whitewashed entrance hall of the manor house.

It is not quite like the earlier days though, for Mother Kleist is absent and there are no longer small children who sit on the floor, adding their young voices to the singing of the final hymn. There have always been children in the Kieckow manor house, and Father Kleist's hope is that there will be again soon.

Along the walls are simple wooden benches, space enough for all to sit. Father Kleist alone remains standing as he reads a text from the Bible and then expounds upon it. Ruth is deeply moved by the clarity and simplicity of these messages and by the singing of the final hymn, which has become a theme song for the Kleist family: "Come, Thou Bright and Morning Star."[7]

Jürgen remembers a particular singing of this hymn in his childhood, as he set off for boarding school at sunrise one fall day, seated next to his father in one of the Kieckow wagons with his school trunk behind them. He was shivering with cold and filled with trepidation, for it was dark when they rolled down the path from the manor house. But by the time they passed through Klein Krössin and on to the stage road, the heavens brightened with the red of the rising sun. Just then Father's voice burst into song with the words so familiar to Jürgen. The coachman joined in (no one who lived at Kieckow in those days did not know this great hymn), and finally the boy, too, raised his timid voice. Miraculously, his fear of the unknown school vanished. Ruth now knows this story as well as Jürgen, for it is part of the Kleist inheritance she has taken unto herself.

When Father and Mother Kleist resided at Kieckow, each morning and evening devotion was announced by the ringing of the great iron bell that still hangs from the roof outside. In that earlier time, all of the village attended these services, and Ruth also takes this bit of history to heart; when she and Jürgen become the patrons of Kieckow, they will indeed ring the bell and summon all of the villagers to these household rites. Ruth has come to believe that Kieckow is a place of God, and despite her youth, her instinct tells her that it will be her charge to keep it so.

This first Easter at Kieckow, however, is beset by uncertainties having to do with more temporal matters. They present themselves principally in private conversations between Jürgen and Father Kleist, yet they also impact Ruth's relationships with Hans Anton and with Elisabeth.

In Prussia, without special arrangements to the contrary, all landed property passes to the oldest son. By law, estates are never divided, and historically this has been a source of strength for the kingdom. Within families, however, it has often sown the seeds of discord.

Hans Anton, the oldest son, is afflicted by a paralysis that seized him as a child; hence, he was unable to serve in the military. Yet he completed his studies and now pursues a career in the Prussian bureaucracy. Jürgen, the second Kleist son, wanted most of all to have a career in the military—to be a Junker* in its original sense. But Father Kleist ordained otherwise and instead selected a military career for his third son, whose prospects for study were poor. But while serving in the military, this son, Friedrich Wilhelm, namesake and godson of the late king, fell sick and died. Then there is Elisabeth, namesake and godchild of the former queen. She is companion and helpmate to her father in his widowed years, and by tradition, she is also the mistress of Kieckow. Like Ruth of Grossenborau, Elisabeth was expected to marry one day and become mistress of some other great estate; this is the life for which she is prepared. But this has not happened, nor will it ever. Elisabeth remains wedded to Kieckow, and whenever she is there, like her mother before her, she wears the simple dark gown of the land. On Sundays and during Lent, also like her mother before her, she wears around her neck the jeweled black Stolberg cross, symbol of the Kieckow mistress.

OCTOBER. Once again, for the third time in this nineteenth century, a Kleist from Kieckow is named Landrat of the Belgard District.

The appointment and the move both have much to recommend them. Jürgen's rising so quickly into this Belgard position has been a surprise indeed, for there are elements in the district that believe the Kleists are too entrenched and too powerful. But Father Kleist has been diligent on his son's behalf, and his efforts have succeeded.

*Originally the word *Junker* referred to the younger sons in the families of Prussia's landed aristocracy. From the days of Friedrich the Great, each oldest son inherited the family estate intact. Thus the younger sons were destined to serve in the officer corps of the Prussian army. In time, *Junker* came to mean the entire class of landed aristocracy in Prussia.

The flat for the Landrat of Belgard is modest indeed. It encompasses the second floor of an old half-timbered building situated on the edge of a stream that meanders north from Kieckow on its way to the Baltic Sea. The owner of the building lives on the ground floor and operates a dyeworks next door. The two apartments and the dyeworks share a busy courtyard and stables. Besides the stream, the only redeeming exterior feature of this Belgard home is the parklike garden across the street, which belongs to the building owner. From their little balcony, Ruth and Jürgen can gaze across the courtyard to the old oak tree that dominates this garden and envision the lilac bushes they will plant there as soon as spring arrives.

NOVEMBER. Hans Jürgen von Kleist, the namesake of his great-grandfather and the joy of his parents, is born at home in Belgard. His baptism is arranged so that all three living grandparents can be present. The count and countess of Zedlitz and Trützschler are there from Posen, where Grandfather Robert is governor-general of Prussia's largest Polish province; Hans Hugo von Kleist has abandoned a particularly acrimonious parliamentary debate in Berlin and has hurried back to Kieckow so that he too can be present to witness this portentous event. Hans Hugo personally carries to Belgard the Kieckow baptism bowl, from which two generations of Kleists have previously been christened. Because of the inclement weather, the ceremony must take place at home in the parents' modest flat. Afterward there is a small banquet. And of course there are the indispensable speeches! Both grandfathers are gifted orators, and each finds the appropriate words to bring home the significance of this family event and to place this baby within the eternal and temporal order of the universe.

1887: MARCH. Kaiser Wilhelm I of the German Reich is celebrating his ninetieth birthday at the Hohenzollern palace in Potsdam, just outside Berlin. The entire Prussian House of Lords is invited for the occasion, including Hans Hugo von Kleist and Robert, count of Zedlitz and Trützschler. The event is more a gathering of the Prussian aristocracy, a reunion of the old guard, than a state occasion of the German Reich. As usual, Chancellor

Ruth's father Robert, left, count
of Zedlitz and Trützschler, and,
above, her father-in-law
Hans Hugo von Kleist

Bismarck is at center stage. On this day he is visibly agitated, obviously irritated with Crown Prince Friedrich and his wife Victoria over something to do with the arrangements.

Princess Victoria is a daughter of the British Queen of the same name, and the chancellor believes she has brought a number of dangerous English political ideas to her adopted country. He also believes that these ideas have infected her husband. Whatever affection Bismarck might once have had for English women (in his youth he was known to have been in love with two English beauties), he despises Princess Victoria and despairs over what will become of the German Reich when Wilhelm dies. So disturbed is the aging chancellor that he looks for some divine intervention in the matter, perhaps even hoping that the crown prince will die before his father. Although the court has never admitted it, the whole world knows that Friedrich is not well; thus on this festive occasion in the great hall of the palace, Otto von Bismarck has at his side Friedrich's son Wilhelm—grandson of the kaiser and second in line to the German throne. Through a lifetime of attending such social and

45

political gatherings, Hans Hugo and Count Robert have learned to extract political insights from something as ordinary as the movements of the chancellor during a birthday celebration. The two men discuss their observations in whispers, and they are apprehensive.

Far from the uneasy state of affairs in Berlin, the young Landrat at Belgard pursues his new career with energy and optimism. In a roomy flat beside the Belgard dyeworks, a young mother contentedly nurses her baby son.

If there is anything at all amiss in the second year of this celebrated marriage, it has nothing to do with the uncertainties that plague the older generation in Berlin. Rather it is the fierce possessiveness the young wife displays toward her husband. She chides herself over this selfish, childish behavior—her inordinate fear that she will lose Jürgen as she once thought she had so soon after meeting him. Unfortunately she has difficulty controlling herself when Jürgen is gone overnight, and this happens at least once a month.

Sixty kilometers south of Belgard lies Bad Polzin, the prosperous second city in the Belgard District. Each month Jürgen makes a two-day visit to Polzin, and each time he departs, Ruth watches from the balcony and then dissolves into tears when his carriage pulls away toward the south stage road.

Jürgen views his district with immense optimism. He is most conscientious in performing his everyday duties and relishes each visit to Polzin. He questions and he observes, in the hope of applying the innovative notions practiced there at Belgard. Fortunately he is not distracted by thoughts of Ruth, sobbing at home on the balcony; neither she nor the servants will ever tell.

For Jürgen, the Polzin visits are a source of energy and inspiration. This city is unlike Belgard in all ways except size; both have approximately three thousand inhabitants. Whereas Belgard's roots go back to his original Klest ancestors, who in the thirteenth century followed the Teutonic Knights to Pomerania, Polzin is a sixteenth-century city, founded during Polish times and originally inhabited by Jewish settlers. The population is now ten percent Jewish, and the city is a model of modern enterprise—an energetic island set amidst the sluggish Pomeranian economy. The Jews are principally engaged in cattle buying and leather manufacturing. Alongside them are the non-Jewish weavers, whose diligence and skill have earned the city a reputation throughout all of Prussia and have generated an enviable prosperity. The streets of Polzin are lined with substantial residential and commercial buildings built of brick and stone. These are surrounded by carefully maintained public boulevards and parks and a level of carriage traffic not to be found elsewhere in rural Pomerania. The Belgard District is blessed to have this rich center within its boundaries, and Jürgen dreams of transporting the energy and skills of Polzin to the northern corners of his district.

He has discussed this with his father Hans Hugo, who thirty years ago made similar observations and comparisons. In fact, in his time as the Belgard Landrat, Father prevailed upon the district to tax the landowners and subsidize the superior hospital at Polzin so that every person in the district might receive medical care there at no cost.

Father Kleist colors life in black and white, with very few shades of gray. Ten years ago he became enamored with a new political movement, the Christian Social Workingman's Union. The organization was inspired by one of the chaplains in the kaiser's court, Adolf Stöcker, a man of charismatic qualities to whom Father Kleist has become very attached. The name of Stöcker's organization suggests its bent—social reform, the betterment of the workers' lot, a blurring of class distinctions, and above all, a brotherhood based on Christianity. For a man steeped in conservatism bordering on feudalism, yet imbued with the nineteenth-century Pomeranian Christian revival spirit, Stöcker's radical social concepts offer rebirth in an evangelistic sense.

The other side of the Workingman's Union is its virulent anti-Semitism, which is so virulent that Crown Prince Friedrich has denounced it as "a shame and a disgrace to Germany." While Hans Hugo is not unmindful of the underside of Stöcker's ideal Christian state, he defends it by saying that the portrayal of the Jews is somewhat justified, and in any case, it is only part of an agenda that can revitalize the spiritual qualities of all Germany.

What a strange relationship men like Hans Hugo maintain with the few Jews they meet in everyday life. For instance, he

admires the industriousness of Polzin, this jewel within the
Belgard District, where the middle class is dominated by Jews. Yet
he distances himself from all Jews, complaining that they are no
better than street musicians. When his son marvels at this
unlikely comparison, Father Kleist shares with him his frustrations from the days when he managed Kieckow himself.

At that time, there was nothing more disruptive to the estate
economy than a group of traveling musicians. They would arrive
in the morning and remain until evening, entertaining the
entire village while the workers dropped their last hard-earned
coins into the musicians' open hands, a waste of money for the
people and a wasted day for the estate. In Father's opinion, the
Jewish peddlers were no better. They came to Kieckow in order
to purchase hides, invariably arriving on a day when the bailiff
was absent. All work in the village ceased as they bickered and
bargained, offering either money or trinkets in exchange for the
large and small animal skins the men had acquired during the
season. From Father's point of view, the villagers received much
less than the hides were worth, and since those days he has
allowed no Jews at Kieckow.

Jürgen reminds his father that the Jewish peddlers at least paid
the villagers in money, of which there was otherwise mighty little
to distribute at Kieckow. And anyway, Jürgen concludes cheerfully, with the railroads expanding and new ways of farming, both
the peddlers and the musicians will soon disappear. He has no
time for naysayers and even less for demagogues.

What Jürgen does not completely understand is that ideas die
slowly and the collective mind remembers little and forgets
nothing. Thirty years after Father Kleist's involvement with Adolf
Stöcker's misbegotten crusade, one Adolf Hitler will rework
Stöcker's theses, eliminating some of the Christian biases and
expanding on the Jewish themes. Hitler's efforts will result in a
book entitled *Mein Kampf.* Very few Germans will read this book.
Among those who do, some will be captured by its idealistic portrayal of the state and the people. They may even excuse those
racial themes that appear unacceptable or preposterous, much
as Father Kleist did in Stöcker's time.

A few voices will speak up, readers of *Mein Kampf* who choose
to believe Adolf Hitler means what he says when he expounds his

racial theories, be they directed against the Jews or the Slavs. Among these will be two Kleists from Pomerania, Kleist of Kieckow and Kleist of Schmenzin. They will spell out their warnings in a printed tract that will go unheeded. Yet sixty years later, a hundred years after Stöcker's crusade, Germans will whisper to each other: "Yes, the Kleists of Pomerania; historically they were anti-Semitic always."

1888: MARCH. Ruth is expecting her second child, yet there she is on hands and knees next to Jürgen in the garden across from the Belgard dyeworks. Together they are planting lilac bushes brought from Kieckow while little Hans Jürgen looks on.

At Potsdam, Robert, count of Zedlitz and Trützschler, stands bareheaded outside the Hohenzollern family church. Before him, the casket of Wilhelm I, the king and kaiser, is carried from a horse-drawn caisson into the crypt below. The king's guard salutes the casket, then turns to salute the new king and kaiser—Friedrich III. Robert marvels at the precision of the guards and recalls that he once was one of them, and as if by reflex, he also salutes. How far the world has come in these years.

Standing nearby, Hans Hugo von Kleist is absorbed in his own thoughts as he too watches the movement of the casket and the salutes to the fallen kaiser and to his successor. Wrapped in scarves, the pale kaiser bears mighty little resemblance to the proud ancestor whose namesake he is; and his wife, now the queen, looks distressed indeed. The chancellor stands between her and Crown Prince Wilhelm, as if to isolate the young man from his mother. Only Wilhelm looks fit and confident, wearing the full uniform of the German navy with a military bearing that ought to inspire every German officer. One would hardly believe he has a withered arm. Yet to Hans Hugo this young man is still a stranger, and this day is indeed a day of mourning for Father Kleist. The wind blows cold; the kaiser is ill; and Otto von Bismarck will not cast one glance in the direction of his Uncle Hans.

JUNE. At Potsdam, Robert, count of Zedlitz and Trützschler, and Hans Hugo von Kleist again stand bareheaded next to each other outside the church of the Hohenzollerns. Before them, the

casket of Friedrich III, their king and kaiser, is carried into the
family crypt. This king's reign has lasted but ninety-nine days, for
he was already gravely ill with cancer when he assumed power.
The king's guard salutes the casket, then turns to salute the new
king and kaiser, Friedrich's son Wilhelm II.

The Christening Bowl

1888: JULY. In the afternoon of a day filled with sunshine and
warmth, a daughter is born to Ruth and Jürgen von Kleist. The
name they have chosen for her is Spes, the Latin word for
"hope"; the very next morning, Ruth carries the infant from her
bedroom to the balcony of their flat in Belgard in order to view
the garden across the street, so lovingly planted in spring.

A week later the families of Ruth and Jürgen gather for a
second christening in Belgard, this time at the ancient Church of
St. Mary, to which Ruth has become deeply attached. This four-
teenth-century edifice, with its arrowlike nave, is considered to
be the jewel of Pomerania. Once more, Father Kleist has brought
with him the Kieckow christening bowl, which now stands on the
baptismal font below St. Mary's famous seventeenth-century
altar. Flowers Ruth has picked herself from the garden across the
stream surround the bowl and fill the two vases on the altar.

Flowers have always played a significant part in her life. On
ordinary days, flowers in bloom bring joy to the most mundane
tasks; on occasions of celebration, such as this christening, they
magnify the joy already felt; later Ruth will discover that the blossoms from her garden can comfort and lighten the burden in
times of intense sadness and deep tragedy.

The family has formed a little procession from the church
back to the flat, where the christening banquet will take place.
Despite the fact that the banquet hall is reached from a dark
flight of stone steps above a cluttered courtyard, and that the
young mother and her servants are constantly battling mice in
the dining room cupboards, this celebration is not to be fore-
gone. Among the Prussian aristocracy, a banquet such as this is
the glue that holds together a tradition, a class, and indeed an
entire nation. At least this is what the child's parents and grandparents believe, and it is assumed that the child in turn will grow

to accept this view of the world. Yet it will be Spes, among all of Ruth's children, who one day will question, then rebel, and finally go a different way.

Later that day, Father Kleist returns by wagon to Kieckow to return the christening bowl to its honored resting place. He is tired; he worries about the Socialists and the Polish nationalists, and about business—all the interests that portend future change for Pomerania. The lease on Kieckow still has eight years to run, but Hans Hugo knows that he will not last that long. His greatest wish is that Ruth and Jürgen will take over the estate when it is free again, and he has stated this wish clearly in his last will.

In the meantime, the young parents rejoice in their small son and their infant daughter, and increasingly participate in the society of Belgard. They have acquired a circle of friends with whom connections go back for generations, including several families who were initially opposed to another Kleist from Kieckow taking over as Landrat of the district. And somewhere in the back of Ruth's mind, the thought that she will one day be mistress of Kieckow kindles her imagination and enlivens her hopes for the future.

1889. The Landrat of Belgard has proposed that the district council acquire an official residence, not only to provide decent accommodations for his own family, but also the offices and reception rooms the post of Landrat ought to command. One must assume that Jürgen has memories of the elegant governor's residence in Oppeln, where he once courted and later married his bride. Naturally there is some reluctance to approve the proposal, for such a residence will cost a great deal of money, and the chronic shortage of money in Pomerania is not limited to the landowners and peasants.

Although Jürgen's proposal is ridiculed in some quarters, the council nevertheless approves it, and soon the district purchases a substantial building at the intersection of Belgard's main boulevard and the equally lovely Luisenstrasse. Behind the building lies an undeveloped meadow, which the district also purchases. Together Ruth and Jürgen draw up plans for the formal garden and park that will become part of the Belgard Landrat's residence. The design of the park and the supervision of the stonework and planting will be among Ruth's fondest memories from the Belgard years—not only the hours of planning alone with Jürgen, but also the discovery of hidden talents in herself that otherwise may never have surfaced.

The family quarters in the new residence are a far cry from the modest flat next to the dyeworks. To begin with, there are no mice, and Ruth has every intention of keeping it that way. The rooms are spacious, so large in fact that additional pieces of furniture are brought by wagon from Kieckow to fill the empty corners. Then there are the balconies, one in every room that faces the garden. Very few weeks in the year go by without Ruth and Jürgen having afternoon tea on a balcony while overseeing the upkeep of the gardens.

Jürgen's office and the district reception rooms are located in the same building as the living quarters. From Ruth's perspective, Jürgen is always at home, and for a wife as possessive as she, this is a happy state of affairs.

1890. Otto von Bismarck resigns as chancellor of Germany and prime minister of Prussia, submitting his resignation to the young Kaiser Wilhelm in protest over the kaiser's decision to abandon the Reinsurance Treaty with Russia in favor of a closer alliance with Austria-Hungary. But this is only an obfuscation of the real issue—Wilhelm's leanings toward a more democratic Germany in which even the Socialists will play a role. On the threshold of a new decade, the young kaiser understands the need for a more democratic government much better than Bismarck and most other Junkers in Pomerania. Unfortunately it is Bismarck who understands foreign policy better. Without him, Wilhelm will embark on policies that eventually alienate Russia on the east and help pave the way to the First World War.

This is not the first resignation that Bismarck has tendered to a kaiser. When Wilhelm's grandfather ruled, Bismarck did this quite regularly, whenever it appeared that his base of power was slipping away. The difference is that the grandfather eventually always came around, for he wanted least of all to lose his chancellor, but the grandson has no such compulsion; hence he has accepted the resignation, with outer regret but inner satisfaction.

After forty years of service to five Prussian kings, three of whom were also German kaisers, Otto von Bismarck abdicates with great bitterness and, no doubt, deep sadness. He is seventy-five years old, while the kaiser is but thirty-one. The only member of the government to leave with him is his son Herbert von Bismarck, godchild of Hans Hugo von Kleist. Otto always hoped that Herbert would eventually succeed him; hence he had him appointed secretary of state, in charge of Germany's foreign affairs. As the faithful son, Herbert must also resign and share in his father's bitterness and sadness.

And Hans Hugo von Kleist? He too is seventy-five years old, with forty years of public service behind him. To him the resignation means that his nephew Otto is finally returning to the Junker fold after years of estrangement and abandonment. Unlike Otto, Hans Hugo holds no bitterness. He has never manipulated and never behaved in a politically expedient manner. He has simply been true to his ideals, serving God, the Fatherland, and his own family. Although he has not risen to the heights of Bismarck, neither has he fallen to the depths his nephew has. Hans Hugo will remain in Berlin and in the House of Lords, casting his vote among the conservatives as he has done for forty years. He now places his hopes in the new kaiser's own choice for Prussian prime minister and German chancellor—Leo von Caprivi, a Silesian aristocrat who has more in common with Count Robert than with this old Pomeranian Junker.

1891: FEBRUARY. On a Sunday morning, the first day of the month and just three days before his mother's birthday, Konstantin von Kleist is born at the Landrat's new residence in Belgard. Outside, the church bells are ringing, as if to announce the arrival of this Sunday child.

AUGUST. The Landrat, his wife and three children are spending their summer holiday near the Oder River in the old Stolberg family castle, childhood home of Mother Kleist and still home to Jürgen's great-aunt, Elisa Stolberg. Even for Ruth, the daughter of a manor house, the Stolberg castle has a fairy tale quality about it. It is surrounded by a deep forest, and inside there are rooms upon rooms upon rooms, each more elaborate and imaginative than the other. An entire wing of the castle has been set aside for Jürgen and his family, plus the nursemaid, with supplies and servants furnished far beyond the needs of the visitors. In the children's nursery, three beautifully dressed dolls lie on the nursemaid's couch, each with a delicate porcelain face framed by a satin bonnet. But for the quick intervention of the nursemaid, Hans Jürgen and sister Spes would quickly have taken the pretty dolls to use them in their favorite game of "let's pretend." Tante Elisa proudly relates how these three dolls go back to her own childhood and how she has preserved them carefully for future children who might one day live in the Stolberg castle.

In the winter of 1945, four of Ruth's grandchildren, the oldest just twenty, will arrive at the Stolberg castle by horse and wagon; they too will be sheltered in rooms along this wing, but just for one night. Like Ruth and her children in 1891, these later grandchildren will marvel at the porcelain dolls with their exquisite dresses and satin bonnets. These visitors will move on quickly the next morning, supplied with fresh provisions and leaving the dolls just as they found them. A week later the castle and everything in it will be bombarded by heavy cannon fire until it is nothing but rubble.

1892: JANUARY. Father Kleist is ailing badly, but he refuses to leave Berlin. For the first time in years, the government is proposing a law that is dear to his heart, and it may in fact have a chance for success. The catalyst for this bold new move is none other than Ruth's father Robert, count of Zedlitz and Trützschler. Only a few months earlier, Caprivi summoned Count Robert from Posen and appointed him Minister of Culture in Prussia. In this capacity, he is responsible not only for education in all of the Prussian provinces, but also for maintaining the delicate relations between church and state.

Count Robert is now fifty-five years old, with a vigor and an energy that belie his age. His genius has always been the ability to moderate crises, particularly those that arise from the enforcement of harsh legislation. While Bismarck was chancellor, relations between church and state in Germany followed an uneven course, depending on the chancellor's need to court the Center Party, in other words, the Catholic vote.

Chancellor von Caprivi has taken a more universal view of church relations, particularly as these affect education, and his appointment of Count Robert confirms this. The new Minister of Culture has prepared legislation that will permit religious education in the public schools and will also reverse other harsh legislation against the churches, laws that go back to the first years of Bismarck's administration. Historically, these measures were part of Bismarck's strident and emotional battle with the Catholic church and particularly with the Jesuit order of priests, who are influential in Catholic education. Although the Pomeranian Junkers have lost no love on the Catholic church, they are increasingly opposed to these laws, which also rob the Protestant church of its role in the education of its children. Hans Hugo stands firmly with the pietistic Junkers who oppose these laws; Count Robert stands with the Pomeranians in their opposition. He also sees beyond the religious consequences of these antichurch laws and opposes them on political grounds; in Prussia's Polish provinces a rising national consciousness is being reinforced by issues that are viewed as religious persecution by these deeply Catholic subjects.

On behalf of Chancellor von Caprivi and with the support of the kaiser, Count Robert has introduced a revolutionary education bill in the Prussian Chamber of Deputies. Hans Hugo is ecstatic. He hopes the debate will be short, however, for he is plagued with a constant cough, and the weather in Berlin is terrible. His daughter Elisabeth, ever at his side, is worried about her father's health and wants to take him home to Kieckow.

MARCH. For two months the debate has raged in the Prussian Chamber of Deputies, filled with the kind of acrimony not heard in Germany for a decade. One might almost believe that a new religious war is in the making. At Belgard, Ruth reads her daily letter from Father Kleist in Berlin, in which he reports faithfully on the progress of Father Zedlitz's legislation, summarizing Father's speeches on the floor of the Chamber as well as the glowing statements of his supporters. Reading his letters, Ruth anticipates that the vote will be soon and that her father's bold vision of church and state will become a reality.

Unexpectedly, though, the kaiser begins to vacillate and subsequently withdraws his support. Dumbfounded, Count Robert recalls his bill immediately and resigns his post as Minister of Culture in Prussia. Chancellor von Caprivi is furious, and twenty-four hours later, in protest over the kaiser's weakness, he resigns as prime minister of Prussia, retaining his post as German chancellor. For the first time ever, these two offices are no longer united in one person, a turn of events that bodes ill for Caprivi's effectiveness as chancellor and, more seriously, for the stability of the German Reich.

After four decades of politics, Hans Hugo leaves his flat in Berlin and returns with Elisabeth to Kieckow.

APRIL. The master of Kieckow is now a familiar sight in the village church, and as in earlier years, no Sunday service begins without his presence. The sermons are always long at Kieckow, and on his first Sunday home, the master snored loudly all the time the pastor preached. But no more—the old man has vowed never to fall asleep again! At the beginning of every sermon, he rises from his seat and remains standing until the end. No one among the congregation casts an embarrassed glance; not even the children smile. At Kieckow, what the master does is by definition correct.

Elisabeth, now the reigning mistress of Kieckow, is seated next to her father. Over her dark dress and mantle, she wears the Stolberg cross. Privately the villagers wonder when the new young mistress will take over and what will then become of the familiar Elisabeth. There is much talk in the village about who will wear the magic cross. "Wait and see," the wise ones say.

Festival at Harvest Time

1892: MAY. Hans Hugo von Kleist is dying. From Kieckow to Belgard to Stettin to Berlin the word has gone out. Kaiser Wilhelm sends a personal message, wishing him a complete recovery. Hans Hugo, still conscious, smiles at the news, knowing that the kaiser only sends such greetings when the condition is hopeless. Nevertheless he is immensely pleased; among the Prussian aristocrats, one is always pleased to have the king take notice.

Early in the morning on the twentieth of the month, Father
Kleist breathes his last. His children, Hans Anton, Jürgen and
Elisabeth, are at his bedside. By nightfall they are joined by Ruth
and the grandchildren, Hans Jürgen, Spes and Konstantin. This
funeral is Ruth's first family funeral as an adult, and she doesn't
even own a mourning dress. The housekeeper quickly comes to
her aid, and within twenty-four hours a complete mourning
ensemble, including hat and full veil, has been created by a
seamstress from the village. Ruth hardly recognizes herself in the
mirror; hopefully, she will not need this gown again for many,
many years.

She has no way of knowing that in just five years she will put on
the gown again and wear it day after day for twelve long months.

The Kieckow church overflows with mourners; the pews are
filled, and many stand against the walls and even listen as best
they can from outside. Aside from the family members and those
from the village, there are landowners and other acquaintances,
mostly from the Belgard District but some from as far away as
Stargard, where the Puttkamers and Bismarcks have their estates.
Although most of Father Kleist's contemporaries are gone, a few
remain, among them Philipp von Bismarck, Otto's nephew and a
long-time friend of Hans Hugo. Noticeably absent is the former
chancellor; at seventy-seven years of age, Otto von Bismarck is
traveling about the country on a lecture circuit, courting the
people of Germany with the intent of coming to power once
more. Old friends and family only shake their heads in dismay
and remember that once when they were all much younger, they
called him the Mad Junker.

Then there are the official guests, whose presence will be
immortalized for three generations of Kieckow Kleists by the
names they enter in the manor house guestbook. The assem-
blage includes the kaiser's aide-de-camp and personal representative, Captain Jacobi, as well as Puttkamer, the Prussian prime
minister, Reich Treasurer von Maltzahn-Gueltz, and the vice president of the House of Lords, Baron Manteuffel.

Fifty years later, Ruth's son Hans Jürgen will burn the guestbook, for in the Third Reich, one becomes known by the friends
who come to call.

The master of Kieckow is dead. His successor will not take over for four more years, until the Kieckow lease expires, for he cannot afford to buy out the tenant manager. In the meantime, Elisabeth von Kleist presides as mistress while Hans Anton comes and goes as suits his nature; Jürgen and Ruth return to Belgard with their children. Jürgen has little to say regarding the future of the estate, but only comments wistfully to Ruth, "Oh, if we could only live together at Kieckow, but that would be too much happiness."

In the crypt under the Kieckow church there are now two coffins, as Father Kleist's remains join Mother's. Jürgen, who shares with Ruth every joy and sadness of his life, does not explain. She senses there is disagreement with his brother and sister as to where their parents should be buried.

SEPTEMBER. Jürgen has been called up as an army reserve officer and ordered to report for a month's military training. It is the first time since his marriage he has received such orders, for his name is not on the active reserve list. This particular callup, however, is termed an emergency maneuver; obviously it is related to the kaiser's increasingly ambitious foreign policy, which his detractors have dubbed "saber rattling." Jürgen is not ignorant of these political dynamics. Nevertheless, as a reserve officer, he is obliged to fulfill his military duties and demonstrate once again his unwavering loyalty to the kaiser.

Ruth has always taken pity on those young wives whose husbands are in the active reserve and must leave them for an entire month out of every year. Now she too must share this experience. Upon hearing the news, Father Zedlitz has immediately sent Ruth an invitation to visit Grossenborau for the month. After so many years in public service, he and Mother are now on the estate and he is managing it himself. It will be Ruth's first visit to her Silesian homeland since her marriage, and it will be the children's first visit ever.

At the Belgard railroad station, Ruth waves a tearful farewell to the children. Six-year-old Hans Jürgen holds tightly to the hand of his sister Spes to keep the active four-year-old from falling out onto the railroad tracks. Little Konstantin smiles bravely and waves at his mother from the nursemaid's arms. The four are leaving by train for Grossenborau, where Ruth will join them later. First she will travel to Berlin with Jürgen, who wants her to see his regiment on parade before it moves into the field.

From a reserved seat at the Tempelhof parade grounds, Ruth watches the magnificent parade. Like her husband, she is easily caught up in the martial airs of the German Reich. Her heart is stirred to see the troops marching with their colorful banners and the bands playing their regimental tunes. She is after all a Prussian and imbued with the ideals of her ancestors, generations of loyal vassals of the king.

In the years since her childhood, the German army has become a modern machine, and on parade, an ever grander spectacle to behold. She is slightly disappointed that from her vantage point, she cannot distinguish her lieutenant from the others, but cheers herself with the thought that she and Jürgen still have one night together in Berlin's Bellevue Hotel.

Early the following morning, in full uniform, Jürgen says goodbye. It is an emotional farewell on Ruth's part; she is not always the good soldier that she would like to be.

A day later, at the Friedrichstrasse railroad station, Ruth is settled in a compartment of the train to Freystadt. She has arrived well ahead of the scheduled boarding time and is gazing idly out the window when her eyes fall on a banner spanning the street. To her amazement, it announces the trooping of the First Garde Field Artillery Regiment—Jürgen's regiment—on its way to the field. She is dumbfounded, for she can already hear the military band in the distance. Rushing from her compartment and out of the train, she dashes across the street to a position where she can see the band as it comes into full view. Behind the band are the commander, his adjutant, and the captain, all three on horseback, followed by one platoon after another, each led by a lieutenant, marching with spectacular precision. And then comes Jürgen's platoon, with Jürgen in the lead. He looks straight at her with not even the smallest change in his expression and then is gone. Yet she knows he recognized her, for he dipped his sword ever so slightly.

So Jürgen is now all soldier, torn from the one who loves him more than anything in the world! Ruth cannot bear the thought. Tears streaming down her face, she returns to her compartment, where she buries her head in the upholstered seat, sobbing inconsolably all the way to her destination. Not until Freystadt, at the sight of her three happy children on the station platform, does the young wife and mother regain her composure. Later Ruth will scold herself for such unseemly behavior, but she will forgive herself also, believing that her heart must already have known what would ultimately happen.

1893: MAY. A second daughter, Maria, is born to Jürgen and Ruth at the Landrat's residence in Belgard. Her head is covered with a mass of thick black curls, and even on her first day in this world, the tiny infant's face wears a joyous look.

Maria's christening is the first without Father Kleist, but the Zedlitz grandparents are present and so are sister Anni von Tresckow and her husband Hermann. The baby is healthy, and the Kieckow christening bowl shines brilliantly. What more is there to wish for in a family?

1896: MAY. Everything happens at once, the good and the bad together! The Kieckow lease has finally run out, and the entire estate, along with its debts, now belongs to Jürgen as Father Kleist had ordained. For days, empty wagons are sent to Belgard, returning to Kieckow laden with boxes and furniture. Mother, four children, a cook, a maid and a children's nurse all are being moved from the Landrat's residence to the Kieckow manor house for the summer. Half the village is involved in the preparations, for it has been years since the manor house received any attention. As if to welcome its new mistress, Kieckow is now in full bloom—the chestnut trees, the lilacs, the snowballs and even the beginnings of the azaleas, which are normally not expected for another month.

Except for Elisabeth's leave-taking, this would be a time of immense joy for Ruth. The homecoming she has looked forward to ever since her first visit ten years earlier is perceived by Elisabeth as an eviction, even though Jürgen has assured her that her room will be waiting whenever she wishes to visit. She is leaving for Berlin, where she will live in the flat she once shared with Father Kleist and Hans Anton. Before his death, Father bequeathed this to her so that she would always have a home of her own. For Elisabeth, the arrival of a new mistress at Kieckow is a bitter pill to swallow. She will return again to her childhood home but twice, each time for a brother's funeral. With Elisabeth goes the Stolberg cross; Ruth silently chides herself that she ever coveted this symbol of feminine power at Kieckow.

The breach with Elisabeth is soon overshadowed by Jürgen's complaints of ill health. It is obvious the move has been stressful for him, and added to that he is alone in Belgard during the week. Each Friday afternoon the Kieckow carriage stands at the Landrat's office, ready to take the husband and father home to his family. On one occasion, after Ruth has thrown her arms about Jürgen's waist to greet him on his arrival, he admonishes her: "Ruth, my love, do not press so." And one night in bed he tells her apologetically, but firmly: "I must turn away from you tonight, my dear; there is a pain in my side when I face you." This admission causes an equally painful lurching in Ruth's heart.

Ruth finally convinces Jürgen that a vacation is needed—at a health resort, where he can bathe in the hot spring waters. They are gone for an entire month, leaving the children in the care of servants, the estate in the care of the bailiff, and the affairs of the district in the hands of Jürgen's assistant. It is good when one has trustworthy employees.

SEPTEMBER. The vacation has helped a little; the pain is still there, but Jürgen at least feels stronger. It is he who suggests that the traditional Kieckow harvest festival be instituted once again, and Ruth is ecstatic. It has been twelve years since the last festival was held; after Mother Kleist died, Father could never bring himself to revive this popular celebration. Since coming to Kieckow, Ruth has made regular visits to the village, and in just four months she has learned much about the people—their hopes, their memories and their traditions. She has come to know every family by name, and in her conversations with them, she has heard over and over how much they loved the Kieckow festivals. She vows to her husband, "Oh Jürgen, this year it will be as never before!"

OCTOBER. It is Sunday and the church service has finished early. In honor of the occasion the pastor has given his shortest sermon ever! Two entire villages, Kieckow and Klein Krössin, are gathered outside the Kieckow schoolhouse. The village spokesman is shouting orders, trying to get the excited, unruly children to line up for the procession—"boys with the men and girls with the women." Each man carries a scythe and each woman a rake, and every implement is bedecked with a garland of flowers.

On the carriage ramp at the manor house, Ruth and Jürgen await the procession. Standing beside them are their four children, Hans Jürgen, Spes, Konstantin and Maria, and behind them are Jürgen's Kleist cousin from Schmenzin to the east, Ruth's sister Anni von Tresckow with her husband, and a host of friends and colleagues from the Belgard District. Shortly after the sounds of music reach them from the village, they catch a glimpse of the procession—first only bits of color from behind the thick stand of trees, but then in full view as it rounds the corner and winds up the road to the manor house. Leading the parade is a single trombone player, trying his best to make one instrument sound like an entire marching band. Directly behind him walks a very old woman carrying the harvest crown, her own handiwork—a thick garland of flowers into which she has entwined a stalk or leaf representing every crop grown at Kieckow and Klein Krössin.

With a wave of his arms and a nod of his head, the spokesman gathers the villagers into a group in front of the carriage ramp. When all is quiet, the reviewers express their approval with enthusiastic applause. When they too fall silent, the spokesman steps forward and, taking the harvest crown from the old woman, ceremoniously presents it to the master of Kieckow and Klein Krössin.

Once more the trombone sounds, this time with the notes of a harvest hymn that has been sung on this Sunday in every church on every estate throughout Prussia, as long as anyone can remember:

> Now thank we all our God
> With heart and hands and voices . . .[8]

Now it is the master's turn. Conscious of the fact that he is walking in his father's footsteps, Jürgen addresses the large gathering, still holding the crown in his hands. He takes his theme from this hymn of thanksgiving—thanks be to God for the bountiful harvest and thanks be to all who dwell at Kieckow and Klein Krössin, for their hard work, their honesty, and their loyalty to God, to the Fatherland, and to the House of Kleist. Finally, he expresses his gratitude to the late master of Kieckow that the family Kleist is once again engaged in its traditional agricultural pursuits on these ancient Prussian lands. The speech is short, in line with Jürgen's limited energy, yet some of the listeners are moved to tears.

Now the harvest foreman steps to the front to speak the traditional words of response to the master. On this occasion, he is especially sincere, for the village too has suffered under years of tenant leases. When he is finished, he turns to his men, who join him in the age-old cheer to the landowners of Pomerania: "Er Lebe Hoch, Lebe Hoch, Lebe Hoch."* By tradition, the cheer is given three times—once for the master, once for the mistress and once for the children of the manor house. With each word, the men strike their scythes in unison. Once again, the villagers break into song while the master hangs the harvest crown in a conspicuous spot on the front wall of the house, where it will remain until another harvest.

This is only act one. Act two is the banquet meal, served in an empty granary. A dozen long tables are set up for the meal; on one side are those for the landowner, his family and friends, and on the other side, those for the village workers. When all are seated, the pastor stands to give the table blessing. Next comes a "Hoch Leben" to the kaiser, and there is a flurry of activity as everyone rises to stand at attention. At last the meal is served, thanks to the efforts of all forty servants attached to the manor house in one way or another. The cavernous building echoes with the pleasant sounds of good cheer and hearty laughter.

When the eating is finished, Jürgen von Kleist rises from his seat, holding a huge silver goblet filled with wine. Inviting his guests to drink with him, he takes one sip, then passes the goblet to Ruth, who also takes a sip; it is then passed in turn to each person at their table. A servant stands ready to carry the goblet

*May he live well!

to the next table, to be passed around again, then on to the next table, until everyone has drunk of the wine.

Out on the lawn the children are running hither and yon, barely able to contain their excitement, for they know that act three is especially for them. Not the least of these are Hans Jürgen, Spes, Konstantin and Maria of the manor house. Now the new mistress has her moment in the sun. Ruth has organized a number of children's games—a sack race, blindman's bluff, and a climbing maze, all remembered fondly from her own childhood. She has arranged little prizes for the competitions, and each is presented formally with a handshake to the winner.

In preparation for the final act, the men of the village have brought the long tables and the chairs outside and placed them under the trees. Once again, servants are busy bringing pitchers of coffee and trays of cakes as the tables are quickly occupied. Following the tradition established two decades earlier by her mother-in-law, Ruth goes from table to table with pitchers of hot coffee, filling empty cups and heating up those partially filled, not stopping until the setting sun and the evening chill send the villagers back to their homes. Over and over again, the villagers express their thanks, often with tears in their eyes, and bid farewell until next year.

But next year there will be no harvest festival; there will not be such a festival at Kieckow for another generation.

"Faithful Unto Death"

1896: NOVEMBER. The festival has buoyed Jürgen's spirits immensely, but it has done nothing to stem the relentless progress of his physical illness. Ruth is proud that the day she planned all on her own was so enjoyable for him and for the villagers, but her spirits sag as Jürgen's pain increases. He now has trouble eating, and as he grows thinner, the doctor prescribes another month away, this time at a sanatorium in the south.

For an entire month Jürgen and Ruth, who is pregnant with her fifth child, rest together at a mountain resort. Dutifully they drink the water, bathe in the soothing mineral springs and partake of the bland diet that is supposed to restore the ailing patient to health and benefit the expectant mother. Jürgen's condition does not noticeably improve.

1897: MAY. A third daughter is born to Ruth and Jürgen in the Landrat's residence at Belgard. A few days later, in the ancient Church of St. Mary, she is christened Ruth, with water dipped from the Kieckow bowl. Her mother weeps in joy and in sadness, for she has a premonition that this daughter will never know her father.

OCTOBER. The Landrat's Belgard residence is all but abandoned since the Landrat can no longer fulfill his professional duties. Jürgen has come home to Kieckow. He drags his ailing body slowly about the estate, then sits alone on the terrace, drawing comfort from looking into the forest. Neither his wife nor his children, especially not his infant daughter, can give him any solace, for the pain is more than he can bear. The physician has determined that it is a disease of the kidneys whose effects will eventually reach Jürgen's brain. He speaks the truth; Jürgen hardly recognizes his own children these days. Although he offers no hope for a cure, the doctor suggests once more that Ruth take her husband to a sanatorium.

By now Ruth is painfully torn between the needs of husband and children; still she chooses the former. Although winter is at hand, she musters all of her strength to take Jürgen to a sanatorium in the Austrian Alps. With the help of the coachman and the bailiff, she loads him into a carriage for the drive to Belgard, where they place him in a train compartment made into a berth. Alone with her patient, Ruth comforts him as best she can. At Dresden they are to change trains for the final lap of their journey, but long before the train reaches that city, Jürgen's condition deteriorates so profoundly that Ruth decides they cannot go farther. In Dresden she summons help and takes her dying husband to a hotel room.

NOVEMBER. Jürgen von Kleist leaves this world from an unfamiliar room in a Dresden hotel. Ruth returns to Kieckow by train, with her husband's body already encased in a coffin. She who throughout life has shed a surplus of tears when none were required is now unable to produce a single one.

The great hall is draped in black, and Jürgen's coffin is set down in the center of the room, where it is to remain until the funeral. Unused to death in the family, Ruth at first feels comforted that the younger children go about their play, seemingly undistressed by the coffin in their midst. One afternoon as she passes the closed door of the boys' room she overhears a piteous sobbing; opening the door, she discovers seven-year-old Konstantin lying on the floor in tears, consumed by his grief. As she takes the child into her arms to quiet him, the boy pleads with his mother to open the coffin so that he might look at his father one more time. Ruth must tell him no. Never again in his life will Konstantin shed tears. On occasion, they will well up in his eyes, but he will hold his jaw firmly until they go away. It is unseemly for a Junker boy to cry.

Jürgen's sister Elisabeth, his brother Hans Anton, Father and Mother Zedlitz, and Ruth's sisters and brothers and their spouses are all gathered at Kieckow. Elisabeth is dressed in deep mourning garb, and from around her neck hangs the gold-rimmed Stolberg cross. Consumed by her own grief, Ruth does not even take notice. She is wearing the black gown that was made for her when Father Kleist died, and she asks herself over and over again, "Who would have dreamed that it would come to service again so soon?"

From far and wide, visitors arrive to attend the funeral and pay their condolences to the young wife, whose husband represented their hope for the future of Prussia and the German Reich. The Kieckow church is filled to overflowing, but the master's seat remains vacant, a painful reminder to Ruth that she will never have Jürgen at her side again. A grave has been dug in the church cemetery, but after the service the widow orders a change in plans. Instead, the pallbearers should place the coffin in the crypt beneath the church, next to the coffins of his parents.

When the coffin has been laid to rest, she asks to be left alone. Then, carrying the infant Ruth in her arms, she leads her four older children down the three steps into the crypt, Hans Jürgen holding tightly to Spes's hand and Maria clutching the hand of

Konstantin, quietly seeking his protection. Gathering her off-spring around the coffin, the mother instructs them with words they do not yet understand: "Faithful unto death[9]—so has your father been and your grandfather before him. And so shall we be. This is my creed; let it be yours also—faithful unto death." The mother bows her head in silence, and the four children lower their eyes also. They are afraid.

One by one, over the next few days, family and friends take leave of the mourning Kieckow family. Finally only Father remains. Alone with him for the first time, Ruth throws herself into his arms. All of the tears she has suppressed since Jürgen's death come pouring out in a torrent. "Father, I cannot do it," she cries. Without hesitation, he replies, "You cannot now, my child, but you will learn." What father and daughter are talking about is the future of Kieckow.

Among the Junkers, it is rare to find an estate that is retained by the widow of a deceased landowner. It happened once before in the Kleist family, when the widowed mother of the first Hans Jürgen dared to hold on to Gross Tychow and Klein Krössin until her son grew to adulthood; her courage has been talked of ever since. Father insists that Ruth is made of equally sturdy material and that it can happen again. Ruth agrees to accept the challenge, even though as yet she has little confidence in her own ability to manage.

When Father leaves, Ruth is left alone with her grief, her children, the manor house, two villages and a large agricultural enterprise. As soon as his carriage is out of sight, she goes to the buffet in the dining hall where she finds two tin candle holders, two long candles, matches and a flint. Then hurrying to the large wardrobe cupboard in the entry hall, she selects a hooded cape to throw over her dress and leaves the house quietly. The sun is long gone, even though it is not yet supper time. Down the road, left through the village, past the pond, around to the back of the church, then down the three steps to the crypt—Ruth opens the door and enters the dark, musty cavern. Making her way to the altar, she sets the candles into the holders, then fumbles with match and flint, and soon there is light. For more than an hour she remains alone with Jürgen, until the housekeeper appears at the door. "Madam? Madam von Kleist, your children are waiting for you and the baby is crying. Please come to supper."

Together, the two women return to the manor house. The villagers watch from behind the window curtains of their houses and shake their heads.

1898: JUNE. Father Zedlitz arrives at Kieckow from Grossenborau, confident and vigorous, ready to discuss affairs of the estate with his daughter and the bailiff. He is brought by carriage from Belgard and met at the door by Ruth and a bevy of children. It disturbs him to see that even at home, this young mother, barely thirty-two years old, is dressed from head to foot in black, with her face swathed in a black veil. Nevertheless the reunion is joyful as they all adjourn to tea in the library. Afterward a servant shows Father upstairs to a guest room, and no sooner has he opened his bag than there is a knock at the door. It is the housekeeper. "Excuse me, Count von Zedlitz, I must speak with you for a moment." Count Robert bids the housekeeper to enter his room and shuts the door; both remain standing. "It is about your daughter, Madam von Kleist; things are not normal with her. Every night she is down in the crypt of the church, sitting with the dead people. She even takes the children there at least once a week. I know it is not right for them, but I have no influence in this. I just want you to know how it is. Please excuse me, Count von Zedlitz." With a curtsy, the housekeeper backs her way to the door, opens it and is gone.

For two days, Father bides his time and observes. He is particularly aware of his oldest granddaughter Spes, now ten years old, who reminds him a little of his Conti Ruth; she has the same high spirit, but unfortunately without the reining in that only a father can provide. Father makes a mental note that perhaps later he can be of help here. Otherwise he finds the children exemplary in all ways, and this is confirmed in private by both the nursemaid and the governess, the latter a new addition to the family household.

Spring planting is well under way and the agricultural enterprises appear to be in good hands, at least so the bailiff reports. The Kieckow debt, however, can only be discussed with Ruth. Father decides it is not the time.

On the third night of his visit, he confronts his daughter in the library. "Ruth, it is time now to come out of your mourning period. Take off the hat and veil; they no longer become you. Pay attention to your children, before you come to regret it. And leave the dead in peace, including your husband Jürgen. Tomorrow order the workers to dig three graves. Bury the coffins and bolt the door to the crypt. I consider the situation under the church barbaric—un-Christian, above all." Shocked by her father's sharp words, Ruth retreats into sobbing and is unable to speak. Father is patient, and when she regains her composure, she explains that the coffins of Father and Mother Kleist lie unburied because when Father Kleist died, Jürgen's brother and sister were reluctant to bury their parents in the Kieckow cemetery. Why, Ruth does not know, for Jürgen would never discuss it. As to Jürgen, Ruth knows it cannot go on this way. In truth, she cannot stand seeing her husband's coffin lying there in the dark crypt, but alone, she simply could not bring herself to give the order to have it buried. Going to her father, she embraces him gratefully.

On the morning of Father's last day at Kieckow, the order goes out for the immediate burial of the late master. That afternoon, Ruth, her father, and her five children make their way to the cemetery, where the pastor conducts a burial service that is sober and prayerful, without undo emotion. When the benediction is done, Father raises his hand as if to bless the group. Instead he invokes his most parliamentary voice and announces: "The time for mourning at Kieckow is past."

In the morning Ruth rides with Father to Belgard in the open wagon, sharing the bench with him and the driver. She wears a simple black dress with a black and white cape and her black hat, and she is no longer veiled. On the stretch of road between Kieckow and Klein Krössin, the men in the field turn from their work and wave to the mistress and the visitor. Both wave back and smile broadly.

JUNE. No longer compelled to make her way to the crypt, Ruth has found a new means of alleviating her overwhelming loss. She intends to write down the story of her marriage so that she and those who come after her will never forget the man she so loved,

Jürgen von Kleist of Kieckow. In the long summer twilight, she
sits at her desk with pen in hand and begins her story:

> When was the first time his name came into my life? It
> must have been the spring of 1882 in Oppeln, when my
> father came to the dinner table and said . . .

The chronicle is never finished. Ruth adds to it from time to
time in her long life, particularly in periods when events of the
present are too painful to ponder. She recalls what it was that distinguished Jürgen from every other man in the world, endearing
him so to her, and she writes this recollection in her distinctive
style:

> He was pious in the truest sense of the word. By piety I
> mean when a human being stands under God's will in
> attitude, deed and character. He led a disciplined life,
> bridling his own impatience, yet doing always what he
> thought was right. And he demanded the same discipline
> from his wife and from his subordinates. He was truthful,
> just and loyal.

In writing this tender memoir, Ruth recovers her spiritual
balance and takes upon herself Jürgen's legacy—a readiness to
mold the future by mastering the present.

III

THE WIDOW OF KIECKOW

1898-1911

A Bismarck from Kniephof

AUGUST. The young widow is seated at a tea table on the terrace, surrounded by her children, reading them fairy tales from the Brothers Grimm. A nursemaid stands by the French doors in case little Ruthchen becomes restless, but even she, just a year and a half old, watches and listens as her mother's voice changes from that of the good princess to that of the bad witch. Then, to the children's disappointment, the afternoon's story is brought to a sudden end when an old family retainer appears on the terrace steps with a telegram for their mother:

DEAR FRIEND STOP ON WAY FROM DANZIG TO KNIEPHOF BY EVENING TRAIN STOP TYCHOW AT EIGHT STOP WISH TO SEE YOU AND KIECKOW STOP YOUR FAITHFUL HEDWIG BISMARCK STOP

Ruth is overjoyed at this news of a visit from the widow Bismarck, a friend in the sense that the Kleists and Bismarcks are all bound in friendship, yet an acquaintance with whom Ruth has spent little time alone. It is high time to deepen this relationship! Ruth turns to the children in an attempt to share her joy, but for the moment, it escapes them.

Ruth has met Hedwig exactly four times, twice at Kniephof and twice at Kieckow. The first time was in the summer of 1886, when Hedwig and Philipp von Bismarck introduced Jürgen's bride to the Bismarck circles. Their second meeting was at Kieckow in 1892, on the occasion of Father Kleist's funeral. Two years later they met again at Kniephof, for the funeral of Hedwig's husband Philipp, and most recently, at Kieckow for Jürgen's funeral. This reunion will be unlike the others—a meeting of two widows, each the mistress of two estates and responsible for two villages, fulfilling alone the heavy responsibilities that fall to a Prussian landowner.

Ruth quickly calls out a list of orders—to the message bearer, "Bring the coachman to me"; to the housekeeper, "Make ready the guest room"; and to the nursemaid, "Prepare the children to greet our guest." Before she sends her brood on its way, she asks which song they will sing for this cousin of Grandfather Kleist. The response is unanimous, "The Old Barbarossa." Ruth reacts with mock surprise, for she knows that this is their favorite. The song retells the legend of Kaiser Friedrich Barbarossa, still sleeping under the mountain, his chin resting on a marble table with his beard grown through, waiting to return after a hundred years.

Like her children, Ruth is enchanted with the spectacle of the sleeping Barbarossa, but unlike them, she also wonders about the symbolism of this beloved folk song. It takes on particular meaning just at this time, for Otto von Bismarck has just died at the end of July, and it is he, not the late or present kaiser, who called forth to his countrymen the memory of Barbarossa. Ruth has mixed feelings about the late Bismarck, who molded out of Prussia and the other German kingdoms a modern nation-state, yet mocked the living kaiser unmercifully. It will be good to share these feelings with Hedwig.

Alone on the terrace, Ruth contemplates the complicated tale of that immensely gifted family, starting with the mother of them all, Wilhelmine Mencken von Bismarck, daughter of a learned Berlin professor.

Ruth once heard that a son of the Mencken family* had emigrated to America against his father's advice and is reminded of her brother Rob's youthful desire to go to America and become a *self-made* man. Why is this so important to these young men when such immense responsibilities and opportunities lie all about them on these vast Prussian lands? Rob gave up this idea at his father's bidding and is now personal adjutant to one of the

---

*Otto von Bismarck was distantly related to the American journalist, H.L. Mencken, whose father emigrated from Germany to Baltimore.

kaiser's sons, more or less playing nursemaid to a young man who insists on embarrassing the royal family. Since Jürgen's death, Rob has visited often, entertaining his sister with stories of the shallow lives such people are destined to lead. As much as she enjoys these bits of gossip, Ruth fears for the House of Hohenzollern. If only those in power would heed the age-old call to God, fatherland and family, as the Kleists and the Zedlitzes, and, yes, the Bismarcks, have done for generations.

Ruth counts through her own five children and wonders which, if any, will ask some day to go to America and become a *self-made* man or woman. Interesting that one must use the English word here; the German language has none to fit.

Her thoughts turn back to the intellectual Wilhelmine Mencken, who married Ferdinand von Bismarck, Prussian military officer and owner of three Pomeranian estates. They say he was the best of the Junkers, lover of the Pomeranian landscape, protector of its forests and fields, and master of that peculiarly Pomeranian pastime, the hunt. How strange that such an unlikely marriage should produce two sons and a daughter as gifted as Bernhard, Otto and Malvina. Almost eighty years later Pomeranians still talk of this unhappy match between the professor's daughter and the Pomeranian Junker!

The country house at Kniephof was the birthplace of Bernhard and Otto and the home of their childhood years with an unhappy and ailing mother. While they were still very young, she sent them away to a boarding school in Berlin, determined that they should be prepared for the university. Miles from home, these two homesick brothers from the countryside bound themselves to one another, the older Bernhard protecting the younger Otto in an alien, unfriendly environment. Their mother's persistence bore fruit, and both sons completed their education. Bernhard, like Ruth's Jürgen, became a Landrat in the Prussian civil service, and Otto became a legend. Ruth marvels at the importance of a mother's influence, even such an unhappy one as Wilhelmine, and silently prays that she might do at least as well as this poor woman.

Otto returned to Kniephof as a young man and took over management of the estate, at the same time carousing and behaving outrageously. He became the "mad Junker of Kniephof" in the eyes of society, yet in those years he brought this debt-ridden agricultural enterprise back to health. Bernhard married a daughter of the adjoining Lasbeck estate; this union produced but a single child, Philipp, for the young mother died a few weeks later. Twenty-two years later, Philipp, a lieutenant in the Prussian army, distinguished himself in the war with France, a war many said was of his uncle's making. The victory belonged to Prussia, and afterward Kaiser Wilhelm granted Otto von Bismarck an estate out of Prussia's newly conquered western lands. Philipp returned from the war to take over Lasbeck from his maternal grandparents and to purchase Kniephof from his Uncle Otto, combining the two estates into one great enterprise.

Philipp began his career as a landowner first by taking a wife and erecting for her a new manor house at Kniephof, then by building a road through the thick forest that lay between the two estate villages, shortening the distance the workers and others must travel back and forth each day. The villagers named this romantic walk "the lieutenant's lane," and after Philipp's death it became a kind of living memorial to this master of Kniephof and Lasbeck. Ruth recalls that shortly after her marriage, she walked the entire distance, both directions, on the arm of Jürgen, spinning dreams of the life they would have at Kieckow.

Like his own mother, the wife of Philipp von Bismarck died shortly after the birth of her first child. The fate of these poor women reminds Ruth of the two village births she recently presided over, the first a healthy baby whose mother could not be saved and the second a healthy mother whose newborn child died within a few hours. Attendance at these village births is expected of the mistress of Kieckow, and Ruth has taken it upon herself to learn about care of the expectant mother and midwifery in the countryside. She counts herself among the fortunate, a healthy young mother with five healthy children.

A short time after the death of his wife, Philipp met and married Hedwig von Harnier from the gentle forests of the Rhine River valley, who took charge of his motherless son. Now Hedwig is both mistress and master of Kniephof and Lasbeck. Ruth ponders the meaning of these two words, each of which denotes ancient privileges and specific responsibilities, a kind of division of tasks that evolved out of a feudal society over hundreds of years. Amazingly, on this eve of a new century it continues to work well as long as the mistress and the master both live, or as in Hedwig's case, the mistress assumes the role of master as well.

Hedwig arrives late at night in the Kieckow covered wagon. There is little opportunity for more than a warm embrace and a few words of greeting. Ruth leads Hedwig to her room, followed by a maid carrying a pot of hot tea nestled in an oversized tea cozy.

At morning prayer in the Kieckow dining room, the children are introduced to Cousin Hedwig, who except for her blue-gray dress, seems much like their own mother. They have almost forgotten that mothers dress in any color but black. Ruth sits down at the organ and improvises on her favorite hymns, a talent the late Jürgen once claimed to envy in his wife; she was equally envious of his ability to read the notes from sight, a skill that still eludes her. Hedwig is seated on one of the dining chairs, turned to face the piano, and the nursemaid and governess are seated on either side of her. The housekeeper, the maids and two older male servants stand behind them. Rising from the organ bench, Ruth picks up her Bible, opening it to a place marked for the occasion of a long-awaited visitor, and reads aloud. Following this prescribed passage, Ruth speaks her own words of welcome, then reminds the assembly of their individual and collective duty to God and offers a prayer of thanksgiving for His bountiful blessings on behalf of all those present. This is followed by the concluding hymn, with Ruth once more at the organ. Her selection for this day comes as no surprise to anyone, for it is Bismarckian as well as Kleistian—"Come Thou Bright and Morning Star." The older children know all five verses by heart, and beneath the melody one hears an alto voice, confident and in perfect tune, giving the rendition a churchlike quality. The singer is Spes, now ten years old, who has understood harmonizing since long before she could read the notes. Her musical ear is a wonder to her mother.

With a visitor in the house, breakfast takes on a festiveness normally reserved only for Sundays. Instead of lard for the bread, there is butter (as a rule, all butter churned at Kieckow is destined to be sold outside the estate); and there is freshly made marmalade from this year's crop of Kieckow pears. Afterward, Ruth and Hedwig retreat to the library, for they have much to discuss.

Back in the dining room, it is the children's task to carry the dishes to the kitchen. Spes is calling orders to the others, and she has assigned little Ruthchen to the napkins. Although the child has only recently begun to walk, she proudly picks up one napkin at a time, each rolled carefully into its engraved silver ring, and tries in vain to place it on the buffet. Noticing her difficulty, Konstantin, who at seven and a half is tall enough to reach the high buffet, takes each napkin from his baby sister and puts it away. Among all the children, it is Konstantin who is most aware of others' needs. He is a gentle fellow except when it comes to the protection of his sisters. Just recently his mother had to reprimand him for striking an older village child, who had turned over the children's little wagon with Maria in it and boldly set himself in her place. In this case the reprimand was as painful for the mother as it was for the son.

In the library over tea, the two women begin by discussing family and children. Hedwig tells Ruth of her own arrival in Pomerania as a new bride—the desolate landscape, the primitive structures, the sober faces, all in harsh contrast to the warm, cultivated surroundings of her childhood in southwest Germany. Ruth laughs aloud as Hedwig relates how forlorn she felt upon first viewing Kniephof, remembering her own disappointment on that first Sunday visit to Kieckow. Already the two women have formed a closer bond.

Hedwig shares with Ruth the tender and troubling moments she experienced as she gradually took over mothering Philipp's small son and the pitfalls and pratfalls that beset her early marriage—her homesickness, her dismay at the coarse and sarcastic Bismarck humor, and her discovery that the name Bismarck, above all else, spells *tradition*. She recalls how foreign she felt after her first social event among the neighboring landowners when she learned that the women objected to a newcomer dressing in white rather than in the grays and blacks of the region. Yet she could always depend on her most loyal ally, Philipp, and take comfort in the lovely Kniephof park and the forest road to Lasbeck. Gradually Hedwig's early qualms faded, particularly

after three more children arrived—Gottfried, Herbert, and
finally, Elisabeth. Each child spent its first months in the
Bismarck cradle, an elaborate piece created from the trunk of
what must have been a magnificent oak. Into the wood are
carved the symbols of forest and field. Hedwig enumerates the
names of those Bismarck offspring who have slept in this family
heirloom. She knows that the first was Otto, for his mother
Wilhelmine commissioned it while expecting Bernhard, but
unfortunately the craftsman, whose name has already been lost
to memory, did not finish it until Bernhard was past the cradle
age. Thus it came to be known as "Otto's cradle," and it now
belongs to Kniephof. Elisabeth was the most recent child to lie in
it, and Hedwig wonders whose child will be next.

Neither woman can know that the last child to be rocked in
Otto's cradle will be one who calls each of them great-grandmother, shortly before the cradle goes up in flames along with
everything else.

Hedwig's most recent memory of Uncle Otto is a bittersweet
recollection of his last visit to Kniephof, just five years ago. He
had come for the funeral of his nephew Philipp. Such an old
man he was, a far cry from the great chancellor before whom all
Europe had once trembled. After the funeral, he came to
Hedwig and asked her to take one last walk with him through the
park of his childhood home. Clearly the old man viewed this as
an occasion of farewell. Arm in arm, the old chancellor and the
newly widowed mistress wound through the park until they
reached an open meadow. Halting before a giant spruce tree, the
old man told her, "As a child, I often sat here with my mother,
out of view of house and village. On warm sunny afternoons,
unbeknown to anyone but me, Mother would take from the folds
of her skirt a magnifying glass and hold it over her lower body,
catching the sun rays to warm and soothe her ailing liver." Otto's
voice broke at these words, and Hedwig gently wrapped her arms
around the old man, conveying her shared grief over the wasted
life of this gifted woman, who was always an alien in the
Pomeranian countryside.

At last Hedwig brings the conversation around to the main
reason for her visit to Kieckow. She has come with the express
purpose of giving advice to this young widow who now walks in a

path so familiar to her. Her youngest child was just eight years old when Philipp fell ill with an influenza and was gone within the week, leaving a mistress without her husband, four children without a father, and an estate without its master. In Pomerania, Hedwig cautions, the estate must always be considered first; above all else is the need to find a bailiff who is trustworthy, skilled, and worthy of respect from the workers. Ruth winces, for she questions all three of these qualities in the bailiff Jürgen hired just before he became ill.

It is also incumbent upon the widow, Hedwig continues, to demonstrate a skill beyond that of anyone in the house or village in the tasks she must personally supervise, whether it be the trimming of the lamps, the planting and nurturing of the vegetable garden, food preservation, spinning, weaving, sewing, or even the slaughtering of pigs and chickens. Ruth nods her head. Except for the weaving and the sewing, she brought few skills from Grossenborau, but in two years at Kieckow, she has learned much. She vows that she will attain proficiency in all these tasks, just as Hedwig advises.

It is also important, Hedwig admonishes, that when it comes to the buying or selling of animals, be they horses or hogs or cattle, it is best left to a man, for there is no woman in Pomerania strong enough to bargain with a Jew! Ruth is amazed at the differences in how these people are perceived. Hedwig's statement could just as well have come from her father-in-law, but it could never have come from her own father or from Jürgen.

Finally, there are the accounting skills, the lack of which in recent decades has doomed one estate after another on these eastern Prussian lands. Ruth has already looked deep into the ledgers at Kieckow and has found the past to be muddy indeed. Under Jürgen, the ledgers became clear enough so that the debts now stand out quite legibly. Ruth intends to clear the ledger, for she vows never to turn over to her son Hans Jürgen, who even at twelve years displays the keen and honest eye of his father, a Kieckow burdened like the one that came into Jürgen's hands.

By midday dinner, the number of children has grown to nine, for down in the village a mother has fallen ill. The father is working in the fields with the other men, and Ruth has ordained that children in such circumstances must take their noonday meal at the manor house. Spes and Hans Jürgen have set the appropriate number of places, even bringing the extra napkins and the wooden rings used in the servants' dining area. For them, table setting ranks with puzzle building as their favorite pastime. Little do they realize that every game their mother invents is designed to prepare them for their lifetime roles.

Today it is five-year-old Maria who asks the table blessing, softly, yet with a clarity and seriousness that touch the visitor deeply. When the meal is finished, mother announces that Spes will play a Mozart selection on the grand piano in the great hall, after which the children will all sing a song in honor of the visitor. Spes's performance of a sonatina is flawless. Ruth is delighted with Spes's talent and with her own success as a piano teacher, but she also realizes that such a talented child needs better train- ing than this mother can offer. Spes too is pleased with her playing and with the applause, which she acknowledges with a grand curtsy. Now the other four rush to her side while Mother sits down at the piano. The children arrange themselves facing their small audience—Hedwig, the governess and nursemaid, the bailiff, and the four village children. After a brief keyboard introduction, the chorus begins:

> The Kaiser Barbarossa, for lo these hundred years,
> Sits beneath the mountain until our call he hears. . . .[10]

Later that afternoon two women stroll from the manor house arm in arm, one in gray and the other in navy blue speckled with white. The sight of the mistress of Kieckow in other than black is enough to catch the eye of every worker. "Madam von Kleist," nods the gardener as he pauses in his hoeing and tips his cap. "Madam von Kleist," greets the blacksmith, rising from his stool and mopping his brow. And so it goes as Ruth leads her friend through the vegetable gardens, the courtyard, the horse stalls, hog barns and haying meadow on a tour of the entire estate. She stops to gather a bouquet of flowers from the new flower garden, her first change in the otherwise unchanging order of things at Kieckow. The two women are on their way to the village to greet a lifelong resident of the estate who today celebrates her nineti- eth birthday.

When it is time for Hedwig von Bismarck to leave Kieckow, Ruth gathers all of her children on the entry hall terrace; each holds a different flower from their mother's garden. Cousin Hedwig gathers the flowers into a bouquet, and when little Maria reaches out with her gift, Hedwig cannot resist scooping the child into her arms. After embracing her friend one last time, the visitor steps into the waiting wagon. Ruth calls out one last farewell, but her words are drowned by the noise of the wheels as the wagon rolls down the ramp, circles the giant courtyard oak trees, then makes its way along the sturdy road through the village, between Kieckow fields, and past Klein Krössin, finally reaching the station at Gross Tychow.

Men Who Come To Call

1898: SEPTEMBER. Within the course of a single month, four men, each of significance in the young widow's life, come to call at Kieckow. The first visitor, not surprisingly, is Father Zedlitz, who is on his way to Berlin from Grossenborau. Kaiser Wilhelm II has called Count Robert out of retirement to serve once again in the Prussian administration, this time as governor-general of the Hesse-Nassau province in southwest Germany. Thus after six years of managing his own estate, the sixty-year-old count is to take up the responsibility of governing and placating an area in which the scars of Bismarck's anti-Catholic edicts are still visible. Father makes a detour to stop at Kieckow and is immensely pleased over his daughter's state of mind and the abundance of this year's harvest.

While he is there, Ruth tells her father of her decision to lease a flat in Stettin so that the children can attend school while living at home. Taking care not to offend him, Ruth explains that education at home is not adequate for these modern times and that she is in no position to fund boarding schools for Hans Jürgen and Spes, and very soon for Konstantin also. In fact, Ruth asserts, an education for Konstantin is most important of all. As the second son, he will never be heir to an estate; nor does he appear to be suited for a military career; whatever remains certainly requires a gymnasium education and then the university. Father quite agrees with Ruth's proposal, still he feels obligated to raise the issues that are bound to develop when a landowner resides apart from the land. Ruth feels these problems can be avoided if she spends two days each month at Kieckow and assures him she intends to do just that. Father is inwardly over-joyed at her increasing confidence and promises to visit once every three months.

In the Belgard District news travels swiftly. While father and daughter are touring the outbuildings and overseeing the farm chores together, they spy two figures on horseback, coming across the meadow toward Kieckow from the east at full gallop. Ruth knows that it must be the Kleists of nearby Schmenzin, Hermann and one of his sons. Five minutes later, a man and a young boy enter the courtyard on horseback, dismount and hand the reins over to the stableman. From the crude cut of Hermann von Kleist's clothes, one would never guess that he is owner of three immense estates. The son follows his father's lead, extending a hand to the familiar neighbor, Cousin Ruth, and to the stranger from abroad. When Ruth expresses surprise that Ewald is home from boarding school, the boy's face breaks into a shy smile: "It is the harvest holiday." Like his father, nine-year-old Ewald is dressed in the homespun garments and leather boots of Schmenzin.

Hermann and Count Robert have met only once before, at Jürgen's funeral. Content to cultivate and protect his ancient Kleist lands in Pomerania, Hermann has never been attracted to either the political or the social life in which so many of his class are involved. Nor has he ever been attracted to the pietistic lean-ings of his Kieckow cousins, insisting that he has made peace with his Maker in his own way. Though his peers refer to him as the country bumpkin[11] from Schmenzin, the peasants and workers on his lands have nothing but deep loyalty and indeed real affection for this coarse but kindly fellow.

Ewald is more his mother's child, quiet and seemingly embar-rassed by his father's rough ways. Hermann's wife Lili is the epitome of a cool, aloof Prussian aristocrat. Always clad in the dark gray high-collared gown of a Prussian noblewoman, she allows no one to forget that she was once a countess from East Prussia. From Ewald she demands the very best; a *good* in his school report will not suffice. Even during this harvest holiday he is compelled to spend most days over his books so that his next report will contain only *excellents*. Ruth is far more attracted to the earthy Hermann than to his high-styled, demanding wife, and she has long since taken the boy Ewald into her heart. She only wishes he had more of the freedom she takes pains to give her own two sons.

Taking advantage of this opportunity to give the boy some enjoyment, Ruth invites the Schmenzin visitors to the house for coffee. The offer is accepted without hesitation. Looking around, she spies one of the stablemen and sends him running to the manor house with two messages. For the housekeeper the message is, "Coffee for three in the library within the quarter hour"; the message to be delivered to the schoolroom is, "Send Hans Jürgen to the library to greet Ewald von Kleist and fetch him for afternoon children's tea."

Over coffee and biscuits with pear marmalade, Hermann von Kleist of Schmenzin pledges his advice and counsel in all matters relating to the Kieckow and Klein Krössin lands. He begins with a warning that money should never be borrowed against one's property, for mortgages are the work of the devil in the guise of bankers, whether Jews or Christians. Ruth quickly lowers her eyes at this admonition, for she dares not admit the depth of the Kieckow indebtedness.

In the children's nursery, the sons and daughters of Kieckow vie with each other for the attention of the sportily clad Ewald. His boots are definitely those of a horseman, and his rugged outdoor clothing is permeated with the pungent aroma of the stables. Hans Jürgen wishes that he too had such an outfit, and a father with whom to ride horseback through forests and across meadows. As if somehow aware of this unspoken longing, Ewald invites Hans Jürgen to ride with him soon on the hidden forest paths near the estate.

Thirty years later Ewald and Hans Jürgen will ride horseback together on one of these hidden forest paths, to discuss with Mother Ruth a book they both have read, *Mein Kampf* by one Adolf Hitler.

Not more than a week after Father Zedlitz's short visit, Ruth receives a letter from her sister Anni von Tresckow, who is presently living in the city of Marburg. Since the birth of her first child, a son, earlier in the year, Anni has been depressed and in frail physical health; the letter merely confirms this. On a happier note, Anni informs Ruth that her husband Hermann, on his way home from maneuvers in the east, plans to stop at Kieckow. She calls it a brotherly visit, but Ruth knows that Anni worries about her and that she has sent this stern husband of hers as her investigator and emissary.

Two days later, dressed in her white-spotted navy blue dress, Ruth receives this brother-in-law whom she barely knows with a warmth to which he is hardly accustomed. The family resemblance between the two sisters is extraordinary, yet there is a marked difference in their outlook on life. Where Hermann anticipated this visit as an occasion to lighten the burden of his widowed sister-in-law, instead Ruth listens as the husband grieves over his wife's ill health and unhappiness. In her forthright manner, Ruth tries to motivate this stern husband toward a more tender familial stance. It is clear that the life of this army officer's wife is not a happy one—always in transit, no roots, and worst of all no place to call home. Ruth urges Hermann to consider the future carefully in light of his family, which will no doubt grow larger year by year. Afterward she cannot decide whether the visitor was mellowed by their meeting. She prays to God that Anni's future may be blessed.

The fourth and last of the September visitors is Fritz von Woedtke, a cousin of Ruth's late husband (as all Belgard landowners are cousins in one way or another). Speaking with Cousin Fritz behind the closed library doors, Ruth unfolds her plan to move the children to Stettin in the new year.

But what to do about Kieckow? Ruth turns to this cousin for his opinion. She intends to be at Kieckow two days each month to inspect everything and to balance the accounting books herself. Smiling at the immense confidence of this woman, Fritz Woedtke suggests that he could be of service between visits. Has he not managed the Woedtke family estate for years, and is it not true that there is no finer example in the district? Ruth interrupts to declare that the Woedtke estate is indeed the showplace of the entire countryside. By the time Woedtke leaves the Kieckow manor house the pledge is sealed. He will come by Kieckow and Klein Krössin at least once a month, more frequently during planting and harvest. With a click of his booted heels and a kiss of Cousin Ruth's hand he is gone.

NOVEMBER. On the days that Fritz von Woedtke is at Kieckow, he always takes dinner in the manor house. When the children are present, he sits at the family table where the master used to sit. In this and in other small ways, the widow of Kieckow sends a message to the world, and in particular to every person on the estate: When Herr von Woedtke is present, all of the master's power lies with him. Taking her new advisor into her confidence, Ruth has shown him the account books, the stables and barns, the blacksmith's shop, the harness shop, the carpentry shop, the milkhouse, the village, the church and the crypt beneath, the manor house, including the ground floor and attics, the school, the pond, and even the cemetery. In so doing, she has learned to know Kieckow better than any mistress, and probably any master, before her.

At Home in Stettin

1899: APRIL. "The children's boardinghouse"—this is how Ruth describes the partially furnished flat she and the children, plus the Kieckow cook and a maid, are now occupying in the new residential section of Stettin, a city as old as the Kleists of Belgard. The original town lay in a valley to the west of the Oder River, watched over by a castle and surrounded by a wall, all dating back to the time when Stettin belonged to the Hanseatic League. It was the trading link between the hinterland of Pomerania and the Baltic Sea, and over the centuries its fortunes rose and fell with those of the league to which it belonged. Had it not been for the industrial revolution, this backwater haven for ships might have more in common with other Baltic ports hundreds of miles distant than with the great land mass that spans its perimeter.

Within Ruth's lifetime, the entire character of this old city has changed. Just fifteen years ago the ancient city walls were torn down to encourage the development of residential areas on the hills beyond. The result is a pleasing garden city outside the old town, with lakes and parks and other green spaces occupying the low areas along the river.

The children's boardinghouse encompasses the entire first floor of a substantial residential building. It has a music room, a sitting room, a dining room and four bedrooms, as well as a kitchen, a bathroom, central heating and plumbing. The children are immensely intrigued by the plumbing, something that doesn't exist at Kieckow, nor even in the grander neighborhood manor houses, not to mention the villages. No more servants carrying porcelain pots up and down stairs—fortunately, for there is but a single maid here in Stettin. At first the bathroom water spigot and the flushing toilet provided untold amusement for Maria and Ruthchen, until their mother put a quick end to this form of entertainment.

Spes is mistress of the girls' bedroom, where a double bed, a cot, and a huge clothing cupboard fill the space. The boys' room is shared by Hans Jürgen and Konstantin on an equal basis, despite the difference in their ages. These two brothers, quite unlike in so many ways, have a close friendship that is amazingly free of conflict. Ruth has reserved for herself the smallest of the bedrooms. When the ever-curious Konstantin inquires as to why his mother has taken the least for herself, she replies with an affectionate smile, "Why, I consider the entire flat to be my room." Konstantin, still just eight years old, does not fully understand this point of view.

The fourth bedroom, with its double bed, spacious cupboard and writing desk, is the guest room. Even at the expense of the children's privacy, Ruth insists on having an extra sleeping room available at all times. She is too much ingrained with the mentality of the manor house, where there is always room for one more unexpected caller to spend the night.

Everything at home in Stettin is smaller than at Kieckow. The music room is completely filled by the grand piano, which has been brought by wagon from Kieckow. In the country house this large piano stood in the great hall and was hardly ever used, mostly for Spes to practice on, and then only in warm weather. For morning and evening prayer services, Ruth always played the organ in the dining room, and in cold weather she also gave Spes her music lessons there. At Stettin, the grand piano is the center of life—morning and evening devotions, Spes's daily practicing and the frequent four-handed concerts that take place whenever Ruth is able to find a suitable partner. Ruth not only enjoys the camaraderie, she is also intent upon improving her ability to read music. One of the regrets that often plague her when she thinks about Jürgen and her marriage is that she failed her husband as a piano partner. Too often did Jürgen chide her, "Ruth, my love, if you would just practice a little in between these times together."

The dining room is much smaller than at Kieckow. The table and the buffet are also much smaller, but then so are the number of people—just a mother and her five children. Not even the tutor for the younger children lives with the family. She is from Stettin and comes each day to give lessons to Maria in the sitting room. This family room even looks like a schoolroom, furnished with two small school desks from Kieckow.

For the three older children, Stettin means the end of their tutored education in the manor house schoolroom. Hans Jürgen and Konstantin are enrolled at the Kaiser Wilhelm Gymnasium, which will eventually prepare them for the university. Spes attends a private lyceum, a sort of girls' equivalent to the gymnasium, though not at all comparable in its academic content. Yet for Ruth, whose entire education was at home or in the parsonage near Oppeln, her daughter's education seems avant-garde indeed. In Spes's case it will begin her serious study of piano and eventually lead to a performing career of sorts, something never before achieved by one of the Kleist women from Pomerania.

Even for the cook and the maid, life in the Stettin flat is a new and adventurous experience. They share a room three stories above, under the roof, where the servants for all of the flats have their sleeping rooms. In this respect, life is not much different from Kieckow, except that it is lonelier, for there is no large circle of servants nor friendly village community nearby. But in many ways life is much easier at Stettin. There is a modern kitchen just behind the dining room, rather than in the foundation of the house, as at Kieckow; and there are no longer the porcelain pots to be carried, just hot water, and that only at bathing time. In one way Stettin is less convenient than Kieckow.

In the city the cook must go out daily to buy fresh milk, meat and other items that cannot be stored over time. Otherwise the Stettin larder is stocked with the fruits and vegetables and other products of the estate economy. Since the maid cannot perform all of the household tasks herself, Ruth insists that all five children help with such things as bed making, table setting and dish drying.

For the first time in her life, Ruth is observing society from within an industrialized city, and it occurs to her that the world is changing much faster than she had ever imagined. She reckons with the possibility that the way of life she has always known might quietly disappear before her children, and for certain her grandchildren, are grown.

This mistress of Kieckow has witnessed too often the grief of village families when their sons and daughters announce their intent to leave the land and seek their fortune elsewhere in the world. Most often these youthful ambitions end in the factories and slums of Germany's industrialized cities. Sometimes the fate of those who leave is even worse—poverty, disease and early death. Once in a while a son who has prospered returns to visit his childhood village. His parents rejoice and the neighbors gather in awe. But no matter what befalls the village offspring in the world outside, no emigrant from Kieckow has ever returned to live on the land again.

JUNE. Ruth has remained faithful in her commitment to personally oversee Kieckow affairs. Throughout the spring she has made the trip once each month, by train from Stettin to Gross Tychow, then by wagon to Kieckow, returning the following afternoon by wagon to Gross Tychow, and by train to Stettin.

It is noon of visiting day for the mistress of Kieckow. At the Gross Tychow station, a covered wagon is already waiting to receive its passenger from Stettin. Fritz von Woedtke has come from his estate to meet the young mistress and is waiting on the platform with his son Jürgen, a boy about the age of Hans Jürgen. Fritz settles Ruth on the upholstered seat toward the back of the wagon, then takes his own place on the front seat with his young son and the driver. There is always a bittersweet tug at Ruth's heart when she sees a father and son in close intimacy with one another, for she is reminded that her own two sons will never have this experience.

The horses are set in motion and the vehicle proceeds south on the road to Klein Krössin. Like a cathedral arch, the full-leaved maple trees tower over the road from both sides, their branches meeting in the center. Beyond are the fields and pastures that were once all Kleist lands, and in the distance the forests. Farther on Ruth recognizes the outline of her own lands—the village forest and then the sharp turn to the left, which brings into view the village of Klein Krössin, where a child waves as the wagon passes. It is another three kilometers to Kieckow, then again to the left and up the short road to the courtyard. The wagon winds around the old oak tree, then up the ramp to the main entrance, where the faithful housekeeper stands ready to welcome her mistress.

Thus begins the busy afternoon at Kieckow. Ruth goes directly upstairs to her room, where her Kieckow clothes lie ready. Since time is always of the essence on these estate visits, a maid is waiting to help exchange her heavy traveling wardrobe for the plain dress and shawl of the manor house. Ruth goes immediately to the office to go over any new entries in the ledgers with the bailiff. Afterward there is dinner alone with Fritz, to lay out plans and resolve any difficulties.

Then it is time for Ruth to review the month's activities, going first on foot to the animal barns, the stables, the milkhouse, and the granary, then climbing into the wagon for a tour of one field or another, usually with the bailiff at her side. Ruth is still uncomfortable in dealing with the field workers, although she is completely at home with these same men and their wives down in the village. But as Father Zedlitz once said, this too will come in time.

Back at the manor house, it is time for tea. Ruth has arranged to have the pastor of Gross Tychow, the Kieckow village teacher and Fritz join her in the sitting room. It is a good time to inquire about details of school and of crises and problems to be dealt with in the village.

Afterward, Fritz and his son return to their own estate, and Ruth retreats to her room to read the month's mail. The housekeeper has arranged her correspondence, and on top of the pile

is an envelope postmarked Kniephof and sealed with the
Bismarck crest, a letter from Hedwig. The contents concern
Hedwig's sons, eighteen-year-old Gottfried and fifteen-year-old
Herbert. Both are boarding in Stettin and, like Ruth's sons,
attend the Kaiser Wilhelm Gymnasium. Hedwig wonders
whether Ruth can recommend a boarding arrangement that
might provide a more disciplined environment for these fatherless adolescents, who now reside in an elderly widow's home near
the school. As Ruth considers the possibilities, an obvious solution comes to mind—of what use is the Stettin guest room if not
to provide shelter for those in need? She promptly takes up her
pen to write, "Dear Cousin Hedwig, . . ."

Late the following morning Ruth makes her monthly visit to
the village. The street is alive with activity. The children have just
been dismissed from school and they are everywhere, playing
their games of marbles and tag while elderly men and women sit
in front of their houses and watch. Several women are churning
butter outdoors, and the smell of fresh-baked bread is in the air.
Ruth carries two bundles of flowers in her arms, the first for a
new mother and her infant. Despite Ruth's absence at the time
of the baby's birth, both mother and child are doing fine. Inside
this village house, Ruth takes time to sit and talk with the woman,
reminding her about cleanliness and diet and fresh air, all necessary for a healthy infant.

From there, Ruth moves on to another house, where a man
lies gravely ill and near death. Along with her bundle of flowers,
she brings the man's family a spiritual message of solace and
comfort. Her words have much meaning for them because she
too lost a husband in the prime of life, and he too suffered
greatly in his last illness.

Although this couple is relatively young, even by nineteenth-
century standards, their children are grown. One daughter is a
servant in the manor house and will soon be married to the
driver of the Kieckow wagon. Another daughter and two sons are
already married. The sons both have children and are therefore
entitled to houses of their own in the village, but the married
daughter and her husband must live with the parents. A single
glance tells Ruth that this is a crowded household; the kitchen
area is far too small for the two women to share, and there is no

place for privacy. Inviting the sick man's wife to walk with her along the street, Ruth tells her that more than likely she will not be there to sit with her husband in his last hours, but promises to return for his funeral. The family should notify the manor house so that a telegram can be sent to Stettin.

AUGUST. Hans Jürgen, Konstantin and Spes have a whole month free from school. Ruth has moved all of the children, the cook and the maid back to Kieckow, where the children will spend four weeks on the land and in the forests. The tutor remains in Stettin, which means that it is vacation for little Maria also, a time of freedom within the broad limits set by her mother. Ruth has determined that August is to be "French month" and that all mealtime conversation is to be conducted in that language. She herself turns out to be the principal conversationalist, but she discovers that the participation of the children is inversely proportional to their age, with little Ruthchen the most vocal and the most perfect in accent, and with Maria a close second.

August is also the month of thunderstorms, those frequent occurrences that strike fear in the hearts of landowners and villagers alike. Thunder means lightning, and lightning means the prospect of fire. There is no estate in Pomerania that does not have a living memory of some building being consumed by flames while its inhabitants looked on helplessly. Throughout the centuries, the forests of Pomerania have provided these flammable building materials to house the people, the animals and the products of the fields. Only lately are the half-timbered buildings giving way to a few modern, all-brick structures.

The Kieckow manor house stands on a knoll well above the village and courtyard structures. Its stucco exterior belies the wood construction underneath; only the roof and floor, both of burnt-red tile, are fireproof. The outbuildings and village houses are even more vulnerable, for their roofs are made entirely of straw.

On this particular August evening, the air is heavy with humidity, and in the distance one can hear the low rumbling of a thunderstorm. Generations of Kieckow residents have grown up in fear of this sound and the deadly storms that can follow. In the manor house, the children are in bed, but Ruth remains dressed, knowing that after midnight the storm will probably reach Kieckow. She chooses to await its onset downstairs in the servants' dining room, drinking tea with the housekeeper and the old retainer from Father Kleist's time.

At two o'clock in the morning everyone is roused from sleep. The children are told to bring their rain clothes, for there is always the chance that the house must be abandoned. While the servants wait in the kitchen, rain gear in hand, Ruth gathers her sons and daughters in the dining room to sing what she calls her three storm hymns because they contain words of divine petition—"May God comfort the fearful and protect the endangered." The two boys assume a protective stance over their two youngest sisters and put up a brave front, singing with a gusto that is normally lacking. Spes alone is immune to the threatened calamity. Announcing coolly that she will be sleeping on the sofa in the library, she asks to be awakened when the excitement is past. Another time, Ruth might challenge this willful daughter of hers, but tonight she views her nonchalant behavior as a good example for the others. And anyway, if lightning should strike the house and set it afire, they must all pass by the library on their way out the door.

OCTOBER. The number of children at the Kleist boardinghouse has swelled from five to seven with the addition of two foster sons—Gottfried and Herbert von Bismarck—who share the double bed in the guest room.

There is an expression in German literature, specifically from an early work by Goethe, the greatest writer of them all, that accurately describes the perils of a boy growing into manhood. The words are "storm and stress,"[12] and so it is with Gottfried. At almost nineteen years of age, he is not a happy young man, and still a long way from taking his graduation exams. Yet he is filled with talent when it comes to music and art. At the Kaiser Wilhelm Gymnasium, Gottfried was recently reprimanded severely after he became incensed over the unjust treatment of certain students by the director of this private school. Consequently Ruth prevailed upon Hedwig to have him transferred to the state-supported gymnasium. Her heart goes out to this sensitive youth who wrestles so with life.

Letters fly back and forth between the two widowed mothers, discussing whether or not Gottfried should be required to finish school or allowed to go directly into a business apprenticeship. He will of course take over the Kniephof estate one day, and wouldn't a business background be much more useful than a university education? At least this is how Ruth reckons with the "storm and stress" of her friend's son.

Ruth handles Gottfried's day-to-day affairs in her own way, without bothering his mother. Three years ago he began dancing lessons, along with other students of his gymnasium class and lyceum girls of the same age. These lessons are considered to be a kind of apprenticeship, preparing the youth of both sexes for their later participation in society. Ruth, who took part in the Oppeln ball season when she was still just sixteen, is no stranger to these affairs nor to their ultimate purpose. But Stettin is not Oppeln and the unfettered girls in the dancing classes here are quite different from the sheltered countesses of Grossenborau. Worst of all they are a distraction to Gottfried von Bismarck beyond reason.

Diversion is Ruth's strategy. Fortunately Gottfried is immensely talented at the piano, and Ruth has introduced him to the four-handed music she and Jürgen used to play together. Amazingly, he is immediately caught up in this pleasant pastime, and for the entire two months in Ruth's home he devotes three or four nights each week to playing these compositions with her. Ruth considers this a victory of sorts for her view of the world.

As for fifteen-year-old Herbert, this is his first year of dancing school, and the bold girls of Stettin flock to him like bees to honey. Yet Herbert adjusts easily to his foster mother's demands, and his good nature endears him to everyone in the household.

1900: APRIL. Maria and Ruthchen are in tears, for Gottfried and Herbert have packed their bags and are about to move to bachelor quarters. From the girls' reaction, one would think they were leaving for America! Herbert swings seven-year-old Maria high in the air, making her dark curls swirl about her head in a broad circle. He promises her that one day he will come riding his white horse to Kieckow and carry her away to his castle on the highest mountain. Observing his intense sincerity, Ruth muses

that this must be what endears him so to his dancing school partners. Never does she dream that one day he will indeed carry
Maria away to his castle, though the mountain will be but a knoll
on the Lasbeck landscape. Thus will the Kleists and the Bismarcks of Pomerania be united for a second time in history.

As she watches Gottfried lift little Ruthchen into his arms,
Ruth is reminded of a father lifting his small daughter, for he is
already a young man, complete with broad mustache. Yet Gottfried's son will one day marry Ruthchen's daughter, and thus will
the Kleists and the Bismarck's of Pomerania be united for a third
time in history, just before Pomerania and Prussia disappear
forever.

The Answer is No

1906. Within certain circles, the younger Count Robert of Zedlitz
and Trützschler has become almost as well known as his father.
For the past three years, Rob has been Controller of the Royal
Household, meaning that he is responsible for all of the finances
related to the kaiser's principal residences in Potsdam and
Berlin, as well as for his various other royal residences scattered
throughout Germany. The most recent addition to this bevy of
palaces is a giant monstrosity constructed in the city of Posen, a
place the kaiser hardly ever visits due to the distinct lack of affection his Polish subjects have displayed toward him. The agitation
among these Slavic peoples seems to have been increasing for
more than a decade, coinciding with the departure of the senior
Count Robert from his position as governor-general of Posen. At
that time the principal Polish-language opposition newspaper, in
a tongue-in-cheek tribute, praised his departure as a step forward
for Polish nationalism. The reason for this backhanded compliment was that during his term as governor, the count had so mit-
igated the oppressive government measures against the Polish
people that the population was losing its impetus and its drive
toward independence from Germany!

Later, as Prussian cultural minister, Count Robert's politics of
moderation prompted him to resign his office when the kaiser
failed to lend his support. Now his son, the younger Count
Robert, finds himself bound to the kaiser at the most familial

level, yet powerless to bring about any sort of reform in what he believes to be a Byzantine circle of hangers-on who distract, mislead and even infect the kaiser with their gossip and their pettiness.

Rob's inclusion in Kaiser Wilhelm's inner circle comes as a surprise to many, particularly since he married out of the aristocracy, albeit the daughter of a prosperous banker. She is the former Olga Bürgers, and she will stand faithfully by Rob and Grossenborau through the best and the worst of times to come. For those close to the family, and particularly for his sister Ruth, Rob's new position is proof not only of the kaiser's high regard for her brother, but also of this leader's ability to overcome the traditional narrowness of Prussian royalty. Rob teases Ruth by insisting that she is more devoted to the Prussian royalty than the kaiser himself! He qualifies this by saying his sister's devotion lies in her ignorance of the kaiser's household, a condition that will prevail as long as she closes her ears to the distasteful truth he would willingly share if only she would listen.

Proof of a narrowness of view at court that borders on stupidity is the recent fiasco involving the "Jewish question." This issue is regularly laid to rest, at least once in every generation, only to rise again in the next, usually under some new guise. Currently it is the practice of withholding from unconverted Jews commissions in Germany's elite Reserve Officer Corps, to which men with names like Kleist and Zedlitz have belonged for generations.

In 1898, when the kaiser called the senior Count Robert out of retirement and named him governor-general of Hesse-Nassau at Kassel, the count unwittingly became embroiled in this latest re-examination of the Jewish question. Soon after assuming his duties at Kassel, he met a young man whose family represents the last of the Rothschild dynasty still residing in Germany—Baron von Goldschmidt-Rothschild. Count Robert was immensely attracted to this young man, finding him to be highly gifted, well-educated, handsome, and of impeccable manners. What more could one say to recommend this young friend? In the opinion of Count Robert, there was much more to be said about Goldschmidt-Rothschild. He was ambitious and would have liked to become an army reserve officer, but he refused to be baptized a Christian just to gain entrance into this select group, a common capitulation among Jews with similar aspirations. Count

Robert viewed this refusal as a sign of superior character in his friend, and he exerted whatever influence he could muster to obtain this commission for him. In spite of the count's efforts, Rothschild did not receive the coveted commission.

In 1903, precisely at the time of Count Robert's intervention in this matter, the kaiser appointed him to a post that represented the culmination of the count's ambitions—governor-general of Silesia, his homeland and the land of his ancestors. The count and countess now reside in the beautiful governor's residence at Breslau, that jewel among Germany's eastern cities. The count is among old friends again, and he is near his beloved Grossenborau. Although the estate has fallen into some neglect since he came out of retirement, he still holds onto the lands in the hope that one day Rob will take over and bring Grossenborau back to prosperity.

The count is still very uncomfortable with Kaiser Wilhelm over the Rothschild affair. Is it possible that this coveted appointment was meant to distance him from Goldschmidt-Rothschild and from the controversy? If so, the old count might consider it a compliment to the strength of his political influence. Instead he grieves for the future of a nation whose leaders refuse to abandon their historic prejudices. In Silesia, where Jews have lived for centuries, Jewish issues have passed into oblivion. In education and the law, among the landowners, and above all in the banking and business world, Jews and non-Jews study, work and socialize in a common community. Would that such a community existed among the Germans and the Poles. But what Count Robert fails to grasp is the nature of nationalism. While German Jews consider themselves Germans, the Poles want to have back their own nation!

SEPTEMBER. Far to the north of Breslau, and no less distant from the reserve officer controversy, Ruth von Kleist and her brood go about their daily affairs in the flat at Stettin. It is their seventh year in the city, and Ruth still makes the monthly trip to Kieckow, to be met at the Gross Tychow railroad station by the Kieckow coachman. All that has changed for Ruth after nine years of widowhood is that she now knows her own mind much better. Fritz von Woedtke is still her trusted advisor, and the housekeeper is still in charge of the manor house.

The changes in life have most to do with the children. Ruth rejoices daily at their development and thanks God morning and evening that she has come so far with so few problems in this lonely responsibility with which he has entrusted her.

Hans Jürgen, almost twenty years old, has passed his graduation exams from the Kaiser Wilhelm Gymnasium. Now a man, he is leaving the children's boardinghouse to study forestry, all to prepare himself for the landowner tasks ordained to be his as of the first moment he appeared in this world. But first he will spend a few weeks at Kieckow—his future landholding. Fritz von Woedtke has always taken a fatherly interest in this eldest Kleist son, and already the two men are exchanging letters regarding the Kieckow hunts. This year will see the first hunts since before Hans Jürgen was born! The men have agreed that there will be just two days, one for small game in October and one for the great bucks in November. Hermann von Kleist over at Schmenzin is offering advice (more than Hans Jürgen really wants) as to where to place the principal guests and in which direction the beaters should move. Hermann claims to know the Kieckow forests better than anyone in the Belgard District. His son Ewald spends more time at Schmenzin now, preparing to take over that estate from his own stern father. Hans Jürgen welcomes the thought that this kind, thoughtful boy of his childhood, who could ride like the wind, will one day be his colleague and neighbor.

Hans Jürgen does not yet know that Ewald will become his closest friend and most loyal ally and will remain so until the Gestapo take him away from Schmenzin forever.

Spes, Ruth's oldest daughter, who displays such marvelous talents, yet is the one with whom the mother seems to have the least rapport, has just turned eighteen. This is the year when she must be introduced to society, and Ruth is beset with uncertainty. First of all, there is the financial commitment. Money is always a scarce item, particularly with four children now in private schools and Spes receiving the best piano instruction Stettin has to offer. And then there is the question of the Stettin society, somehow lacking in taste, at least so it seems to this mother. She thinks back to her own maidenhood, when one gown saw a young lady through an entire season. Not so in Stettin! Nowadays if there are six balls, there must be six gowns, each more beautiful than the other. And the styles—in these this Kieckow daughter can't even compete!

Fortunately, Grandfather Zedlitz is wise not only in matters of politics and religion. When it comes to his family, he is the source of wisdom and the rock on which all else rests. Again and again, he unravels the quandaries that baffle those of lesser stamina, and Spes's future is no exception. Grandfather's solution begins with a letter from Breslau, unsolicited by Ruth. As governor-general of Silesia, the count is required to give the first ball of the winter season, in the magnificent governor's residence. Since an old count and countess need some reason for such an entertainment, would it be possible for Spes to take leave from school and spend the time with her grandparents in Breslau? A new Steinway grand stands silent in the great hall, awaiting the touch of Spes's talented fingers. Two young ladies, one French-speaking and one English-speaking, are available for tutoring, and there are dressmakers galore eager to create a gown or two for the lovely Spes von Kleist of Kieckow! Such is Grandfather's proposal and such is his way of presenting it. Ruth is moved to tears, recalling the brilliance of the Silesian ball seasons.

NOVEMBER. Invitations to the opening event of the Breslau ball season in the glittering governor's residence are for the moment the most coveted item in the city. Grandfather has had the final say in selection of the guests, and today he is arranging all of the place cards himself on the festive banquet table, while Grandmother supervises the positioning of every glass and plate and the folding of every napkin.

Among those who have received invitations to this ball is a count reputed to be one of the richest landowners in Silesia. It is also known that he openly admits to having a Jewish grandmother, an unusual concession in Germany, even for these modern times. Grandfather Zedlitz dismisses such topics as unworthy of consideration. He has great admiration for this count, knowing him to be a man of maturity and integrity, as well as a Christian and a true believer in the tradition of the Zedlitzes and the Kleists. Furthermore, he is a member of the upper nobility in Silesia, and he is unmarried. Just as the father once selected table partners for each of his daughters, the grandfather now looks over the guest list and selects a table partner for his oldest granddaughter. Spes von Kleist of Kieckow will sit to the right of the bachelor count.

1907: JANUARY. For Spes, this winter visit to Silesia is like a fairy tale—the thrill of practicing in the great hall on the wonderful Steinway, the theaters and the concerts, and most of all the parties in one or another of the immense country houses outside Breslau or in one of the elegant city homes. Spes begins to understand her mother's caution as she bid this daughter farewell in Stettin: "In no way can one compare Silesia to Pomerania!" There are many young men who dance with Spes and talk with her over a glass of punch. And at every ball there is Grandfather's friend, who asks for no more than a few friendly words and the single dance to which each man is entitled.

For all of the count's discretion, Spes is well aware of his interest in her. She surmises that he will appear in Grandfather's office any day, and so he does. Afterward Grandfather seeks her out at the piano and draws up a chair beside her. This suitor has asked for her hand; it is only a preliminary proposal, for he must of course obtain her mother's consent. "Spes, my child, before we go any further, I want to know your mind and your heart." For a long time Spes sits with her hands resting in her lap, her eyes on the keyboard. So much is at stake here; but Spes knows her mind well.

The answer is a firm no. Grandfather asks if there is more to it. Is the count somehow personally displeasing to her? Does she wish to know more about his background or his future prospects? Spes's reply is, "Grandfather, I cannot marry that man. I know that he is one-fourth Jew, and he even looks it."

FEBRUARY. Spes is home in Stettin, a month before her mother expected her. It was Grandfather's decision. A letter from Count Robert explains that it did not work out as he and Grandmother had hoped; they are not used to a young lady as headstrong as this daughter of Ruth. No doubt Spes would be better off with a young man from Pomerania, and the count and countess are not in a position to be of much help there. It is an immense disappointment for Ruth; in a way, she was reliving her own youthful fairy tale romance in her expectations for Spes.

The musical demands on Spes are enough to put thoughts of marriage far out on the periphery of her dreams. She barely has the time to prepare for a piano concerto performance here and a solo recital there, for this serious and gifted pianist has been *discovered* by the musical circles of Stettin.

NOVEMBER. Spes has received an invitation to the first party of the Stettin ball season. It will be given by the owner of a prosperous trading company, and the guests will mainly be the owners of the manufacturing and shipping businesses that dominate the life of the city, along with their eligible sons and daughters. Above all, the ball season is the mechanism for creating the matches that will carry society forward to the next generation. At the Stettin parties there are very few families from the aristocracy, for the city is certainly not a center of Prussian nobility. Furthermore, the Pomeranian landowners, whose presence could provide the missing ingredient, are inclined to avoid this commercial enclave.

The names of Spes von Kleist of Kieckow and her mother, the former Countess von Zedlitz and Trützschler, are high on every party list of the season. Ruth plans to attend several of the affairs, but she chooses with care, weighing the many issues that must be considered in accepting or rejecting an invitation. For Spes, there will be but a single ball gown, which in itself will limit the number of parties mother and daughter can attend. Ruth will wear the lavender ball gown from her wedding trousseau, which has served so well for weddings and christenings throughout the years. For Spes, she has purchased a ready-made white gown with a lace collar, an incredibly simple dress by Stettin standards, but one that will carry Spes through a number of seasons. Ruth finds it impossible to view one's wardrobe as something to be turned over as styles change. To spend money on one's own adornment is foreign to her, as it has always been to the Kleists of Kieckow.

1908: JANUARY. At a magnificent ball in the country house of the Stettin harbormaster, Spes von Kleist meets Walter Stahlberg,

fifteen years her senior and owner of a prosperous oil manufacturing company. Herr Stahlberg is very tall and he is very handsome. He is also a great deal more forward than the men Spes
has known in her family circle. He is above all a relaxed young
man, sure of himself and not shy in voicing either his convictions
or his intentions. In fact, this bold suitor inquires as to which
parties Spes has on her schedule so that he can arrange to attend
each of them.

For the remainder of the winter season, Walter Stahlberg and
Spes meet and dance and talk. What Spes learns from Walter—
no longer the formal "Herr Stahlberg"—is that the Stahlbergs
have lived in Stettin for at least three generations. Walter's
grandfather founded the family firm at a time when Stettin's
economy derived more from the Baltic Sea than from the
Pomeranian hinterlands. In fact, the Stahlberg mills still take
their raw materials out of the ships that arrive at the harbor from
places as far away as east Asia and South America. For Spes,
Walter and the Stahlberg mills represent a bright window to the
vast world beyond the Oder River and the Baltic Sea. In Spes and
her family, Walter perceives a continuity and a stability that he
has yearned for since childhood. His parents died young and he
is essentially without family.

It should come as no surprise therefore when Walter Stahlberg
proposes marriage just before the Easter holidays. Spes calmly
informs her suitor that she intends to have a career as a concert
pianist. Not only that, as soon as she passes her lyceum examina-
tions, she hopes to continue her music studies in Berlin. With
such a future in store, she can't possibly think about marriage!
Her answer to Walter Stahlberg is an unequivocal no.

An Unlikely Marriage

1908: APRIL. Ruth has brought four children back to Kieckow for
Easter. Hans Jürgen continues to study at the Prussian forestry
academy in preparation for his life's work as a landowner and
estate manager.

On the afternoon of Good Friday, when the house and village
are in a subdued and reverent mood, Spes knocks on the door of
her mother's bedroom and quietly enters. Ruth is sitting in a

high-backed chair next to the window, reading from the New Testament, all about the Lord's suffering and his death on the cross. Though Spes's visit is an interruption to her Good Friday meditation, Ruth welcomes it, for seldom does this daughter approach her mother with any sort of intimacy.

Spes sits down on the floor, taking her mother's right hand between her own two hands and placing her head in her mother's lap. It is a position she has not taken since she was a small child, and Ruth is startled by it. At first Spes says nothing. Ruth waits patiently until by and by the girl begins. "Mama,[13] Walter Stahlberg proposed to me two months ago. It was at the Landrat's ball in Stettin. He wants to marry me, but I turned him down. I told him I was going to Berlin to study music. I made it all sound so definite and so important so that he wouldn't try to change my mind. I know you want me to get married like everyone else, so I was afraid to tell you."

"And why did you turn him down?" the mother asks.

"Mostly because I want to be a great pianist one day. I want to go to Berlin, maybe even to play before the kaiser. And anyway, Walter is not like us, Mama. He grew up in the city, and we don't even know his family."

Withdrawing her hand from her daughter's grasp, Ruth reaches for a handkerchief as great tears begin to roll down her cheeks, giving way to such anguish as Spes has never before seen from her mother. What is it that she has done to bring her mother to this? Eventually the sobbing subsides and it all spills out—the worry over what to do about three daughters who will never have dowries, for there will never be enough money; the need to find a good and loving man who will settle for nobility over material goods. And now within twelve months there have been two proposals—and each one rejected!

As the true nature of things closes in on Spes, she too breaks into tears. So this is what Stettin and the lyceum and the hours at the piano are all about, to make a good match, to attract some man who will take a wife with the name Kleist sans dowry. The injustice of such a system infuriates the girl and she starts to bolt from the room. But by now her mother has regained her senses, and for the first time ever, she speaks to this daughter as an equal. "Spes, my child, we are powerless to change the system, and perhaps the system is not that bad. Look about at the women in our family, particularly at the many widowed women in the history of the Kleists. We have kept the lands together and we have passed them on intact to our sons.

"Walter Stahlberg knows that Spes von Kleist is of such a fabric, even though she has no dowry. That he wants to marry you is in itself a mark of his character. I imagine he too would like to see you become a concert pianist. I know enough of the young man to believe he is immensely ambitious. Reconsider, Spes, so that you will not later live with regrets."

Spes rises from the floor, embracing and kissing her mother, moved by this candid assessment to see it all in a different light. Then she goes immediately to her room, and sitting down at her desk, writes a letter to Herr Walter Stahlberg. It is a declaration of her change in heart, written without apology, and an invitation to visit Kieckow in order to speak with her mother.

On the day after Easter, the first automobile ever to enter the Kieckow lands rolls into the Belgard District, turns left off the main stage road south from Gross Tychow, rumbles past the Klein Krössin village, between the newly planted fields, through the village of Kieckow, then left up the lilac-rimmed road to the manor house. In its wake are huge clouds of dust, the squawking and lowing of startled animals, and clusters of field workers with mouths agape. It is the first time they have ever set eyes on this amazing four-wheeled machine.

Upon receiving Spes's note that very morning, Walter Stahlberg put on his touring outfit and drove straight to Kieckow from Stettin, determined to arrive before nightfall. Grandfather Kleist's old retainer greets the visitor at the door, relieving him of goggles, dust cap, coat, and rubber boots. The old man has seen much in his long life, but never anything like the contraption that stands just outside the entry terrace. He quickly delivers the visitor to the library and raises the housekeeper from the kitchen so that he can join the other Kieckow servants, who are rapidly gathering on the ramp in front of the manor house to examine this latest scientific invention.

The housekeeper hurries to the schoolroom, where Ruth is sorting books with Maria and Ruthchen. "Herr Walter Stahlberg of Stettin is in the library, Madam, waiting to see you."

A short time later, Ruth greets the unannounced visitor: "Herr Stahlberg, yes, of course we have met, several times last winter. Sit down, please." First there are the obligatory preliminaries, those polite inquiries with which relative strangers take the measure of each other. But Ruth has never been one to tolerate lengthy preludes to serious business, and today she perceives that Herr Stahlberg is of like mind. He comes to the point very quickly. In recent months he became acquainted with Madam's daughter, Miss Spes, and admittedly developed a great admiration and affection for her. For a time, he thought he was in love with her and did indeed propose marriage, but Madam's daughter rejected his proposal forthwith. Then just this morning he received a letter from Miss Spes—Herr Stahlberg pulls it from his pocket—expressing a change in her feelings toward him and declaring an acceptance of his recent proposal. Herr Stahlberg falls silent for a moment, as if to gather his strength before addressing this formidable mother further.

"Madam, after your daughter's refusal of my marriage proposal, I thought over the entire circumstances of our meeting and our friendship. I don't think I knew my own mind at that time. After considering our relationship and all of the other circumstances, I realized that the proposal was very premature. Had I any inkling that your daughter would reconsider her response, I would certainly have withdrawn the proposal long ago. I hope you understand; we young men can be very impetuous when it comes to charming and talented young ladies. I will be most appreciative if you will kindly inform your daughter how it stands between us. I in no way wish to hurt her feelings; I think, as her mother, you can do it much better."

Herr Stahlberg rises from his chair, prepared to say good-bye and take his leave. If he thinks this will be the end of it, he is sorely mistaken. Although thirty-five years of age, never before has this young man faced the likes of Ruth von Kleist, former countess of Zedlitz and Trützschler. Rising to her full height, shoulders back, she declares, "Herr Stahlberg, you have behaved most indecently toward my daughter, and in so doing, you have insulted an entire family. No, I will not be your message bearer. You will speak to her yourself!" Ordering him to stay in the library while she locates her daughter, Ruth is out the door in a

flash and into the dining room, where Spes is seated at the
organ, trying to remain calm; like the entire neighborhood, she
knows that Walter Stahlberg is with her mother in the library.
After whispering a few words into her daughter's ear, Ruth
accompanies the girl to the library, sending her in alone and
shutting the door behind.

Ruth goes to her sitting room to wait out the drama in the
library. After a few moments, her anger begins to subside and a
cloud of remorse settles over her. Never in her life has she
spoken so rudely to another human being. And what did Herr
Stahlberg do that was so wrong? Isn't it better to know one's
mind before committing to marriage than to find out too late?
Certainly Spes should marry into the Pomeranian aristocracy.
Perhaps this whole Stettin adventure was a mistake. Will Maria
and Ruthchen be as troubled when their time comes? Eyes shut
and hands clasped tightly in her lap, Ruth turns to her Maker in
a prayer of supplication. Afterward, she feels chastened. For the
rest of her life, she will remember the incident in the Kieckow
library, when she treated Walter Stahlberg so abominably, as the
one time she was seized by the devil himself. And whenever the
memory surfaces, she will find herself humbled by it.

Twenty minutes after the door to the library closed behind
her, Spes von Kleist emerges on the arm of Walter Stahlberg, her
eyes somewhat reddened by tears. The handsome pair walks into
the room where the girl's mother sits alone. As she rises to meet
them, each of the young people seizes one of her hands. Herr
Stahlberg announces that he and Miss Spes are engaged to be
married.

OCTOBER. The ballroom of Stettin's Hotel Preussenhof is a mass
of autumn blossoms. The civil marriage took place yesterday, at
the city Rathaus, and the religious ceremony just before noon in
the chapel of the Bethany Order Deaconess Home. The require-
ment that the civil ceremony precede the religious ceremony
dates back to the days of Otto von Bismarck; it is still very much
resented by the Kleists of Kieckow.

The bridal couple is receiving the guests informally at the
entrance to the ballroom, where the wedding banquet is about to
begin. Two long tables have been been placed end to end to

accommodate exactly forty people. The guest list reads like a reunion of the entire Zedlitz and Trützschler family from Grossenborau—Father and Mother, now Grandfather and Grandmother, then son Rob and Olga from Berlin, daughter Lisa, now a teacher, daughter Anni and Hermann von Tresckow of Wartenberg (finally a place Anni can call home, for Hermann has resigned his commission to take over this newly inherited estate), son Stefan and Lene from Frauenhain, and Etti, the youngest, with her husband Carl von Rohr. It is the first time in the twentieth century that all of the Zedlitzes have been gathered under one roof.

Without Cousin Hermann von Kleist from Schmenzin and his wife Lili, the countess, the Kleist component of this family gathering would be mighty slim. Of Jürgen's generation, only Elisabeth is still alive, unmarried and residing in Berlin, and she has declined the invitation. Lili is looking every bit the East Prussian aristocrat that she is, and by comparison Ruth feels dowdy indeed. And there is also Hedwig von Bismarck from Kniephof, bound to Cousin Ruth by that peculiar thread of shared widowhood.

Then there are the sons of the families, those who will carry the names of Kleist, Zedlitz, Tresckow, and Bismarck forward to the next generation—Hans Jürgen and Konstantin; Rob's three sons; Anni's sons Gerd and Henning; the Schmenzin sons Hermann Conrad and Ewald; and Hedwig's sons Gottfried and Herbert, Ruth's foster sons from the children's boardinghouse.

And on the female side? Foremost there is Spes, the bride, never leaving Walter's side and graciously accepting everyone's good wishes. Hedwig's grown daughter Elisabeth has Maria and Ruthchen in tow, along with the two little daughters of Tante Lene and Uncle Stefan.

The Stahlberg family is represented only by the groom and two of his friends.

Forty women, men and children of three generations stand behind their chairs in the banquet hall as the pastor, who has already spoken his piece during the marriage sermon, offers a short dinner prayer. Following the "amen," each of the guests sits down at a place marked with his or her name. Then all forty rise again. Holding partially filled wineglasses in their right hands, they stand silent while Grandfather Zedlitz offers the first toast: "To his majesty, the German kaiser and king in Prussia, Er lebe hoch!"

Many toasts and many courses later, the table is cleared and the guests begin to break off into conversational groups. Ruth finds herself drawn much more to the young men in her family than to her own contemporaries. She particularly enjoys talking with Ewald von Kleist, whose intense conservatism makes her own orthodox views sound positively liberal and whose religious pronouncements Ruth finds bordering on heresy. Yet she dearly loves this passionate, driven son of the Schmenzin land.

The Tresckow sons possess an austerity Ruth has never before seen in young children. Gerd is just ten years old, yet he is already the image of his aloof officer-father. Thankfully Henning, the younger of the two boys, still has something of Anni in his personality. Ruth worries about her frail, timid sister, who seems unprepared for the strenuous responsibilities of an estate as large and diverse as Wartenberg.

While the other guests are absorbed in conversation, two men slip away quietly to a secluded corner where they can speak privately. Grandfather Zedlitz has an urgent matter to discuss with his son, who he hopes might have influence on the kaiser. The old count finds Wilhelm's actions and pronouncements a continual source of class embarrassment as well as personal pain. Only a week ago, Chancellor von Bülow, Germany's third chancellor since the dismissal of Bismarck, called on Grandfather in Breslau. It seems the pesky matter of the Goldschmidt-Rothschild affair is about to blow up again, this time right in the face of Bülow. He recently appointed Rothschild to the diplomatic corps and posted him in London in order to gather sensitive information on British military preparedness, which Rothschild is privy to through his English banking connections. Now the opposition press is about to create another uproar over the fact that this Jew who handles the most sensitive matters of the Reich cannot obtain a commission in the Reserve Officer's Corps. Bülow is afraid to approach the kaiser himself because he has already earned Wilhelm's displeasure in other areas. A confrontation over Rothschild might well lose him the chancellorship. Thus the chancellor wants Count Robert to intervene through his son Rob.

"Father, when Bülow comes face to face with the kaiser, he has feet of clay. In my opinion, he is a coward. I will make inquiries, but I am certain that it will have no effect. His majesty has the knack of listening only to the worst advice in these kinds of matters."

Rob's words will prove to be the truth, for within a few weeks the kaiser will have dismissed Bülow as chancellor of Germany. After that, Bülow's days at court will be numbered.

Just then Grandfather Zedlitz's eyes stray to a point above and behind Rob's head. Curious, the younger count turns around to find Ruth standing just behind him. It is obvious she has heard every word. Going to this sister and taking her into his arms with a surprising intensity, he pleads, "Ruth, my love, may this kaiser never cause a breach between you and me!"

"My Prodigal Sons"

1910. A lonely kind of quietness pervades the Stettin flat. Ruth stands at the French doors in the music room, looking out at the garden, which once served as the children's play yard. This year, as in every other year, the crocuses blanketed the earth in early spring, and now the garden glows in quiet splendor, undisturbed by the games and sports of growing children. If ever quiet spelled loneliness, it is the garden in early spring.

At one time Ruth's flat was home to her five children plus the two Bismarck sons; now all are grown but two—seventeen-year-old Maria and Ruthchen, going on thirteen. Both girls are enrolled at the lyceum, and Maria has just one more year to go.

And what of her other three children? Hans Jürgen is about to take his forestry exams and embark on an apprenticeship. Young as he is, he has begun to take on some of the responsibilities of an estate owner. At Kieckow, Fritz von Woedtke continues to advise the bailiff, while Hans Jürgen visits often to listen and to learn. Grandfather Kleist's old retainer has died and been buried in the Kieckow cemetery. The housekeeper, now in retirement, has taken over his old room. It is a small space, but there is a certain prestige in being located on the main floor, normally reserved for the landowner's family and guests. The room has been whitewashed and furnished to the housekeeper's comfort. She generally spends her days mending the Kieckow linens and Hans Jürgen's clothes, or crocheting items to be given away to the workers on special occasions such as baptism and confirmation. In summer, she tends the garden of the mistress, who is mostly away in Stettin.

Hermann von Kleist rides from Schmenzin to Kieckow whenever he knows that Hans Jürgen is there. This senior Kleist has already turned over his Dubberow estates to his older son, Hermann Conrad. Schmenzin will eventually go to Ewald, and the father waits impatiently for the day when his son will quit his position in the Prussian administration and return to the land. In the meantime, Hermann cautions Hans Jürgen to resist the economic and social pressures that will undoubtedly be placed on him by the Kieckow workers. He is one of those old conservatives who laments the innovative laws enacted to mitigate the exploitation of industrial workers in the cities. Like many of his peers, Hermann believes that these measures merely encourage more of the agricultural workers to abandon the rural lands. If the trend continues, eventually these great estates, the eastern bulwark of Prussia, hence of Germany, will go to rack and ruin. Hans Jürgen listens and questions. He is not yet ready to agree.

On the water's edge just outside Stettin, Spes and Walter Stahlberg have built an elegant country house, furnished in the good taste with which Spes was raised, but with material means far beyond anything known in the Kieckow household. They also have produced a daughter and have named her Ruth Roberta—after her grandmother and great-grandfather. The child is the absolute delight of her grandmother, who lives for her occasional visits to the Stettin flat. Ruth wishes Spes would bring little Raba more often, but this is hardly possible since the Stahlbergs also maintain a flat in Berlin, where Spes is studying piano. Walter usually stays in Stettin during the week, occupying a small flat near the Stahlberg vegetable oil mills. On weekends there is a great deal of coming and going between the two cities, always with a nursemaid in tow.

Ruth does not really agree with this gypsy existence, comparing it to her own marriage and her idealistic view of the wife living happily in the aura of her husband. Yet she questions these romantic notions, and wonders what Jürgen would think of her now, this decisive and independent woman who was once his naive and sheltered bride? Ruth tries to imagine how their marriage might have changed under the pressures of modern life. The scene is always clouded, most of all the figure of Jürgen, who would now be fifty-six years old and probably graying. She puts away these useless thoughts lest they obscure the memories she once treasured above all else. She also wonders about Maria and Ruthchen. Will they too abandon the Prussian landscape? Will they, like Spes, lay aside a way of life that has been hewn and smoothed for more than seven hundred years? She hopes not, for Germany still lives off the lands of Pomerania, and each estate still requires a mistress as well as a master.

Konstantin—so joyful yet gentle, so radiant and kind—is the most like Jürgen of all the children. He is Ruth's Sunday child! His fate is that of the younger son, the Junker as they were called in earlier times. Almost a year ago this second son passed his gymnasium exams with ease, then said good-bye to the home in Stettin. Through Walter, whose business contacts span the entire German Reich, Konstantin obtained an apprenticeship in a Karlsruhe banking house. There he learns accounting procedures and the other skills required for his chosen career in business and commerce. Konstantin insists that business is where he belongs, though his mother surmises he is simply making the best of his lot. Ruth lives for the letters she receives from this son, who crowds enough for three lifetimes into his limited spare time away from the bank—the theater and concerts in Karlsruhe, Spanish guitar lessons, lectures on politics and philosophy, and even a drama reading group, where the latest works are read aloud by the members. "Mama, last night we read Shaw's Candida," he writes. "I am saving the book for you as you will especially like it."

His salary from the bank is minuscule; nevertheless Konstantin puts together enough funds to spend a week in Munich, visiting the old and the new Pinakothek galleries. By chance he meets Gottfried von Bismarck, his tempestuous friend who once shared the Stettin flat. Gottfried is studying philosophy and art at the university, hoping, he says, to unravel the mysteries of creativity; but subconsciously he is postponing the future to which he is unalterably bound. His mother Hedwig von Bismarck holds Kniephof together, anticipating the day when her older son will return home and take the reins from her hand. How strange is the fate of these young men from two such similar families; the one who is destined to stay on the land would prefer to leave it, and the one who must leave wishes that it could be otherwise.

Konstantin's letters are full of Kieckow references. "Are the chestnut trees in bloom? . . . How is Mama's garden and Frau Hannemann's* rheumatism?" And when his mother writes of her wish to accompany Spes and Baby Raba to Kolberg on the Sea by way of Belgard and Kieckow, Konstantin sends one hundred marks with the message, "This bank note just turned up by accident; if you don't accept it, I will be obligated to give it to the Red Cross."

SEPTEMBER. Maria is practicing vocal scales in the music room of the Stettin flat. Her teachers praise her remarkable talent and recommend that her voice be trained. "She is so musical and her voice is quite exceptional," they report. As yet, her mother hasn't had time to make inquiries. On this afternoon, Ruth is reading nearby, a book on modern biblical interpretation. Ruthchen is also in the room, studying her English lesson. So proficient in English is this youngest daughter that her mother calls her "our English tutor." This comfortable Sunday afternoon scene is soon interrupted by the maid's announcement of a visitor: "Herr Herbert von Bismarck asks to see you, Madam." Maria's voice falls silent as her mind races back to the charming Herbert, who broke her heart when she was hardly seven years old. She wonders how many hearts he has broken since then.

Ruth, who still tends to react like a schoolgirl when news of some long lost friend comes her way, rushes to the front hall with her two daughters following demurely behind. And there stands Herbert, who is indeed a man of distinction now, with his bowler hat and business suit, and even a cane to set in the corner stand. Herbert is not as tall as either Hans Jürgen or Konstantin, and not nearly as tall as Walter Stahlberg. But then the Bismarcks were never particularly tall, more the size of the Zedlitz men.

*Frau Hannemann, the old housekeeper at Kieckow.

Maria is drawn to his clear blue eyes, which give off such happiness and warmth and a distinct tenderness toward her mother.

Ruth leads the visitor to the sitting room. She is so delighted to see this foster son again, she can barely contain her excitement. "Now sit down on the sofa, in the middle," she instructs him. "Maria, you sit down next to Herbert here, and Ruthchen on the other side. I will sit across and feast my eyes on all of you, particularly on this dignified gentleman from the Prussian administration—your great-uncle Otto would have been so proud of you!"

Tea is on the way, and for a change Ruth decides to pour a bit of cognac from the cupboard. "We must celebrate this homecoming. Herbert, I often think of you and Gottfried as my prodigal sons. I once loved you both so dearly, and then you went away. Of course I had no right to love you—how long were you with us? It must not have been more than a few months."

For the next hour Herbert reports on the intervening years—completing his university studies, serving six months as a reserve officer in the army, then passing his law exams. After that there was his Landrat apprenticeship in two different provincial capitals, and now he has been appointed district attorney in Stettin.

Herbert also brings joyful news from Kniephof. His mama, Cousin Hedwig, sends greetings and the announcement that Gottfried is to be married—to Gertrud Koehn, an artistic and musical young lady from Berlin. Herbert says that she will no doubt rank as the most intellectual of all the Bismarcks, at least since Great-grandmother Wilhelmine. Though this last is said with a twinkle in his eye, Ruth does not let it pass. "Herbert, you know you oughtn't make comparisons in this way. Your great-grandmother was indeed brilliant, but she was also tormented."

Maria, on Herbert's right, does not move a muscle, waiting for what she fears is sure to follow. Will Herbert now also announce his own engagement? Where are the girls he used to speak of, the ones who came to church just to see who was sitting with him?

Later, after Herbert has left, Maria confesses to her mother that she used to spin fairy tales, and that Herbert was always the prince. Ruth smiles tenderly, remembering her own dreams of Jürgen and her own painful insecurities. She must do her best to smooth the waters for Maria.

OCTOBER. As if having Herbert back in Stettin weren't joy enough, Konstantin too arrives unexpectedly one afternoon, knocking on the door and announcing that he is to begin work as a salesman for the Stahlberg mills. Both Walter and Konstantin have kept the arrangements secret, wanting to surprise Ruth in person. They are well rewarded by her joyous embrace and her barely contained tears of happiness.

Konstantin has established his own residence, but he reserves Sunday afternoons for tea at the children's boardinghouse (he alone still uses this fond epithet for his mother's flat). He usually brings Herbert with him, and they often invite friends whom Ruth remembers from the gymnasium days. She calls these get-togethers the golden hours.

Ruth has enrolled Maria in sewing and tailoring classes in addition to her academic courses, and she has procured a private voice teacher as well. Mother and daughter also share a secret, which they are keeping from Herbert and Konstantin. Under supervision, Maria is sewing her own dresses for the ball season, and by November she will have completed three gowns, two to wear alternately for the parties and one for the theater and concert hall. Ruth is immensely proud of Maria's versatility, and she knows that this girl will be well prepared to take on the serious tasks of a landowner's wife.

1911: FEBRUARY. It has been a glittering ball season by Stettin standards, filled with beautiful memories that Maria will cherish the rest of her life. From November until Ash Wednesday, there was at least one party every weekend. And beginning with the first party in November, Herbert von Bismarck has had eyes for no one but the "maid of Kieckow," as he now refers to her. In addition, there was the philharmonic series, the chamber ensemble, two theater series—one classic and the other modern drama. And of course there was the opera.

Ever since the first year in Stettin, Ruth has always bought several series and taken each of her children in turn to at least one performance of each series. This year she seems to have tickets to every kind of season Stettin has to offer. On one evening it is Konstantin with Maria, then Herbert with Ruthchen, or Maria and Ruthchen alone, with Konstantin picking them up afterward, but mostly it is Herbert with Maria, and hardly ever anyone with Ruth. She has begged off in every instance—"too strenuous a day," . . . or "both girls must see this play," . . . or "I am too old for Strindberg." She has as many reasons for declining as there are performances. No one believes a word of it, but they understand it is this mother's prerogative.

MARCH. Herbert and Maria have just returned from church and they are standing awkwardly together in the sitting room. Herbert seems nervous, quite unlike himself. When Maria asks him to sit down, he moves toward the chair, but then swings around to face her, taking both of her hands in his. In a few, well-formed words, he declares his love for this lovely dark-haired Kleist daughter and asks her to be his wife. Like her mother a quarter century ago, Maria flies into her lover's arms and buries her head in his chest. Unlike her mother, she speaks not a word, letting the joy on her face speak for her. In this way Herbert von Bismarck, the heir to Lasbeck, and Maria von Kleist of Kieckow become engaged to be married.

They rush to Mother's room to find her smiling through her tears, for Herbert has already spoken with Ruth. In fact, the carriage from Kniephof is expected momentarily. The three of them will drive directly to Hedwig von Bismarck so that Herbert's mother might also share in their happiness and become acquainted with her new daughter. One has reason to suspect that the two widows, who have shared so many joys and burdens with each other, might also have spun dreams together about a union such as this.

1912: FEBRUARY. The wedding of Herbert von Bismarck and Maria von Kleist is celebrated in Stettin at the Bethany Order Deaconess Home.

Maria's two sisters and her two brothers are all present, along with her brother-in-law and the two Stahlberg children, little Raba and the infant Alexander. Grandfather and Grandmother Zedlitz have come from Berlin, where they are now living in retirement. Two years ago, Grandfather resigned as governor-general of Silesia, citing ill health, but even then the kaiser was reluctant to accept his final retirement.

Rob and Olga are not in Stettin for Maria's wedding. Rob too has resigned from the kaiser's service, laying down his responsibilities as Controller of the Royal Household. Although he does not admit it publicly, he is disgusted with the foibles and follies of the royal household and with the complicity and pettiness of the kaiser's closest advisors. Rob writes from Silesia that Grossenborau was in shambles when he assumed control and that he is just now completing a total renovation of the manor house. He cannot leave the estate until the work has been completed. Ruth is disappointed, for among her siblings, Rob occupies the most tender place in her heart.

Mostly it is the Bismarcks who make up the entourage at this wedding. Although Herbert's immediate family is very small, there are cousins and second cousins who have come in automobiles or by train from one end of Pomerania to the other. For the widow of Kieckow, there is much to be happy about in the joining of these two families. Her affection for Herbert now finds an even more legitimate place in her heart, surpassing her affection for his brother Gottfried, which has been tempered by the fact that he is now a married man.

Perhaps Gottfried remembers the evening hours with Cousin Ruth at the piano in Stettin, or perhaps he recalls Ruth's sharp, yet loving reproofs to his youthful escapades. In either case, he introduces her to his wife Gertrud as "my Stettin mother." Gertrud von Bismarck, a young woman more at home in the intellectual society of Berlin, is now the mistress of Kniephof. She and Gottfried were married in Berlin just a year ago, and their first child is expected very soon. The couple has settled at Kniephof, and Gottfried has taken over the estate management from his mother. Yet a cloud already hangs over this marriage, for on the honeymoon Gottfried became very ill with an influenza, which he has not yet overcome. It is the prayer and hope of all that Gottfried will recover his strength in the bracing Pomeranian climate.

One is tempted to make comparisons between the two Kleist weddings in Stettin—first Spes's and now Maria's. Whereas the banquet table at Spes's wedding held forty people, the number at Maria's is double that. Otherwise the occasions differ very

Ruth's brother Rob, count of Zedlitz
and Trützschler, in the kaiser's court

little. Grandfather Zedlitz begins with his toast to the kaiser, but
there is a sadness in his voice that cannot be explained by age
alone. Like his son Rob, Count Robert knows too much. He
laments the lack of leadership in Berlin and the foolhardiness of
the kaiser, who has stepped into this vacuum himself. The count
views this as a potentially disastrous development, since Wilhelm
is indecisive to the point of being dangerous. In domestic politics
the kaiser pontificates and in foreign policy he threatens, yet he
fails to act consistently in either arena.

A marriage into the royal Hohenzollern family itself would not
have generated more joy for the Kleist family than this union
with the Bismarck family. Yet the grandfather's apprehension
overshadows the entire occasion. One is tempted to ask, "Is this
the last time?"

Following the First World War, historians will write books upon
books analyzing this prewar period. It will come to be known as a

watershed signifying the end of the Bismarckian era, the crumbling of the monarchy, and the final demise of feudalism in Germany. For Maria and Herbert and those who come after them, it will be remembered as the beginning of a long and happy marriage that flourishes through worse times than any of these historians could ever have imagined.

IV

THE GOOD SOLDIER

1912-1930

Konstantin

SEPTEMBER. Mother and daughter—Ruth and Ruthchen—go about their affairs in the flat at Stettin. For the mother, the months since Maria's wedding have been a time of readjustment and a time for reflection. The frenetic pace of life that was hers for almost fifteen years, ever since Jürgen's death, has now diminished to the point where she waits each day for Ruthchen to return from school. Even the maid and cook find themselves with time on their hands, a situation unknown at Kieckow and until now at Stettin. It is as if the three women are anticipating some dimly perceived event still to come.

One might say that these women, in their personal lives, are not much different from the nation as a whole. Increasingly over the past decade, a kind of premonition is in the air—the expectation that there will be war in Europe and that Germany will be engulfed along with all the other great nations, from Russia on the east to England on the west, and of course everything between. At Maria's wedding, Father Zedlitz's toast hinted at this foreboding. Everywhere in Prussia there seems to be an unspoken consensus that the kaiser and his chancellor simply do not have the skills to steer a course of limited risk in the perilous waters of modern Europe. Would that Otto von Bismarck still lived! With him one might hope for victory without war; and if there were indeed war, one at least could count on its being victorious.

These days the intellectual naysayers in Berlin (and even in Pomerania, if one counts Gottfried von Bismarck's wife Gertrud)

117

go so far as to predict the downfall of the kaiser and an end to the monarchy within Ruth's lifetime. Such predictions fill her with immense sorrow. Ruth admits that Kaiser Wilhelm is sorely lacking in imperial qualities; she knows too much of Rob's years at court not to accept this fact. Still, one man's reign is nothing in comparison to the five centuries that have gone into the building of an orderly system in which every man and woman has a designated place and a set of responsibilities and privileges to go with it. Besides, it is all part of God's plan, a secular order in parallel with, yet subservient to, the spiritual order in which Jesus Christ reigns supreme. Whatever the future holds, if the monarchy is threatened and duty calls, Ruth will be there, and she has absolute confidence that all of her children, from Hans Jürgen to Ruthchen, will be there too.

Konstantin in fact has just completed his reserve officer's training. A year ago, sensing that war might not be far off, he left his position at the Stahlberg mills and voluntarily reported for training so that he might be prepared for any eventuality. Konstantin's nature is such that one would never expect him to have a career as a military officer; yet he is no less the loyal soldier than Hermann von Tresckow, Ruth's stern brother-in-law, for whom the military is still the only way of life. Hermann reluctantly resigned his commission, for he deemed it his duty to take over the Tresckow lands on Prussia's eastern flank. Ruth considers Hermann and Anni and herself, and now her children—those men and women whose lives are devoted to these ancient lands—to be soldiers every bit as much as the men in uniform who bear arms.

Fate, however, has gradually led Konstantin away from the Kleist lands, in fact out of Prussia entirely. He has accepted a position in a firm at Frankfurt am Main, a city that is a long, long way from Pomerania in attitude, if not in distance. From his modest financial means, he continues to contribute toward improving the condition of the estate. Why? "Because," he assures his mother, "when Kieckow is strong, we are all strong."

Konstantin has become private secretary to Wilhelm Merton, founder of a prosperous metallurgical firm in Frankfurt. This coveted position was obtained through Grandfather Zedlitz, who as governor-general of Hessen-Nassau had established a strong personal friendship with Merton. To his mother, Konstantin asserts that he has never met a man with more integrity in his financial dealings than Wilhelm Merton, this Frankfurt Jew. These are strong words for the grandson of Hans Hugo von Kleist!

Old Merton has taken Konstantin into his social and family circle, and Konstantin has responded with an enormous enthusiasm. Through Merton he has met a Professor Stein from the Frankfurt University. Konstantin has enrolled in Stein's evening lectures, which deal with trade unions, workers' housing and other social issues. Unlike most university professors, Stein even encourages discussion after his lectures. Konstantin is stimulated and uplifted by the new ideas that are evolving out of changing conditions in Germany.

With Professor Stein he visits a Socialist labor union headquarters, and of course he relates everything in his letters to his doting mother back at Stettin. Ruth reads Konstantin's letters in wonderment, then rereads them with fond amusement. How far has this son traveled from the land of the Kleists! Possibly she even covets his freedom. When one is bound to the land as Ruth and Hans Jürgen and Maria are, one is also bound to a certain view of the world. Only Spes and Konstantin are truly free since they have left the land, for better or for worse. And Ruthchen? Ruth hopes that she will follow in the footsteps of her mother, and of her grandmothers and the women before them, as ordained by history if not by God himself. Konstantin is of the same mind. He takes a fatherly view of this youngest sister, the only one who never knew her father, and he is quietly laying aside funds for her dowry so that one day she might be married to a man of her own kind and live on her own estate somewhere in Prussia.

1913: FEBRUARY. Ruth is celebrating her forty-sixth birthday, alone with Ruthchen at Stettin. A mountain of letters rises before her, each one a declaration of family solidarity at a time when events seem to separate the family members more than ever. Konstantin's letter is wrapped around three bank notes, but there is no mention of them in his message, as if they just fell into the envelope by accident. He writes:

Dearest Mama, Once again you are at the point of a new year in your life. We all are hoping and wishing that this new year will bring you the best and the most beautiful of all that is good. If only it could be arranged so that you might enjoy this one year free from all cares. There is nothing that your children would rather see. And to the extent that this lies in my hands, I will at least not lay on you any additional burdens.

So far away and yet so close is this second son. More than all of the other children, he represents Jürgen in Ruth's life these days.

MARCH. At Kieckow, Hans Jürgen is now fully in command, and he has a huge building project under way. A second story is being added to the manor house and the entire main floor is being renovated. Even the ground floor is not neglected, for the kitchen and laundry also benefit from the indoor plumbing and central water system that are being installed.

When it is all completed, the manor house barely resembles the modest rambling structure that first greeted Ruth more than a quarter century ago. Now it rivals any of the country houses in Pomerania. In the new second story are the bedrooms and sitting rooms, and even a schoolroom, for Hans Jürgen intends this to be a house inhabited by children. The second-story windows are symmetrically arranged within the new mansard-style roof. Above them are the attic windows, still peeking out from the little coves in the tile roof.

With most of the bedrooms moved upstairs, there is now a spacious salon, an office and a bedroom suite for the master and mistress of Kieckow. Indeed there will presently be a new mistress of the estate, for Hans Jürgen is engaged to be married!

It is the grand central hall, however, that most distinguishes the remodeled house from its earlier state. From the exterior, the central hall is framed by five glassed Roman arches, each topped with a finely cut fan of glass, and fronted by a full second-story terrace over the carriage entrance. Inside, a grand stone staircase rises from the old burnt-tile floor. The staircase merges into a balconied area above, which is framed by a heavy wooden banister, and a massive chandelier hangs from the high ceiling. Upstairs and downstairs, there are tall wooden doors on three sides that lead to the many rooms beyond. All in all, counting the ground floor and attic, there are now more than fifty rooms in the Kieckow manor house!

JUNE. In a resort town on the Baltic Sea, Hans Jürgen von Kleist is married to Maria von Diest, daughter of a military officer and barely twenty years old. Ruth has sworn that this bride will not be hostage to her mother-in-law's longevity, for she remembers too well her own time of waiting and watching while Kieckow languished in the last years of her father-in-law's life.

After the wedding Ruth returns directly to Stettin, knowing that she must feign a busy life there, at least until Hans Jürgen's Maria has found firm footing on Kieckow's soil. Ruth has no worries about this daughter-in-law, who will always be known as Mieze. Yet the former mistress of Kieckow cannot help but question the usefulness of her own life—so far from the place of her roots, occupying a rented flat in an industrialized backwater city.

OCTOBER. In Frankfurt, for certain not a backwater city, Konstantin spends more and more time in the Merton family enclave. During the opera season, Konstantin is a regular among the opera buffs, often sitting in the Merton family box. Like cultivated Germans everywhere, Jew or Gentile, his imagination is captured by the operas of that greatest of all modern German romantics, Richard Wagner. On the stage of the Frankfurt Opera House, performances that Konstantin first heard in the less cosmopolitan opera houses of Stettin now become experiences of unforgettable emotion. It is as if Wagner, more than anyone before him, has probed the emotional depths of the German psyche and laid bare its soul; so Konstantin writes home to his mother at Stettin.

1914: JUNE. Afterward they will say it was bound to end in disaster. By this they will mean not only the Hohenzollern monarchy, on which so much in life has depended for so long, but also the confrontation that is to be its undoing. In the early summer of 1914, the smell of conflict is in the air; yet there are mighty few who have any notion the expected clash will engulf an entire continent and employ weapons that bring the death tolls to numbers never dreamed of in the well-organized and long-practiced European endeavor called war. And who would imagine it happening in the Austro-Hungarian Empire, with whom Prussia has lost little love over the past century?

Yet on the twenty-eighth of June in Sarajevo, Bosnia,* a young Serbian nationalist draws a pistol and kills Archduke Franz Ferdinand, nephew of Austria's Kaiser Franz Joseph and heir to the Austro-Hungarian throne.

JULY. Two weeks later, on a beautiful Sunday afternoon in Pomerania, with the garden in full bloom and the grain waving in a gentle wind, an entire clan is gathered at Kieckow for a celebration and a dedication. Members of three distinct families—Bismarcks, Diests and Kleists, appropriately merged—are gathered in the manor house along with Puttkamers and Blankenburgs, two families that always gather with Bismarcks and Kleists from generation to generation.

Luitgarde von Bismarck, infant daughter of Maria and Herbert, and Ferdinande von Kleist, infant daughter of Mieze and Hans Jürgen, have just been baptized with water taken by the pastor from the Kieckow christening bowl.

After the ceremony in the great hall, the company adjourns to the long banquet table in the dining room, where Grandmother Ruth has arranged the seating hierarchy according to Prussian tradition. She has placed herself in the place once designated for her father-in-law, Hans Hugo, and later for her own father, Count Robert. Grandfather Zedlitz still lives but is too frail to make the trip to Kieckow. In his place, Ruth rises to offer the initial toast, to Wilhelm, the king and kaiser, followed by sentiments about the future that echo her father's at Maria's wedding two years earlier. Only now the future is imminent. The peace that Otto von Bismarck established forty years ago has come to an abrupt end with the gunshot at Sarajevo. There is only the waiting for what is to follow.

In late afternoon, with the sun due west of the manor, the entire gathering moves through the French doors out onto the

*In 1914, Bosnia was part of the Austrian Empire. Under the Versailles Treaty, Bosnia became part of Yugoslavia.

The christening of Ferdinande von Kleist and Luitgarde von Bismarck,
Ruth standing behind the two mothers holding their infants

glass-roofed terrace, there to be recorded on film by a photogra-
pher from Belgard. Ruth will think back on this day as a blessed
one indeed. It will grow in significance as the years pass, for it
will be remembered as the last time they all gathered and prayed,
not only for the children and for their families, but also for the
monarchy and for the king and kaiser—may he live forever!

AUGUST. Clearly Serbia was at least partially responsible for the
archduke's assassination; it followed as only reasonable then that
Austria issue an ultimatum to the Serbian government. But the
situation began to muddy when Serbia acquiesced to the ultimatum, except in certain details. The aging Austrian kaiser, Franz
Joseph, might have hedged; but Kaiser Wilhelm of Germany,
allied by treaty with Austria, encouraged his colleague to stand
firm. Less charitable historians will even say that Wilhelm's chancellor urged the Austrians on. In any case, on the twenty-ninth of
July Austria declared war on Serbia. Two days later Russian forces
were mobilized on the Austrian border since Russia, Serbia's
giant ally, was committed to protecting that small nation. The
German government responded to this partial mobilization with

a twelve-hour ultimatum, demanding that the Russian armies withdraw. If only Otto von Bismarck were still in power!

By noon of August 1, Germany is at war with Russia. At 7:00 P.M. Germany issues another ultimatum, this time to Belgium, demanding the right of military transit through that country in the event of a state of war.

On the third of August, Germany declares war on France, a nation tied to Russia through a mutual defense pact; the following morning German troops cross the frontier into Belgium. Wilhelm's advisors are counting on neutrality from England, considering that the kaiser and the king of England are first cousins. The advisors prove to be wrong. Before the night is out, England has entered the war on the side of France and Russia. This is not what Franz Joseph had in mind to avenge the death of his heir, but by the time he realizes the folly of his declaration against Serbia, circumstances are far beyond his or anyone else's control.

It will later be said that these first days of the World War were a heady time for the leaders of the German military machine. Historians will theorize that they had been preparing years for the event, but whatever the validity of this supposition in general, it can hardly be applied to one family of reservists—the Kleists of Kieckow. However, loyal soldiers that they are, their response to war is prompt and it is unquestioning.

Ruth has just returned to Stettin following the christening at Kieckow. Ruthchen is back at the lyceum in this next to last year of her schooling. Instead of being a time for peace and quiet, these first calamitous days are ones that require quick decisions. The news of Germany's general mobilization is relayed to the public in the morning newspapers on the street, and before noon Ruth is at the post office sending a telegram to Kieckow:

NEED TWO WAGONS AT STETTIN TOMORROW STOP COMING WITH RUTHCHEN AND SERVANTS TO KIECKOW STOP MAMA.

By mid-afternoon she has penned a note to Spes across town in the Stahlberg villa, to be hand-delivered by messenger:

Spes, my dear, I leave for Kieckow late tomorrow or early the following day. We must speak before I go. Can you

and the children still today come to the flat? . . . God
bless us all, especially our brave young men.

In time for tea, Spes and her three children, Raba, Alexander
and Hans Conrad, who was born in February, arrive by carriage.
Walter has no time to bring his family by auto, for he is busy
arranging his affairs at the mill. He is to report to his cavalry regiment tomorrow. The mother is forthright and purposeful with
her equally strong-willed daughter. Ruth is closing her flat immediately, taking Ruthchen, the cook and the maid back to
Kieckow. She insists that Spes, too, must close her house, even
though it is a major undertaking to close a villa with an entire
staff of servants. It is an extraordinary request, but then these are
extraordinary times.

A day later, three telegrams arrive at the flat, one from Hans
Jürgen at Kieckow, one from Konstantin in Frankfurt, and one
from Maria at Lasbeck. From Hans Jürgen:

> WAGONS LEFT KIECKOW AT DAWN STOP MASTER BEDROOM
> READY FOR YOU STOP AWAIT RUTHCHEN AND SPES WITH
> CHILDREN STOP HANS J REPORTS TUESDAY AT KÖSLIN STOP
> KISSES FROM MIEZE AND HANS J

From Konstantin:

> MAMA STOP LEAVE FOR BERLIN TODAY STOP EXPECT TO
> GO EAST AND SOUTH STOP EVERYTHING LEFT AS IS IN
> FRANKFURT STOP SHOULD BE BACK BEFORE CHRISTMAS
> STOP FOREVER YOURS KONSTANTIN

And from Maria:

> DEAREST MAMA STOP HERBERT REPORTS TO DUTY TOMOR-
> ROW THOUGH GOVERNOR DOES NOT WANT HIM TO GO
> STOP HERBERT SAYS IT SHOULD BE OVER SOON STOP HE
> WANTS US AT KIECKOW STOP WILL TAKE L AND ME TO
> TRAIN THIS EVENING STOP HAVE WIRED HANS J STOP YOUR
> MARIA

In the twelfth century, when the battle cry sounded, loyal
vassals of Kaiser Friedrich Barbarossa rode off to war while the
women and the children, soldiers all, barricaded themselves
behind the moats and walls of their fortress castles. Not unlike an

early Zedlitz of Zedelic or a Kleist of Belgard, Ruth von Kleist leads her brigade of women and children into the Kieckow kingdom. There she will reign as general, if not as queen, until the Fatherland is safe once more and the men come marching home. Ruth turns to her God to plead that it may all be over soon, yet grateful that she has been called upon now to protect the family bastion and hold down this eastern flank of the Hohenzollern kingdom. How could she ever have thought that her days of work were done!

"With Wings Like Eagles"

1915. Christmas has come and gone and the war is not yet over; in fact it rages with increasing vengeance on two fronts and at sea. At Kieckow, Ruth looks around her small kingdom and senses the import of her presence—that she and her four daughters (for Ruth also considers Mieze a true Kleist daughter) are the keepers of the castle. They are no less significant to the future of Prussia and Germany than the young men whose lives are in jeopardy at the front. This insight both comforts and disquiets this leader of the Kieckow women.

The news from the fronts is bewildering. Initially, Germany's grand successes on two fronts created a heady confidence at home; Belgium was easily conquered and the kaiser's armies moved deep into France, all within a few weeks. But then it all came to a halt. Armies no longer advance nor do they retreat, but only hold their same muddy positions and call it a stalemate. The western front has become a network of trenches and tunnels, from which men emerge like moles for intermittent forays that invariably end in mammoth casualties. The swift cavalry charges for which the Hohenzollerns were once famous have given way to a strange and slow-moving warfare—motorized lorries and men who languish in deep, muddy trenches. If there was ever beauty in warfare, it no longer exists on Germany's western front.

Yet Walter Stahlberg of Stettin continues to ride horseback in parade dress, reproducing the same polished movements that Robert, the count of Zedlitz and Trützschler, practiced three-quarters of a century ago. Grandfather Zedlitz is now gone, having died in October of last year. Walter carries on this ancient tradition as riding master at the training grounds of the kaiser's guards, teaching others the discipline that combines man and horse into a single entity, moving with artistic precision, but to what end?

On Germany's eastern front, armies still move across the landscape, often at high speed, and the cavalry still rides, though it is a poor match for twentieth-century machine guns. Russian armies have conquered parts of East Prussia and have moved into Germany's Polish provinces, lands that provide a buffer between Pomerania and the Russians, whom these Germans view with a mixture of awe and disdain. But as long as Junkers dwell in Pomerania, there will always be loyal officers to lead the kaiser's armies on this eastern front—the likes of Hans Jürgen and Konstantin von Kleist, Herbert von Bismarck, Ewald von Kleist and Hermann von Tresckow. And such men as these fight with confidence that places like Kieckow, Klein Krössin, Schmenzin, Lasbeck, Kniephof, and Wartenberg are in the hands of women whose mindsets match their own.

At Lasbeck, Hedwig von Bismarck rules as she has for years, while at neighboring Kniephof, her son Gottfried lies ill. His wife Gertrud, the musician's daughter from Berlin who is still viewed as a stranger to Pomerania, takes hold of the estate as if she were born to run it. Her interests lie not only with the threatened Fatherland, but also with her two small sons, for whom she intends to maintain and strengthen the Bismarck lands, as her mother-in-law did before her.

At Schmenzin, Lili von Kleist, once a countess and now a widow, holds her head high. Hers is the largest among all the Kleist estates, and she holds the land with a tight rein, awaiting the day when her son Ewald comes marching home. This young man, now an archconservative who brooks no compromise, is viewed as a misfit even in Pomerania.

Forty years later, the Nazis will behead him, and others will enshrine him as a hero. Such are the vagaries of twentieth-century Germany.

Likewise at Wartenberg another former countess, Ruth's sister Anni, manages the enterprise, caring for the village and her three young children. Her husband and her two older sons,

Gerd and Henning, fight for the Fatherland and for their land. Of all these women, Anni is perhaps the least suited to her task. Raised at Grossenborau in gentler Silesian surroundings, she will never fully adapt to the stern demands of the Neumark countryside and of her stern Junker husband, Hermann von Tresckow.

Quite the opposite is her sister, Ruth, *general* of Kieckow and Klein Krössin. Since her return from Stettin she has turned the manor house and the villages into a single unit, as well organized as they have been at any time in the history of this ancient Kleist stronghold. In fact the entire district of Belgard feels the presence of this purposeful woman. She has organized a drive for resources to undergird Germany's war effort—the collection of gold and precious stones for the kaiser's army from every landowner and townsman in the district. To set an example for others, this mother and her daughters have emptied their jewelry boxes of all that is valuable. In the mother's case it is substantial—bridal gifts from the Zedlitzes, the Rohrs, the Blankenburgs, the Bismarcks, and of course from Jürgen and Father Kleist. What does it matter that all of these items were originally given with the expectation that they would be passed on to future generations. When the Fatherland demands sacrifice, every soldier must heed the call!

Quite apart from the jewelry, Kieckow has been severely sapped by the wartime demands of the Fatherland. Eighty of the workers have reported for military service, and all of the best work horses have been conscripted by the government, leaving the old and weak animals to provide food for the nation. To further impair any kind of productivity on the estate, some government bureaucrat has decreed that each animal be given no more than three pounds of oats per day, a ration far below the minimum requirements for a reasonably healthy, working horse.

Nor is there any man to replace the master. Hans Jürgen himself took care of the accounting, procurement and sales activities of the estate, with the help of an accountant and a clerk. They have all been gone since August. Without his guidance, the bailiff tends to manage this five-thousand-acre agricultural enterprise with a rigidity that further exacerbates any hope for decent productivity, not to mention prosperity.

In the manor house, the four daughters are under Ruth's command, each with her own area of responsibility. Mieze, the current mistress of the estate, remains in charge of the household, although she has gratefully given over to her mother-in-law the overall responsibility for the estate. A nursemaid is in charge of the three babies—Spes's Hans Conrad, Mieze's Ferdinande, and Maria's Luitgarde. The Kieckow nursery, expanded now to include an additional, larger room, is the liveliest corner of the entire house, with three mothers coming and going during the day between their assigned tasks.

Sometime in her life, every mother will reflect on the way in which she raised her children, usually with satisfaction, but always with a regret or two. Ruth is no different, particularly as she contemplates the relationship between herself and her oldest daughter. She acknowledges that mistakes were made from the time Spes was a small child, with her incredible ear and sense for music. Too often this talented daughter was exempted from the mundane tasks with which others wrestled. But in today's situation, no one is exempt from responsibility. Ruth assigns to Spes and Maria the tasks she believes to be above all others in importance. Maria has become the teacher in the family schoolroom, where Spes's two older children are to obtain their primary education. Spes is assigned to the Kieckow village school, where fifty children would otherwise be without a teacher since the schoolmaster was conscripted into the military along with all the other young men. Spes has risen to the occasion magnificently, and Ruth feels vindicated.

To Ruthchen, the mother assigns the most unlikely task of all—responsibility for the accounts of this tenuous financial enterprise encompassing Kieckow and Klein Krössin. While Ruth may believe that the teacher is most important in this feudal community, every villager and every worker knows that his or her fortune ultimately rises or falls with the balance sheet in the master's study. There sits Ruthchen, in her single dark gray skirt, entering the numbers and extracting their meanings day in and day out. She receives the bailiff at the same hour each morning and gently prods him in light of the deteriorating economy. Yet she is aware of her own powerlessness in the presence of this de facto master.

For Ruthchen there will be no ball season or house parties or theater benefits, or any of those time-honored events that provide the opportunity for the maidens and bachelors of the aristocracy to meet and mate, all in the interest of the family and the Fatherland. Her sisters wonder among themselves—will Ruthchen be the unmarried one, another Elisabeth von Kleist, or perhaps a deaconess at some church hospital? Spes, whose sharp tongue is often capable of inflicting pain, has named this sister Saint Ruth, and not without cause. Ruthchen generally appears for morning and evening prayer, but seldom ever between. Not unlike the ancient heroes of the Kleist and Zedlitz families, Ruthchen von Kleist is bound to the Kieckow ledgers for the duration of this war.

1916. With horses and machines and guns, and above all, with men of courage—many now dead—the armies of the kaiser have pushed the enemy from Germany's eastern lands. Before the year is out, these armies will have moved through Prussian and Russian Poland, deep into Mother Russia itself. The troops of the Russian czar are demoralized, and there is a revolution brewing. It is a year of cautious optimism in Germany.

If only this optimism could be extended to the western front, a sinkhole where immense numbers of brave young men have died for the Fatherland, yet there is nothing to show for their sacrifice. For better or for worse, these German armies are under the direct command of Crown Prince Wilhelm, son of the kaiser. His competence may be questioned, but the symbolism is not without its importance.

Konstantin von Kleist is transferred to Verdun in response to an offensive mounted by English and French troops. Before the year ends, more than a million young men, German, French and English, will die or be severely wounded in the contest for this one village, yet there will be no victor. One of those to die will be Konstantin's closest comrade in arms. To this young man's mother he writes:

> . . . nevertheless I cannot mourn for him. Since I have seen so many men fall, I know that death is a natural event and that it marks the end to just a part of our existence. I live in the certainty that I will one day be reunited in some form with my friend.

In December another death, more like a death in the family, moves Konstantin to write his own mother from Verdun:

Old Merton has died. Surely you read it in the newspaper. This death has moved me more than any other, even in this time of dying. I know that he felt a special tenderness toward me. No doubt this has changed the form that my life will take. Of all the people I have come in contact with since I left my parental home, Merton has had the greatest influence on me, both in his example and in his fatherly interest for my welfare. I value this man not just as the genial businessman and organizer that he was. I revere him even more as a human being. His generous philanthropy has given me the greatest inspiration in my professional life. Would that I could thank him once again.

As Konstantin's mother reads and rereads this eulogy, as she does every word this son writes, she is reminded of a scene from the past—little Konstantin crying his heart out that he could not look at his dead father one more time. She wishes she had had the privilege of knowing her son's surrogate father, Merton the Jew.

1917. This is the year in which one dangerous enemy nearly collapses, only to be replaced by an even more deadly one.

In Russia, the Czarist government falls to revolutionary forces. Normally such an event would strike fear in the hearts of loyal monarchists like the Kleists of Kieckow. However, the revolution in Russia is good news for Germany—a peace of sorts and an end to war on the eastern front.

In France, the stalemate continues, but under a changed constellation. Tired reinforcements being transferred from the eastern front are little match for the strengthened alliance on the other side. The United States of America has entered the war, providing fighting forces, but more importantly, providing military supplies and badly needed food for the ravaged civilian populations. Even the great estates of Pomerania run a poor second compared to the unlimited supply of food now available to Germany's enemies from across the Atlantic.

SEPTEMBER. Konstantin has just been qualified as a replacement aviator after less than three months of training. These heroes of

the air, who will take on mythological qualities in the eyes of
their battered countrymen, drop from the skies at least as frequently as their comrades in the field. From an airfield behind
the Verdun lines, Konstantin writes home:

> Dearest Mama, . . . It is an experience beyond descrip-
> tion, like no other in this earthly life—to ascend with
> wings like eagles . . .

OCTOBER. At Kieckow, the harvest is in; it is not the best but
neither is it the worst. Ruthchen enters the quantities into the
estate ledger and wonders what these will later convert to in currency. It is Sunday afternoon, and Ruth sits nearby, rereading
aloud from Konstantin's latest letter:

> The promise for our Kieckow harvest is less than opti-
> mistic. Still we must realize that the size of the total
> German harvest is most important of all. May the
> [Kieckow] crops come in good and timely; still, I cannot
> help but be anxious about an early frost . . .

Ruthchen decides to write that very day. Konstantin must not
worry; he should know that all is well in the homeland, at least as
well as can be expected with poor horses and only old men and
women to bring in the harvest.

On Monday morning, two telegrams arrive for Ruth von Kleist
of Kieckow, delivered by bicycle from the railroad station at
Gross Tychow. So many telegrams have arrived during these last
two years, always for one family or another in either of the villages. And always the news is of casualties—sometimes wounds
from which the young man might recover, but more often death.
For three years the flag of the German Reich, always visible from
the mast in the Kieckow courtyard, has flown at half-mast almost
as much as it has flown at full height. Yet the manor house has
been immune for so long that Ruth is inclined to believe it will
be spared forever. She has not seen the bicycle drive up the
entrance ramp. Others have seen it, and the question has spread
like the wind through the two villages—"Has the master fallen?"

Ruth receives the telegrams at her desk, surrounded by four
daughters who have been summoned by the servants. She
already guesses the contents, for these telegrams are addressed
to her, not to Mieze, nor to Spes, nor to Maria. For sure, the

master has not fallen. The mother opens the first telegram and reads:

FROM THE FIELD COMMA OCTOBER 7 STOP 1917 STOP LIEUTENANT VON KLEIST TODAY CRASHED WITH AIRPLANE COMMA BADLY WOUNDED STOP LETTER FOLLOWS STOP

Frantically she tears open the second telegram and reads:

FROM THE FIELD COMMA OCTOBER 7 STOP 1917 STOP LIEUTENANT VON KLEIST HAS SUCCUMBED TO HIS WOUNDS COMMA REQUEST TELEGRAM AS TO WHETHER BODY SHOULD BE RETURNED STOP SQUADRON 3 STOP

Ruth's first words are to the servant at the door, standing a discreet distance from the family members: "The flag must be lowered to half-mast again."

Out of the cupboard comes the blackest of gowns, now twenty years old, frail and too tight to wear. But the Kieckow seamstress quickly accommodates the gown to Ruth's widening figure. Within a few hours of receiving the news, Ruth is once more dressed in mourning.

On Wednesday morning a third telegram is delivered, again to the mother:

FROM THE FIELD OCTOBER 9 STOP 1917 STOP YOU AND YOUR FAMILY PLEASE ACCEPT MY SINCERE SYMPATHY IN THE HEROIC DEATH OF YOUR NOBLE SON WHOSE FAITH- FUL SERVICE AND SACRIFICE TO OUR CAUSE WILL BE PRE- SERVED IN GRATEFUL MEMORY STOP CROWN PRINCE WILHELM STOP

Surprisingly, this telegram is a great comfort to the mother. She hopes that from their places in eternity, Jürgen and Grandfather Zedlitz, and most of all, Grandfather Kleist, have also taken note. The message in some small measure lifts the weight of this mother's immense loss; it is a reminder that for the Fatherland some must die.

On Friday, Konstantin's last letter is delivered to Kieckow. It was written the day before his death.

Dearest Mama, . . . It is the third day of bad weather and this makes me really angry. In addition I am bored to death. At Verdun nothing can be done in the air, so we must keep ourselves busy on the ground. . . .

It was on a Sunday that Konstantin was born, and it was on a Sunday that he died. A week later, also on Sunday, his body is delivered in the Kieckow wagon from the railroad station at Gross Tychow, and a week after that, on Sunday the twenty-first, Konstantin von Kleist is laid to rest next to his father in the cemetery at Kieckow. His funeral service is not the first nor will it be the last the Gross Tychow pastor preaches for fallen soldiers from Kieckow. On each of these occasions, he rises far above his own capacity, which Ruth interprets as a clear sign of divine intervention. In memory of the fallen Konstantin, the pastor eulogizes:

> He was a Sunday gift to his parents, always Sunday's child. He had the sun in his heart and he leaves behind with us a trace of this sunshine. He is not lost, nor has his sunshine set. . . . One Sunday morning the angels carried his soul on high to . . . a soldier's destiny—a sweet destiny. That which we love remains, and it remains forever. . . . 'With peace and joy aloft I soar, a child of God forevermore.' In God, all death is conquered . . .

For all the eloquence and comfort of the pastor's words, it is those of Konstantin's comrade that strike closest to his mother's heart. He is Lieutenant Zernick, and though he is not from Pomerania and is not even a Junker nor any other sort of aristocrat, the officers and enlisted men in Konstantin's squadron have designated him to deliver their comrade's body to its final resting place.

Outside the church under a cold October sky, men of the village have lowered Konstantin's coffin into the open grave. Zernick looks down upon the coffin and speaks earnestly to his fallen comrade. He first describes the sorrow Konstantin's death has brought to his fellow aviators and to all those who knew him. He then concludes with the words that will be remembered as long as there are Kleists to remember:

> I shall not complain, nor shall I speak at length. This is not the nature of the soldier and certainly it would not be your way. Just take with you our fervent pledge: That you will live on in our hearts and that even if you are not among us, we will keep you in our minds as our most

shining example in the great purpose toward which we strive. For you have given your life in a holy love for the Fatherland. That indeed is your way. Live well, Konstantin!

NOVEMBER. Five women, five small children and a baby—Maria von Bismarck's second child Jürgen, nestled in his mother's arms—make a circle surrounding the still-fresh grave at the Kieckow cemetery. The oldest among them, Mother Ruth, offers a simple prayer to dedicate the newly laid headstone. Cut deeply into its surface are the following words, meant to last longer than any of these survivors:

Konstantin von Kleist-Retzow
1891-1917
"With wings like eagles"

This time there are no tears.

Betrayed by the King

1918: MARCH. Nature and life have conspired to create an aura of hope at Kieckow. Spring has come early to these lands, and the Russian front has disappeared with the stroke of a pen. It is quiet on Germany's eastern frontier, and battle-hardened troops are being shipped west as rapidly as there are rail cars available for transport. One hears the steam whistles as the trains race west through the Kieckow lands on their noble journey.

This unlikely development began in October when the Bolsheviks seized control in a second Russian revolution, which continues to be far bloodier than the first revolution, the one that toppled the czar a year ago. The Bolsheviks have signed a treaty of virtual capitulation with Germany, and for this the Junkers of Pomerania have the most radical of all Red revolutionaries to thank—Vladimir Lenin. This indebtedness will turn out to be as ephemeral as every other German victory in this final war of the Hohenzollern monarchy.

It is said that the death of a child leaves a deeper scar than the death of any other loved one. Ruth von Kleist and her children and her children's children will later speak of the fallen Kon-

The Kieckow manor house

stantin as the "most gifted of all the children," the "son of greatest promise," and his mother's "favorite child." In every century
and in every language, words like these have been spoken by
mothers who have lost sons and daughters, including the fifteen
mothers in the combined villages of Kieckow and Klein Krössin
whose sons have fallen for the Fatherland.

Ruth has shed her dress of deep mourning. She must be an
example to these mothers and also to the widows and orphaned
children of Germany's fallen. In the fresh air of spring, she
makes her visits not once nor twice, but almost every day of the
week, alternating between Kieckow and Klein Krössin. Invariably
she has in tow nine-year-old Raba—Ruth Roberta Stahlberg—
and Raba's six-year-old brother Alla—Alexander.

It is a mother's privilege to harbor regrets in looking back over
her years of child rearing. In Ruth's case, an overwhelming
regret is that her children know little of the deep feudal roots
and the relationships that bind together those who live on a
Pomeranian estate. Raba and Alla, like their mother, are children of the city. This grandmother knows that their days at
Kieckow are numbered. The war cannot last much longer, and

when it is over, they too will be lost to the land. She hopes that these village encounters will remain with them in some way.

The village streets are better than a puppet theater to the wide-eyed Stahlberg children—women in country clothes sitting before their huts, churning butter while the wonderful smell of baking bread wafts from the open doorways; young girls dressed in milkmaid skirts, playing hoops in the street to while away the time until they must milk again. On this Kleist estate there are twenty milkmaids and eighty cows, besides the cows that belong to the villagers themselves. Even if the English blockade holds forever, there will be milk and butter and cheese and bread for Germany from this Kleist stronghold!

A village woman offers Ruth a bouquet of early crocuses, which she gracefully accepts. The same woman then brings from her house slices of freshly baked bread covered with butter and honey for the two children. With their hands clasped tightly behind their backs in an act of immense self-discipline, this granddaughter and grandson of the manor house politely refuse the delicious offering. Raba speaks for both: "We may not take honey and butter while there are children in Stettin who go hungry."

Walking back up the road to the house on the hill, the grandmother tenderly acknowledges the sacrifice of her two charges. For almost four years there has been no butter on the manor house dining table, and honey only on Sundays. Raba and Alla have not disappointed their grandmother, and it shall be mentioned at evening devotions.

AUGUST. These days much is left unsaid at Kieckow. The news of the war is far less hopeful than it was in spring. The unexpected peace with Russia and General Ludendorff's bold initiatives in the west were short-lived victories. One hears that morale on the front is lower than it has ever been. Worse than that, there are rumors that the navy is riddled with treason—mutiny on one ship after another. But then what can one expect from the German navy, that grandiose fantasy of a foolish kaiser! No one contemplates mutiny in the army; whatever changes history brings, Germany can count on Prussian soldiers of every class to be the bulwark of the nation.

On a warm, hazy August morning, all six children of the
manor house, even two-year-old Jürgen von Bismarck, are out on
the meadow romping in the sunshine, while in the distance half-
grown boys and girls, with their mothers and their grandfathers,
work to bring in the Kieckow harvest. Old wagons drawn by old
horses and driven by old men and old women stand quietly
awaiting their turn in the field. The Kleist grandchildren amuse
themselves under their nursemaid's supervision and presume to
help by feeding pieces of clover to the docile animals. It is not
the custom of the land that the women of the manor house participate in these agricultural tasks. Therefore they are out of
sight but equally busy in Ruthchen's countinghouse. There are
messages to relay between field and office, particularly news of
current prices, with each wagon that returns from Gross Tychow.
What a shame that prosperity on the land must come at the
expense of war; nevertheless in rural Pomerania, good harvests
and good prices stand very near to godliness.

The last returning vehicle has driven right through the village
and up to the manor house. The driver disembarks and walks
around to the back door, from which one can enter directly into
Ruthchen's office. He lays on her desk the day's mail, a pile of
letters that must be sorted and distributed throughout the
village. As modern as Kieckow pretends to be, there is still no
mail service to this remote outpost.

Ruthchen searches through the pile, hoping for news from
Hans Jürgen or Herbert or Walter, or from one of Mother's
cousins. Right now there are so many men to keep track of, and
each one stationed in a more dangerous place than the other.
Today there is no word from any of the men, but there is a letter
to Mother, addressed in a magnificent handwriting, from
someone whose name is not at all familiar to Ruthchen—Hans
von Wedemeyer. Dropping her pen, she runs to her mother's
sitting room, where Ruth is at her desk writing to one or another
of her men in the field.

Inviting Ruthchen to stay a moment, Ruth reads the name on
the envelope, remembering a couple she and Jürgen met long
ago at one of the sanitoriums they visited while he was ill. The
Wedemeyers are fine people from an estate near Wartenberg,
and they are friends of Anni and Hermann von Tresckow. Ruth

recalls they had children, three daughters and two sons. Possibly one was named Hans.

She opens the letter and reads aloud. It is the same family; the father is now dead and the mother alone holds the estate together. Hans, the younger son, recently returned from Palestine, where he served under Franz von Papen. Now Hans von Wedemeyer is at nearby Köslin, learning to fly airplanes. It is a short training course, not more than three months; he would like to call on Madam von Kleist and her daughters in order to bring greetings from his mother. Ruth nods, but says nothing; without being told, she knows that Hans von Wedemeyer is not married and that he is looking for a wife. Even in wartime, without the balls and receptions, the Prussian aristocracy is determined to find ways to perpetuate itself.

Ruth pens a message to the young man, and Ruthchen delivers it to the servant, who will see that it is on the milk wagon early tomorrow. With an uncharacteristic lightness in her step, this daughter returns to her ledgers and figures. From her little office she can see directly into the forest, and she imagines her prince charming emerging from its dark green depths on a white steed. It is not so easy to bring one's mind back to the price of oats and the number of bags delivered today at Gross Tychow.

On the last Saturday of the month, Lieutenant Hans von Wedemeyer is to visit Kieckow. The entire household is involved in the preparations for Mother Ruth's visitor from Köslin. She has spent the entire morning arranging late summer flowers in the dining room, in her sitting room, on the veranda, and most importantly, in the guest room where the young man will sleep. Each of Ruth's married daughters, without putting into words what is common knowledge, has dressed herself in a summer garden dress from her trousseau. Ruthchen, the Cinderella, has no trousseau. Laid out on her bed is her one and only summer frock, plain and somewhat threadbare from constant use through four long years, but washed and pressed for the occasion.

From the door below, two men's voices can be heard and the sound of footsteps as the servant leads the visitor to Ruth's sitting room. She feigns business at her desk, but clearly she has been waiting and watching through the window for the Kieckow wagon with its welcome load. One by one the daughters make their appearance, and by the time Ruthchen arrives there is pleasant conversation with Mother at its center. Within a few minutes Hans von Wedemeyer has become an old family friend. He is tall—taller than any of the men in the family with the exception of Walter, and in uniform he is every bit the prince this maiden had imagined. But most surprising of all is his uncanny resemblance to the fallen Konstantin—the glow in his eyes, the lighthearted repartee, and the underlying serious nature of this man have endeared him to all five women. Even Ruthchen's embarrassment over her worn out dress disappears at the kindly glances that come her way.

Supper is served, and during the meal the conversation turns to topics of a more serious nature. In fact, the lieutenant is prompted to ask for a Bible. Later on the family files into the great hall, where the tea table makes its final appearance of the day. Spes sits down at the keyboard and directs her sisters in a choral performance of Brahms's *Lieder*. Ruth's eyes fill with tears—a mixture of joy and tenderness, this last for Jürgen and Konstantin and the hope that this beautiful music might be heard in Paradise.

Sunday morning means the customary family attendance at church services. Ruth is seated in the forward family pew between Lieutenant von Wedemeyer and Maria. Ruthchen is seated on the visitor's other side, and Spes is at the organ; the children fill the other family pews, with Mieze somewhere in the middle. The common pews are occupied by the villagers, and those who care take note that Miss Ruthchen appears to have a suitor, tall and good-looking, which is what she certainly deserves.

After dinner, there is a pilgrimage through the forest, to a far corner where a small meadow is formed by a circle of ancient oak trees. Over many decades, workers have gathered stones from the Kieckow fields and have laid them here out of the way. As a child, Konstantin often led his sisters into this secret fort, from which he guarded the land and kept one-eyed pirates at bay. Since his death, mother and daughters have turned this secluded spot into a kind of memorial to Konstantin, and they come here frequently. The stones have been arranged around the perimeter, piled so that visitors can sit facing one another. The women lead their new friend into the circle with a mixture of religious reverence and childlike delight.

For the next hour, the Kieckow women sit quietly while Hans von Wedemeyer talks of his early war years in France, behind the lines where it is not always easy to distinguish friends from enemies. Ruthchen follows these adventures like a wide-eyed child. How will the man who one day comes to call on her ever compare to Mother's extraordinary visitor!

Before nightfall the visitor is gone, by wagon to Gross Tychow, then by train to Belgard, where he must change for the train to Köslin. Rather than waiting on the station platform, Hans chooses to visit the old St. Mary's church on the market square, pausing there to contemplate the events of the past two days. At this moment he resolves to ask for Ruthchen's hand in marriage.

Later Ruthchen will learn of this and will view it as an act of God, who sent her prince charming unknowingly into the church where she was baptized. Such is the legacy of Ruth von Kleist—that her children and her children's children will frequently believe events in their lives to be touched by the hand of God.

SEPTEMBER. Hans von Wedemeyer makes an urgent visit to his widowed mother to report that he intends to marry a daughter of Frau von Kleist, the Landrat's widow. He has not yet approached her mother, for he first wants his own mother's approval. In answer to her questions—"How old is she? What do you find appealing about her? What does she looks like?"—Hans can only shrug. In truth, he couldn't pay that much attention, so distracted was he by this entire family of females—each of the young women so straight and slender in appearance, so open and uninhibited in temperament, a quartet of beauty for the eye to behold. He will inform himself on the details later; for now it is enough to say that he intends to marry the youngest of them— Ruth, whom they all call Ruthchen.

OCTOBER. Germany has issued to America an appeal for an armistice—a way out of this bitter, hard-fought war. There is bickering in Berlin and immense restlessness everywhere in the land.

One hopes for at least an end to the killing on the western front, yet is fearful that a bloody Bolshevik revolution might follow a military cease-fire.

Still there is a hunt at Kieckow this year, and Hans von Wedemeyer is invited from Köslin as the principal guest. Except for Fritz von Woedtke, there is not another man in the whole district of a standing sufficient to warrant an invitation. Fortunately, there are a few left among the workers strong enough to beat the forest and rout out the animals for the visiting hunter.

There are twenty-four for breakfast this weekend of the hunt. Halfway through the meal, and seemingly oblivious to everyone else present, Hans stops the conversation by addressing Ruth across the table: "Madam, there is something I wish to discuss with you alone."

Alone with Ruth in the sitting room, Hans von Wedemeyer petitions for the right to propose marriage to her daughter Ruthchen. The mother responds with a not unreasonable question: "Do you love my daughter?"

The suitor's response is most unusual for its honesty: "No, but I do know that I would like to marry her and that I must marry her; I believe that this assurance is the most important basis for a marriage."

"Do you believe then that my daughter loves you?" Ruth continues.

His response is equivocal at best: "I have no idea whether or not she loves me. Why, I have hardly spoken a word with her!"

There is much consternation in the manor house when Ruth reports the situation to her daughters. She has arranged a wagon ride through the countryside for tomorrow—herself in the forward wagon with a female companion and the coachman, while Ruthchen follows with the young man at the reins of a second, smaller wagon. The older sisters are incensed. Just because the mother is captivated by this young officer in uniform doesn't mean that she should hand over her daughter on a silver platter. Spes and Maria, and even the docile Mieze, rise to the defense of the helpless Ruthchen.

Ruthchen is uncomfortable and proposes to cancel the whole ride because tomorrow is pay day for the workers and she must, under all circumstances, spend the afternoon in the office.

Mother Ruth, however, is not to be trifled with. Her instincts tell her that Hans von Wedemeyer is no less Ruthchen's prince charming than Jürgen von Kleist was her own. If necessary, the workers will just have to wait for their pay, for the afternoon ride shall go forward as planned.

The next day Ruthchen finds herself riding beside Hans in the wagon. Along the way he speaks easily of his childhood and family. Ruthchen only listens, fearing she has nothing to contribute. That night, with a lighted candle, this youngest daughter makes her way to her mother's room and sits down on the edge of the bed. Ruth speaks first: "What would you say to marrying Hans von Wedemeyer?" Ruthchen is unsure. She finds it difficult even to carry on a conversation with the young man; it must be that she was not meant to marry. The mother says nothing, but only kisses her daughter and sends her on her way.

On the following morning, the day on which the lieutenant is to leave Kieckow, Ruthchen encounters him in the corridor before breakfast. "And how did you sleep?" Hans inquires.

"Very well, thank you. And how did you sleep, Lieutenant?" Ruthchen asks in turn.

"Oh, I slept very badly; in truth I hardly slept at all." The young man looks into her eyes, with deep seriousness and not without pain.

Ruthchen's eyes drop shyly to the floor. "I lied to you, Hans; my night was no better than yours."

With this unlikely exchange of words, Ruthchen von Kleist and her indefinite suitor Hans von Wedemeyer are betrothed.

Two weeks later Hans is back at Kieckow again, this time temporarily relieved of his military duties after a bout with influenza. War or no war, it is the obligation of every young man in the aristocracy to introduce his intended to his own mother within three days of the marriage engagement. Ruthchen and Hans travel by wagon to Gross Tychow, then by train south to the home of Hans's widowed mother.

Like her mother before her, Ruthchen travels a new road to a land she has never seen before—Prussia's Neumark, bounded on the north by Pomerania and on the south by Silesia, all of it east of the Oder River. Unlike her mother a generation earlier, Ruthchen is overwhelmed by the beauty of her husband's childhood home. At the entrance of the manor house stands his widowed mother, dressed elegantly in the traditional gray gown of the land, her silver hair pulled back into a bun. She greets this new daughter with such warmth and open affection that Ruthchen ceases for all time to view herself as the Cinderella from Pomerania.

NOVEMBER. Time has run out. Germany's allies—Bulgaria, Turkey and Austria—have all capitulated. Furthermore, America's response to Germany's peace overtures is a demand for an armistice and the creation of a democratic Republic of Germany. Revolution has spread to most of Germany's cities, and Kaiser Wilhelm has dismissed the last of his many wartime chancellors. Friedrich Ebert, a socialist, is now chancellor of Germany. As if this is not enough to test the devotion of the Prussian aristocracy, the kaiser has yielded to demands that he abdicate the throne and leave the country.

Of all the misfortunes that are to beset families like the Kleists and the Wedemeyers, the Bismarcks, and the Tresckows after this world war is over, the one that will be remembered with greatest bitterness is Wilhelm's decision to abdicate as German kaiser and to slip away under cover of darkness, abandoning these loyal vassals who would gladly have given their lives in defense of his person and of the Hohenzollern dynasty. As long as the sons and daughters of Ruth von Kleist live, Wilhelm of Hohenzollern will never be forgiven.

A Wedding at Kieckow

1918: NOVEMBER. A mob of German citizens hoisting bright red banners and armed with clubs and pitchforks has attacked the air base at Köslin. Lieutenant von Wedemeyer is prepared to respond with gunfire, but his commander refuses to give the order. The kaiser has left the country; this must mean Germany is a republic, and if the people want the air base, let them have it. Disgusted with his superior for surrendering without resistance, the lieutenant decides to quit his post immediately. Fearing for his mother's life, Hans boards a train for home. En route, the train is overrun by revolutionaries who force their way through

Germany, 1920-1933

the passenger cars accosting the officers and tearing the epaulets and insignia from their uniforms—but not from the uniform of First Lieutenant von Wedemeyer! When a man in a red cummerbund approaches, Hans dares him to touch this uniform of the kaiser. The man backs off momentarily, and Hans jumps from the train. He is still thirty kilometers from home and must make the rest of the journey on foot, but he finds his mother safe and well protected by the loyal villagers.

A day later, in a rail car somewhere in a French forest, Germany signs an armistice with its enemies. In a hastily written letter to Ruthchen, Hans pleads that she make her way to the Neumark immediately so that they can be married in haste. If there is to be a Bolshevik revolution, at least they should hang from the same tree. The situation seems no less urgent from the Kieckow perspective, but Mother Ruth, while agreeing that an immediate wedding is called for, dictates that it shall take place at Kieckow in Pomerania.

On the seventeenth of November, Ruthchen and Hans are married in the Kieckow church. She is the first bride from the manor house to be married there, and all who are present agree that no bride in history ever looked as radiant. Dressed in the bridal gown of one sister and the slippers of another, Ruthchen's transformation can only be compared to that of the fairy-tale princess Cinderella. No one even notices that the wedding rings are of molded steel.

On the following morning, in gently falling snow, the bride and groom set out for their home in the Neumark—Pätzig, the Wedemeyer estate that now belongs to Hans. Ruth bids the young couple farewell with tears of joy and sadness, and after the Kieckow wagon has rounded the corner into the village and disappeared from sight, she retreats to her sitting room to reflect and to remember. Whatever the fortunes of their kind in a new and different Germany, this mother is comforted that her youngest daughter at least is bound to a man and to a home for which she is eminently suited. There could be no greater destiny for this most vulnerable of her daughters, the one who had not a penny of dowry. Would that Konstantin still lived to share his mother's joy!

DECEMBER. By train, by wagon, and on foot, the men of the manor house and the men of the villages return to the land and to their families. Hans Jürgen is the first to return to the manor house, arriving at Gross Tychow by train and carried home in a wagon covered with evergreen branches—a gesture of welcome by the Kieckow workers for the long-absent master. Ruth insists on vacating the master bedroom, her wartime sleeping quarters, now that the master has returned. Mieze and Hans Jürgen protest, but the mother as usual prevails. Two days later Herbert von Bismarck arrives by automobile, the first such vehicle to be seen at Kieckow in almost four years. Farewells and tears are exchanged on the entrance ramp as Maria and Herbert leave for home, with Luitgarde barely visible on the seat between her parents and little Jürgen perched on his mother's lap.

Within nine months two more grandchildren will be added to Ruth's healthy six, Konstantin von Kleist and Hans Otto von Bismarck.

Ruthchen and Hans von Wedemeyer

Finally there is word from the last of the returning soldiers, Walter Stahlberg. In a brief letter, Walter reports that he is in Stettin, taking control again of the Stahlberg mills, which are in a state of dismal disrepair. He is also opening up the family villa in preparation for Spes's return to the city. Then without any announcement, he appears one afternoon on the snowy landscape, driving an automobile fit for a king (were there still a king in Prussia). There are more farewells and more tears on the entrance ramp as the last of Ruth's daughters drives off with her husband. Despite their grandmother's sadness at being separated from them, the departing grandchildren are in the highest of spirits. Raba, Alla and Hans Conrad, bundled warmly for the long winter journey, are sitting proudly on the leather-covered rear seat of their father's shiny seven-passenger sedan.

1919. The quiet sitting room that was Ruth's during four years of war is now the scene of an intense discussion between mother and son. Ruth has decided to return to her flat in Stettin, where her few pieces of furniture still remain, to pick up the threads of her widow's existence. Hans Jürgen is vehemently opposed to the idea. There will be lean years ahead for Kieckow, and he intends to run the combined Kieckow-Klein Krössin enterprise with the help of a single bailiff. Hans Jürgen proposes to convert the bailiff's house at Klein Krössin into a retirement home for his mother. Kieckow has more than enough skilled craftsmen to do the work, and with the estate running more smoothly than ever before, some workers can be spared. He has thought this over carefully during the long periods of boredom that separated the bursts of terror and death on the front, and he insists that his mother not renew the lease on her flat.

Hans Jürgen's offer is too enticing for Ruth to refuse. The bailiff's house stands on the edge of the forest just outside the village of Klein Krössin. Of all the buildings on these Kleist lands, this cottage is the most traditional—single-storied, with half-timbered walls covered by a thatched roof, and an interior more spacious than the exterior suggests.

During the quiet winter evenings, Ruth happily plans the details of her new home. First of all, it must have three guest rooms, each one spacious and comfortable, with names to inspire the guests who sleep there: Hope, Contentment and Joy. And there must be a well-equipped kitchen and pantry, and she will hire a cook. Never in her life has she had so much input into the planning and arranging of her surroundings.

This newfound freedom carries over into other areas of Ruth's consciousness as well; her lifelong interest in the Bible and all that flows from it begins to take on a new dimension. In reading the periodicals of the Pomeranian church, she has discovered new trends in biblical interpretation and new perspectives on the church and society. These ideas pique her curiosity, and she is surprised at the gentle shifts in her own understanding. Ruth begins to see quite clearly that her role in the growing family circle is to reconstruct the foundations—both spiritual and secular—to which this family can cement its traditional ethical and moral values.

Ruth von Kleist, mother of four families and confidante to at least as many more, vows that she will devote her remaining years to this divinely ordained task.

APRIL. At the Palace of Versailles in France, where less than fifty years ago King Wilhelm I of Prussia was crowned kaiser in Germany's Second Reich—an event inspired by Cousin Otto and described to Ruth countless times by both her father and her father-in-law, both of whom were present—representatives of the German government sign a treaty that causes strong men and women to weep for themselves and for the Fatherland.

In the east, a Polish nation is to be reconstructed from lands seized by Prussia, Austria and Russia in the eighteenth and nineteenth centuries—a Slavic nation-state within a few miles of the Belgard District! In the west, Germany will cede to France the long-contested area of Alsace-Lorraine. The west bank of Germany's Rhine River is to be occupied by the troops of Germany's wartime enemies, the east side of the river permanently demilitarized. For the next fifteen years, Germany's coal-rich Saarland is to be governed by an international organization, with France administering the coal mines. After fifteen years there is to be a plebescite, at which time the inhabitants will be permitted to choose between France and Germany. And the German army, that bastion of the Junkers and millions of other loyal Hohenzollern vassals, is to be limited to 100,000 men, with military aircraft and certain other modern weapons forbidden.

AUGUST. In the new democratic Germany, outrage and resentment envelop every region and every class. Despite Ruth's quiet way of life in the Pomeranian countryside, even she is not immune to the storms that rage throughout the Fatherland.

In the Belgard District, in fact throughout all of rural Germany, there is a situation unheard of in the history of Prussia—a strike by agricultural workers. Wheat and corn and oats remain in the fields, long since ready for harvesting, and the dreaded field rot has begun to appear. In the town of Belgard the strike is particularly fierce. At Kieckow, the once-loyal workers refuse to enter the fields. A Red-inspired agricultural workers' union is being organized, and all of the men have gone to a meeting in Gross Tychow, either out of curiosity or in sympathy with the cause. One hopes it is the former rather than the latter.

There is a flurry of activity in the Kieckow courtyard as Ewald von Kleist trots up to the manor house ramp and dismounts, having covered the distance that separates his six thousand acres from his cousin's four thousand in record time. This cousin and neighbor, who taught the fatherless Hans Jürgen to ride horseback and introduced him to the hunt, and whose demeanor demanded respect from Hans Jürgen even as a boy, is now master of Schmenzin. Not yet thirty years old, he returned home after the armistice to take over the inheritance his mother had faithfully managed—five large estates and five villages, all in the district of Belgard. He promptly held gatherings with all of the people on his lands, conveying to them a single message: "The Prussian king has abdicated; I consider it a betrayal of us by the person Wilhelm. For the moment, the Hohenzollern throne is empty. Do not believe that anything has changed, though. We are still all vassals of the Hohenzollern kingdom—I am and so are you—let no one tell you otherwise. Until a king comes forward to fill the empty throne, consider me king at Schmenzin, at Hopfenberg, at Wilhelmshoehe, at Dimkuhlen and at Gross Freienstein. Long live the Prussian king!"

As Hans Jürgen arrives to greet his boyhood friend and cousin, he is amazed to see that a pistol hangs conspicuously from Ewald's belt. "Hans Jürgen, we must not give in—not you, not I and not the others," Ewald declares. "I intend to ride into Gross Tychow, right into their midst, and demand a chance to speak. If someone seeks to topple me from my mount, I will shoot him. There is more at stake than this harvest or my life. Never mind what they ask in wages and hours. We can give them all that and more later. What we have to protect is our position relative to the land and to the people who work it. As long as I live, no red-girdled Bolshevik will dictate to me in my kingdom."

Hans Jürgen agrees to hold firm and allow the harvest to spoil if need be, and his cousin is off, this time through the forest behind Klein Krössin, there to catch the Gross Tychow road. No sense in further alarming the villagers; he'll save his energies for the confrontation with the mob.

It is close to sunset before Ewald von Kleist is finally permitted to speak outside the ancient Kleist castle in Gross Tychow. This most resolute of all the Kleists rises in his stirrups and addresses the angry gathering, yielding not one inch to the demands of the listeners. Still, no one comes forward to challenge his person.

SEPTEMBER. The Belgard District strike is broken, but not before most of the crops have spoiled in the fields. The leaders of the union have all but disappeared, and the workers are back in the fields, picking up any residue that might still have some value. It will be a hard winter throughout the district, but the landowners have promised better wages for the year to come.

For sure, Hans Jürgen rules his domain with a lighter hand than does his cousin Ewald, and it may also be true that Hans Jürgen stands in Ewald's shadow on the Pomeranian landscape. Yet between these two men there exists a bond of friendship and an unspoken loyalty that will both protect and expose each of them in the time of terror that lies ahead.

1920. The German economy is in shambles; hunger, unemployment and despair have embittered the population, particularly in the cities. Resentment that was at first directed against the foreign victors of the war is now turned against Germany's first democratically elected government. In places like Pomerania and the Neumark, spring planting and fall harvesting take place in peace. If any part of Germany is immune to the current economic and political debacle, it is these lands of the Prussian Junkers.

Spes and Walter Stahlberg's marriage has been severed, not without pain on both sides. Walter will remain in Stettin, although the family villa is to be sold. Spes is taking the children to Berlin, where she has found a flat in Grunewald, now a center of Berlin society and culture. It is one of the few suburbs of the city that continue to prosper in the wake of disastrous inflation. Spes will have her grand piano, and Raba will attend the Kaiserin Augusta Gymnasium; the two boys will study violin and cello. This divorced mother has come a long way from provincial Stettin, and a long, long way from Kieckow.

Ruth's feelings are mixed. She wonders if Spes's fierce streak of independence is at the root of this marriage dissolution, or whether the marriage simply could not surmount the cultural differences between the city-bred businessman and the country aristocrat. Ruth knows Spes's side of the story well and she has rallied to this daughter all of the forces at hand. No one in the family will ever know Walter's side, for neither the divorce nor Walter Stahlberg will ever be mentioned again.

Deep down Ruth is inclined to blame herself for this ill-fated marriage. She was the one who dared the reluctant suitor to withdraw a proposal already rejected by her daughter, and in so doing ensured the marriage. For this she could never forgive herself were it not for Raba and Alla and little Hans Conrad. This grandmother will never say that any grandchild is favored more than the others, yet Spes's three are very dear to her heart.

For all of the difficulties and the trauma this year has brought, there is at least one joyful event to be celebrated. Ruthchen von Wedemeyer, at home in Pätzig, gives birth to her first child, a girl. Mother Ruth is present to assist in the delivery, along with Hans, the baby's father. The child is named Ruth Alice, after her mother and her grandmother.

From Pätzig, Ruth continues on to Grossenborau, her first visit with Rob and Olga since before the war. If Kieckow represents the old ways in Prussia, Grossenborau definitely stands for all that is new—a city-bred mistress, a master who feels at home under Germany's republican government, and a village filled with *Bauern*, freeholders of land, notwithstanding their commitment to the estate at large. Still it is the same old Rob who once chided his sister over her girlhood flirtations, yet continues to encourage her to rise to every new challenge. Seldom do this brother and sister meet, yet they are closely bound by their common childhood memories.

Mother Zedlitz, widowed now for six years, is aged and frail. Like her daughter Anni von Tresckow, this countess of Zedlitz still stands in the shadow of her much-admired husband. Without him, life is empty. Ruth wonders whether she too would be like Mother Zedlitz and Anni if her husband had lived. There was a time in her maiden life when Ruth wanted only to live in Jürgen's shadow. What a different life God chose for her!

Like Anni and Hermann, Rob and Olga have three sons. Two of them were old enough to serve in the war, and one has not recovered; he lives at home, stricken with tuberculosis, the dreaded disease that knows no class and for which there is no cure. Their youngest son Friedrich Carl, still in school, is the one in whom Rob places his hope for the future of Grossenborau.

From Grossenborau, Ruth travels to Berlin for a talk with Spes and a glimpse of the three children who are never far from her thoughts, then on to the flat in Stettin, where two trucks from Kieckow are waiting. Even in Germany's defeat, one discovers that the clock of progress cannot be turned back. It is barely a year since the armistice, and already the Kieckow barns are lit by electricity and the estate equipped with two motorized vehicles.

Ruth oversees the dismantling of the Stettin family home without sentiment, for she believes as never before that Kleists were not meant for city life. On the trip back to Kieckow, she insists on riding in one of the trucks, next to the driver. She prevails on him to turn left at Klein Krössin and drive directly to the renovated house. In the darkness of a moonless night, the men unload her bed and place it in one of the bedrooms. Without undressing, Ruth lies down alone to sleep for the first time in her new home.

The Garden at Klein Krössin

1923. The garden surrounding the old bailiff's cottage outside Klein Krössin is like no other garden in the Belgard District. It was designed by Ruth as a place to sit and commune with nature and to converse with friends over tea. It is her pride and joy, despite her pretensions to the contrary.

The house itself serves as a place to write, a place to receive visitors—Ruth is hardly ever alone for afternoon tea—and a place to read, to contemplate and to sleep. Its layout is remarkable in that the size of the combined sitting and dining room is modest compared to the size of the four sleeping rooms.

Ruth's bedroom doubles as her study and is dominated by the great writing desk that once belonged to Jürgen, which Hans Jürgen had sent over from the Kieckow manor house. Given its deep drawers and hidden cubbyholes, a more superstitious person might imagine the desk to harbor the spirit of its departed owner. For Ruth it is a fond reminder of the gentle young man she accompanied to this land so long ago. From this private corner Ruth can look out through large windows, toward her garden on one side and the forest on the other, to be inspired by the fruits of God's hand in every mood and in every season.

Ruth can count on one or two grandchildren arriving each year, and she insists on being present at each birth. How could she not be? All through the war she presided at every birth in the Kieckow village, and since her move to Klein Krössin no birth

Ruth's cottage at Klein Krössin, from the garden

there occurs without her involvement. Ruth simply does not trust the rural midwives enough to leave any infant or mother in their hands alone. How could she do less for her own family than she does for the families of the village?

There are now four children in the manor house at Kieckow—Ferdinande, Konstantin, Jürgen Christoph and Hans Friedrich; four children at Lasbeck—Luitgarde, Jürgen, Hans Otto and Spes; and two at Pätzig—Ruth Alice and Maximilian. There are also three children far from the land in Berlin—Raba, Alla, and Hans Conrad. The children are enough to capture the complete attention of any grandmother, but this grandmother has energy to spare. In this age of change, a sense of duty drives her into examining her own values and ideas as well as the political and social structures that are under siege. Ruth is by instinct conservative, yet she feels obligated to deal with the changes that are overwhelming her world, to understand the new ideas and to evaluate them against the old values. It is a responsibility that she has taken on, not so much for herself, but rather on behalf of her children and grandchildren. In fact Ruth is writing a book, putting down on paper her thoughts on the values and the institution that she knows best, the role of the landed aristocracy in an age of democracy.

Understandably Mieze and Hans Jürgen are involved with their own growing family and the affairs of the estate. Still Ruth does not lack for intellectual stimulation and a sounding board for her thoughts as long as Ewald von Kleist is in the vicinity. She is frequently visited by this free-thinking neighbor and cousin to her children, who would rather discuss political and religious issues than entangle himself with the daily tasks of Schmenzin.

Ewald has finally married. His wife is the former Anning von der Osten from Warnitz in the Neumark, friend and neighbor to the Tresckows of Wartenberg and to the Wedemeyers of Pätzig. Anning is taller than Ewald, which gives rise to a malicious kind of gossip among his opponents around Belgard. She is also fiercely loyal to her husband, a trait that from the beginning of the marriage requires courage and assertiveness, for Ewald has enemies as well as friends. Anning's father is Oskar von der Osten, elected leader of the conservative German National People's Party in the Neumark. This marriage completes a circle that will have immense ramifications in future years—the Pomeranian cluster of Lasbeck, Klein Krössin, Kieckow and Schmenzin tied through marriage, religious beliefs and political conviction to Pätzig, Wartenberg and Warnitz in the Neumark.

Ewald is now the elected leader of the conservatives in Pomerania; however, it is not politics that he and Ruth discuss for hours at a time in Ruth's sitting room or garden, depending on the time of year. The point of contention between these two neighbors is the Bible itself—whether divine inspiration engenders every word to flow from the pen of the Almighty and whether Jesus Christ is in fact God. Ewald refuses to accept either of these theses, and Ruth feels obligated to challenge him with every weapon in her arsenal of scriptural sources. Ewald is not an easy man to deal with on such questions. He claims to be a Unitarian Christian, and Ruth endeavors to show him that one cannot be a Christian without the Trinity. The discussions are energetic, but fruitless. Ewald remains with his dogma and Ruth with hers; yet the mutual affection grows and the friendship is deepened.

Years later, Ewald will write from a prison cell that he has come around to accept what Ruth always proclaimed—the living God in Christ. His letters will one day be published for all the world to see, but long after his own death and the death of his friend and counselor Ruth von Kleist.

What Ewald and Ruth together hold as a truth above all else in the secular sector of life is the ordering of society within the monarchical tradition. In more practical terms, this means that both refuse to abandon the validity of a king and kaiser as the head and heart of Prussia and the German Reich. It is an unpopular position to hold in modern Germany, but neither Ruth nor Ewald shies from discomfort or pain imposed by one's own conscience.

1924: APRIL. A new book has been published in Germany, under the title *Twelve Years at the Imperial German Court*.[14] It is causing a sensation, for it reveals the most intimate details of Kaiser Wilhelm's administration in the crucial years preceding the World War. Never before has someone so close to the kaiser and his family as this author published a day-to-day diary of the activities in the Hohenzollern court. And never before has someone so close to the kaiser revealed the frivolities, the gossip, and the mean-spiritedness that sapped the decision-making strength of his government, which represented the dominant nation in central Europe.

It is enough to strike discomfort in the hearts of those Prussians whose loyalty to the monarchy has already survived extraordinary changes. But it is much worse than that for Ruth. The author of this exposé is the kaiser's former Controller of the Royal Household, Robert, count of Zedlitz and Trützschler and owner of the Grossenborau estate in Silesia—the brother for whom her affection runs deepest among all her siblings.

From Klein Krössin the call goes out—through letters, over telephone wires, and when possible by personal visits. There will be no further associations with the count and countess and their children, except in the case of illness and death, and their names shall be stricken from the *Almanac de Gotha*, that geneological Bible of the European aristocracy. Ruth has agonized over this, she has reviewed it intellectually, she has weighed it in her heart and she is prepared to stand by her family and her class: Rob, his wife Olga, and their sons are to be written out of the Prussian aristocracy.

Ruth has passed this hardest test in her life so far—she has overruled her heart by supporting without reservation the harsh sentence meted out to Rob and to all who will come after him. The sentence is far-reaching. Beyond the immediate family, the Kleists, the Bismarcks, and the Wedemeyers, there are Ruth's two sisters, Anni von Tresckow at Wartenberg and Etti von Rohr in Silesia, and her second brother, Stefan, who inherited the old family estate at Frauenhain. Like Rob, he is also the count of Zedlitz and Trützschler. All are pledged to cast out their brother in order to defend the honor of Wilhelm II, that vain and foolish man who brought down the House of Hohenzollern without a single bullet being fired.

Ruth thinks back on her youthful attachment to the dramas of Friedrich Schiller, in which good men and good women over and over again brought tragedy upon themselves, their families and their kings by failing to choose duty over the desire of their hearts. One can live with heartbreak more easily than with duty failed. Such is the mindset of the loyal soldier at Klein Krössin.

MAY. "The Lord giveth and the Lord taketh away."

On a sunny morning at Kieckow, the lighthearted Ferdinande von Kleist and her shy brother Konstantin knock on Papa's office door, asking if they might take a bouquet of straw flowers to Grandmother's house. These two oldest children of Hans Jürgen plead so charmingly, with bouquets already gathered and in hand, that he agrees to take them along on his morning round to Klein Krössin. He lifts ten-year-old Ferdinande and four-year-old Konstantin into the wagon, where they perch themselves firmly on the seat. Papa himself will drive them to Grandmother's house.

Papa and the children are in high humor as the wagon rolls out of the courtyard, down the path from the manor house, and makes a right-hand turn onto the village road. The horse trots easily along the three-kilometer stretch of fields that separates Kieckow from Klein Krössin. Yet in the heat of the day, the flies insist on bothering the animal. As he shakes his head to rid himself of the pests, his bridle and bit come loose. The frightened horse bolts into a fast gallop homeword, dragging the wagon behind. The frightened animal is out of control.

Papa grabs Konstantin and throws him feet first into the ditch; he seizes Ferdinande and does the same, then jumps from the runaway wagon himself. Konstantin rolls as he falls and in a moment he is sitting up. He looks startled, but he does not cry. Ferdinande does not get up. Her head is bleeding where it struck a sharp stone, and she is unconscious. Several men come running from the village, and one of them picks up the frightened boy while Hans Jürgen lifts his daughter gently into his arms. The following day Ferdinande dies without regaining consciousness, and shortly thereafter she is buried in the Kieckow cemetery.

Far away in Berlin, Elisabeth von Kleist, the estranged aunt of Hans Jürgen, is so moved by this child's death that she places the Stolberg cross into a mailing envelope and sends it to the child's mother at Kieckow. Mieze is so moved by this act of reconciliation that she sets aside her own sorrow and immediately boards the train for Berlin to thank Tante Elisabeth, whom she has never even met.

As long as Mieze lives at Kieckow, she will wear the Stolberg cross on Sundays and during the Lenten period. This somber black ornament will be a constant reminder of her lost child Ferdinande and also of the lonely Tante Elisabeth, who died soon after. Later Hans Jürgen and Mieze will erect a monument to their daughter, in the form of a stone cross, at the spot of her fatal injury. Into its face will be chiseled the words *Gott Rief 25 Mai 1924*—God called. Of all the monuments erected to Kieckow's dead, this one alone will survive the final cataclysm.

JULY. At Pätzig, another daughter is born. She is Maria von Wedemeyer, and she will later be tied to her grandmother in strange and wonderful ways.

1925. At a time when despair and doubt permeate the Fatherland, there are corners of Pomerania where spiritual renewal, national consciousness, the nation's youth, social welfare, and even world peace and ecumenism are discussed in the quiet confines of ancient castles and secluded manor houses.

Within Ruth's own circle of family and friends, there are three such estates, each of which will forever after be associated with one or more of these questions and the organizations they spawn. Ruth will be present at one time or another on each of the estates, addressing each of the questions and involved in some way with each of the movements, which will go in many different directions when the day of reckoning finally arrives.

Less than one hundred kilometers from home, at the historic Trieglaff estate, new ideas are once again taking shape under the protective cloak of Adolf von Thadden, a prominent Prussian Landrat. He has a daughter whose legacy will become part of German history. She is Elisabeth von Thadden, who will die before her time in the manner of Marie Antoinette.

In the first desperate year after the war, Elisabeth von Thadden put together a meeting at Trieglaff, inviting from Berlin a group of leading personalities in church and social matters, and from Pomerania, friends and neighbors like the Bismarcks and the Kleists. At this gathering, leading intellectuals and social scientists put forth proposals for the church and society—ideas that went far beyond religious issues to encompass the welfare state, the plight of the under classes, ecumenism in the Christian church, and the possibilities for permanent world peace. Every year since there has been a Trieglaff Conference, as the meetings have come to be known, and every year the ambitious agenda has been redefined and refined as ideas and conditions change. Year by year the number of participants grows and the deliberations take on more significance. Even though Ruth does not agree with all of the notions that emerge from these conferences, she has taken particular note of Elisabeth von Thadden, the originator and director of these Trieglaff gatherings. She appears to be a young woman with an immense sense of responsibility for others, and one who is uncomfortable in her own plush surroundings. Ruth shares her opinion of these, for the present Trieglaff castle, built in this century, is so pretentious as to be considered in bad taste.

Closest to home in the realm of new ideas are the Schmenzin Summers, annual events during which adolescent boys from Berlin are brought by their pastors to the free and open Kleist lands of Pomerania. Ewald and Anning open their entire estate to these young visitors, and they arrange their activities to nurture sturdy bodies, a love for the Fatherland, a sense of nationalistic fervor, and a fondness for Germany's romantic past. From time to time during the summer, the boys put on performances of folk songs and gymnastics, and Ruth is always there. Her heart yearns for the sense of history and passion she knew in her youth, yet is so lacking in these modern times.

Ewald's young guests receive other training also, principally in the military arts. In the spacious courtyard at Schmenzin they practice military formations, and in meadows remote from the village they learn to use rifles. In this way does Ewald broadcast his disdain for the Versailles Treaty provision limiting the German army to 100,000 men.

If Trieglaff and Schmenzin differ in their response to these uncertain times, they have a distinct similarity—their bias toward the secular sector of life. This similarity is not shared by the activities associated with a third estate—Berneuchen—whose name will become permanently attached to a movement that emphasizes the spiritual sector of life.

Berneuchen belongs to the family Viebahn, members of the Prussian aristocracy of course. At Berneuchen there have been three conferences in as many years, the participants principally clergymen and academicians, with a scattering of laymen. At this year's conference, there were sixty-three participants, sixty-one men* and just two women. One of the women attended as the wife of an invited architect. The other woman was invited in her own right—Ruth von Kleist of Klein Krössin. She arrived in the company of her son-in-law, Hans von Wedemeyer of Pätzig.

The Berneuchen gatherings represent a quest for spiritual enrichment within Germany's Protestant church. By going back to the roots of Christianity and biblical scholarship, these men and women hope to renew the waning vitality of the church. They examine in detail the role of prayer, liturgical forms, music and even church architecture in facilitating each individual's search for God. In so doing, they hope to surmount the estrangement of Germany's youth, the breakdown in family and morality,

*Including Dr. Paul Tillich, one of the great twentieth-century theologians, whose opposition to the Nazi regime forced him to leave Germany in 1933.

and the rise of revolutionary political forces on both the left and the right.

An American observer of the Trieglaff, Schmenzin and Berneuchen agendas might well expect the most from Trieglaff and Berneuchen and the least from Schmenzin when the reign of terror breaks over Germany. In fact, there are men and women associated with each of these agendas who will be counted among the most courageous resisters, indeed reluctant martyrs, when the Nazis eventually take hold. There are also others who will become apologists for and collaborators with the regime.

Two New Books

1925 (*continued*). Of the thousands of books that are published in Germany this year, two have prompted gatherings at Klein Krössin. One of them was written by Ruth von Kleist, the other by Adolf Hitler.

AUGUST. The book Ruth has written is a testimonial—her statement on the legitimacy of a feudal institution in a modern democratic nation-state. It is a small volume, appearing under the title *The Responsibility of Landed Property in This Social Crisis.*[15] In it Ruth first lays out the difficulties inherent in any discussion of the issue:

> The question as to whether social misery is worse in the city or in the rural areas cannot be answered in a few words. First of all, conditions are very different in these dissimilar environments. Whoever views the countryside from an urban perspective is inclined either to romanticize and idealize it or to paint it gray upon gray.

Then, in her direct and uncomplicated style, she enters the fray by outlining her own view of the economic, the social and the human conditions on the large estates in eastern Germany. She is optimistic in that she sees a bright future for these estates, even with the apparent contradictions they present in a democratic industrialized nation. Her final paragraphs are directed to all whose lives are bound in one way or another to the land:

I consider the [landowner's] self-awareness of his responsibility to be most important of all. We were not given our
landed estates so that we might enjoy them; rather we
were appointed householders of God. Hand in hand with
the land goes a veritable sea of responsibility that must
be shared by all those who live on it, including the pastor,
the teacher, and the peasants. If there is suffering, if
there is disorder, if there is injustice in our village, we
must all share the responsibility. We are all responsible
for the economic health of the estate, for its productivity,
and for its further development. . . .

Someone once said that the landowner is a little king.
Rightly so—and we want it that way. But the statement
should go further. The landowner has royal duties and
royal responsibilities. Like a royal monarch, he must day
and night keep in mind the well-being of his land and his
people. . . .

No, the life of the landowner is not so easy, nor so
comfortable as it first seems. It involves tasks and responsibilities that can only be fulfilled when we feel closely
bound with those whose lives are dependent on us. The
people must mean more to us than numbers in the wage
column of the account book. They must be viewed as
living souls who have been entrusted to us. Have our
hearts not grown up together? Are we not on the same
land that our forefathers worked together? Are we not
one in the land, both in prosperity and in failure?

Thus we are obligated to fight and to suffer together—
for ourselves, for the German nation and for this land
that God has given us!

OVER THE CENTURIES on these old Prussian lands, the grandmother of the family has traditionally been revered as the wise
one; not only are her opinions to be sought, but they are to be
given consideration above all others. Yet the respect that Ruth
commands derives less from tradition than from her own
forthrightness. To acknowledge their respect, Hans Jürgen and
Mieze have arranged a small reception in their mother's garden,
which is still displaying its midsummer glory.

Herbert and Maria have driven across from Lasbeck, and Ewald and Anning from Schmenzin. The Woedtkes and other neighboring landowners have also come to praise Ruth's clear statement on their raison d'être. The district Landrat has driven down from Belgard, and the district church superintendent and the pastors of Schmenzin and Gross Tychow are also present.

There are a dozen toasts and speeches, each speaker outdoing himself to honor the author of this thought-provoking work. In mock consternation, Ruth protests what are beginning to sound like eulogies: "But, this is not yet my funeral!" All in all, the afternoon is nothing short of a love affair between the generations.

If there is anything to mar the celebration, it is the purported joint authorship of the book as displayed on its cover—"Carl Schweitzer and Ruth von Kleist-Retzow"—for Dr. Schweitzer's contribution consists entirely of a short introduction to the book. The author herself waves aside any sense of belittlement. She surmises that the pastor's name helped more than a little in finding a publisher. Her admirers are not so charitable.

This book will reach a rather limited circle of readers in Germany. It will be read for what it is—the statement of one Pomeranian aristocrat. Some will dismiss it as the sentimental meanderings of an old woman (Ruth is now fifty-eight years old). Yet twenty years later, Ruth's thesis will be fully validated in one last dreadful test; and after that it won't make a difference anymore, for the land will all be gone.

SEPTEMBER. The Klein Krössin gathering prompted by the Adolf Hitler book is of a far different kind. It involves just three people—the wise woman, her son, and her friend—and it happens in the following way.

The children of the Kieckow manor house are all out in the courtyard, for this is the most exciting time of the year. The harvest is under way, and the grain is being hauled into the elevators. There are horses and wagons and tractors to watch and a nursemaid to keep one from interfering with the activities of the men. But this is only the beginning; everyone knows that there will be a harvest festival this weekend, the first in almost thirty years. Prosperity is slowly finding its way to these Kleist lands, and it is evidenced in the faces and in the talk of people everywhere.

One's attention is directed for a moment away from the busy courtyard. From the northeast, along a corridor between the forests, a horse is galloping across the fields toward Kieckow at high speed. It must be Cousin Ewald, for he alone among the neighbors would come on horseback rather than by auto. A few minutes later he dismounts in front of the manor house. The children have already surrounded Uncle Ewald, and the chattering group follows him as he ties his horse to a convenient railing. Then, one by one, he lifts each of them high into the air and plants them firmly on the pavement again before shaking their hands. Even two-year-old Hans Friedrich extends a small hand and bows ever so slightly from his waist.

A stableman steps up to take the visitor's horse, but Ewald waves him away. The visitor intends to be here only a few minutes. He has come to summon Hans Jürgen from his countinghouse.

Ewald carries a book under his arm, and he urges his cousin to ride with him to Klein Krössin. There are confidential developments that they should discuss, out of the range of others. (By others Ewald does not mean Mieze or the children. From earliest childhood, landowners' children are taught never to relay anything spoken within the family to those on the outside. Nor do the children have any trouble distinguishing between the family, which is wide indeed, and the outside world.) Ewald is referring to the servants. He knows that at the home of Ruth von Kleist at Klein Krössin there is but a single cook, who goes down to the village in the afternoons.

Ewald's message is relayed and Hans Jürgen appears on the ramp precisely at the moment the stableman arrives with his mount. The two men are off through the woods behind the manor house, on the short ride to the bailiff's old house beyond the village of Klein Krössin.

Ruth is still napping when her visitors arrive, and it is much too early for tea. Still she quickly dons her shoes and spectacles and prepares the hot water. She has already guessed that what is to be discussed demands at least a double portion of tea.

When the three are settled in the sitting room, Ewald begins: "Everyone now knows about the National Socialist German

Workers' Party in Bavaria. It is a nest of radicals; its leaders are ruffians and goons at best; and its spokesman, Adolf Hitler, is a demagogue. We conservatives at least have seen beyond their seductive rhetoric. We know them for what they are—proletarians of the worst kind."

Ruth and Hans Jürgen nod in unison. Ewald continues: "And now that the economy is recovering we ought to have more influence politically; isn't that so?"

Once again, there is agreement. At this point Ewald lays open the book on his lap, *Mein Kampf.* It appeared a month ago, but he did not read the entire treatise until yesterday evening. "I received a great jolt last night. I read this diatribe, and I cannot rest until I share it with you to whom I am bound so closely. This book has the potential for great evil, precisely because in many ways it speaks to the longings of us all. Until last night I had some concern that the masses, under certain conditions, might succumb to this man's rhetoric. But now it is clear that the situation is more critical than that.

"This man has taken our Prussian history and corrupted it; he has stolen our heroes—the great Friedrich and Bismarck—and turned them to his own ends. Hans Jürgen, Cousin Ruth, we must pray for stability and for prosperity—and you, Ruth, know how to pray better than I—else our kind too is in danger of being seduced."

Ewald goes on to describe conversations he has had with the conservative politicians and his colleagues in the Belgard Agricultural Council. Some of them have read parts of *Mein Kampf,* and they are enamored with the vision it projects—a rebuilding of the Fatherland spirit, the emphasis on family and decency, the purging of Bolsheviks, Jews, and other outsiders from the land, and a renewed reverence for the land itself. The devil himself could not construct a more seductive thesis than the obscenities of this "Austrian bastard."

Thinking that Ewald has finished, Hans Jürgen attempts to speak, intending to declare a common front. But Ewald·will not be interrupted. He has marked a number of passages he wants to read aloud, lest either of these Kleist friends should equivocate. He begins with:

Prussia, in particular, demonstrates with marvelous sharpness that not material qualities but ideal virtues alone make possible the formation of a state. Only under their protection can economic life flourish, until with the collapse of the pure state-forming faculties the economy collapses too; a process which we can observe in so terrible and tragic a form right now. The material interests of man can always thrive best as long as they remain in the shadow of heroic virtues.[16]

Ruth is amazed. Granted that the writer's language is obscure at best, still the gist of the paragraph is not far from her own thinking. With careful selection, Ewald explains, he could read them dozens of passages from *Mein Kampf* to which they could all say "amen." But he has something else in mind as he selects another page, one that obviates the crass cynicism of this demagogue:

In general the art of all truly great national leaders at all times consists among other things primarily in not dividing the attention of a people, but in concentrating it upon a single foe. . . . It belongs to the genius of a great leader to make even adversaries far removed from one another seem to belong to a single category, because in weak and uncertain characters the knowledge of having different enemies can only too readily lead to the beginning of doubt in their own right.[17]

All propaganda must be popular and its intellectual level must be adjusted to the most limited intelligence among those it is addressed to. Consequently, the greater the mass it is intended to reach, the lower its purely intellectual level will have to be.[18]

The purpose of propaganda is . . . to convince the masses. But the masses are slow-moving, and they always require a certain time before they are ready even to notice a thing, and only after the simplest ideas are repeated thousands of times will the masses finally remember them.

When there is a change, it must not alter the content of what the propaganda is driving at, but in the end must always say the same thing. For instance, a slogan must be presented from different angles, but the end of all remarks must always and immutably be the slogan itself. Only in this way can the propaganda have a unified and complete effect.[19]

Ruth and Hans Jürgen are becoming more uncomfortable with each passage Ewald reads. They are beginning to get a sense of the insidiousness of this work. But Ewald is not finished yet. In *Mein Kampf* Hitler has already selected a victim group on which to inflict this cruel exercise, and Ewald insists on bringing it to light:

> If the Jews were alone in this world, they would stifle in filth and offal; they would try to get ahead of one another in hate-filled struggle and exterminate one another, in so far as the absolute absence of all sense of self-sacrifice, expressing itself in their cowardice, did not turn battle into comedy here too.

> So it is absolutely wrong to infer any ideal sense of sacrifice in the Jews from the fact that they stand together in struggle, or, better expressed, in the plundering of their fellow man.

> Here again the Jew is led by nothing but the naked egoism of the individual.[20]

> In judging the Jewish people's attitude on the question of human culture, the most essential characteristic we must always bear in mind is that there has never been a Jewish art and accordingly there is none today either; that above all the two queens of all the arts, architecture and music, owe nothing original to the Jews. What they do accomplish in the field of art is either patchwork or intellectual theft. Thus, the Jew lacks those qualities which distinguish the races that are creative and hence culturally blessed.

> No, the Jew possesses no culture-creating force of any sort, since the idealism, without which there is no true higher development of man, is not present in him and never was present.[21]

> The Jew has always been a people with definite racial
> characteristics and never a religion; only in order to get
> ahead he early sought for a means which could distract
> unpleasant attention from his person. And what would
> have been more expedient and at the same time more
> innocent than the 'embezzled' concept of a religious
> community? For here, too, everything is borrowed, or
> rather, stolen.[22]

> Protestantism combats with the greatest hostility any
> attempt to rescue the nation from the embrace of its
> most mortal enemy, since its attitude toward the Jews just
> happens to be more or less dogmatically established.[23]

"Well I should hope so!" Ruth is becoming increasingly impatient with Ewald, who continues to read without giving her the privilege of rebuttal.

> This Jewification of our spiritual life and mammonization
> of our mating instinct will sooner or later destroy our
> entire offspring. . . . The devastating consequences of a
> lasting disregard of the natural requirements for mar-
> riage can be seen in our nobility. Here we have before us
> the results of procreation based partly on purely social
> compulsion and partly on financial grounds. The one
> leads to a general weakening, the other to a poisoning of
> the blood, since every department store Jewess is consid-
> ered fit to augment the offspring of His Highness—and,
> indeed, the offspring look like it. In both cases complete
> degeneration is the consequence.[24]

Ruth is now on her feet, projecting a stature even taller than that of her large body. "Stop it, Ewald, what you are reading is all nonsense, if not blasphemy." Ewald concurs; he simply wants those near and dear to him to know what can be expected of this man and his organization.

Turning to the tea table, Ruth removes the giant cozy and pours the two men their cup of tea, not forgetting the cream and sugar—"our peacetime luxury," she calls it. The discussion concludes with the pledge that there will always be a common front among these Kieckow and Schmenzin Kleists. In a more positive vein, Ewald then expresses the hope that improved economic conditions will minimize the dangers from radicals of any bent: "We Germans are much too sensible a people."

But Ruth must have the last word. With a twinkle in her eye, she chides, "But Ewald, since when have we ceased to be Prussians?"

Reunion at Wartenberg

1926. Anni von Tresckow is dead at Wartenberg. After years of frail health, this gentle sister of Ruth's has finally succumbed to pneumonia. Anni is survived by her husband Hermann, twenty years older, who now has outlived two mates. She is also survived by two sons, Gerd and Henning, and Hermann's three children by his first marriage. Jürgen, Hermann's oldest son, has already taken over management of Wartenberg, and when the time comes, he will inherit the manor house and the entire estate. Gerd and Henning have both recently reentered the German army. Like their father, these two were born to the military. Each one agitates impatiently for Germany to throw off the shackles of the Versailles Treaty and rebuild a military organization worthy of their nation.

Henning recently married Erika von Falkenhayn, daughter and namesake of Erich von Falkenhayn, who during the World War was chief of the Reich general staff and a trusted confidant of the kaiser. There are some who now question his competence as Germany's military chief in the early years of the war; still the family considers this marriage of a Tresckow son to Falkenhayn's daughter a very good match indeed.

It is Hermann and Jürgen's wife Hete who greet the arriving mourners and show them to the guest rooms in the manor house. Anni's coffin lies in the great hall, closed to view and covered with flowers and greens from the nearby forest and garden. Tomorrow it will be taken by wagon to the village church, and after the funeral, carried by pallbearers to its final resting place in the Wartenberg cemetery.

Hans Jürgen, Mieze and Ruth have driven down from Pomerania by automobile. Hans and Ruthchen will drive over from Pätzig tomorrow, just for the funeral. These days automo-

biles and paved roads are turning what were day-long trips into
just a few hours.

Even Stefan and Lene[25] and Etti and Carl[26] now live close
enough that they will drive up just for the day to attend this
sister's funeral. But what of Rob and Olga, whom no one has
seen in at least three years? They have been notified, but they
aren't really expected to attend. Without embarrassing anyone,
this outcast brother has a ready excuse to stay at Grossenborau.
He and Olga care for Mother Zedlitz, whose memory has faded
to the point of making her totally dependent. When Ruth visited
her just before the family break, she was saddened to discover
that her mother no longer recognized her. At least, Ruth comforts herself, Mother Zedlitz is spared the family tragedy with
which her children must all wrestle.

Thus it comes as an immense surprise when a servant enters
the great hall, where visitors and family are gathered in prayer, to
announce that the count and countess of Zedlitz and Trützschler
have arrived from Grossenborau. Forgetting all manner of
decorum, let alone the protocol demanded by Rob's banish-
ment, Ruth bolts from the room as the puzzled Hermann calls a
halt to the family service.

In the grand entrance hall of Wartenberg, an elegant
reminder of the powerful Bismarckian times, Ruth throws her
arms about brother Rob with a fierceness that nearly topples
him. Then she turns to Olga and tearfully embraces her sister-in-
law. Rob alone remembers this Ruth from another time and
place—emotional, passionate, and prone to both ecstasy and
agony—for he alone among all those present shared her childhood years.

By now Mieze and Hete have followed Ruth's lead and joined
in welcoming the count and countess with emotional embraces
and kisses, as if to compensate ahead of time for what they know
is to come.

With these initial greetings complete, Rob turns to face the
men of his family, Hermann von Tresckow, with sons Jürgen,
Gerd, and Henning, and Ruth's son Hans Jürgen. The five men,
each dressed in mourning black, stand abreast of each other,
hands clasped behind their backs. Rob, also clad in black, walks
first to his brother-in-law, then to each of his nephews. He does

not offer his hand, for he knows the rules at least as well as the rest. Rather he makes a slight bow, and each man responds with a brief solemn greeting.

The women watch in silence. Ruth does not weep, for she too understands the implications of ostracism from the Prussian aristocracy.

1927. Grandmother Ruth attends three births followed by three christenings in three different manor houses, all within a single calendar year—Elisabeth at Kieckow, Hans Werner at Pätzig, and Herbert at Lasbeck. Herbert's arrival is celebrated with particular joy and thankfulness, for not many months earlier little Maria von Bismarck was taken in death.

This is also a year of tentative but continued prosperity on the land, and even more noticeably in the cities. Unemployment is down, and the government has passed significant legislation to provide unemployment insurance for the workers. As viewed from Klein Krössin, though, this prosperity is a double-edged sword. Each step forward in the condition of the industrial laborers attracts additional migrants from the land. Ruth laments the conditions of the workers in the cities, and even more, the breakdown in values accelerated by the urban environment.

It is not only the workers who fall victim to this moral decay. The news from Berlin's social and intellectual elite is regularly relayed by Spes at the Kleist family gatherings, and it is nothing short of scandalous. Ruth's sensibilities are offended by the new music, the modern dances, and worst of all by the visual arts. She sees anger and rebellion in every work, as if each painter does his best to depict the ugliest aspects of life. Ruth would be the last to rejoice in the legacies of the war, yet she cannot abide the sordidness and the depravity that Berlin's most highly touted artists insist on portraying.

Ruth's world view is challenged not only by her daughter, but even more sharply by Gertrud von Bismarck, wife of the ailing Gottfried. After fifteen years at Kniephof, Gertrud is still not totally acclimated to her adopted homeland. Her heart and head continue to take their inspiration from Berlin, that fountain of European creativity, which Ruth insists on labeling a veritable "den of iniquity." It seems that in every generation, the tensions and the loyalties between the Bismarcks and the Kleists are destined to be balanced anew.

Despite these family involvements, Ruth maintains her island of independence at Klein Krössin. She is concentrating on her New Testament studies, looking for fresh insights to enliven the Christian message in this secular age. Certainly Germany is badly in need of a more relevant spiritual message to answer the tremendous needs of the times. When one's life is relieved of many daily tasks, one is obligated to take on more universal responsibilities. The matriarch at Klein Krössin takes these responsibilities in earnest.

1928. In Silesia Mother Zedlitz departs from this world. Ruth pays a bittersweet visit to Grossenborau, the land of her childhood and of her innocence. Fortunately it is not a farewell to Rob, for brother and sister decide to meet once a year, at Marienbad. This scenic spa was once the trysting spot for German kaisers and literary giants, where Goethe in his last years fell in love with a twenty-year-old beauty. Although Marienbad now lies in the heart of democratic Czechoslovakia and is called Marianske Lazna, it is still a mecca for the old aristocracy, a place where one talks more of the past than of the future.

1929. There is a birth at Kieckow—Heinrich von Kleist—and a birth at Pätzig—Christine von Wedemeyer. There is also a death at Lasbeck—two-year-old Herbert von Bismarck. He is the third child Maria and Herbert have lost in their seventeen years of marriage, the second in the past three years. Still, the Kleists and the Bismarcks have faith in God's infinite power and wisdom.

1930. There was a time in history when events in places as close as Frankfurt and Munich had virtually no effect on life in Pomerania. Yet today Germany is being engulfed by an economic crisis that had its origins on the far side of the Atlantic Ocean. In October of last year, the economy of the United States collapsed in the wake of the crash of the New York stock market—or perhaps it was the other way around. In Germany, the sequence of events leading to this collapse makes no difference. The outcome is a rapid and complete disintegration of the German economy; unemployment, already high, has trebled, foreign trade has caved in, and there is a national epidemic of bankruptcies.

The political repercussions are also immediate and fierce. For an entire decade, Germany has been ruled by weak political coalitions. If there was any political stability at all, it was in Prussia, where a rather stable coalition of the Social Democrat and Center parties governed effectively, though not with the support of the Kleists, the Bismarcks or the Wedemeyers. Even Prussia is not immune to this catastrophic breakdown.

The worldwide depression is gravely affecting the fragile political structure in Germany. Ruth's sons and daughters are members of the conservative German National People's Party, which stands to the right of the Catholic Center Party. Like all Germany, Prussia also has its extremists—the Communists and more recently the Nazis. (Ruth still has difficulty adopting the modern term *communist* to describe the long-feared Bolsheviks; she has even more difficulty believing that the National Socialist Workers Party has a significant following, not only in southern Germany, but even in Prussia.)

Adolf Hitler and his supporters have been ranting and raving now for almost a decade, and the latest edition of Hitler's *Mein Kampf* includes a detailed program that is almost prescient in its response to the current calamity. This outspoken leader has solutions for every economic, moral, and spiritual ailment that confronts the nation. The masses, in their ignorance, seem to sway from one extreme to the other, depending upon the pressures and the propaganda that each extreme brings to bear. One does not expect much from those whose lives are entwined with the godless industrial cities, and one certainly cannot count on the intellectuals, who have been flirting with socialism and communism for decades. Whatever stability and decisiveness remain in this battered nation can surely be traced to the land and to those who own the land. Has that not always been so in German history?

One may well believe all of this, but it provides small comfort at the moment. Even Ruth feels pressed to confront the mounting chaos. In her attempt to delineate between that which is permanent and that which is only transitory, she has unwittingly stepped directly into the world of politics. Curiously, Hans Jürgen and Ewald have stepped into the realm of ethics and religion in their effort to provide leadership through the political maze they view as a one-way trip to disaster. Both men are active in the conservative Nationalist Party, and Ewald, in fact, is chairman of the Pomeranian Party Council. Ever since the war, the Kleists have stood with the Nationalists in opposition to the Social Democrats and to the Center Party. Any one of this old family could rationalize his adamant refusal to enter coalitions with either of these mainstream parties. Are not the Social Democrats just a step or two away from the Communists? And is the Center Party not the last bastion of papal influence in Germany as well as a front for the industrialists and other free trade advocates? What reason have men and women from Prussia's eastern lands to compromise their long-held allegiances for the mere expediency of the moment?

JUNE. One is amazed at the privacy provided by the garden at Klein Krössin. On this hot afternoon, the sunlight enhances the vibrant shades of violet in the clematis and the creeping phlox, while the oak tree's spreading branches shelter a round tea table and five chairs. Today is the wedding anniversary of Hans Jürgen and Mieze, and Ruth has arranged a modest celebration. The only other guests are Cousin Ewald and Anning, whose ties grow ever closer as the years march on. The garden table is covered by a linen tablecloth, woven almost a hundred years ago from Kieckow flax. Forty years ago the village seamstress embroidered the cloth for the young mistress of Kieckow. As long as Ruth lives, this will be her *wedding cloth*. In the center stands a most remarkable pastry, one reserved for the most festive of occasions—the *Baumkuchen*. Shaped like an evergreen tree, it is filled with almonds and covered with chocolate from top to bottom—as much to be admired as to be eaten.

In celebrating such a happy occasion—and the marriage of Hans Jürgen and Mieze is in all ways happy—one might expect everyone to be in the highest of humor. But as usual, Ewald is leading the conversation, and the subject is one that now nearly dominates his life, the rise of National Socialism.

It seems that even the landowners are not immune to the

seduction of the National Socialists. The Belgard Agricultural Council, of which Ewald is chairman and on which Hans Jürgen also serves, must take a stand on the Nazi Brown Shirts, a mob of thugs that operates as a security force within the Nazi Party. They are creating chaos and in fact wresting police power from the hands of the legitimate law enforcement agencies. Ewald reports that the situation in Belgard is out of control; the bloody weekend encounters between the red-belted Communists and the brown-shirted Nazis invariably result in severe injuries and deaths. But these incidents would never take place if it were not for the incendiary tactics of these Nazi mobs. The police have failed to intervene for weeks now, and it is unclear whether this is due to sympathy with the Nazis or out of intimidation by them.

Ruth chooses to play the devil's advocate. "Ewald, if the Nazis will bring back decency and morality and stability and prosperity and a sense of nation in our people, what have we to fear and what then is this violence all about?"

Ewald could not have asked for a better entré to put into words his deepest concerns. It is precisely this quality that endears him to the matriarch of the Kieckow Kleists. Regretfully most of his colleagues—Junkers all—fail to grasp the underside of the Nazi promise. He points out that the insidious theme of National Socialism, brought out repeatedly in the second edition of *Mein Kampf*, is its godlessness. Adolf Hitler has substituted the state and the people for God. In some ways he is subtle, careful not to attack the traditional religious institutions. In other ways he is disgustingly blunt, particularly in his indecent attacks upon the Jews. Granted the Kleists have never had much to do with these people; in fact, as far as Ewald knows, there is no Jewish blood in the Kleist family. But that is beside the point. "Such virulent and obscene assaults against any of God's human creatures constitute an assault on the human race itself, hence can be none other than the work of the devil," he declares. Strong language from this Kleist of a more liberal theology—yet the kind of language that Ruth understands.

Furthermore, at Belgard it is not that the Landrat is sympathetic to the Brown Shirts, nor does the Belgard police director willingly abrogate his responsibility to keep the peace. It is worse than that. The current occupant of that lovely Belgard Landrat's residence acquired in Ruth and Jürgen's time is half-Jewish. So intimidated is he by the Nazi propaganda and the terror of the Brown Shirts that he has ordered his police to walk softly. One must weep for the man even as one chides him for his cowardice.

They will weep more later, for in three years the Landrat will be dismissed by the Nazis and he will see no other way out than to take his own life.

It is still broad daylight on this midsummer evening when the guests prepare to leave. Ewald hands over to Ruth a manuscript he has prepared for publication entitled, *National Socialism—A Danger*. Would she look it over and make suggestions, for he values above all her independent perspective? Ruth assures him that she will; has not God Almighty himself positioned each of them in this struggle for a nation's soul?

The two Kleist couples make their way on foot through the forest to Kieckow, along the way discussing all that has transpired. Hans Jürgen and Ewald will carry the message throughout the district, where too many are blinded by the Nazi rhetoric. Yet neither man dares suggest the boldest of all solutions—a coalition of the conservative German National People's Party and the Center Party, and if necessary, the Socialists, to create a majority sufficient to save the republic. In this twentieth century, such an idea seems much too Bismarckian!

V

GRANDMOTHER RUTH

1931-1938

An Unhappy Surprise

Ruth Roberta Stahlberg, Ruth's oldest grandchild, is a student at the University of Berlin. Raba is tall and striking, like her father, but she has the fiercely independent spirit of her mother. Grandmother Ruth is immensely proud of Raba and perhaps a bit envious, for this granddaughter is the first female in the family ever to attend a university. Ruth continues to have a special feeling for this child, to whom she became so attached during their wartime years together at Kieckow and who is now virtually fatherless. Although Walter Stahlberg continues to support his divorced wife Spes and his children, as is expected of a well-to-do German industrialist, Raba does not see much of him.

FEBRUARY. In these years of turmoil, one has come to expect the unexpected, particularly when it comes to news from Berlin. Still Ruth is unprepared for the announcement Spes makes on this visit to Klein Krössin. Raba, now twenty-one years old, has joined the Nazi Party. In fact she is the delegated leader of the party's female student faction, meaning that she shares an office with Nazi student leader Baldur von Schirach at party headquarters in Berlin. Raba even has a half-time secretary to help in her organizational efforts, for her responsibilities go far beyond the organization of students at the Berlin University. Raba's office is next to that of Dr. Josef Goebbels, the Nazi Party propaganda chief, who is her nominal supervisor.

Nor is Raba an exception among the young people studying at German universities. Even the theological departments can now

177

count on most of their students being party members; at one university, ninety percent of the Protestant theology students wear their party badges to class. Berlin is not much different from other academic centers. Its overcrowded theology department has more than a thousand students, the majority of whom apparently find no conflict between their God-centered theology studies and the state-centered Nazi philosophy; Adolf Hitler's program is as yet more a philosophy than a plan of action.

AUGUST. At Berlin there is a new lecturer in the theology department. His name is Dietrich Bonhoeffer. He is no stranger to Berlin, having grown up in Grunewald, and his parents travel in the same circle as Spes Stahlberg. Raba even attended the same Grunewald gymnasium as Bonhoeffer, a school considered by many to be the best in all of Germany, but at the moment Raba and he have very little else in common. Bonhoeffer is not only lecturing in the department of theology, he is the focal point of that group of theology students who find *Mein Kampf* and the subsequent propaganda of the Nazi Party to be totally incompatible with God-centered, or in Bonhoeffer's case, Christ-centered theology.

The German National People's Party, the party of the Kleists, the Bismarcks, the Wedemeyers, the Ostens and the Tresckows, is gradually dissolving under the pressures of the Nazi movement. Certain party leaders are in favor of joining forces with the Nazis in an effort to build a governing coalition. Others in the party, among them the Kleists, the Bismarcks, the Wedemeyers and the Ostens, are unalterably opposed to cooperation with the Nazis and cautiously suggest moving the Nationalists in the direction of the fragile center-based governing coalition. With such fragmentation, the death knell of the party is already sounding.

Raba has come upon a tremendous idea that can be implemented at the university in parallel with these political developments. She has invited herself into Dr. Goebbels's office, a Spartan room furnished with only two sofas, a table and a wooden chair. Were it not for her innate self-confidence, Raba might have trouble speaking with the tiny Goebbels, for she towers over him. The good doctor asks her to be seated on one of the sofas. When he sits down across from her and nearly disap-

Ruth Robert (Raba) Stahlberg
(portrait by Sophie Knobloch)

pears into the cushions, it occurs to Raba that the effect is not conducive to his finding favor with her suggestion. Goebbels must realize his ridiculous appearance also, for he quickly extracts himself from the cushions and walks across to Raba, positioning himself jauntily on the arm of her sofa. Now the talk can begin.

Raba proposes to Dr. Goebbels that the Nazi student organization at the university offer to share offices with the beleaguered German National People's Party student organization. The Nazi students would agree to pay half the rent, then promptly move into the offices. After a few months, the Nazi students would

179

simply take over. Leaving his perch, Goebbels paces thoughtfully back and forth across the room, then turns back to face this female student faction leader. "No, the idea is not a good one," he chides her gently. It would not be honorable, and the Nazis, above all, are honorable men and women!

SEPTEMBER. Raba and her mother are spending the week at Klein Krössin, Spes in the guest room called Contentment and Raba in the room called Hope. Ruth has assigned the rooms with care. She prays often that Spes might be fulfilled and content with life through her children and her music. As for Raba, like grandmothers everywhere, she wants to believe the Nazi Party is just a phase of the girl's maturing process, a belief she also holds for the nation at large.

Raba has spent the entire morning with pen and paper at the desk in her room. She is preparing a talk to be given next week at a Nazi student rally in the Berlin Sport Palace—a great honor and an even greater challenge to this young woman who has never before spoken publicly.

By chance, on this Saturday afternoon there is to be a gathering of the Agricultural Council—the Belgard District landowners—at the estate of Jürgen von Woedtke. Hans Jürgen and Mieze have just arrived to pick up Ruth and Spes. Raba originally declined to join the family on this outing, but she has changed her mind. She is so filled with new ideas that she wants to share them with others, and neither Grandmother nor Mother is inclined to listen.

The Woedtke estate still holds fond memories for Ruth from the days when she was the mistress at Kieckow. She remembers how Jürgen's father Fritz encouraged her first feelings of self-confidence and worked with her to bring Kieckow back to prosperity. With fondness and affection, Ruth recalls the monthly wagon rides with her bailiff and Fritz, through the village and across the fields, while this good friend cajoled or complimented the bailiff as conditions required.

The Kleists are immensely welcome at the Woedtke estate. Fond memories go in many directions among this closely knit group of Belgard landowners; at least that is how it used to be. Nowadays the Agricultural Council is divided, just as the entire nation is divided. There are those who support the Nazi movement and those, like Woedtke and the Kleists, who vehemently oppose it. Ewald von Kleist has spoken his piece many times to this group; today one of the Nazi landowners is scheduled to speak. Raba looks the situation over and sees this as an opportunity to practice her own Sport Palace speech—to give it a first try among these backward Junkers who are not as discerning as the sophisticated Berlin listeners will be.

And so it comes to pass. The local landowner addresses his colleagues with a message akin to that of Adolf Hitler, exhorting his listeners to come aboard and help bring about the new Germany. There is polite applause. Then Raba asks the host if she might also speak. The cordial Jürgen von Woedtke calls for order and introduces the tall Kleist offspring from Berlin. A hush falls over the assembled group, for these Junkers are not accustomed to hearing a woman speaker. Raba steps up onto the raised platform where the Woedtke grand piano stands and begins to talk. She gives an impassioned statement of what one might expect for Germany, in Europe as well as internally, if the listeners were to join forces with the Nazi Party. Mostly she emphasizes the humiliation that Germany has experienced in the twelve years since the Versailles Treaty. She challenges her listeners to explain how the descendants of the great Prussian Junkers can continue to be party to a government that does not stand against the forces of international treachery and of bolshevism? Raba makes no reference to the Jews.

The grandmother is visibly moved by her granddaughter's words. She wonders to herself, "Why is it only the Nazis who understand our plight?" When Raba is through, there is tremendous applause. She steps down to shake hands with everyone who presses forward to congratulate her, and as she does so, she spies a figure standing behind the hall drape, the man who until now has been conspicuous by his absence. It is Cousin Ewald, and he has heard every word.

"Raba, I would like a moment with you, in the garden." Coming from Cousin Ewald, this is not an invitation, but a command. Raba quickly extricates herself from the well-wishers and follows her mother's cousin through the terrace door. Ewald leads her to a bench under a huge maple tree, far beyond the ears of any listener. In the afternoon shade of its spreading branches, Ewald lays out for this cousin his perception of the dangers ahead should Hitler and the Nazis prevail. He urges her not to be seduced by looking at just a part of their program, and he cautions her against quoting anything from Hitler's writings without examining everything he has written. Ewald urges Raba to take stock of the misdeeds so far—those committed by the Brown Shirts, in particular. He warns that it will only get worse if these hoodlums ever gain legitimate power. Raba's confidence melts under his tirade, for this is the stern Cousin Ewald at his very sternest. When he has finished, Ewald rises and, after helping Raba to her feet, embraces her warmly. It is a spontaneous gesture on his part and is followed by a declaration of devotion and faithfulness to Raba, to her mother and to her grandmother, who are after all Kleists like himself.

Raba decides not to give her speech at the Sport Palace in Berlin. She informs Dr. Goebbels that speechmaking is not her forte and begs to be excused, but she still joins the Nazi students in the cabaret after the rally. The wine and beer flow freely, and the loosened tongues soon inspire impassioned toasts and forbidden songs. In their frenzy, the students raise their table knives high in the air and chant lustily to the tune of a familiar folk song:

> When Jewish blood is on my knife,
> So much better is my life.[27]

Raba suddenly feels sick. She races to the lavatory, where she violently regurgitates the beer, the sausage and her untold feelings of guilt. Without saying good-bye to her friends, she goes straight home to Grunewald, that elegant enclave in Berlin where Jews and non-Jews, aristocrats, academicians, physicians and judges live together in harmony, convinced that they are not like the others, but rather are Berlin's chosen elite.

Coming so soon after the gathering at the Woedtke manor house, this dreadful night has awakened doubts that Raba cannot quiet. She begins to wonder where she really belongs— maybe not in the Nazi Party, maybe not even at the university, certainly not at Kieckow, for she doesn't even have a *von* to fall back on. Perhaps Raba belongs to Grunewald; she longs to talk it over with either Mother or Father, but such things are never discussed among the Stahlbergs.

OCTOBER. On Sunday morning Raba is still in bed when the phone rings. It is Baldur von Schirach, Nazi Party student leader, and he comes straight to the point: "Raba, I have bad news for you. Dr. Goebbels gave me a report yesterday showing that you are one-fourth Jewish blood, on your father's side." Baldur pauses for a moment before continuing. "Of course you know what this means; you must give up your post. You know the rules as well as I. But as far as I'm concerned, you may certainly stay in the party."

The coldness in Baldur's voice causes ice to form in Raba's heart. It cannot be! With Baldur, she has no trouble maintaining her composure; she had almost decided to quit the party anyway. Once she has placed the receiver back on its hook, however, the former Nazi female student faction leader bursts into tears.

Between the Stahlberg parents there is a scene far worse than any that preceded their divorce ten years ago. Spes accuses Walter of hiding his ancestry; Walter accuses Spes and all her family of bigotry. A bitter exchange ensues until both finally realize their children's futures are at stake. Walter promises to look into the state birth and marriage records and see to it that any incriminating evidence is removed. And Spes phones Klein Krössin to inform her mother.

Once again Ruth is forced to recall Walter Stahlberg's first visit to Kieckow, now more than twenty-five years ago. Her thoughts begin with mild annoyance—that brash young man who dared declare to her face that he did not want to marry Spes. The annoyance fades as Ruth confronts her own response—the arrogance with which she ordered Walter to speak directly with Spes. It is a memory that even the divorce has not obliterated, and now the situation is worse than ever. The affair is almost biblical and Old Testament in its ramifications—that it should be the three Stahlberg children, already so vulnerable and so loved by this grandmother!

In life there is a time for prayer and a time for action; Ruth decides to try action first and to pray afterward. She writes a journalist in Hamburg with whom she made contact when her small book was published. Would he please investigate? She must know if it is true that Walter Stahlberg is half-Jewish.

NOVEMBER. On a rainy Sunday afternoon, Walter Stahlberg arrives unannounced at his former wife's Berlin flat. He has never been there before; in fact, Walter and Spes have not seen each other for almost ten years. There is immense tension in the first greeting and handshake, but then eyes meet and a long-forgotten tenderness emerges. Walter grips Spes's hand with both his hands while Spes's eyes fill with tears. It goes no further; Walter clears his throat and asks politely whether he may set his umbrella on the floor. Of course—in this burst of emotion Spes had forgotten the normal social amenities. Walter extracts three documents from his pocket and hands them to his former wife, explaining that they are certified documents direct from the Stettin Provincial Registry—one for Raba, one for Alla and one for Hans Conrad. The documents name the paternal ancestors of the children back four generations. Spes carefully reads through each name and religious designation. There is no trace of a Jew. She relaxes somewhat but still looks puzzled: "And what about you, Walter?"

Spes's former husband takes her hand tenderly and assures her that any Jewish blood in the Stahlberg family has been totally purged from the Provincial Registry. "In Stettin, Spes, we Stahlbergs still count for something!" When Walter turns to leave, Spes can only muster a feeble "thank you." After the door is closed behind him, however, she sits down with her head in her hands and weeps quietly. It is too late to undo the past, particularly in these times.

It takes just two phone calls for Raba Stahlberg to resign from the Nazi Party—one to Dr. Goebbels and the other to Baldur von Schirach. Raba is surprised at her own confidence in dealing with the matter. Still she decides to adopt a new family name, and she begins to attend church for the first time in years, a Catholic church in Berlin. God has returned to Raba's consciousness, but she is not yet ready to tell Mother or Grandmother.

DECEMBER. At Klein Krössin the phone rings and rings as Ruth makes her way from her bedroom. It is her afternoon nap time, and the cook is down in the village. Fortunately the caller is patient, still there on the line when Ruth finally picks up the receiver. It is the Hamburg journalist, and his message is short and succinct. Through trusted contacts, he has checked the Stahlberg family records in Stettin and Hamburg for traces of Jewish descent. "Madam von Kleist, I advise you to leave the affair alone; it is worse than you think."*

Crisis in the Nation

1932: JANUARY. *National Socialism—A Danger,* Ewald von Kleist's statement of conscience, which Ruth first read and critiqued three years ago, has been published in Berlin. It is somewhat expanded from the original version, for the author has now read Volume II of *Mein Kampf* and been exposed to the more blatant Nazi propaganda. He is also increasingly aware of the trends that are gradually leading the conservatives into the Nazi net. Kleist's little booklet is a heartfelt plea to his fellow conservatives: "Do not be misled; do not be seduced." There is no reason to believe that it is widely read.

FEBRUARY. Oskar von der Osten, former Landrat in the Neumark, is now retired. He spends his days in the administration of his estate, Warnitz, while at the same time assessing the political winds from his village, through the district, and all the way to Berlin. Osten is the leader of the Neumark conservatives, though his views more nearly match those of some liberals. When his colleagues urge him to join a national political party so that he might gain national influence, Osten replies in mock surprise: "Why should I become a politician when the politicians come to *me* for advice?"

Osten is also no stranger to the Pomeranians. His daughter Anning is married to Ewald von Kleist, and the ties that bind the Kleists of Belgard extend far enough to include Oskar von der Osten as well as the Wedemeyers and the Tresckows, all landown-

---

*Walter Stahlberg's maternal grandfather was Moritz Heckscher, Minister of Justice for a short time during the 1848 German revolution. Moritz's father was president of the Hamburg synagogue.[28]

ers of the Neumark. So when old Osten twists the tail of the young Nazi Party, reverberations are felt not only in these hinterlands, but all the way to Berlin. It happens in the following way.

There are Nazis living in the village of Warnitz, but in this twentieth century the landowner can do nothing about this. However, when the Nazis decide to have a rally at the village inn, Oskar von der Osten chooses to exert feudal rights that have not been enforced for at least fifty years. Technically every building in the village still belongs to the landowner, although the inn business is owned by its proprietor. Osten makes known his ownership of the building and forbids the rally to take place there. He is not challenged, for the Nazis are not yet brave enough.

MARCH. A nationwide election is held for the office of president of Germany. The incumbent is eighty-four-year-old General von Hindenburg, a hero of the World War and the revered father-figure of the country. Challenging him is Adolf Hitler, leader of the upstart Nazi Party. There are other candidates also, but they turn out to be of little consequence. Hindenburg receives 49.6 percent of the popular vote, but Hitler, running a strong second, receives an astounding thirty percent. Since Hindenburg does not capture the majority of the votes, a second, run-off election is scheduled for next month.

APRIL. For the first time in the history of the frail German republic, all of the democratic political parties are of one mind, urging their supporters to vote for Hindenburg as defender of the constitution. Hindenburg is handily reelected, with fifty-three percent of the popular vote against Hitler's thirty-seven percent. Nevertheless the depth of Hitler's support is a sobering reality.

With the Nazis now demonstrating their substantial voting power, new pressures are being exerted on the office of German chancellor. Heinrich Brüning of the Catholic Center Party is the incumbent, backed by a coalition that includes neither the Social Democrats on the left nor the German Nationals on the right. In the Reichstag, the German Parliament, the left and right mainstream parties ally with the Communists and the Nazis and form a hostile majority to the government. Brüning, now powerless to deal with the collapsed economy and the collapsing government,

Ruth in her Klein Krössin garden

makes a move his critics call a betrayal of German democracy, although it pales when compared to what is to come later. To deal with the economic turmoil, he declares a state of national emergency, enabling him to exercise a range of emergency powers.

The German National People's Party, the party of the Kleists, the Bismarcks, the Wedemeyers and the Tresckows, is totally alienated now from Brüning, though deeply divided as to who should take his place.

Twenty years later Hans Jürgen will look back in sorrow and say to his son that they all erred by not supporting Brüning in those critical last months of the republic.

MAY. For the moment the key to the struggle lies with President von Hindenburg, who alone has the power to appoint and dismiss the German chancellor (shades of the Bismarckian era). He has already decided to dismiss Brüning, but as yet he has not selected a replacement.

East of Berlin in the Neumark, there is excitement at the Warnitz village. A black Mercedes automobile bearing a government license plate has just raced through the quiet street and up to the Warnitz castle. Two men exit the auto; the chauffeur remains seated. A surprised servant receives the two visitors, taking their cards and promptly leading them to the master's cluttered office. Oskar von der Osten is in his slippers and shirt sleeves, but still very much the advisor to politicians when he greets President von Hindenburg's personal representatives. Of course, the president is an old friend, and the arrival of his emissaries demands a cup of tea at the least. The servant bows and departs.

Through these emissaries, Hindenburg is inquiring whether Osten will take the chancellorship and form a government cabinet that includes both Social Democrats and German Nationalists. The president actually believes that this old Junker, above all others, is suited for this formidable task.

To call Osten a liberal conservative is not a contradiction. This older man has seen his nation defeated, its monarchy collapsed, the Fatherland humiliated, and now the people betrayed by extremists from the left and the right. He is pleased and touched

that old Hindenburg should think of him as the man to pull the
decent majority together. Without hesitation, the retired bureaucrat offers his strong hand and his affirmative answer to each of
the emissaries.

Over tea and ham and freshly baked bread, the three men
spend the next hours forming a cabinet—writing down names,
making phone calls, scratching names, then adding new ones,
until after sunset. When the visitors finally gather up their papers
and leave Osten's office, they have in their briefcases the
makings of the next chancellor's cabinet, the future hope of
their nation. All that is required now is Hindenburg's decision
and the confirming phone call from Berlin.

The call never comes, for Hindenburg is being pressured to
appoint Franz von Papen, like Brüning a member of the Center
Party but much more conservative than Brüning. Papen proposes to the president that he form a nonpartisan cabinet of conservatives who lean toward the return of the Hohenzollern
monarchy. Suddenly the old dishonored kaiser is seen as a possible bulwark against Hitler, the man who threatens to become a
new kind of German kaiser.

Traditional monarchists see hope in such a government. Certainly the twin threats of communism and nazism demand
unusual and creative responses. Down at Pätzig, Hans von
Wedemeyer is tentatively supporting Papen, the Catholic from
western Germany whom he knows and trusts from a time when
he served under Papen during the World War.

Hans and Ruthchen, with their new baby girl, drive up to
Kieckow, ostensibly to show off the infant Werburg to Grand-
mother Ruth. In truth the trip is meant to enlist support for
Franz von Papen from Hans Jürgen and Ewald. On the manor
house terrace are gathered the matriarch Ruth, Hans Jürgen and
Mieze, Hans and Ruthchen, and of course Ewald and Anning.
Hans is speaking in favor of his old comrade in arms, Franz von
Papen. Ewald is blunt in stating that he does not totally trust
Papen. Instead he is supporting Osten, his father-in-law, as next
chancellor. This comes as a great surprise to Hans and Ruthchen, since no one outside of Hindenburg's inner circle knows
of the president's proposal to Osten; but it will not change anything for the Wedemeyers. It is Hans Jürgen, with his mother and

his wife, who are caught between. Hans Jürgen, out of immense respect for his brother-in-law Hans, does not speak in opposition to Papen as chancellor; and Hans understands his Kieckow brother-in-law well enough to know that he will support Osten, for he stands politically at the side of his cousin Ewald in all matters.

JUNE. President von Hindenburg appoints Franz von Papen chancellor of Germany. Papen forms a nonpartisan government with General Kurt von Schleicher as Minister of Defense, for Schleicher controls the army. The government is not opposed by the Nazis.

It will later become evident that Schleicher had made a deal with the Nazis, to tolerate their uniformed storm troopers in return for their tacit approval of the Papen cabinet

Papen promptly outdoes Brüning in misusing the emergency dictatorial powers granted under Germany's constitution.

JULY. Franz von Papen dismisses the entire government of Prussia and names himself Reich Commissioner of that land. New national elections are held and the Nazis gain a resounding victory, more than doubling their seats in the Reichstag.

SEPTEMBER. All Nazi Party members attend the Reichstag sessions in full Nazi uniform. This is a clear violation of German law and can only be construed as an exhibition of the their total disdain for constitutional government. Still they are able to gather enough additional opposition in the Reichstag to demand Papen's resignation. He refuses and again dissolves the Reichstag, calling for new elections and governing in the meantime by emergency decree.

OCTOBER. Belgard is the scene of bloody encounters between the Nazi Brown Shirts and the Communists. Each weekend one hears of deaths among the combatants. At Kieckow and Klein Krössin, at Schmenzin and elsewhere, astonished landowners blame the police for their inability to control the populace. The situation is one of virtual lawlessness.

NOVEMBER. In the national elections the Nazis lose substantial power and the Communists correspondingly gain. In addition to its widespread economic problems, Germany now appears to be on the road to anarchy. Papen is forced to resign as chancellor of Germany. The support he once enjoyed, including that from Hindenburg and from his old friend Hans von Wedemeyer, has rapidly dissolved as events continue to resist any sort of control.

DECEMBER. President von Hindenburg reluctantly appoints Kurt von Schleicher as the new chancellor. The Kleists, the Bismarcks and the Wedemeyers applaud the appointment, for at the moment the issue of law and order overrides all others. However, at Warnitz Oskar von der Osten laments the appointment as a definite move toward a military dictatorship. Nearby at Wartenberg, Osten's young friends, Gerd and Henning von Tresckow, are of another mind. These two sons of Ruth's late sister Anni look to Adolf Hitler for the restoration of Germany's place in the sun. Before very long these two idealists will find themselves sorely disappointed.

1933: JANUARY. Franz von Papen, still Reich Commissioner for Prussia, appoints Herbert von Bismarck State Secretary in the Prussian Interior Ministry. This means that Herbert is to be responsible for the law enforcement agencies of Prussia. Appointed as his aid is a young attorney who has just completed his judicial studies, Fabian von Schlabrendorff.

Like Herbert, Fabian is the scion of an old Prussian political family. His academic credentials are from Halle, an old distinguished university where the study of law and justice still holds to the old truths. He brings to the Prussian Interior Ministry a healthy distrust of Adolf Hitler and a strong aversion to the Nazi philosophy and program. Fabian also brings a young man's energies and an acute curiosity. Herbert immediately takes the young Schlabrendorff into his confidence, though neither man is yet aware of the dangerous depths to which their mutual trust will lead them.

Ewald von Kleist of Schmenzin, active member of the German National People's Party and well known in certain circles, makes

his way to Berlin. During his stay, he will be a guest at the apartment of Herbert von Bismarck. The two men are well acquainted
in many ways, though not always in total agreement politically.
Lasbeck and Schmenzin have always had close familial and geographical ties. In this generation the Bismarcks and Kleists are
bound through the marriage of Herbert to Maria von Kleist of
Kieckow, who is a cousin to Ewald. Both men have known Maria's
mother Ruth since their childhood, and they feel equally bound
to this Pomeranian matriarch.

Ewald has heard that Franz von Papen is working behind the
scenes to put together a coalition of conservative parties that is
to include both the German Nationalists and the Nazis. Ewald
abhors the idea, believing that this course will mean the destruction of Germany. He intends to discuss the matter with President
von Hindenburg, then with Papen. If Papen cannot be dissuaded
from this fatal step, then Ewald will go to Hugenberg, leader of
the German Nationalists. Still Ewald has enough doubts as to his
own instincts that he first wants a personal meeting with Hitler.

Hitler is not easily accessible, but thanks to the ties that still
unite the members of Germany's aristocracy, Ewald prevails on
Papen to arrange a private meeting between him and the leader
of the Nazi Party. As leader of a party represented in the
Reichstag, Adolf Hitler has access to an office in the Chancery;
but whereas most party leaders vie for the largest windows and
the best views of the Wilhelmstrasse, the leader of the Nazi Party
has chosen an interior office with no windows.

Ewald meets Adolf Hitler outside the party leader's office at
the desk of his secretary. Ushering his visitor inside, Hitler invites
him to be seated, closing the door behind them. Ewald finds it to
be a mighty strange office with but two pieces of furniture, a
comfortable chair and a footstool. He presumes his host means
for him to sit in the chair, which he promptly does, expecting
Hitler to take his place on the well-cushioned footstool. Not so;
instead Hitler suddenly begins pacing back and forth across the
room, simultaneously embarking on a lecture. The more he
speaks, the more agitated he becomes and the faster he walks.
Ewald can only listen and follow the peripatetic figure as it moves
from left to right, then back to the left, then back and forth
again. What Ewald expected to be a two-way political conversa-

tion turns out to be a one-man harangue. Hitler lays before this eastern Junker his plans for Germany, for Lebensraum, for the soon-to-be-German lands of Poland, the Ukraine, and eventually all of European Russia. Ewald's resolve grows as the minutes pass. Two hours later, he bids a quick farewell, totally exhausted and amazed that his host seemingly could go on talking forever.

That night, from Herbert's apartment, Ewald phones home to Anning: "There is no chance for compromise; the rest of my life will be dedicated to the destruction of that man before he destroys our nation and our history."[29] Ewald does not mention the man's name, for one must be careful in these treacherous times.

The meeting with the president of Germany is easier to arrange—no need to involve Papen nor any other influential person. Ewald simply makes a phone call to Hindenburg's office and identifies himself as the son-in-law of Oskar von der Osten. A day later the president and Osten's son-in-law, fellow Pomeranians, sit alone together in the sumptuous presidential office overlooking the Wilhelmstrasse.

After reporting to Hindenburg on his meeting with Hitler, Ewald puts forth the widespread rumor that Franz von Papen is only interested in ousting Schleicher, and that to achieve this he will propose a cabinet that includes the leader of the German National People's Party (Hugenberg) and members of the Nazi Party also, possibly with Hitler as chancellor. Ewald expresses his horror at the thought.

To this Hindenburg replies, "Look, I am pleased that you are telling me this. I know that my chancellor [Papen] wants me to make Hitler the Reich chancellor. My sense of duty and responsibility will not allow me to do that. [Hitler] is not a statesman; in my view he is fit for the Postal Ministry at best."[29]

Believing in Hindenburg's integrity, Ewald spends the following week in conversations with Papen, pleading in vain that he desist from his plans, and when this fails, cajoling Hindenburg not to appoint the coalition. Neither man can be moved, for each believes that with a minority of Nazis in the government, the conservative majority can prevail.

Two weeks later, Hindenburg dismisses Schleicher and appoints Adolf Hitler chancellor of Germany, with Papen as vice chancellor and Reich Commissioner of Prussia. Papen boasts that he has tied the Nazis' hands, for they have but three of the eleven posts in the cabinet.

Ewald makes his last visit ever to the German Chancery. There he confronts both Papen and Hugenberg, declaring each of them to be a traitor to the Fatherland—harsh words from a gentleman of the Pomeranian aristocracy.

The Kaiser's Likeness

1933: FEBRUARY. Within twenty-four hours of Hitler's becoming chancellor of Germany, "the lake has turned over," as they say of the Pomeranian lakes in spring. Hitler's closest associate, Hermann Göring, is now Minister of the Interior in Prussia and the superior of State Secretary Herbert von Bismarck. The Nazis are thus assured control of all police powers in that state. Josef Goebbels's organization seizes the German radio (although this won't be official until the middle of March when Goebbels is appointed Minister of Public Enlightenment and Propaganda), and Baldur von Schirach is designated leader of two organizations that together will ensure control into the next generation—the Hitler Youth for boys and the League of German Girls.[30] One can only imagine what position might have awaited Raba Stahlberg had she not had her eyes opened by Cousin Ewald!

One day later, the regularly scheduled radio program of the German Protestant church features a lecturer from the Berlin University. He is Dietrich Bonhoeffer, who is speaking on the dangers of a führer cult as currently promulgated by the Nazi Party. Twenty minutes into his radio lecture, Bonhoeffer warns that a leader [führer] who succumbs to the idolatry of those whom he is leading will inevitably lead them astray: "This is the leader who makes an idol of himself and his office, and who thus mocks God."[31]

In the middle of this last sentence, the microphone is disconnected at the control box. One suspects that Dr. Goebbels's organization is already in operation.

On the night of the twenty-seventh of February the Reichstag building is destroyed by fire. The following morning, Herbert von Bismarck and his assistant Fabian von Schlabrendorff make their way to the Prussian Interior Ministry. The ruined Reichstag building is still smoldering, and the smell of smoke has found its way deep into the Ministry's corridors. Still, from inside the office of Hermann Göring come the sounds of unmistakable mirth. Göring is engaged in a jovial conversation with the normally staid Franz von Papen, who still wields considerable power as Reich Commissioner for Prussia. Herbert enters the office and exchanges greetings, more out of courtesy to Papen, a fellow Junker, than out of deference to Göring. He has difficulty taking seriously this buffoon who is now his superior. Göring is in high spirits. He makes no effort to suppress his enthusiasm for the smoldering fire and all that it portends.

Just then Adolf Hitler walks in. Göring's countenance overflows with joy at his führer's unexpected visit. For Hitler's benefit, he reports on all of the events surrounding the fire, includings its probable cause—Communists, of course. He accentuates certain delectable details by slapping one thigh or the other. Hitler stands stone-faced and silent. Later that morning he announces an emergency edict. For the protection of the people and the state, he has abolished all personal rights formerly guaranteed by the German constitution.

MARCH. After church on the Sunday of the German Reichstag elections, Ruth, Mieze and Hans Jürgen von Kleist drive to Gross Tychow to cast their ballots. For weeks they have been subjected to glorious promises and hateful denunciations generated by the new government, both on paper and over the airwaves. Outside the polling place, storm troopers are everywhere, and not a single district policeman is in sight.

Ruth, Mieze and Hans Jürgen all cast their votes for the slate of the Catholic Center Party. No one can remember when Kleists from Kieckow last cast their votes for a Catholic candidate, certainly not since the time of Hans Hugo. But these votes come too late to save the Fatherland. When the election is over, the Nazis and what is left of the German National People's Party will together make up the Reichstag majority. Franz von Papen, who so cleverly constructed the coalition that was to keep the Nazis in the minority and himself in control of Prussia, is turned out as

Reich Commissioner. His replacement is none other than Hermann Göring.

Under this portentous cloud, Herbert von Bismarck resigns his position in the Interior Ministry. He closes his Berlin apartment and returns to Lasbeck to take up in earnest his duties as husband, father, landowner and administrator of the Bismarck lands. Perhaps he can even assist his now-widowed sister-in-law Gertrud, who bravely carries on at Kniephof, holding the estate together for her son Klaus.

And Fabian? He will disappear into the national bureaucracy, hardly to be heard from for more than a decade. But Fabian will not disappear from the Bismarck circle, for he has already been introduced to Herbert's oldest daughter Luitgarde, just graduated from the lyceum. She is now in the Neumark at Pätzig, that showplace among estates east of the Oder River, in the position of tutor to her Wedemeyer cousins.

While Herbert von Bismarck and his trunks make their way by rail to Pomerania, Fabian von Schlabrendorff is crossing the Oder River by automobile. He is bound for Pätzig, ostensibly to report first-hand to Hans von Wedemeyer on the recent calamities in Berlin. In truth, Fabian has thoughts only of the lovely tutor Luitgarde, picturing her surrounded by the six lively Wedemeyer children. One hears tales of the Pätzig household, where even in winter the children are herded outside after gymnastics to run barefoot three times around the broad manor house. Fabian smiles indulgently at the eccentricities of this unconventional clan. After crossing the Oder bridge, he opens the throttle to its fullest.

APRIL. On April Fool's Day, by popular consent, a national boycott of Jewish-owned businesses is declared.

At Klein Krössin, Ruth von Kleist, widow of the late Landrat of Belgard, invites the current, half-Jewish Landrat to tea. One can only guess how much longer he will retain his position.

At Warnitz in the Neumark, old Oskar von der Osten, former Landrat of Küstrin, hands back his certificate of honorary Küstrin citizenship and pays a social call on a neighboring Jewish landowner whom he never much cared for.

In Berlin, Julia Bonhoeffer, the ninety-one-year-old grand-mother of the controversial theologian Dietrich Bonhoeffer, crosses a heavy cordon of Nazi storm troopers to enter Kaufhaus des Westens, the city's largest department store. It is Jewish-owned.

Neither Ruth nor Oskar von der Osten nor Grandmother Bonhoeffer is challenged by neighbors or onlookers. Even in Nazi Germany one is indulgent of the peculiarities of the elderly.

Less than a week after the boycott, by government decree, non-Aryans are purged from the German Civil Service.

MAY. It is May Day, a workers' holiday originally conceived by the Communists and Social Democrats and very handily usurped by the Nazis. The government has declared that on this day all churches and all public buildings must fly the swastika flag, emblem of the new Germany. At Naseband, an estate village owned by Ewald von Kleist, Pastor Reimer of the village church refuses to fly the swastika flag.

Even on Kleist lands there are now Nazi enthusiasts eager to inform on recalcitrant clergymen and landowners. Thus word of the pastor's refusal spreads quickly to the Belgard Nazi leader, as well as to Schmenzin and to Kieckow, where Pastor Reimer is well known and admired by Grandmother Ruth and her family.

It is expected that storm troopers will visit Schmenzin rather than the pastor at Naseband, for the man who owns the Naseband church is Ewald von Kleist. These brown-shirted storm troopers will certainly be armed, but the Kleists of Belgard do not lack for confidence in times of crisis. Ewald phones Hans Jürgen, and Hans Jürgen makes three phone calls of his own—one to Jürgen von Wödtke and one to each of two other Belgard landowners on whom he can count. Within ten minutes, four automobiles are making their way over little-known back roads to Schmenzin, each driven by a Junker landowner dressed in riding pants and boots; each man also wears a leather shoul-der strap and a holster containing a loaded pistol.

Some time later, a caravan of six automobiles, each carrying four storm troopers, pulls into the Schmenzin cul de sac. Ewald von Kleist stands by himself before the tower entrance to his home, hands at his side, a loaded pistol hanging conspicuously from his belt. Through the full-length windows in the house behind, four men in similar garb are clearly visible. A storm trooper steps out from one of the automobiles, intending to walk toward the house. Ewald threatens to shoot if the man comes one step closer. All eyes are on the brown-shirted leader. He remains motionless for few seconds, then clicks his heels and makes an about face. Without a word, he returns to his auto. Moments later, the six autos are gone, leaving an angry cloud of dust in their wake. As the four armed men exit the Schmenzin manor house, Ewald extends to each a handshake of deep gratitude. The landowners of Belgard still count for something.

JULY. The Nazi Party is formally declared the only political party in Germany.

1934. The *nazification* of Germany is proceeding well on many fronts, not the least of which are religion and education.

In religious matters, there is immense pressure on Protestant clergymen to declare themselves one with the newly organized German Christian Church. At best this emerging form of Christian doctrine glorifies the German Fatherland and the führer as the secular equivalents of the kingdom of God and his son Jesus Christ; at worst it rejects non-Aryan Christians, mixed marriages and non-Aryan Scripture, meaning the entire Old Testament of the Bible. In all cases it is anti-Semitic. There are islands of resistance to these pressures, and the name of one man and one parish stand above all others—Pastor Martin Niemöller of the Dahlem Church in Berlin.

In education, the government has taken over the administration of the Internats, those boarding schools where the old aristocracy and the newly rich industrialists send their children to be educated. For the moment, the paying public secondary schools are still under local control and relatively free of state indoctrination.

MARCH. Generations of Junker sons, and more recently daughters also, have attended the select Internats, or boarding schools, in Prussia. This generation is no exception. Two Kleist sons,

Konstantin and Jürgen Christoph, aged fifteen and thirteen, and one Bismarck son, fifteen-year-old Hans Otto, are students at Templin, a private Internat west of the Oder River, near Berlin.

Hans Otto is gathered with some of his classmates in the school library, awaiting the arrival of a proctor to supervise their study hour. A plaster statue of the last Hohenzollern kaiser, Wilhelm II, stands on a wooden pedestal. In a spontaneous burst of mischievousness, the boys decide to destroy the kaiser, for now they have a new führer—Adolf Hitler. The boldest among them picks up the statue, raises it above his head and prepares to throw it to the stone floor, but at that moment Hans Otto von Bismarck accosts the taller boy and attempts to wrestle the kaiser's plaster likeness from his arms. The sculpture falls to the floor in splinters, and Hans Otto is beaten down with it. Amidst the taunts of his classmates, but without a word in response, the bruised boy picks himself up and flies to his room, consumed with guilt for having failed to prevent this insult to Germany's last kaiser.

That night young Bismarck is awakened from his sleep by a proctor, who orders him to put on the uniform of the Hitler Youth and report to the parade grounds. The boy complies and arrives to find all of his classmates also in uniform and in parade formation. Two proctors from the Hitler Youth position the boy between them and order him to face the class. A drum begins to sound, and in the darkness the two proctors, one to the left and one to the right, tear from Hans Otto's uniform all of his polished brass buttons. From this moment on, none of the other boys is permitted to speak to him. Still, Hans Otto does not cry.

When word of Hans Otto's humiliation reaches Lasbeck and Kieckow, parents and grandmother spring into action. Herbert, the boy's father, leaves immediately for Templin, there to pick up Hans Otto and all of his belongings. The letter of protest will follow later. Hans Jürgen is not far behind; he too withdraws his two sons from the school. Back at Kieckow, Mieze is on the phone to her sister-in-law Spes Stahlberg in Berlin. Something terrible has happened at Templin, and her two sons are being taken out at once. As there is no good gymnasium in Belgard, could Spes take Konstantin and Jürgen Christoph into her home at Grunewald so they can finish the gymnasium there? And what about confirmation? Under the Nazis, Templin has not provided preparation for this important event of a boy's life. Does Spes know a trustworthy pastor? Spes claims there are no trustworthy pastors in Berlin, but then that is typical of her nature. With genuine enthusiasm, she agrees to take in her Kleist nephews after the Easter holidays, for she is now entirely alone; even her youngest child Hans Conrad has left home for the military.

Ruth sees a similarity between this sudden development for Spes and her own life twenty-five years ago, for at that time she took the two troubled Bismarck boys into her Stettin flat. How much easier it all was when one could trust the schools and above all the pastor. Right now this grandmother has but one thing in mind—to find a pastor in Berlin who will prepare these two grandsons for confirmation. The search begins with a phone call to Pastor Reimer of Naseband. The second call, at his suggestion, is to Pastor Niemöller of Berlin.

APRIL. After Easter Konstantin and Jürgen Christoph are delivered to the Stahlberg flat in Berlin and registered at the Grunewald gymnasium. Arrangements have also been made with Pastor Niemöller for religious instruction to prepare them for confirmation in the Dahlem Church a year hence. It is a gracious commitment on the pastor's part, for he is also leading a new organization of churches and pastors called the Pastors' Emergency League, which is the nucleus of the emerging Confessing Church. Although not yet declared illegal by the government, this sturdy core of anti-Nazi Christians lives under constant tension.

Hans Otto von Bismarck is being taught at home. His mother cannot bring herself to let this son go away again so soon.

JUNE. Fabian von Schlabrendorff is often seen at Lasbeck now, and not even the most suspicious Nazi raises an eyebrow, for everyone understands that the Bismarcks will soon be announcing the engagement of their daughter Luitgarde to the bespectacled young lawyer from Berlin. On this early summer day, Luitgarde is not the only subject on Fabian's mind. He has driven to Lasbeck to inform Herbert of a bloody plot being hatched in the Chancery. Hitler intends to do away with those he perceives to be his rivals. It is not clear who is meant, but there is no reason to believe it is limited to certain well-known party members. And how does Fabian know these things? "Don't ask, but expect it to happen soon."

Before the day is out, Herbert is on his way to Kieckow. By nightfall he is on his way back to Lasbeck, and Hans Jürgen and Ewald are sitting with their heads together in the Schmenzin library.

At noon on the thirtieth, German radio announces that the führer has foiled an attempted Putsch by traitors in his own party. The villain is Ernst Röhm, leader of the powerful storm troopers, now under arrest along with many others. Anning von Kleist hears the report and relays it to Ewald. She has a premonition that he is in danger.

In June, darkness comes late in Pomerania. Thus it is still daylight when the four small Kleist children of Schmenzin are put to bed in their clothes. The oldest child, Ewald Heinrich, sits with his parents in the dining hall of the manor house; all eyes are on the cul de sac outside, until the interminably long twilight finally fades into darkness. At last, the outline of an automobile is visible. Ewald and Anning run to wake the sleeping daughters. All seven family members are loaded into the automobile—an unfamiliar vehicle, but with the Schmenzin chauffeur at the wheel. The motor is incredibly quiet, and there are no lights. The vehicle crisscrosses back and forth across the Belgard District, on roads rarely used, until long after midnight, eventually arriving at Dubberow, the home of Ewald's mother Lili. After the children are put to bed, Ewald suggests they all retire until morning. Anning insists otherwise; she will stay, but Ewald must leave immediately.

Anning von Kleist, daughter of old Osten, who but for Papen might have become German chancellor and saved them from all of this, has instincts well out of the ordinary. A quarter hour after Ewald leaves with his chauffeur, a Gestapo van, fresh from an exhaustive search of the Schmenzin manor house, arrives at Dubberow. One of the officers asks Anning where her husband is. "I don't know; he has driven away," she replies.

"When I am away, my wife always knows where I am," the officer counters.

"But I am not your wife," she retorts. The Gestapo leave without searching the Dubberow manor house.

It is clear to Anning that Ewald is driving into a trap, for all the roads will certainly be posted. Telephoning Kieckow, she begs Hans Jürgen to rouse the forester, his most trusted employee. Ewald is probably headed for Kieckow, but he would be better off driving to a train station. With a jacket over his nightclothes, the forester heads for the Klein Krössin village road by bicycle, intent on intercepting Ewald's vehicle before it enters the main road to Gross Tychow; but he is too late. The vehicle speeds past without seeing the man frantically pedaling a few meters from the road.

Then a miracle happens; Ewald's vehicle strikes a badger and comes to a full halt, giving the forester time to catch up and relay Anning's warning. The automobile turns around and heads in a different direction, to a small railway station where the early morning milk train stops. Still undetected, Ewald von Kleist boards the train and is on his way to Berlin.

By noon he arrives incognito at the capital city of the new Reich and makes his way to the apartment of Ernst Niekisch, a left-wing intellectual possessed with revolutionary zeal. No one would ever expect Niekisch to be a friend of the bookish Fabian von Schlabrendorff, who has given Ewald this address. Niekisch greets the well-known conservative Junker with an amused quip: "Why Herr von Kleist, if you can stand me, I can certainly tolerate you."

For three weeks, until the Gestapo loses interest in this particular pursuit, Ewald remains in hiding—one week under Niekisch's unlikely protection and two more in the Swedish Embassy.

When the purge finally runs its course, Hitler's former confidante Ernst Röhm and hundreds of his supporters are dead, as is General Kurt von Schleicher. The total number of victims from these bloody weeks will never really be known. Röhm's organization of storm troopers is rendered impotent. The SS, under Heinrich Himmler, is now the all-powerful police force, reporting directly to Hitler. Only the army is not yet in Hitler's hand, for it is nominally controlled by President von Hindenburg.

AUGUST. Eighty-seven-year-old Hindenburg is dead, and Adolf Hitler has taken on the presidency of Germany. All provincial parliaments are abolished. In a national plebiscite, more than thirty-eight million Germans, eighty-eight percent of all those voting, cast their ballots in favor of the Nazi government.

Finkenwalde

1935. Over the centuries, the children of Prussian Junkers have been taught that an invisible wall separates them from the children of the neighborhood, whether it be the estate village or the nearby town. Without it being put into words, they are encouraged to keep within the manor house all that is said within their family circle. These attitudes are hardly to be recommended in a society of democratic institutions, and in fact, after the German republic was created in 1918, there was harsh criticism of such lingering Junker traits.

In the Third Reich—the new name for Hitler's Germany, successor to the earlier two Reichs—a minority of Junker families will choose to stand against the Nazis. They will be somewhat more successful than like-minded Germans of other classes and circumstances, for under Hitler, the peculiarities of the Junker class will confound the government to the very end.

The four children at the Kieckow manor house (the two oldest are away at school in Berlin) and the five children at Schmenzin (three more have yet to be born) are each others' best friends and constant playmates. All are being educated at home, hence they are not pressured to join the Hitler Youth or the League of German Girls, and beside that, their parents have forbidden it. All participate vicariously in their elders' plots to avoid flying the swastika on Hitler's birthday (April 20), on May Day, and on other designated holidays. At Kieckow the game is to remove the flagpole from the courtyard and fly the black, white and red flag of the Hohenzollern Reich from the housetop (technically not a violation of the law). At Schmenzin the game is played differently; the master of the estate orders the village flagpole moved to the center of the manure pile and gives the village schoolteacher responsibility for raising the flag at appropriate times. A dedicated Nazi, the teacher nevertheless chooses not to fulfill his duty. The Kleist children take delight in these antics, not realizing that the parents are acting in dead earnest.

MARCH. To the south of Kieckow lies the estate of one of the men who so recently stood with Ewald von Kleist, pistol in hand, behind the glass windows of Schmenzin. This man's father is celebrating his seventieth birthday, and the entire trusted Belgard circle is invited. It is the kind of party for which Pomeranians are famous—a gathering of three generations to commemorate the patriarch's long life with food, speeches, dancing and conversation, much of which is often political. Nowadays in Nazi Germany political discussions take place only between men and women of like mind, and such are the guests at this seventieth birthday party.

Two days later, the patriarch is arrested and taken to the Belgard jail for questioning. He is detained overnight and released. On returning home, the older man summons to his manor house every man, woman and child who attended the birthday celebration. Inside the great hall of the house, behind closed doors, he confronts his family and friends: "Who was it that denounced me?"

The silence is immediately broken by the sobs of his ten-year-old granddaughter. She confesses that she told her schoolteacher the following day about what had been said, for is that not what one is supposed to do?

JUNE. The experience of one family is not lost on the others. At the recent christening of the newest Lasbeck son, Fritz Christoph von Bismarck, the children of Ruth von Kleist came to a common decision. The three families will lease a flat in Stettin; Grandmother Ruth will come out of retirement—"one can't just read Karl Barth's theology day after day"—and all the grandchildren of gymnasium age will attend public school in the city, with Grandmother in charge of them all.

Back at home after the christening, Ruth begins to comprehend the dimensions of this new responsibility. It will require unusual stamina, for she is now sixty-eight years old and no longer used to children in large doses. But it will be an immense opportunity to have influence on those she loves most in these godless times. When God makes a demand and one submits to his will, he will provide what is needed. Life has demonstrated this to Ruth time and time again. Even now, as she anticipates her new task, unexpected energies are rising within this determined matriarch, and she begins to feel young again!

AUGUST. After a noontime picnic on the Bismarck terrace, a caravan of three automobiles proceeds out from Lasbeck, each loaded with children's belongings, pension provisions, and the designated inmates for the second children's boardinghouse in Stettin. In the lead vehicle, Grandmother Ruth is seated next to the driver, Herbert von Bismarck, an alumnus of her earlier boardinghouse. In the back seat are his son Hans Otto and his daughter Spes.

The second vehicle is driven by Hans von Wedemeyer, who came up from Pätzig early this morning to rendezvous with his brothers-in-law at Lasbeck. Next to him is Ruth Alice, the oldest of the Wedemeyer tribe and the one on whom Grandmother will rely most. Behind them, Hans's son Maximilian and his younger daughter Maria are squeezed amid hams, heads of cabbage, carrots and duffel bags. Ruthchen and Hans have discussed at length whether this lively daughter is mature enough to come under her grandmother's care, and for the time being, Maria will stay at Grandmother's boardinghouse on a trial basis.

The last automobile of the trio is from Kieckow, with Hans Jürgen at the wheel and the Klein Krössin cook on his right. In back are Hans Friedrich and a young woman from the Kieckow village, who will be kitchen helper to the cook. The two passengers are surrounded by cartons of kitchen utensils and a hefty supply of the food with which Kieckow abounds. It is the great irony of the times that thanks to Hitler's economic policies, this once debt-ridden estate, which Hans Jürgen came close to losing in 1933, is now prospering. One is reminded again and again that the Lord often moves in ways that are beyond understanding.

As the caravan draws nearer to its destination, Herbert spots a village sign and announces to his passengers, "Five kilometers to Stettin."

They are passing through the tiny village of Finkenwalde, which at one time belonged to the estate of an aristocratic family. Today it is just a collection of ordinary cottages along the highway, with the run-down manor house behind, which appears

to be inhabited. Ruth also notices the sign and declares to no
one in particular, "Here lives a man of great repute. This man I
intend to meet."

SEPTEMBER. It has taken several weeks to get organized, but all
six children are now in school. Extra furnishings from the
various estates have all arrived and are in place, including the
grand piano from Klein Krössin. Music teachers have been
engaged; Ruth Alice von Wedemeyer, at fifteen the oldest of the
Stettin children, has agreed to be house tutor for "English"
suppers every other day of the week; now all that remains is to
find a tutor to oversee the alternating "French" suppers. For
Grandmother Ruth, there is a strong sense of déjà vu. Thirty-five
years ago she made precisely these arrangements for her own
five children.

Lately Ruth's circle of interests has spread far beyond her own
family, and in Stettin, rather than narrowing the circle, she
intends to widen it even more. She already has church-based
contacts in this provincial capital city, for she is a delegate to the
Belgard District governing body of the Confessing Church—that
band of Protestant clergymen, lay people and congregations who
have refused to participate in the newly structured German
Christian Church. The support structure for the Confessing
Church is the Council of Brethren,[32] organized at the parish, district, provincial and national levels. It seeks to be the legitimate
Protestant alternative to the German Christian Church, which is
now filled with Nazis and Nazi apologists.

By good fortune, the office of the Pomeranian Council of
Brethren is just down the street from Ruth's flat, hardly a
minute's walk. Ruth has already announced herself at the office,
offering her services for anything from consulting to letter
writing and prayers of intercession. In this early period of the
church struggle in Nazi Germany, the offer of prayers might
seem a bit ludicrous. Very soon such prayers will be of overriding
consideration.

Just as Nazi inroads into the churches have led to the creation
of a new church organization in Germany, so has the Nazi invasion of the universities led to the demand for new, independent
seminaries. A guiding force in this development is Dietrich

Bonhoeffer, ordained pastor and theology lecturer at the Berlin University, where his lectures are considered nothing short of brilliant. Bonhoeffer has also developed an international reputation. He has studied and worked in America; for a year and a half he had a pastorate in London; he has close ties with several English bishops; and he is at home in European ecumenical and peace organizations. At twenty-nine years of age, Dietrich Bonhoeffer has an immense reputation on which he could easily rest for the remainder of his career.

Bonhoeffer, however, has chosen to resist the spread of the godless Nazi philosophy and its corollary edicts in the way he knows best—through his lecturing and his theological stance. Even before nazism was perceived as a threat to spiritual life, Bonhoeffer strayed from modern theological opinion and worked out a Christ-centered theology that draws more deeply from the Bible than does much of modern theology.

Dietrich Bonhoeffer now has the task of establishing and directing a seminary in Pomerania under the auspices of the Council of Brethren and the Confessing Church. He selected Pomerania as a seminary location a year ago when he made his first trip ever to these eastern German lands. Here he discovered a conservatism, a piety, and a leisurely way of life that gave hope of nurturing the kind of Christian community that could never survive in Berlin. The seminary site lies just east of the Oder River, two hundred and fifty kilometers from Berlin—Finkenwalde, an old manor house recently used as a school. It is shabby and unfurnished, but with interior spaces and grounds well suited to a theological institution. For some three months now, the seminary has been in operation, its twenty-three male students performing most of the tasks required to upgrade and maintain the facilities while the seminary director travels the countryside begging and borrowing from friendly churches and sympathetic landowners. Though very few comprehend Pastor Bonhoeffer's revolutionary theology, those who care understand that the Finkenwalde seminary stands in opposition to the Nazis. On this basis alone, doors are opened in the most unexpected places.

Grandmother Ruth has learned that Pastor Bonhoeffer holds Sunday morning services at the seminary, to which the public is

At Ruth's Stettin flat: standing, Max von Wedemeyer; seated, left to right, Spes and Hans Otto von Bismarck, Ruth Alice and Maria von Wedemeyer, Hans Friedrich von Kleist

invited. On the last Sunday of September, a beautiful, warm fall day, she and her six charges board a local train at Stettin and twenty minutes later disembark at the Finkenwalde station. Walking on the arm of sixteen-year-old Hans Otto, the aging Kleist matriarch makes her way up the ill-kept road. The five other children follow behind. Outside one wing of the house, a group of young men waits quietly while familiar hymns sound from a piano inside. Before the visiting delegation reaches the door, the group of seminarians breaks up and enters what must be a chapel, each one in turn greeting the pastor. He is dressed in a simple black vestment, with Bible in hand. The last to enter are the visitors, who have not yet identified themselves. Pastor Bonhoeffer—it can be none other than he—ushers the grand-mother and her brood to the front of the chapel and invites them to be seated in the empty chairs. The service promptly begins.

During the opening hymn, Ruth looks around the Finken-walde chapel—four bare walls decorated with hand-drawn banners, an ordinary cloth-covered table as an altar, a plain but beautiful wooden cross, a small lectern for a pulpit, and a dozen or so rows of classroom chairs. It is so austere it cannot even be compared with the simple church at Kieckow. The pastor now leads the congregation in prayer, after which the seminarians sing again. When at last the pastor preaches, the grandmother is transfixed by his message. Amazingly, ten-year-old Maria von Wedemeyer appears to be transfixed also.

Later it will turn out that the child was counting the number of times the pastor said "God"—sixty-eight if one includes the sermon and all the prayers!

Outside on the lawn, Ruth von Kleist finally introduces herself to Dietrich Bonhoeffer and presents the six children to him. The genial pastor insists that they all stay for dinner an hour from now. Ruth politely declines—her cook expects them back at Stettin for dinner—but perhaps next week! Still there is time for a short visit. Three young men are already carrying chairs from the chapel, placing them in a circle for themselves and the visitors. Two other students carry a Ping-Pong table from the glassed-in solarium, and while the children are occupied with the game, the pastor and the grandmother become acquainted.

Pastor Bonhoeffer is amazed at Ruth's connections in the religious community—this old woman is well acquainted with Harnack, Barth, Tillich, the Berneuchen factions—and at her familiarity with the protagonists and the issues that have been driving the churches in this century. Yet she appears to be a restless woman, dissatisfied with what passes for twentieth-century theology and still searching for a higher truth.

By coincidence the pastor has experienced a similar crisis in his own system of beliefs. He now views each individual's freedom to select moral options under God as bounded by the responsibility to act out these options in the real world. It is a demanding position he has chosen for himself and for others, given the harsh realities of Germany today. Yet, ever the teacher, Dietrich Bonhoeffer sees in Frau von Kleist a keen mind to be taught, a vessel to be filled, and a soul to be led through the minefields of the church in these Nazi times. By the time the visitors leave for the train, a number of arrangements have been made. They will all return next Sunday, for dinner as well as for church; Ruth will investigate further sources of support for the seminary; and Werner Koch, the seminarian best trained in the

Dietrich Bonhoeffer

French language, will have dinner once a week with the children in Stettin.

During the week following the initial meeting of pastor and matriarch, Ruth is in a state of high excitement. After numerous phone calls to each of the estates within her captive circle—Kieckow, Lasbeck, Pätzig, Schmenzin and even Dubberow—she has commitments for mountains of food, a scattering of used furniture, kitchen and writing utensiis, books, garden tools and even that most valuable staple of all—money—for the seminary at Finkenwalde. What joy to share this news with Pastor Bonhoeffer!

NOVEMBER. Sundays at Finkenwalde are as much a part of the Stettin children's lives now as school days at the gymnasium or lyceum. When the weather precludes table tennis on the lawn, the seminarians organize Shakespeare readings in the library. How much more fun for them all when Ophelia, Juliet and Lady Macbeth speak in female voices!

One can only imagine what the grandmother and the pastor are discussing. In truth, it is the pastor's latest manuscript, almost complete, from which he reads particular passages to elicit Frau von Kleist's response. Ruth has already formed a study club in Stettin, women like herself but younger, who are reading and discussing Bonhoeffer's published tracts. She encourages and cajoles the pastor to finish this latest work, already titled *The Cost of Discipleship*. The readers of Stettin are impatient! And what of the Bible, in which the pastor claims lie the weapons for these times? At his suggestion, Ruth is studying Greek. Under the guidance of her mentor, she hopes to read the New Testament in its original form.

The children under Ruth's care are somewhat oblivious to the plans their grandmother and the pastor are devising these days. As far as they are concerned, Grandmother's days are devoted entirely to them. To begin with she has purchased small accounting books for each of them—Hans Otto, Hans Friedrich, Spes, Ruth Alice, Maximilian and Maria. Each week the children are given their allowance with the instruction that every expenditure must be recorded in the little books, to be examined by grandmother at the end of the week. The children faithfully record their expenses daily and dutifully submit their books for inspection each Saturday morning. Only later does the truth come out that certain entries for "pencils" and "paper" have been masking purchases of candy.

Every day after school Grandmother is waiting at the flat. She questions each child in detail as to what he or she has learned this day, afterward correcting the facts and attitudes she feels are erroneous. It is perhaps the most depressing task of the day for Ruth, for she is now acutely aware that the Nazi propaganda has infiltrated the local schools. In the evenings there are often concerts, and Grandmother has two tickets to everything—one for herself and the other used alternatively for each of the children. They have season tickets to the Stettin philharmonic; they hear visiting orchestras, chamber music and piano recitals; they attend a concert by the famed Don Cossack Chorus and performances of Schiller's popular dramas. Always before a theater performance, parts of the drama are read aloud at the flat so that each child gains familiarity with the work to be performed.

Even with a cook and a kitchen helper, the children have their regular assignments at mealtime—to set the table, to clear the table, or to wipe the dishes. The Stettin flat is a busy little world, and everyone in it takes his or her turn.

Nor is Grandmother concerned only with duty, honesty, thrift and work. One of the challenges of this family pension experiment is to provide the children with a rich life in an environment where all public youth activities are now incorporated into the programs of the forbidden Nazi youth organizations. Ruth takes pains to make the flat a place of indoor recreation. She encourages card games, rummy and whist when several are present, and patience when one is alone. Of course with music lessons, to which every child must submit at one time or another, there are practice schedules and even recitals from time to time. Ruth Alice, who is more her grandmother's accomplice than her charge, even creates an opera with five singing parts. It is performed by the children when any of their parents or Finkenwalde friends come to Stettin to visit.

Above all else, undergirding and reinforcing this family circle is the evening prayer service, with Max at the piano and one child or another reading from the Scriptures. The homily is always left to Grandmother Ruth—even when the pastor from Finkenwalde comes to supper.

A Birthday Coincidence

1936. The Confessing Church in Germany, which just a year ago had hopes of being the bulwark against a Nazi takeover of the church, is under attack from within and without. Pressure from without comes from international organizations, namely: The World Alliance, Life and Work, and Faith and Order. In these institutions, the leadership bends over backward to treat the Confessing Church and the German Christian Church with an even hand. Bonhoeffer is dumbfounded that leading international Christian organizations continue to recognize an official German church that promotes Aryan Christianity and a führer concept that does battle with Christ. Bonhoeffer now refuses all speaking invitations at gatherings to which German Christians are invited. Instead he works to tighten his bonds with certain

English and Swedish bishops, who he believes understand the true nature of the church struggle in Germany.

Would that the German clergy understood it so well. Even a colleague like Martin Niemöller, whose passion is to keep the church separate from the state, is inclined to be tolerant of the new regime, provided that it doesn't interfere with the activities of the Confessing Church. Among the theological professors at the Berlin University, Bonhoeffer alone is dismissed from his lecture position. His twin sister's husband, Gerhard Leibholz, is also dismissed, on the basis of his Jewish ancestry.

The latest government edict denies accreditation to all of the Confessing Church seminaries, including Finkenwalde. Still Finkenwalde prospers.

FEBRUARY. This year, on the fourth of the month, Ruth's sixty-ninth birthday is celebrated with a tea party in the Stettin flat. There are flowers and cakes and letters and telegrams, and even poems by two of the grandchildren.

For all of the joy surrounding each birthday, a corner of Ruth's heart is always stirred by the thought that it is also the anniversary of her marriage to Jürgen—gone now for many decades but still able to call forth in this bride a distant longing. This year in particular, the fiftieth anniversary of her marriage, one might expect the day to be bittersweet for Grandmother Ruth. Indeed that is not the case. The fourth of February has taken on a new dimension, and Ruth will later attach to it eschatological meanings. It is also the birthday of Dietrich Bonhoeffer!

This year Dietrich (no longer Pastor Bonhoeffer to Ruth) is thirty years old, and his presence at her birthday tea party lends an aura that even the children cannot ignore.

Almost as exciting for the children is the reunion with their larger-than-life cousin, Alexander Stahlberg, who arrives bearing in his long arms the largest bouquet of flowers any of them has ever seen. Grandmother is so overwhelmed that she blushes to a deep pink, also a spectacle the children find extraordinary.

Alla, who as a small child spent his first years at Kieckow before moving so far away to Berlin, is now living and working at Stettin. His father's mills are extremely prosperous under the new economy, and Alla is expected to take them over one day, of course in partnership with his younger brother. Alla Stahlberg steers very clear of politics, but nevertheless he has heard of Pastor Bonhoeffer. Stettin is a stronghold of the controversial Confessing Church; one cannot help but know of Bonhoeffer and his seminary at Finkenwalde. Alla is pleased to meet the pastor and prepared to be helpful in any way. The pastor makes a mental note of this.

A few days later, on Sunday, there is a large celebration for Pastor Bonhoeffer at Finkenwalde. Of course Frau von Kleist and her brood are there too. In a turnabout on gift giving, the seminarians present to their beleaguered director a birthday wish—that he use his ecumenical connections to organize a trip to Sweden. Their spokesman is Eberhard Bethge, the pastor's closest friend if not his alter ego. Would such a trip not strengthen international support for their position as well as raise the seminarians' morale? Such is Bethge's tack. Dietrich is persuaded and promises to explore the possibility. Of course not everyone at Finkenwalde can go along, only as many as there are funds for ship passage. But the director makes light of this by suggesting that "while the cat's away . . . "

MARCH. It will take more than money to get Dietrich Bonhoeffer and his seminarians to Sweden. The trick is to make all of the arrangements in Sweden, including land transportation and places to stay (for money is not permitted to be taken out of Germany), then to obtain a visa and a ticket before the information can be relayed to the headquarters of the German Christian Church. As soon as these church officials discover a leader of the Confessing Church about to go abroad, they report it to the government authorities. One cannot have churchmen traveling about the world spouting anti-Nazi propaganda. Luckily, Dietrich and his companions succeed in reaching Sweden before the news reaches these unfriendly offices.

The scandal will unfold upon their return, however, when it is learned that they met with the Archbishop of Sweden.

There is no reason to believe that while Bonhoeffer is away, anything unusual is happening at Finkenwalde. However, the same cannot be said about his friend Ruth von Kleist.

Ruth with Bonhoeffer and Konstantin von Kleist,
on the Kieckow lawn

On the seventh of March, German troops invade the Rhine-
land, that portion of Germany lying west of the Rhine River
which has been demilitarized ever since the Versailles Treaty of
1920. The demilitarization of these lands, to which Germany has
acquiesced for sixteen years, has been a constant source of irrita-
tion to Germans of all political persuasions. For the old Prussian
soldier, Ruth von Kleist, it has been a particularly painful thorn
in the side. The image of the German army now marching
through these ancient lands induces a long-forgotten joy in her
Junker heart, and the news that there will be a Sunday parade in
Berlin to celebrate the shedding of the Versailles shackles is
something Ruth cannot resist. She phones her daughter Spes
and invites herself for a weekend in the capital city.

Fortunately, Konstantin and Jürgen Christoph, the Kieckow
grandsons, are also at the Stahlberg flat. Ruth suggests that these
two boys attend the parade with her. She also asks that Jürgen
Christoph carry a wooden chair from Spes's kitchen out to the

215

street, onto the streetcar, then by foot down to Unter den Linden, Berlin's most elegant thoroughfare. From just inside the great Brandenburg Gate, they will all watch the new German army on parade.

Too many years have passed since Ruth has seen a parade that really stirred her heart. Wasn't the last time also in Berlin, almost fifty years ago, when Jürgen marched by and looked right through her? Granted the Nazi flags are an abomination; one tries to imagine the colors in their old configuration, the black, white and red of the Hohenzollern flag and the uniforms of the kaiser's guard. The music is the same; the precision is magnificent, and the numbers—the sheer numbers—of keen young men parading by, all eyes left, are a feast for this Prussian grandmother's soul. She is oblivious to the spectacle she herself is making, an old woman in an outdated gown, flanked by two adolescent boys and standing at attention atop a kitchen chair.

Only later, back in Pomerania, does Ruth have second thoughts. In any case, she does not intend to tell the pastor of her excursion, which substituted for the Finkenwalde service one Sunday while he was away.

MAY. Ewald von Kleist and Dietrich Bonhoeffer both possess a special knack for seeing through the obvious to life's hidden dangers, long before these dangers are visible to ordinary eyes. Ewald's domain of course is politics and the secular state, though his judgments are handed down in a manner not unlike those of the Old Testament prophets. Dietrich, on the other hand, is a theologian, and his domain is the organized church of Germany. Here his vision is no less keen.

The German Christian Church is embarking on a nationwide revival crusade that presumes to be the answer to every Pietist's prayer. The spiritual and genetic descendants of the Thaddens, the Puttkamers, the Bismarcks and the Kleists, in their churches and in their manor houses, for years have prayed that the living spirit of God might enter the hearts of their people and fill the churches as they were filled in earlier times.

The clergy of the new German Christians, many of them wearing their Nazi Party membership badges under or over their robes, are leading a religious revival throughout the Fatherland,

and especially in the fertile lands once dominated by the Prussian Pietists. The pews of churches that formerly drew two or three people to a Sunday service are now filled with the young as well as the old.

Bonhoeffer is not blind to these developments, nor to the seductive message being brought to the people, a reinterpreted Sermon on the Mount that promises, "Happy is he who always observes good comradeship, for he will do well in the world," and an enfeebled call to the cross: "Take pains to maintain a noble, calm attitude, even to those who insult and persecute you."

The Confessing Church, on the other hand, is so deeply involved in legal disputes with the government, so ridden by internal doubts, and so pressed by financial problems that it offers no contest to its competing giant. Dietrich has plans to change all that. He has prevailed upon the Pomeranian Council of Brethren to establish a Brethren House that will share facilities with the Finkenwalde seminary. Here newly graduated seminarians and other pastors will be trained in evangelism, to go about the country and establish mission parishes within the Confessing Church. Bonhoeffer is confident of success in this land of once-feudal estates, where the landowners are still patrons of the village churches; and in places where the patrons are not sympathetic, these mission parishes can meet in village homes. If there is to be a revival in Germany, Bonhoeffer has hopes that at least in Pomerania it will be a godly undertaking.

The Council of Brethren concurs, but promises nothing in the way of financial support. However, a unanimous decision is made to establish the first mission at Belgard. The hand of Ruth von Kleist is clearly visible.

JUNE. The entire Finkenwalde seminary, all twenty-five students and faculty, has moved to Belgard. Six village churches have been selected as mission targets, of which three are under the patronage of Ewald von Kleist and one is under that of Hans Jürgen von Kleist. This initial experiment, which is to last a week, promises some hope of success.

Four brethren are assigned to each church, their task to spend five days of the week in the village. Sunday is carefully avoided,

for the pastors of the target churches are appointed by the
German Christian Church and not under control of the landowner patrons. For example, the pastor of the Schmenzin
church is now a hard-line German Christian—ignoring the Old
Testament completely, editing the New Testament to avoid all
references to places like Jerusalem and Israel, and denouncing
the Jews from beginning to end. Among Ewald's villages, only
Naseband is blessed with a clergyman from the Confessing
Church—Pastor Reimer, who will later be jailed repeatedly but
will never be silenced.

These conflicts do not play on weekdays, leaving the missionary brethren free to visit homes and to conduct Bible discussions
with the school-age children. Every evening the village families
are invited to the church, where each of the four visiting
brethren speaks for no longer than ten minutes from the pulpit.
The format turns out to be successful beyond anyone's expectations. The evening meetings last less than an hour (normally
unheard of in the Belgard District) and the churches are full.
Dietrich, well cared for by Mieze and Hans Jürgen at the Kieckow
manor house, visits each of these village church meetings on
alternate evenings. If there is any disappointment during this
mission endeavor, it is that Grandmother Ruth must stay in
Stettin to mind the six grandchildren and miss out on the whole
adventure!

Ruth's family has committed to Dietrich all of the resources
under their command. Still that is not enough. What is needed is
an organized system of broader support for the seminary and for
the House of Brethren. So on the last day of the Belgard mission,
Hans Jürgen invites family and friends, as well as neighbors and
patrons from the district, to Kieckow for a reception and
meeting with Pastor Bonhoeffer, director of the mission and of
the Finkenwalde seminary. The Bismarcks, the Woedtkes, the
Braunschweigs, and of course the Kleists of Schmenzin, are all
present. And accompanying the Bismarcks is Fabian von
Schlabrendorff, Herbert's former colleague, now seen often in
the company of Herbert's daughter Luitgarde. For better or for
worse, this initial introduction of Dietrich to Fabian and to Ewald
lays the groundwork for their later association, one that will
prove to be far more deadly.

Before the afternoon is over, Dietrich gives a sobering report
on the state of affairs in the deepening church struggle, offering
no easy solutions nor even a hopeful outcome. Yet he leaves the
gathering with pledges of support that will guarantee Finkenwalde's existence for another year. Not the least of these guarantees is the promise of padded seat covers—fifty of them—from
Ewald's mother Lili, still the countess of Kleist. Dietrich bows in
gratitude and assures the countess that all of the seminarians,
and above all Madam Ruth von Kleist, will appreciate this gift
more than she can possibly imagine.

OCTOBER. Ruth and the children are back in Stettin after the
harvest holiday; only the French-speaking seminarian is missing.
Werner Koch, who always presided at the foot of the table on
French evenings, has taken a position in Berlin as journalist for
the Confessing Church periodical. Grandmother Ruth, whose
French has remained next to perfect over a lifetime, is left to
carry on without this charming conversation partner.

Dietrich, after a summer of meetings and travel, has returned
to Finkenwalde, where the sense of community grows in propor-
tion to the deepening anxieties.

Ruth used to tell her children, as she now tells her grandchildren, that friendships do not come free. By this she means that
the deeper the friendship, the more one is obligated to the
friend. Such is the case with Dietrich Bonhoeffer.

It began more than a year ago and didn't seem so serious
then—a detention here, a questioning there, an arrest, maybe
even imprisonment, but not for long if one had friends. Clearly it
is changing now, for one by one, here and there in Germany,
seminarians, pastors and minor church officials are being picked
up by the Gestapo on charges of spreading false propaganda at
home or abroad. With his superb organizational talents, Dietrich
is keeping a list—dates of arrest, locations, accusations, prisons,
contacts and, one hopes, dates of release. At first there were just
eight names on the list, then only six; now suddenly there are
seventy, but still Dietrich is on top of it all. And he is making
assignments—who should contact the authorities, visit the prisoner, write letters to his parents and provide support for his wife
if he is married. Dietrich keeps a second list also, the names of

those seminarians and pastors who are Jewish by birth or who have Jewish wives. There are a number of these men and women in the Confessing Church, and he knows that before long they will need special care.

And what of Ruth? Well, Dietrich has given her more than one task. Above all, she is expected to undertake prayers of intercession for every person on the prayer list. At Finkenwalde this is a daily task of the seminarians, who divide the list among themselves. In Ruth's flat, the task is handled a little differently but no less carefully. Each Sunday she picks up from Finkenwalde her carbon copy of the updated list. Before supper, at each family evening prayer, Ruth prays aloud for all those on the list and reads aloud those names that the children recognize. Always she reads the names of those who have been newly released. She and the children then rejoice as if for one of their own.

DECEMBER. The name of Werner Koch, the children's French-speaking friend, is added to the Finkenwalde prayer list. Koch has been arrested in Berlin for publishing abroad defamatory articles about Germany. He is to be tried in January. At Stettin the children pray in earnest.

Carnival at Schmenzin

1937. "Carnival" in Germany is the week of feasting and frivolity that precedes Lent in the Christian calendar year. It is mostly celebrated in Bavaria and other Catholic parts of the country. It is hardly celebrated at all in the old Protestant strongholds of Pomerania. To dilute the effects of this Lenten season, the government has proclaimed a nationwide school holiday at carnival time to coincide with Nazi youth rallies in most of the large cities.

FEBRUARY. At Stettin, Ruth's pension is empty but for the cook and her helper. Over this carnival holiday, all of the children and the grandmother are at their home estates. At Kieckow, this is a quiet time, a time for looking ahead to the sober Lenten period that is to follow. Not so at Schmenzin, where Anning von Kleist has organized an estatewide carnival especially for the children, perhaps as a substitute for the Nazi festivals they are forbidden to attend. It is to be a costume party, with masks and noisemakers, to which the manor house residents from Kieckow and Klein Krössin are also invited. The single resident of Klein Krössin declines, as do the parents at Kieckow. However, the Kieckow children are permitted to attend.

With great care, Mieze and the housekeeper search through the attic and cupboards, looking for materials from which to create carnival costumes for Hans Friedrich, Ruthi, Elisabeth and Heinrich. One wants every children's gathering to be a happy experience, particularly now when one is competing with the lure of the Hitler youth organizations.

No youth rally in the world can compete with this Schmenzin carnival. Each child delights in the costume Mother has fashioned, but the star of the evening is the masked "Herr von Kleist" of Kieckow, who arrives in his best dark suit. In truth he is the children's tutor, whom Mother has dressed in Father's best suit and gold watch chain. The Schmenzin children recognize the impostor immediately, but the Schmenzin bailiff, not so discerning, bows repeatedly before the visiting aristocrat until the final unmasking.

For those who survive the next decade, this Kleist carnival and the masked "Herr" from Kieckow will be among the most joyful memories to be recalled from a vanished childhood world.

MAY. Scarlet fever has invaded Schmenzin. Once the epidemic has run its course, all of the children have recovered, but their mother is dead. There will be no more Kleist carnivals.

Within the year Ewald will take a second wife, Alice von Kuhlwein, twenty years his junior. Early on Alice lived and worked with the Schmenzin family to learn the skills of an estate mistress. In a moment of premonition, Anning asked the young woman to promise that she would marry Ewald if anything should happen to her. Alice will take her marriage vows not for love but out of duty, yet she will be a beloved mother to Anning's children and a devoted helpmate to Ewald in his final years of tribulation.

JUNE. There is now almost a pattern to the activities of the Gestapo organization—first the search and the confiscation of papers, then the arrests, the sealing of the doors, imprisonment, trial and finally the concentration camp. Over and over again the sequence is repeated at various strongholds of the Confessing Church in Germany. The Law for the Protection of the German Evangelical Church, a euphemism for the dissolution of the Confessing Church organization, is being enforced with a vengeance.

Ruth has taken on the spiritual care of the loved ones of several imprisoned Finkenwalde alumni. The one closest to her heart these days is Dita Stockmann, fiancée of Werner Koch, the former French-speaking supper guest from Finkenwalde. Ruth writes to Dita weekly, each letter a declaration of her own faith in God's goodness and mercy. There is so little else one can promise. During the school holidays, she invites Dita to Klein Krössin along with other prisoners' wives in her care, all in response to Dietrich's gentle urgings.

Shortly afterward, Ruth leaves on a long-awaited birthday holiday, an extended trip promised to her by Hans Jürgen on her seventieth birthday in February. It begins with an automobile trip, first to the favorite watering places of her youth, Kolberg on the Baltic and Marienbad in Czechoslovakia, and then to Grossenborau, where Hans Jürgen leaves his mother after exchanging greetings with his Uncle Rob. With the men, nothing has changed since Anni von Tresckow's funeral nine years ago—a brief sober greeting followed by a formal bow, but never a handshake. Spes has come by train from Berlin to share the Grossenborau holiday with her mother and eventually to deliver her safely home.

The days in this Silesian fairyland are filled with both wonderment and nostalgia. The lands are incredibly lush this year, and the village simply glows with prosperity. Even the manor house is perfect in every detail, all as if to mock the growing imperfections of the new Germany.

By coincidence Rob's two sons, Ruth's godchild Friedrich Carl and Konstantin, are both home for visits. Like Ruth's Konstantin twenty-five years earlier, Friedrich Carl is employed by the Merton Metallgesellschaft. But times have changed mightily since those peaceful years before the World War.

Friedrich Carl chose to leave Germany two years ago out of disgust with the Nazi government. Richard Merton, the son and successor to old Wilhelm Merton, gave Friedrich Carl the task of exploring business opportunities in Brazil. Now Friedrich Carl has returned to Europe to assist Merton in moving the firm across the border to Belgium, presumably out of reach of the German government.

The very mention of the name Metallgesellschaft calls forth to Ruth the memory of old Merton, long dead, who took Konstantin into his heart. In this time of Jew-hounding, Ruth does not ask Friedrich Carl about the Jewish owners of his firm. When one knows of injustice, one is obligated to act against it, but in Hitler's Germany, how does an old woman act against the mounting inequities across the land? Until now, Ruth has never thought of herself as an old woman!

Friedrich Carl, the charmer and the delight of all who know him, is now the owner of Grossenborau, though his father is the resident manager.

In the village there are reunions, one more touching than the other, with the elderly men and women of the village who at one time shared their childhood with the Conti Ruth. Then it is time for the good-byes. Ruth suspects this is the last time she will see Friedrich Carl. Neither he nor old Merton's Metallgesellschaft can abide the scent of the new Germany.

Unknown to Ruth, this is also the last time she will see Konstantin. Like her own son of that name, he will fall in battle, though in a different country and in a different war.

JULY. Dietrich's prayer list now contains another familiar name, Martin Niemöller, pastor of the Dahlem Church in Berlin. A year ago he confirmed Hans Jürgen's sons Konstantin and Jürgen Christoph; now he too is under arrest. It all has to do with the Confessing Church, of which Niemöller is the leading figure. On July 1 the Gestapo marched into the church's Berlin offices, ransacked the files and arrested Niemöller. A day later they invaded his home, interrogated his wife and confiscated all of his private papers. He is to be put on trial now, to face charges of "treachery against the Fatherland." At Stettin and at Finkenwalde, wherever Dietrich's prayer lists are found, this pastor is remembered and prayed for. Recalling the pastor's kindnesses to her grandsons, Ruth begins to write regularly to Frau Niemöller.

Although Martin Niemöller will be acquitted of treachery, he will nevertheless be interned at various concentration camps for eight long years; he will survive the war.

AUGUST. Ruth prevails upon Dietrich to prepare three of the grandchildren in Stettin, Hans Friedrich, Spes and Maximilian, for spring confirmation. (Hans Otto and Ruth Alice have already been confirmed.) As for Maria, Grandmother feels the child is not quite ready for such serious matters. Dietrich has promised to teach the children once a week in the Stettin flat when he is at Finkenwalde. When he is away, the children shall ride their bicycles out to Finkenwalde, where one of the seminarians will provide instruction.

At the first confirmation lecture, Dietrich, Grandmother Ruth and the young people are gathered in the music room behind the closed French doors that separate it from the sitting room. Dietrich has his back to the doors, and Grandmother is seated just to his left.

This pastor views preparation for confirmation to be of immense significance in a child's life, not to be trifled with in any way. His goal is to imbue each prospective confirmand with a godly awareness. In this spirit, he addresses the three children in his circle—aged fourteen, fifteen and sixteen years. They appear to be of like mind and are very attentive for the first several minutes of the lecture. Then, one after another, three pairs of eyes drop from the pastor's face to the floor behind his chair. Were Grandmother not sitting at an angle, she might suspect that something is amiss before the pastor's attention is diverted. But alas, he soon realizes he has lost not only the eyes of his audience, but also their attention, and it is clear that each is trying mightily to suppress a laugh. The lecture ceases and the pastor looks around to assess for himself what is happening on the other side of the glass doors. There behind his back is Maria von Wedemeyer, sitting cross-legged on the floor, mimicking him with outlandish faces and exaggerated gestures. Dietrich Bonhoeffer is not amused.

SEPTEMBER. On the twenty-seventh of the month, Alla Stahlberg, in the office of the Stahlberg mill at Stettin, receives a call from Göttingen University in western Germany. The caller is Dietrich

Bonhoeffer, who modestly inquires whether Herr Stahlberg
remembers him from their encounter on Ruth von Kleist's birthday well over a year ago. Of course Alla remembers. Dietrich has
an urgent request. The Gestapo will probably close Finkenwalde
tomorrow; an informant in the SS headquarters at Stettin notified the housekeeper by phone. Could Alla find a place for a
Bechstein piano? The reply is affirmative; everyone would find a
place for a Bechstein grand if it were offered. Dietrich goes on to
explain that this piano was a personal gift to him and must be
removed by the end of the day, for whatever is left will be confiscated. Alla assures his caller that the instrument will be moved
today, and also that it will be maintained and used, for the family
of Spes Stahlberg is above all a musical one. It will be waiting for
Dietrich when this mess is finally over. Alla is immediately in
touch with a mover, and before nightfall the impressive piano
stands in his spacious apartment.

The informant was correct, for on this morning of the twenty-
eighth the Gestapo arrive at Finkenwalde. There are few papers
to be found; what remains are just the simple furnishings of a
near-monastic seminary, including hand-drawn chapel banners
and chair seat covers sewn by the old Countess Lili von Kleist.
The doors are sealed; it is indeed the end of Finkenwalde.

DECEMBER. Dietrich's long-awaited book, *The Cost of Discipleship*,
is finally published. Ruth orders thirty copies from the publisher,
ten for her family and twenty for the Stettin study group. She
reads the book through over several sleepless nights. It is
Dietrich's definitive statement on the Lordship of Christ.
German theologians, who in all generations have a penchant for
cataloging one's statement of faith, will later give it a name—
Christology. Ruth's mind skips to Ewald and his Old Testament
thunder. Will this book do anything to move him in Dietrich's
direction?

Dietrich's prayer list now numbers 804 prisoners of conscience. In her Stettin flat, at each evening prayer, Ruth prays for
the entire group.

1938. Dietrich Bonhoeffer is not permitted to enter the city of
Berlin by recent directive of the district Gestapo. Hence the
pastor is living between the remaining collective pastorates of the

fading Confessing Church. These pastorates are the remnants of the mission parishes that less than two years ago were to be the hope of the church. He is also a frequent visitor at Klein Krössin if the Frau von Kleist is at home, and otherwise at Kieckow.

FEBRUARY. During the annual holiday for German youth rallies, Ruth is at home in Klein Krössin. Dietrich is with her, occupying the guest room called Hope, which is now exclusively reserved for him.

One evening, he confesses his immense frustration in not being able to return to Berlin—to see his parents and to speak with his sisters, his brother and his brothers-in-law. Still viewing herself as the powerful matriarch of a powerful family, Ruth picks up the phone and orders Dietrich to phone Berlin. Why not have Dietrich meet his parents at Stettin—in Ruth's own flat?

Two days later, Dr. and Mrs. Karl Bonhoeffer are reunited with their son in Stettin. Dr. Bonhoeffer brings good news. The Berlin Gestapo have assured him that prohibition of family visits to Berlin by their son is not the intent of the government ban. Once again it is demonstrated that these days one needs friends in high places.

Quite satisfied with herself for arranging such an important meeting, Ruth returns to her reading—Paul's Letters to the Romans in concert with certain difficult sections of *The Cost of Discipleship*. It is certainly an absorbing pastime, but not nearly as absorbing as discussions with the author over tea and cake.

MARCH. There is joy across the land, for the age-old dream of a German Reich encompassing both Hohenzollern and Habsburg lands has now been achieved without bloodshed. German troops march into Austria; the Austrian chancellor capitulates without a whimper; and hundreds of thousands of Austrian citizens line the streets to cheer their German brothers. There is a parade in Belgard, and a nationwide directive orders all land and building owners to fly the flag of the Third Reich in celebration.

A swastika is waving above the manure heap at Schmenzin, but no flag flies at Kieckow or at Klein Krössin. Hans Jürgen is arrested and taken to Belgard, to sit in the not-uncomfortable jail, one of the district buildings constructed while his father was Landrat, until he is contrite. There are three complaints lodged against him, no doubt originating somewhere in the village: Hans Jürgen refuses to say "Heil Hitler" when greeting people on the street; he refuses to fly the flag of the Third Reich; and he does not allow his children to participate in the youth activities of the district.

Fortunately Konstantin, Hans Jürgen's oldest son, has finished the gymnasium. He will inherit Kieckow one day, and until these political problems are settled, he will remain at home, assisting his father with the estate. With Konstantin, Mieze and the bailiff attending to estate matters, this landowner can afford to spend a week behind bars. He expects the local Gestapo to bend eventually, and in this year of 1938 it does.

At Pätzig, the home of the Wedemeyers, the old monarchical flag waves from the courtyard flagpole. On the side of the manor house, somewhat shielded by evergreens, hangs the swastika flag of Hitler's Germany. Hans von Wedemeyer has finally been cowed. He who formerly refused to fly Hitler's flag and who still refuses to say "Heil Hitler" was deprived of the permit required to manage his own estate last year, the equivalent of a sentence to bankruptcy under German law. Only through friends in the Justice Department, most specifically Fabian von Schlabrendorff, was Hans successful in appealing the decision. He and Ruthchen have discussed their situation at length; if flying a swastika flag behind the trees will save Pätzig for the family, this much they will oblige. It is a hard decision, especially when one must explain it to the children.

APRIL. The Kleists, the Bismarcks and the Wedemeyers are gathered at Kieckow for an occasion that traditionally matches both weddings and christenings in importance—the confirmation of two sons and a daughter. The service takes place in the Kieckow church, where the families of the confirmands overflow the patron's pews into the first two rows of the common seating area. Among the attributes often associated with the Prussian aristocracy is its propensity toward large numbers of children, and the congregation gathered on this confirmation Sunday is more than ample testimony to this!

Pastor Bonhoeffer is conducting the service, and he begins with a Scriptural reading from Mark 9:24: ". . . I believe; help Thou mine unbelief."

Confirmation at Kieckow: Jürgen Christoph von Kleist, Max von
Wedemeyer, Grandmother Ruth, Hans Friedrich von Kleist, Hans von
Wedemeyer and Hans Otto von Bismarck. All of the men shown here
were killed at the front during World War II.

The pastor's words include a hard challenge to the old as well
as to the young: ". . . Faith is a decision. Otherwise we have
nothing. 'You cannot serve two masters.' Unless you serve God
alone, you do not serve God at all. . . . And it must be your own
decision! No human being can help you with that. . . . Dear
Confirmands, your faith right now is but at its beginning . . . The
Christian community is the greatest gift of God's abundance. But
God can also take this gift from us if he chooses, as is happening
to so many of our brothers today. Then we stand or fall alone
with our own faith. . . . Your faith will not only cause you tribulation and suffering; it will also cause you to struggle. Confirmands
today are like young soldiers who go to war—the war of Jesus
Christ against the gods of this world. The war is already under

way; it is up to you now to march right in. . . . God leads the battle in us, against us and through us. . . . Amen"[33]

These are strong words for the confirmands as well as for the parents. They are the words Ruth wants most of all to hear.

The final denouement in the struggle of the Confessing Church comes before the month is over in the form of an exhortation by the German Christian Church to the stragglers among the clergy: "Let us make the führer a birthday present by all taking the oath of allegiance to Hitler in parallel with our oath to God." The pressures are immense since it is expected that those resisting will be barred forever from their calling. Ruth is absolutely astounded to learn that the Stettin office of the Confessing Church is encouraging its pastors to comply. She is relieved to learn that Paster Reimer of Naseband has refused to take the oath, and she is disturbed that so few others follow his lead. Ruth forgets perhaps that unlike many of his colleagues, Pastor Reimer has as his patron the unbending Ewald von Kleist. Would that every pastor had such a patron!

When the tally is completed, more than two-thirds of the Confessing Church clergy have taken the oath, albeit with troubled consciences. The stalwart remnant amounts to well under ten percent of the Protestant clergy, of whom half are already in prison. For all practical purposes, the Confessing Church is dead. The religious struggle, like the political struggle, will continue on another plane. Its bywords will be conspiracy, deception, intrigue and assassination—a calling for those few who have the stamina and the courage.

The Silver Wedding

1938: JUNE. In the homes of the villages of Kieckow and Klein Krössin, pressing boards and irons are visible everywhere this morning. Dark suits, normally reserved for weddings and funerals, submit to the hot steam of the heavy irons, followed by white shirts, outgrown confirmation dresses and altered wedding gowns. The entire population of both villages—over two hundred people—is getting ready for the festival to celebrate the twenty-fifth wedding anniversary of the master and the mistress. This inclusive invitation is unique in the Belgard District, where

The silver wedding procession. Above, Mieze and Hans Jürgen von Kleist, Ruth and Hans Friedrich von Kleist, three more Kleist children, the Bismarcks and others. At right, villagers and workers.

ordinarily landowners are not inclined to celebrate family festivals in the company of their workers. But these are not ordinary times, and Hans Jürgen von Kleist is not an ordinary landowner.

In the manor house, the older children carry linens and table settings from the dining hall into the library, the sitting room and the family living room. The plan was to serve on the back terrace and on the front entry platform, but the cold weather has changed all that. One way or another, Mieze intends that all two hundred guests will dine inside the manor house. For once, even the contents of the Kieckow silver chest and china cupboards are not enough. A servant is asked to drive Konstantin to Grandmother Ruth's for additional table supplies. They return not only with Grandmother's flatware, plates and napkins, but also with huge bundles of lavender and white phlox from her garden at Klein Krössin. The two youngest children and their nurse are now called into service to find vases and fill them with table bouquets. Upon viewing the final arrangements, Hans Jürgen declares them to be nothing short of spectacular.

The festivities begin at 11:00 A.M. with a short service in the church. The pastor has come down from Gross Tychow and, as a surprise to the landowner's family, has put together a children's choir to sing the hymns of praise such an occasion requires. The

four family pews behind the communion rail are entirely occupied by the anniversary couple, their six children, one grandmother and assorted relatives from other estates. Their Kleist cousin and neighbor Ewald is also present, though he sits in the first row of the common pews. With him are his six children and the young woman he has just married, barely a year after his first wife's death. These Schmenzin Kleists are a sober lot, even on this day when smiling faces are the rule.

The pastor's pleasant smile belies the strains that plague him daily. So far he has resisted all the pressures brought to bear on him by the government and the church; one fears that his days as a pastor are numbered. Hans Jürgen has nothing but good to say of this pastor: "He is the exception—a theologian with faith!" Fortunate is the parish where such harmony rules.

The pastor is also perceptive, and today he knows that a short service with an even shorter sermon is called for. In fact he suspects that this unusual wedding anniversary service is only an excuse to have all two hundred guests gather with the family at the church before parading to the manor house. The final hymn, "Praise to the Lord,"[34] is sung from memory while the entire congregation organizes for the procession—Hans Jürgen and Mieze in the lead, followed by Grandmother Ruth on the arm of Hans Friedrich, then Elisabeth, Jürgen Christoph and Heinrich. Behind them are Maria and Herbert von Bismarck with their daughter Spes and the other children of the two families. After that come the village families, who have obviously stretched their meager resources to the limit to dress properly for the occasion.

The anniversary banquet, with its toasts, its speeches, and its songs, is nothing short of a love feast. For a time, this day will be spoken of as a relic of the past, not to be compared with the pageantry and festivals of the new, modern Germany. Later, after the pageantry and festivals of the nation have turned to dust, this day will be remembered as the last great Kieckow festival—a gentle farewell to a dying era.

AUGUST. Late summer finds Ruth biding her time in Stettin, faithfully minding the children's boardinghouse. Right now there are only three children in school at Stettin: Spes von Bismarck, Hans Friedrich von Kleist and Maria von Wedemeyer. Ruth Alice, Maria's sister, has completed the gymnasium with honors in every course. Her grandmother misses her terribly, for Ruth Alice has so many qualities that lent peace and stability to this Stettin home away from home. However, Grandmother Ruth has cause to rejoice for her gentle granddaughter and namesake, for Ruth Alice is engaged to Klaus von Bismarck, the heir to Kniephof. He is the son of Gottfried from Ruth's first children's pension and the grandson of Hedwig, once the young widow of Kniephof, who forty years ago advised and encouraged Ruth in her own early widowhood. Earlier in the year, Klaus took over management of the estate after a long apprenticeship at Pätzig. Klaus's mother Gertrud, the intellectual from Berlin, was also an early widow who held together for her son the lands of her husband's forefathers. Gertrud and Ruth have always held divergent views on life, but fortunately they have both mellowed over the years, and their differences are now a source of amusement between the two families. There is only joy over this further binding of the Bismarcks and the Kleists.

Ruth's pension now has two guest rooms, and Dietrich sees to it that they are usually occupied. Among all of his other activities he has now taken on the task of arranging visas for the Jews of his church; some are Christian pastors, some are wives of pastors, and others are friends and acquaintances who have turned to him for help. Dietrich's connections with Sweden are beginning to bear modest fruit, but securing visas for these victims of the Third Reich takes time, and those who pay attention at all can see that time is running out.

Just as Dietrich keeps a list of prisoners to be prayed for, he also keeps a list of Jews to be cared for and a list of homes to provide the care. The list of prisoners is now distributed widely, not only to widen the prayer circle but also to embarrass the authorities. Dietrich alone has access to the other lists.

For the time being, Ruth is sheltering two young Christian women, one of whom she knew from the Finkenwalde days. Both are Jews according to the well-defined statutes of the new Germany, both have families who are not as fortunate as they, and both want desperately to leave the country with their husbands. Evening prayer at the Stettin flat is more fervent than ever before.

Maria von Wedemeyer, the youngest and always the liveliest of the children at the pension, has surprised her grandmother and her cousins this year. It turns out she is gifted in mathematics, and at the Stettin gymnasium she is called upon to assist the other, less talented students. Ruth now regrets how stern she has been with this child, particularly in the presence of Dietrich and the Finkenwalde circle. Even with the distractions at hand, Grandmother Ruth now gives Maria more of her undivided attention.

With Finkenwalde closed, Ruth is forced to turn to the pastors of Stettin for her spiritual guidance. A number of them are affiliated with the Confessing Church; all but three took the oath to Hitler in the spring. Ruth continues to take the grandchildren to church each Sunday, alternating among the three churches whose pastors resisted the immense pressure. Still, without the challenge of Finkenwalde, there is a great void in this grandmother's heart.

All through life Ruth has had trouble sleeping. The positive side of this condition is the immense number of letters that flow from her pen, mostly now to Dietrich and to Eberhard Bethge, the latter usually more accessible than his widely traveled friend. Ruth is working on another book, a kind of collective letter addressed to her twenty-two living grandchildren and entitled, *Why Should One Read the Bible?* It is a compendium of the questions they have asked her at one time or another—questions that are universal in their simplicity. In replying to each of these queries, Ruth draws on a lifetime of experience and her growing arsenal of theological arguments. She is quite satisfied with her modest work and sends a copy of the manuscript for Eberhard's critique. For Ruth, this serious business of the children's religious education is a welcome distraction from the political battles her spiritual friends are forced to wage.

Barely five months after the joining of Austria to Germany, Hitler is talking—in fact screaming—about annexing the Sudetenland, a German-speaking area that was once part of the Austrian Empire but since Versailles has been under Czechoslovakian rule. Ruth despairs over the nation's leadership, but among the masses there is a veritable stampede in support of Hitler's latest objective. However, unknown to the "soldier" in the Kleist outpost at Stettin, a significant change has taken place on the ancient Kleist lands of the Belgard District. Hans Jürgen and Ewald, also two of the Fatherland's most faithful "soldiers," have quietly entered into conspiracy against the German government.

Early on the morning of August 15, Hans Jürgen drives to Schmenzin to pick up Ewald, intent on delivering him to the railroad station at Gross Tychow. Ewald knows that the ride will take longer than usual, due to Hans Jürgen's propensity for driving slowly and carefully, but he needs a few private moments with his cousin before he boards the train to Berlin. With as few words as possible, Ewald explains the nature of the trip, which so far is known only to his wife Alice, for in all probability Hans Jürgen may also be called upon to act in unexpected ways.

The trip has been suggested to Ewald by the Abwehr, the Office of Army Counterintelligence, and all of the arrangements are being made through Fabian von Schlabrendorff, who is like ' family to the Kleists of Belgard since his engagement to Luitgarde von Bismarck. The Abwehr is one of three government agencies the Nazi Party and the SS have not seriously penetrated. It is still relatively free from inquiry and maintains its freedom to act. The other two are the upper echelons of the Army Officer Corps and some segments of the Justice Department. Though in a tenuous position himself, Fabian holds onto his post in the

Justice Department and cultivates trusted contacts in the army. Ewald speaks glowingly of Fabian's role in this delicate matter; Hans Jürgen worries about Fabian's fiancée, the lovely Luitgarde.

Ewald apprises Hans Jürgen of the situation inside the Abwehr. Admiral Wilhelm Canaris, its director, who reports directly to the führer, and Colonel Hans Oster, second in command, are of the opinion that Hitler will destroy the nation if he is allowed to proceed unchecked. Canaris plays the führer's loyal servant, while Oster acts the devious spy. Both are masters of intelligence, and both know how to use this powerful tool to manipulate events in Europe in a manner that will check Hitler before he makes his next offensive move—the destruction of Czechoslovakia. Oster has communicated these interests to General Ludwig Beck, chief of the Army General Staff, and to Baron Ernst von Weizsäcker, deputy foreign minister. Beck is confident of mounting a military coup, perhaps by bringing back the Hohenzollern monarchy to give it some legitimacy, if Hitler fails to deliver the Sudetenland* to the German populace. The strategy of this mission is to raise fears in western Europe sufficient to generate an ultimatum from Czechoslovakia's allies, Britain and France, hoping to undermine the public support Hitler is currently enjoying at home.

But who is to commit the dastardly deed—that is, inform the government of Great Britain, traditionally one of the Fatherland's adversaries, of Germany's military designs on eastern Europe? And that is not all the emissary must do. Whoever carries the message to London must also ask the British government not only to issue an ultimatum to Germany, but to act on it in the event Hitler makes a move toward Czechoslovakia.

Ewald is candid as to why Oster, through Fabian, has turned to him. For all of the bold talk inside the Abwehr, the army and the Foreign Office, no one has volunteered to undertake the mission—no one wants to betray the Fatherland. Ewald sees himself cast in the role of the obscure conservative, unknown internationally, but the sort of person who might speak the same language as the British conservatives who are in power. More

---

*The "Sudeten lands," named for the Sudeten mountain range, are the areas of Czechoslovakia claimed by Hitler.

likely the reason is that he is known to have no fear of the empty-headed majority nor of its leadership.

Ewald concludes with his rationalization for taking on this mission, which many would construe as treason. "Last night I read again from the Old Testament—my old friend Jeremiah. God is with me. Of this I am certain." With that the two men part, and Ewald boards the train. Fabian is waiting at the station in Berlin to meet Ewald and to inform him that all arrangements are in order. For this he is indebted to Ian Colvin, an English journalist working in the city, who is in fact a British spy. He has arranged everything, including visa, airline tickets, hotel accommodations, and the necessary appointments in London.

Through Colvin, Fabian has just learned that there is a hitch. The planned meeting with the British prime minister is in jeopardy, for the British ambassador in Berlin has gotten wind of everything. He has warned leaders of his government not to speak officially with Kleist, an emissary of the German opposition. Fabian is furious, but Ewald will not be disheartened.

The following morning Ewald is aboard the plane to London, and by evening he is comfortably situated at the Park Lane Hotel. During the three days that follow, he is alternately encouraged and he is disappointed. Neville Chamberlain, the prime minister, is unavailable; however, the leader of the opposition, Winston Churchill, spends the afternoon with Ewald and invites him to dinner. Churchill takes to heart his visitor's grim message. Hitler is intent on having hegemony in eastern Europe. Without some move on Britain's part, the Sudetenland will be seized before the middle of September. There are firm plans to absorb all of Czechoslovakia, and after that, to invade Poland. A propaganda barrage to gain support for these measures will be unleashed in late September. Yet there is an underlying reluctance on the part of the Germans to go to war; too many still live with the legacy of the World War. Ewald believes that Hitler's policies of aggression will rally the people to the opposition, and in his view, the generals will refuse to march. If Czechoslovakia's allies rally in defense of that beleaguered land, a coup in Germany is imminent.

What Ewald does not know is that on this very day in Berlin, General Beck has resigned as army chief of staff, for he wants no part in an invasion of Czechoslovakia. To the detriment of the opposition, his resignation is kept secret until October.

Churchill is sympathetic to Kleist's viewpoint, but he offers little in the way of encouragement, maintaining that the current British government is too cowardly to act. Ewald returns to Berlin knowing his mission has failed. A few days later, however, he receives a letter from Churchill through diplomatic channels in which Churchill records on paper the action he would take if he were prime minister of Great Britain. To Ewald's satisfaction, it contains everything for which he had pleaded. He turns a copy of the letter over to Fabian, who in turn passes it on to Canaris. In this way does the name of Ewald von Kleist first find its way into the files of the German Abwehr.

SEPTEMBER. On the last day of the month, British Prime Minister Neville Chamberlain, French Premier Edouard Daladier, Italian dictator Benito Mussolini, and German Führer Adolf Hitler meet in Munich. One of the stipulations they agree to is that it is reasonable for Germany to annex the Sudeten portion of Czechoslovakia.

OCTOBER. The German army crosses the border into Czechoslovakia and occupies the entire western portion of that nation. In Great Britain, on the streets and in Parliament, a tremendous welcome awaits the returning Chamberlain, a hero who has brought "peace in our time." In the House of Commons, Winston Churchill literally sits on his hands and refuses to take part in the standing ovation.

At Stettin a school holiday is declared. Here too there is a tumultuous celebration culminating in a torchlight parade, which Grandmother Ruth and her three grandchildren do not attend. They remain in their flat on this night, playing a game of dice with their two Jewish house guests. It is a game they all know and love—"Hindenburg and Ludendorff." At Schmenzin and at Kieckow, the master and mistress sit together and talk long after the children have gone to bed.

NOVEMBER. *Kristallnacht*—Crystal Night, the two nights and days during which mobs of people in cities and towns all over Germany burn down the synagogues, shatter windows and loot Jewish shops and homes—has come and gone. The German newspapers label it a spontaneous uprising of the citizenry against these subhuman people. All Jews are barred from the government and the professions. Private businesses are confiscated. Most Jews now are without any means of support.

DECEMBER. The Stettin flat is closed for the Advent season. Ruth is at Klein Krössin, and all three guest rooms are occupied. A former student of Dietrich's is recuperating after an operation, and two of his Jewish friends are awaiting visas to Sweden. Dietrich is also there, along with Werner Koch. After two years in prison and concentration camps, Werner has just been released, in accordance with an order signed by Heinrich Himmler personally. Ruth believes Werner's freedom is the result of a combination of fervent prayer and divine intervention. Dietrich knows it also has to do with good connections to those followers of Satan who now sit in high places.

VI

THE PASTOR'S FRIEND

1939-1943

Conflicts of Conscience

JANUARY. The pastor at Gross Tychow has been relieved of his duties, including preaching at the Kieckow church. He bids a heartfelt farewell to Kieckow and especially to Hans Jürgen and Mieze. Unburdening his soul to Mieze, he confesses that he is totally disillusioned with the church organization, as well as with his own spiritual condition. Mieze urges him to call on Dietrich, who is currently visiting his collective pastorates in Pomerania.

The new pastor is an enthusiastic German Christian who eschews the Old Testament and uses his sermon privileges as an opportunity to denounce the Jews. Hans Jürgen, Mieze and Grandmother sit through just one of the pastor's sermons. From then on they drive to Naseband on Sundays, where Pastor Reimer is still preaching, under the protection of his patron, Ewald von Kleist. Mieze is pleased to hear that the Kieckow church is almost empty on Sundays.

FEBRUARY. Dietrich Bonhoeffer is spending his birthday at a collective pastorate near Köslin. In the mail he receives greetings from all three of his recent confirmands. The hand of their grandmother is conspicuous in that all three letters are written on the same kind of paper!

> Honorable Pastor Bonhoeffer, I wish you all the best on your birthday. We are busy with preparations for grandmother's birthday. We plan to celebrate both birthdays joyfully. We are looking forward to seeing you in the future. Best greetings from Spes von Bismarck

Honorable Pastor, I wish you much happiness and God's blessings for your work in the next year. May this work prevail. All is well with me. I look forward very much to your next visit. With many greetings to all the other brethren, I am your faithful Hans Friedrich [von Kleist]

Dear Mr. Pastor, I congratulate you on your birthday and wish you all the best. At Templin all is well with me. I am doing better in school than I did at Stettin. The religious instruction, however, is not so good. The teacher lectures the entire hour and never asks questions. For this reason almost everyone falls asleep. Many greetings, your Max [von Wedemeyer]

Ruth celebrates her birthday in Stettin. Eberhard Bethge sends his congratulations. A day later, she travels by train to Köslin with two objectives in mind—one of a family sort and the other personal.

Hans Jürgen's daughter Ruthi, now twelve years old, is temporarily in school at Köslin, living with family friends. She has outgrown the education provided at home, and her parents don't want her exposed to the Nazi teacher in the village school; yet Grandmother has deemed her too young for the family boardinghouse in Stettin. At Mieze's urging, Ruth has agreed to meet alone with Ruthi, away from home, to evaluate the child's maturity. At a konditorei in Köslin, over tea and cakes, Ruthi and Grandmother discuss school, friends, goals and interests. It is a sober discussion, and Ruthi does her best to be acceptable to Grandmother, whom she has been taught to respect above all others. When the tea party is finished, Grandmother walks Ruthi home, gives her a kiss and announces, "Yes, Ruthi, I believe you are ready. I will tell your mother, and after Easter you may join us in Stettin."

(Ruthi has passed Grandmother's stern test, yet she will never join the Stettin pension, for after Easter it will no longer exist.)

This family issue resolved, Ruth turns to her personal objective in this visit to Köslin. She phones Dietrich, and on the very next afternoon after the tea party with Ruthi, she is once again having tea and cakes at the konditorei, this time with her dear friend. A military call-up is in effect nationwide, and it includes all men

Eberhard Bethge and Dietrich Bonhoeffer,
near Köslin

born before 1907, among them Dietrich Bonhoeffer. Ruth wants
to know how Dietrich will respond. The two of them have talked
at length about objections of conscience to military service.
Dietrich admits to having been a pacifist earlier in his life, but he
insists that events in Germany have demonstrated to him, beyond
a doubt, the fallacy of pacifism in the presence of evil.

Still Ruth worries that Dietrich might declare himself a conscientious objector. A friend in Stettin has done this. He is now in
prison, and Ruth fears for his life.

Ruth's fears are well founded. Her friend Hermann Störr will
be tried as a conscientious objector and subsequently executed.

Dietrich has thought long and hard on the question of military
service under Hitler, and he is determined not to serve. He does
not intend to declare himself a pacifist, for he is not a pacifist,
and to declare himself a conscientious objector would have
serious repercussions on the reputation of the Confessing
Church abroad. Dietrich confides to Ruth that he is making

arrangements to go to England, for how long he is not sure. Ruth wonders if this will be their last meeting, but she is too proud to ask.

Dietrich inquires of Ruth whether the recruiting office director in Schlawe, one Major von Kleist, is a relative. Of course he is, and Ruth knows exactly where this Kleist officer fits into the family tree; she will intercede. It only takes one phone call. Dietrich Bonhoeffer's military service is postponed until further notice.

Upon her return to Stettin, Ruth writes to Eberhard:

> You have again given me to feel what a gift I have in my friendship with you [Eberhard and Dietrich] . . . Your guidance encourages me and it strengthens me. I cannot imagine that I would ever err when it comes to the church of Christ. . . . I feel as if I am a sort of mother to you both, meaning that I not only am comforted by you but also may accept your guidance.

MARCH. Dietrich leaves by train for London. He has information that Hitler will shortly deliver an ultimatum to the crippled Czechoslovakia, and he is relieved to leave the country before this potential war threat is unleashed. In London he meets with the Bishop of Chichester and asks for counsel as to ways in which he might serve the Confessing Church from abroad, perhaps in the spirit of ecumenism. The bishop makes suggestions and is left with the understanding that Dietrich plans to flee Germany.

There are nine German Evangelical Church parishes in England, all affiliated with the Confessing Church. Dietrich meets with the London parishioners, and together they lament the failure of the ecumenical movement to intervene positively in the struggles of the German church.

While in London, Dietrich also has an emotional reunion with his twin sister Sabine Leibholz and her Jewish husband, who left Germany just before all non-Aryan passports were declared invalid.

In Germany, it is happening just as Dietrich predicted. Hitler summons the president of Czechoslovakia to Berlin and threatens to destroy Prague from the air if Czech forces resist German troops. The president yields, and at midnight German troops cross the border into Czechoslovakia. Hitler flies to Prague and declares Czechoslovakia to be a German protectorate. The small nation's army is dissolved, all secondary schools and universities are closed, and a program is implemented to eliminate Jews and intellectuals.

Hitler now turns his attentions to Poland, demanding the Free City of Danzig and an extraterritorial right-of-way through Poland to East Prussia. The Polish government refuses.

APRIL. In Stettin, Ruth reads the most recent pronouncement of the German Christian Church and shudders:

> [National Socialism continues] the work of Martin Luther on the ideological and political side [and thus helps], in its religious aspect, the recovery of a true understanding of the Christian faith . . . The Christian faith is the unbridgeable religious contrast to Judaism. . . . Supranational and international churchism of a Roman Catholic or world-Protestant character is a political degeneration of Christianity.[35]

Dietrich Bonhoeffer does return from England, but he seems totally preoccupied with his military status, intent on postponing his call-up.

Ruth's children decide it is time to close the grandchildren's pension. Spes is in her final year at the gymnasium; Hans Friedrich and Maria will have to go elsewhere. Grandmother Ruth and her cook will remain at the flat in Stettin, but the cook's helper will return to Kieckow and will probably marry the young man who has waited so patiently for nearly four years.

MAY. While Germany and Italy are concluding a "pact of steel," British and French representatives are in Moscow, discussing with the Soviet Union a common front against the Fatherland. The discussions do not go well, and the German propaganda machine makes the most of this dissension among "thieves."

JUNE. On June 2, Luitgarde von Bismarck is married to Fabian von Schlabrendorff, her father's former assistant in the Prussian

Interior Ministry and now his accomplice in activities of which very little is spoken. The wedding takes place at Lasbeck with both of Luitgarde's grandmothers present—Hedwig von Bismarck and Ruth von Kleist. The bride and groom leave for London immediately after the banquet, ostensibly to visit Windsor Castle and learn more about Fabian's great-grandfather, who was an advisor to Queen Victoria. No one questions this combined honeymoon and family research project; it is a little unusual, but certainly acceptable in these modern times.

As a matter of fact the entire wedding trip has been arranged by Abwehr Director Canaris so that Fabian can meet with the most powerful man of the opposition in the British Parliament— Winston Churchill.

A week later in England, while Luitgarde tours the Victoria and Albert Museum, Fabian takes the train south from London to Churchill's country house. His host has agreed to the meeting since Fabian's introduction comes from a very high place, namely the top echelon of Germany's military command. Still the initial confrontation is strained. Churchill invites Fabian to take a seat in his library. Fabian then attempts to clarify his awkward position by announcing that he is not a Nazi, but rather a patriot. Churchill is amused and puckishly replies, "So am I."

With that the discussion commences. Fabian tells this British leader as much as he knows about the various opposition groups. Churchill seems not to be listening. When Fabian finishes, the Englishman asks bluntly if there will be a coup soon. Fabian answers in the negative. Churchill shows his disappointment very clearly by rising from his chair, as if to indicate that there is nothing further to be said. Fabian rises also and extends his hand in farewell. At this point he puts into words the key information that Canaris has given him: This very day Germany is dealing secretly with the Soviet Union, even as British and French representatives are in Moscow discussing mutual guarantees.

Churchill looks stunned; his eyes suggest both surprise and urgency. Yet he recovers sufficiently to clasp Fabian's hand firmly in both of his, a silent gesture of appreciation.

On the way back to London, Fabian imagines that the powerful opposition leader is already on the phone with the British

Foreign Office. He is eager to rejoin Luitgarde. This much he can tell her.

The certainty of war grows stronger, and Dietrich Bonhoeffer is making arrangements for another trip, this time to the United States. From Klein Krössin, it appears that he is abandoning the remains of the Confessing Church that are still tucked away in the Pomeranian hinterland. Worse than that, in Ruth's view, he is abandoning Germany in its darkest hour. She holds her tongue, though, even within the family. The affection she holds for Dietrich is now a familywide affair.

Early in June Dietrich Bonhoeffer leaves Germany for the Atlantic crossing to New York. On board ship he already has doubts as to the rightness of his decision. Writing to his brethren pastors in Germany, he anguishes:

> We ought to be found only where He is. We can no longer in fact be anywhere else than where He is. Whether it is you working over there, or I working in America, we are all only where He is. He takes us with Him. Or have I, after all, avoided the place where He is? The place where He is for me?

In New York Dietrich is welcomed by friends and colleagues. There are offers of lectureships and an offer to work with refugees. In America Dietrich Bonhoeffer is viewed as a distinguished theologian—a German of conscience who has sought refuge from the mad Hitler and his intolerable government. But Dietrich is a troubled man, as his diary entries attest:[36]

> June 13. With all of this, there is only Germany lacking— the brethren. The first lonely hours are difficult. I do not know why I am here, whether it is wise, whether the result will be worthwhile . . . Now almost a fortnight has gone without my knowing what is happening there. It is almost unbearable.
>
> June 14. Prayers . . . in which we remember the German brethren almost overwhelm me.
>
> June 15. My thoughts about Germany have not left me since yesterday evening. I should not have thought it possible for anyone of my age, after so many years abroad, to

be so terribly homesick. . . . The whole weight of self-reproach because of a wrong decision comes back and almost chokes one.

June 22. I have made a mistake in coming to America. I must live through this difficult period of our national history with the Christian people of Germany. I will have no right to participate in the reconstruction of Christian life in Germany after the war if I do not share the trials of this time with my people . . . Christians in Germany will face the terrible alternative of either willing the defeat of their nation in order that Christian civilization may survive, or willing the victory of their nation and thereby destroying our civilization. I know which of these alternatives I must choose; but I cannot make that choice in security.

June 30. I cannot think it is God's will that, if war comes, I am to stay here with no special task. I must leave on the earliest possible date.

JULY. Immense pressures are being exerted on Dietrich to stay in America, but he is unmoved. The night before boarding ship he makes a short entry in his diary:

July 7. The last day. Paul [Lehmann] is still trying to keep me back. It will not do now . . . I go on board with Paul. Good-bye at half past eleven.

Dietrich arrives in London on July 15 and spends ten days there with his twin Sabine and her family. On July 25 he leaves London, and on the twenty-seventh he is home with his parents in Berlin.

IN THE YEAR 1914, on July 17, there was a magnificent gathering of the Bismarck and Kleist families at Kieckow. The occasion was the christening of Luitgarde von Bismarck and Ferdinande von Kleist. It was clear on that day that war was at hand and that this would be the last event within an order that would soon disappear. Even at the christening, the day was spoken of in terms of being "our last." Two weeks later the war began, and as prophesied on that day, it was never the same again in old Prussia.

Now, on July 15 of 1939, there is another great gathering of the Bismarck and Kleist families, this one at Pätzig, home of the Wedemeyers. The occasion is the marriage of Ruth Alice von Wedemeyer to Klaus von Bismarck of Kniephof, a marriage that is rejoiced in at many levels.

The Pätzig manor house, its church, its gardens and its lake are among the loveliest spots in the entire Neumark. The Pätzig church is especially beautiful with its huge hand-chiseled wooden cross towering above a simple stone altar. For this wedding, the altar, the pulpit, and even the window sills are covered with roses, lilies and larkspur from the Pätzig gardens.

Ruth Alice in white and Klaus in uniform stand before Pastor Stählin, founder of the Berneuchen Movement, to which the Wedemeyers are still deeply attached. He is speaking at length about marriage, about Christ, about God, and about godlessness and war. It is an unusual message, but then these are unusual times. Then the bride and groom repeat the traditional vows and are declared to be united in Christ. After the final benediction, the couple turns to face the congregation—a large gathering of the old Prussian aristocracy.

There are the assorted Bismarcks—Klaus's grandmother Hedwig and his mother Gertrud from Kniephof, as well as his brothers and sisters, his aunt and uncle, Maria and Herbert from Lasbeck, their six children, Klaus's cousins, and Fabian von Schlabrendorff, who was married to Luitgarde in June. On Ruth Alice's side, besides the cousins she shares with Klaus, there are her grandmother Ruth from Klein Krössin, the family from Kieckow, Tante Spes and the Stahlberg cousins from Berlin, plus a Wedemeyer aunt and uncle, and of course the bride's parents—Ruthchen and Hans von Wedemeyer—and her three sisters and three brothers, the youngest Peter Christian, just three years old. There hardly seems room for more, but there are also the godparents and a collection of relatives whose relationship to the family is closer than the family tree would suggest.

Like the christening at Kieckow twenty-five years ago, this wedding at Pätzig carries the heavy burden of possibly being the last such gathering. Even the procession to the manor house, always a spectacle to behold, moves at a slower pace than usual, as if to plant it more firmly into each participant's memory.

The wedding procession at Pätzig: marriage of Ruth
Alice von Wedemeyer to Klaus von Bismarck

The banquet begins with the standing silent toast—to
Wilhelm, the Prussian king, now an old man living in Holland.
(Nowadays even this takes courage.) Then come the customary
speeches, the many courses of food, and afterward the dancing
in the great hall of the manor house.

After dinner, out on one of the terraces, Fabian von Schlabrendorff is approached by Gerd von Tresckow of Wartenberg,
cousin to the bride's mother Ruthchen, nephew to Grandmother
Ruth, and neighbor to Pätzig. Though Gerd has not met Fabian
previously, he does not mince words with this new cousin by marriage. Gerd's brother Henning is at Wartenberg this weekend.
The Tresckows know that Fabian was in England, sent by the
Abwehr, and Henning wants desperately to speak with him. How
about tomorrow?

At Wartenberg on the following morning, Fabian von
Schlabrendorff is introduced to Henning von Tresckow, veteran

of the World War and now colonel in the German army. Before the Nazis came to power, Henning was one of those who expected great things from Adolf Hitler. After they took power, this expectation turned to contempt. Alone with Fabian, Henning puts forth his thesis. Hitler will start the war soon; he will have early victories, and he will then be tempted to take on Russia, for his eyes have always been on the East. For a while England will carry on alone and there will be a stalemate, just as there was in the World War. During that time, the industrial power of the West will grow immensely. Then, as in the first war, America will enter and it will all be over.

Henning believes that neither Hitler nor the Foreign Office understands this. The only way to affect the outcome is to intervene and destroy the government. One cannot do this with noble statements and symbolic gestures; one must also use tools that otherwise would be unacceptable—duplicity, falsehood and assassination. Henning concludes by asking Fabian to communicate to Canaris his views and his readiness to act. He sees his role in the opposition as more than a recruiter of staff officers in the field. When the time comes for disposing of the führer, count on him to commit the act.

AUGUST. On August 24, while British and French representatives are still in Moscow talking, the Soviets and the Germans surprise the world by announcing a newly signed nonaggression pact. What is known to only a few, among them Canaris, Oster, Ewald, Fabian and now Henning, is that in a secret portion of this pact, the two giants have agreed to divide Poland between them.

A day later, England signs a mutual assistance pact with Poland, guaranteeing Poland's borders. On this day Ewald von Kleist is in Stockholm, his trip arranged by Canaris and former Army Chief of Staff Beck. His task is to ascertain through Swedish informants whether England will indeed declare war in support of Poland. The information is positive, and Ewald communicates it immediately to Canaris, but he has no illusions. A year ago, for this kind of information, he could have promised a German coup; this time he has nothing to offer. As far as he knows, the centers of opposition within the German military dissolved a year ago with the signing of the Munich Pact.

SEPTEMBER. On September 1, just six weeks after the wedding at Pätzig, German forces invade Poland. The following day England and France deliver a joint ultimatum to Germany. It is ignored. On September 3, both nations declare war on the Fatherland.

Commitment to Conspiracy

OCTOBER. Victory in Poland is swift—thirty-five days, to be exact, from the September 1 invasion. On the seventeenth, Russian troops cross Poland's borders from the east. On the twenty-seventh, Warsaw surrenders to the Germans. On the twenty-eighth the German and Soviet foreign ministers agree on the dividing line between German and Soviet conquests. On October 5 the last Polish forces surrender.

In the wake of the military conquerors come the German SS occupation divisions. For the next six years they will have complete jurisdiction over these lands. By October all Polish Jews are being herded into walled ghetto areas hurriedly constructed in Polish towns. Auschwitz, the first of the concentration and death camps, is also under construction. Others will be added shortly. It will be several months before the massive operation of transporting Jews to these camps gets under way.

By the end of the year, the grim program Hitler announced earlier is being carried out across German-held Polish lands— the systematic internment and killing of Polish intellectuals, clergy and politicians. When it is all over, more than six million Poles will have died, 3,200,000 of them Jews.

1940. Documentation of the atrocities now being routinely committed in Poland has made its way to Berlin through military channels. Other reports are filtering through to the public by word of mouth and from the foreign press. At the Abwehr in Berlin, every military report, some of which are coming from the generals themselves, is being carefully cataloged to be used at the trial being planned for Hitler and other leaders of the Third Reich. The man responsible for building the case against Hitler is Hans von Dohnanyi, a lawyer recruited by Canaris.

Dohnanyi stands with Canaris and Oster as the third man in the Abwehr conspiracy. These conspirators are in touch with a small group of high officers in the army, who see it as their task to gain commitment from enough generals to ensure friendly military control in the event of a political coup. At the moment, the Abwehr plan is to seize Hitler at the time of the coup, then put him on trial so that the entire German nation will learn what the conspirators already know. After the trial, they hope to execute him. The plan also includes a provisional military-backed cabinet, with proposed ministers for every sector of the government. Just as the commitment of the generals is always in flux, so is the composition of this proposed cabinet. At all times it includes the name of Ewald von Kleist of Schmenzin, the leading proponent of monarchy-based legitimacy.

To increase the power base of the conspiracy in the Abwehr, Dohnanyi has recruited like-minded colleagues into the unit, ostensibly for their abilities and connections but in reality for their commitment to the overthrow of the German government. Three of these recruits are Dohnanyi's brothers-in-law—Rüdiger Schleicher and Klaus and Dietrich Bonhoeffer; Hans is married to Christine Bonhoeffer and Rüdiger is married to Ursula Bonhoeffer.

JANUARY. Reserve officers Hans Jürgen von Kleist and Hans von Wedemeyer, Ruth's son and son-in-law, are both in uniform. Six of her grandsons—Konstantin and Jürgen Christoph von Kleist, Alla and Hans Conrad Stahlberg, Jürgen and Hans Otto von Bismarck—are also reserve officers. One by one Ruth's grandsons visit their grandmother in their officer's dress. Her old Prussian heart is still stirred at the sight of young men in uniform, but at the same time her grandmotherly heart breaks to see them marching off to war.

By spring two more grandsons will be in the ranks of the military, Hans Friedrich von Kleist and Maximilian von Wedemeyer.

FEBRUARY. Ruth is at her Stettin flat, a more comfortable place than Klein Krössin during the cold winter months. Hardly a week goes by that she doesn't have a house guest of one sort or another.

Hans Otto is home on furlough from the western front. Proudly displaying his lieutenant's uniform, he makes a birthday call on Grandmother Ruth. Ruth observes that his blue eyes, which once sparkled so with mischief, now betray a serious bent. "Grandmama, my comrades speak so casually of death," he tells her. "I cannot do that. If I should fall, I would have only one wish. I would want to have time enough to prepare myself for it."

"Hans Otto," she assures him, "the fact that you have the wish means that you are prepared."

MARCH. Ruth no longer plays hostess to Jewish and half-Jewish strangers—friends and acquaintances of Dietrich who stayed with her while Dietrich arranged visas and passage to Sweden for them. With Germany now at war, the borders have been closed. It is now all but impossible to leave the country. One did not speak of Ruth's house guests while they lived in her flat or at Klein Krössin; one does not speak of them now that they are absent. Clearly it can only get worse for the Jews. A rumor is abroad that recently a large number of Jewish residents of Stettin were loaded into boxcars and transported to Poland. It is a rumor that everyone knows to be fact. (History will record that this freight train was the first transport of German Jews to the death camps in Poland.)

APRIL. All is quiet on the western front, where the German army stands face to face against French and British forces across an impenetrable wall of defense—the Maginot line. Far to the north of the Maginot line, the army of the Third Reich secures its first western victory. Troops marching into Norway and Denmark meet with very little resistance in conquering those countries for the Fatherland. In Pomerania one waits for the next move.

MAY. Colonel Henning von Tresckow becomes staff officer to General von Rundstedt, commander of the forces on the western front. The majority of the German generals advise against opening this front. When it is clear that Hitler, as commander in chief, will order it anyway, Henning becomes optimistic that it will lead to a stalemate and that the time will be ripe for the coup. Fabian is now in uniform, also on the western front, and Henning has integrated him into the network of military conspirators, this in addition to Fabian's continuing connections with Canaris's Abwehr group.

Reserve Officer Hans Jürgen von Kleist

Henning's optimism is ill founded. On May 10, German forces invade the Netherlands and Belgium, moving swiftly into France. It is no contest. The French troops have no will to fight, and the British commanders make serious tactical mistakes. In England, Neville Chamberlain resigns as prime minister. He is succeeded by Winston Churchill. Fabian and Ewald at least know what can now be expected from this adversary across the channel. Before the end of the month, the Netherlands and Belgium have surrendered and the British forces are routed. Those men not evacuated by ships from Dunkirk are captured.

German casualties are light and Hitler is ecstatic. In the wake of this stunning victory, the coup is his; forever after he will hold in contempt the generals of his army who advised against his bold initiatives.

On May 28, Ruth writes a round-robin letter to all of her "children" in the field—a son and son-in-law, nephews, grandsons, grandsons-in-law, godsons and young friends:

: the many field post numbers before me and I
it I simply cannot write each one as I would like
my eyes scan your dear names over and over
again. My heart tries to visualize you stationed at this
place or that in battle, but it is impossible.

What can I do for each one of you except to include
you in all of my prayers for intercession. It is a wonderful
thing—these prayers and the promise that God will hear
them.

Truly it is not that one simply asks, "Let them not fall."
God knows that this wish is most deeply anchored in our
hearts. We know as well as he does that though this life is
a precious gift, it is not the greatest good. Thus we pray
that God will keep you in every hour and that the
strength from him will always be greater than your suffering, your danger and your fears. . . .

With all my heart I hope that you will read these lines
with the spirit in which they were written. It must be
obvious to you that our thoughts are more out there than
here at home. How beautiful are the spring days here
after the hard winter! And out there the victories make
our hearts beat faster. But we must not forget that victories and blessings are not the same thing and that blood
and tears lie in our hearts.

We are very thankful that we live here at home in well-
ordered circumstances. And what a gift it is that we do
not have the war in our own land! But let us not be pre-
sumptuous.

Greeting you all from my heart, R. v. Kleist-Retzow

JUNE. At Lasbeck, at Stettin, at Kieckow and at Pätzig there is
little rejoicing over Germany's easy victories with so few casualties. Hans Otto von Bismarck, twenty years old, is among the
dead. Ruth writes:

> . . . we constantly live in fear of our faith at these times
> when God deals us such awful blows. How could it be
> otherwise since our faith is not like a reservoir. I remem-
> ber Dietrich's confirmation sermon: "One day is long
> enough for one's faith." I think of that so often when I

awake in the morning and the day greets me like a nightmare. Begin again; become empty again so that God's
grace may fill the vacuum. It is a comfort to be aware that
Christ knows above all how hard it is.

On the night of June 16, Marshal Henri Petain of France sends
to Hitler a request for an armistice. On the following morning,
Hitler replies with the German conditions for France's surrender.

Dietrich Bonhoeffer and Eberhard Bethge are together this
day in a town on the Baltic Sea, drinking coffee at an outdoor
cafe. Dietrich will preach this night to a small group from the
Confessing Church. Over the outdoor loudspeakers, they hear
the fanfare trumpets that signal a special radio announcement,
then the announcement itself: "France has surrendered!"

The patrons at the cafe break into celebration, many of them
climbing on top of the chairs and linking hands with their arms
outstretched. In a burst of patriotic fervor, they begin singing the
German national anthem, "Deutschland, Deutschland über
Alles," and the Nazi Party anthem, the Horst-Wessel song, finally
concluding with the "Heil Hitler" salute. In the midst of this pan-
demonium, Eberhard remains seated, as he and Dietrich have
done on many previous occasions. Dietrich on the other hand is
immediately on his feet, joining in the song while pulling
Eberhard to his feet beside him. Dietrich whispers insistently to
his dumbfounded friend: "Raise your arm! Are you crazy?"
Dietrich then executes the most precise "Heil Hitler" salute
Eberhard has ever witnessed. When it is over, Dietrich turns to
Eberhard and says, "We shall now be running risks for more
important things, but not for this salute!"

Dietrich Bonhoeffer is now fully committed to a conspiracy
that is only waiting for the right moment to set aside the government of Germany. He is also of one mind with the inner circle of
conspirators in that he believes a coup cannot succeed without
the death of Hitler. Still he will continue to maintain his very
visible ties with the pastors and brethren who have taken their
stance against the state church—both out of inner conviction
and as an outward mask.

At Klein Krössin, the sad news of Hans Otto's death is followed
by good news about Alla Stahlberg. He has survived a heavy

artillery bombardment on the western front—one in which most of his comrades were killed. Ruth writes to Dietrich and Eberhard together:

> Dear friends, I want to share with you this hour in which my heart is filled with praise and thanksgiving for the divine safeguarding of Alla. . . . It is a wonder, an indescribable wonder, that he was not harmed. "Though a thousand fall to my left and ten thousand fall to my right, may I still not be harmed." These familiar words ring in my heart. What must happen to the soul of one who experiences that. Is it not worth the whole war? . . .
>
> In the past days, I have had so many painful death reports from friends and relatives. A widow acquaintance, who lost her husband in the World War, in a single day received notice that both her son and her son-in-law were killed. Two distant nephews, both with such hopeful futures, have fallen. Jürgen Bismarck's best friend, recently married, whom I wrote to so faithfully, has also given his life. And still we believe that in all of this there must be some sense.
>
> I thank you, dear Dietrich, for your good letter from Tilsit. I look forward so much to our being together. . . . After the twenty-ninth, 10:00 evening, I will be at Klein Krössin. . . .
>
> I greet you both with all my heart, Your faithful RKR

JULY. Dietrich is absent more often now, and when he visits at Stettin or at Klein Krössin, he is evasive. Some of the intimacy has disappeared, and just now, with so many worries about her family, Ruth finds even more need for intimacy than in previous years. She senses that politics are more on Dietrich's mind than either theology or friendship. She pours out her frustrations and her sadness in letters addressed to Eberhard, who is usually in touch with Dietrich and from whom she is always assured a response.

Bit by bit, Ruth is cementing her connections with the wider Bonhoeffer family. Through Dietrich she has extended summer holiday invitations to the children of Hans von Dohnanyi. They

live in Berlin where, as in other large German cities, there are
frequent bombing raids by the British air force, and it is not
uncommon for parents to evacuate their children to the countryside for a week or two.

At the same time, Mieze has invited two of the children from
Pätzig, Hans Werner and Christine von Wedemeyer, to Kieckow
as playmates for these visitors from the city. With Hans Jürgen in
uniform, Mieze is busy managing the Kieckow enterprise alone,
and although Grandmother Ruth spends a good deal of time
teaching the children to roll dice and play cards, they are often
left to their own devices. As a result, the nearby railroad tracks
have become a special attraction for the boys, a place to pass the
time and exchange boyhood fantasies while watching the constant stream of trains carrying men and supplies to the eastern
front.

Most likely Hans von Dohnanyi has never spoken to his children about his work—neither his official duties nor his conspira-
torial activities. Still these are the children of their father, and
they have absorbed the substance of his political thinking. As
they watch the rail cars pass by, an idea occurs to the boys:
Someone ought to bomb the railroad; then the trains could
never reach the east, where so much damage has been done.

Thirteen-year-old Hans Werner is shocked at this idea, and he
is angry. He too is the son of his father, Hans von Wedemeyer,
who along with Hans's brother is on the eastern front, protecting
the Fatherland. They need food and they need ammunition.
Why would anyone even want to intercept the trains that carry
these necessities to his loved ones? Such are the questions that
plague the children of a country at war; nevertheless Hans does
not tell his grandmother, nor his Tante Mieze, nor even his
mother. He has been trained to keep to himself knowledge that
might bring harm to anyone.

The growing ties with Dietrich's family are a source of
immense satisfaction to Grandmother Ruth, and imperceptibly
she begins to wonder how the threads might be stretched to
include her own family circle.

SEPTEMBER. By order of the SS, Dietrich Bonhoeffer is forbidden
to preach; his name is placed on the list of those whose move-

ments are constantly monitored. Dietrich goes immediately to Klein Krössin, where he takes up residence in his old room, Hope.

It is an awkward location for the SS to surveil—these Kleist lands in Pomerania. The estate roads are often jammed with horses and wagons, and it is not very sporting for an officer to have to leave his vehicle and walk through the village under the sullen stares of the workers. It is even less comfortable to be barred entrance at the door of the landowner's manor house.

For the next four weeks Dietrich will be writing, speaking and listening at Klein Krössin, at Kieckow and at Schmenzin. It is the interlude Ruth has been dreaming of for years, ever since she met this dear friend. It is also a time when Ruth expects Dietrich to bring her dear friend and cousin Ewald around to the truth in terms of theology. Dietrich spends a good deal of time talking with Ewald, but not about this particular truth. Rather they are discussing the intricacies of the current political situation. Dietrich Bonhoeffer and Ewald von Kleist have declared openly in trusted circles that Germany must lose the war in order for western civilization to survive. This view is not entirely accepted, even among these friends!

From his Pomeranian retreat, Dietrich writes to Eberhard in Berlin:

> I rejoice here with the daily morning devotions, which are so necessary for my productivity. The homilies as well as the Bible passages help me in thinking of you and of your work. My day is divided so that I have time for work, for prayer and also for conversation with others, without being bothered by the material and spiritual problems that come from these disordered times. Recently, however, a violent fall storm made me very depressed and it was not so easy to find my equilibrium again . . .
>
> On Sunday we were at Kieckow. We spoke about the situation in the church. It was again made clear to me that the only chance for the Evangelical [Lutheran] Church lies in a restatement of the historical church question. Is it possible to establish a church authority based on God's word alone, or must one return to Rome or submit to the authority of the State? If the authority of God's Word

alone is not sufficient, then the last chance for the
Evangelical Church is gone. The only way then is
through the particularization of the churches . . .

My thoughts are so often with Sabine. . . . How does it
go for you financially and in the air raid shelter? In
Köslin there was another air raid alarm. I wish you well!

Dietrich has reason to worry about his twin sister Sabine
Leibholz and her family in London. Following France's surrender, the commander in chief of the German armed forces, Adolf
Hitler, ordered his staff to begin preparations for the next conquest—Great Britain. The German air force is now bombing
London nightly, a kind of saturation offense to soften up the
target before the invasion commences. At Abwehr headquarters
everything is known, but little can be done.

Though there is much to fear from the bombings of London,
Dietrich's fears of invasion are needless. Inexplicably Hitler will
abandon this idea and turn instead to his long-cherished dream
of conquering Russia.

In mid-October Dietrich leaves his refuge at Klein Krössin. He
has completed a significant portion of the *Ethics* manuscript, his
statement on the accountability of human beings before God in
an evil society.

Divided Loyalties

1941. As though the Kleists of Kieckow did not have enough
worries with three sons at the front, now they must also contend
with illness. Hans Jürgen, well over fifty years of age, was called
up as a reservist just before the war began. Although he was not
sent to the front, he ended up spending most of the time in the
hospital and was then discharged from the military for health
reasons. He is now managing the estate again, but he still is not
well. The problem seems to be an inadequate gall bladder, and
the family hopes it is nothing more serious.

JANUARY. Grandmother Ruth, now seventy-four years old, collapses one morning in the Stettin flat. The cook summons a
doctor and, with the help of a house guest, manages to get her to
bed. The doctor speculates that she has had a small stroke, and

when Hans Jürgen is notified by phone, he is in Stettin within a
few hours to assess the situation for himself. To his astonishment,
he is met at the door, not by the cook nor by the doctor, but by
an elderly man who is a total stranger.

Already distraught over his mother's condition, Hans Jürgen
interrogates the man rather bluntly and is dismayed to learn that
he is a Jew with no resources and no possibility for emigration.
He has been living with Frau von Kleist since September, when
they began transporting Jews from Stettin.

Hans Jürgen is astounded, for he has known nothing of this.
He asks the man to leave the flat immediately; his mother is in
delicate health, and the Jew's continued presence can only make
matters worse. The stranger gathers up his few belongings and
within the hour he is gone, never to be heard of again. To the
end of his life, Hans Jürgen will carry on his conscience the
memory of this man, whom he most likely condemned to death.

FEBRUARY. On February 3, Adolf Hitler convenes his chief generals to present them with "Barbarossa," his plan to mount an invasion and crush Soviet Russia. The meeting is filled with tension
since the Soviets are acknowledged to have far superior numbers
in both tanks and men. Hitler disdains this highly touted superiority of the Bolsheviks, maintaining that the German forces (and
the Germans themselves) are superior in quality. From Army
Commander in Chief General von Brauchitsch on down, the
general staff has serious doubts about implementing the plan.
The führer of course prevails. (Among the generals gathered
here are descendants of Friedrich Barbarossa's loyal vassals.
These men might well wonder whether old Barbarossa will come
out from under his Thuringian mountain now to save Germany,
or whether he will simply turn over in his grave.)

The next day Ruth von Kleist, oblivious of the fateful plans
now in motion, celebrates her birthday in bed at Stettin, surrounded by flowers and letters and a host of well-wishers. She is
gradually recovering from the stroke, but she has lost some of
her spark. From now on there will be a slight weakness on her
right side, and she will always walk with a cane.

Among her birthday letters are one from Dietrich and one
from Eberhard, who reports that his friend will be traveling to

Switzerland. It will be Dietrich's first trip abroad under the auspices of the Abwehr.

The rationale for the trip is a conspirator's nightmare. Publicly anyone who knows of the trip will think that Dietrich Bonhoeffer is trying to shore up international support for his prostrate Confessing Church. However, as an agent of German military intelligence—the Abwehr, Dietrich Bonhoeffer is attempting to gain knowledge as to how various international church organizations are reacting to Germany's aggressiveness in Europe.

At the third level, Dietrich Bonhoeffer, a double agent working for the anti-Nazi conspiracy in Germany, is to set up a communications network with England and the Vatican so that channels will be open when the coup takes place. The urgency of dependable channels is even greater now that "Barbarossa" is under way. Dietrich's pending journey is fraught with risk.

Ruth writes to Dietrich, hoping to reach him before he leaves:

> My dear Dietrich, you must excuse my penmanship for I am writing from a prone position. Today I learned through Eberhard that you are still in the country and I want to express my thanks for your words from the fourth. They lie deep in my heart. In these days of my illness the words go with me and fill me with gratitude. God has blessed you indeed and me also, in that I have won your friendship! . . . That you grant to an old woman space in your young life—this is the greatest gift for me. Yes, in the church the old and the young fuse together . . .
>
> When will we see one another again? It is all uphill with me because God has willed it so. When I am feverish, then I am out of sorts spiritually and I suffer because of it. Then, when the fever has passed, I am once again grateful. Eberhard writes that your book [*Ethics*] makes progress. I follow along in spirit.
>
> Your mother also sent me birthday congratulations. In such good, though embarrassing words. Shouldn't one resist such excessive praise? Yet one is permitted to be thankful for it.
>
> While Spes [von Bismarck] was here to help care for me, we talked much of the beautiful years of our "grand-

children's pension." Again and again we came to speak
of those days when we drove out to Finkenwalde for the
Sunday services! And then the confirmation classes!
Indeed they were such happy and harmless times!

Please greet the Dohnanyi children. I will soon thank
them myself [for the gift of a hymnal]. Yesterday I read
over all the Luther hymns, one after the other, and
rejoiced in them immensely.

And do take care and may God's angel be with you on
your journey. In all faithfulness at all times, Tante R.

MARCH. Dietrich Bonhoeffer has been refused membership in
the National Organization of Writers. This means that in addition to being prohibited from preaching, he is now also prohibited from publishing.

MAY. Hans von Dohnanyi has arranged it so that Dietrich is now
assigned to the Munich office of the Abwehr. This outpost is controlled by the conspirators. It is also reasonably close to
Switzerland, where Dietrich is expected to be traveling rather
often.

JUNE. King Wilhelm II of Prussia, once the German kaiser, is
dead at the age of eighty-two, having lived his last twenty-three
years in exile. In Berlin there is a military funeral. At Kieckow
and Klein Krössin one hardly takes notice.

On June 22, the anniversary date of Napoleon's disastrous
invasion of Russia, three separate German army groups embark
on an offensive that is expected to take them all the way to
Moscow. General von Rundstedt, to whom go the accolades for
the victory on the western front, commands the army group on
the right. Among the hundreds of officers under Runstedt's
command is reserve officer Hans von Wedemeyer, who is in a
staff position. This army group is moving northeast toward
Moscow from its base in southern Poland. The army group on
the left, striking toward Moscow through the Baltic lands, is
under the command of General von Leeb. Among his star
reserve officers is Klaus von Bismarck, master of Kniephof,
grandson of Hedwig, and husband of the gentle Ruth Alice.

Among the tens of thousands of soldiers under Leeb is Ruth Alice's brother Maximilian, an infantryman.

General von Bock commands the Center Army Group, which is to move eastward through the Pripet marshes, always in the direction of Moscow. This central force is the heart of the offensive and the largest of the three army groups. Bock's principal adjutant is Colonel Henning von Tresckow, who has appointed his own adjutant, Lieutenant Fabian von Schlabrendorff. Justification for his appointing an adjutant of such modest rank lies in Schlabrendorff's intelligence skills and his attachment to the Abwehr. In truth, Tresckow has other plans in mind for this cousin by marriage and fellow anti-Nazi.

Among the hundreds of officers under Bock's command are three grandsons of Ruth von Kleist—Konstantin and Jürgen Christoph von Kleist of Kieckow and Alexander Stahlberg of Stettin. A third Kieckow son, Hans Friedrich, is one of Bock's common soldiers.

JULY. The German armies have been moderately successful in this Russian offensive. Bock's Center Army has moved 650 kilometers into Russian territory and is now only 325 kilometers from Moscow. Unfortunately, the Barbarossa strategy demands more than moderate success. Moscow must fall before winter!

Immense numbers of Russian prisoners have been captured, yet immense numbers of Russian soldiers have escaped encirclement. The German armies have sustained large casualties, and now there are torrential rains along the front. The motorized divisions, equipped only with tracked vehicles, are bogged down in mud. The roads in Russia cannot be compared to those in Germany; perhaps this was not accounted for in the Barbarossa plan! In any case, the possibility of capturing Moscow before winter is now in doubt.

The heavy rains plaguing the armies in Russia also find their way to Pomerania. Ruth is at Klein Krössin for the summer, spending much of her time indoors. Her creative skills are put to the test on these rainy days because she is playing hostess to the daughters of Ursula and Rüdiger Schleicher. Ursula is Dietrich's sister; her husband Rüdiger is Dietrich's colleague in conspiracy. Berlin is no place for children these days since the bombing has become incessant. Thus the Schleicher girls are now under Ruth's care and assigned to the Klein Krössin guest rooms named Joy and Contentment; the third room, Hope, is kept available in case Uncle Dietrich decides to pay a surprise visit.

In the evenings Ruth joins the children in the dice game "Hindenburg and Ludendorff" and encourages them to play charades, in which the Kieckow daughters, Ruthi and Elisabeth, often take part. On rainy afternoons, the Schleicher girls are encouraged to write letters home. In this time of shortages, even stationery is at a premium, but for Dietrich's nieces, Ruth will take a few sheets from her stockpile of paper, otherwise jealously guarded for her absent friend.

The oldest Schleicher daughter, Renate, has found her way into Ruth's heart. She is not yet sixteen years old, but will finish the gymnasium in another year. Soon after that one expects she will be married, for Ruth's dear friend and Uncle Dietrich's closest companion, Eberhard Bethge, has recently declared his intentions. Everything waits on her parents' approval and on Renate's completing the gymnasium. Ruth views this pending union as a further binding of Eberhard to the Bonhoeffer family. She wonders if it will ever be possible for anyone from her own family to cross the invisible line that separates them from the Bonhoeffers of Berlin.

The Klein Krössin road is slippery and muddy from the incessant July rains. The horses have been brought into barns or sheds, and all outdoor work on the estate has ceased. Nevertheless Mieze bicycles over from Kieckow to bring her mother-in-law news of a phone call. Going to Ruth with outstretched arms, she gravely informs her that Jürgen Christoph has fallen in battle. The message, which came from the Abwehr office in Berlin, is unofficial—transmitted from the eastern front over military communications by Henning von Tresckow. It will be a few days before the official notification arrives.

Ruth retreats to her room to be alone with her thoughts and her prayers while Mieze bicycles back to her own home—to her children and her husband. The Schleicher children are puzzled that no one is crying.

The next day there is a memorial service for Jürgen Christoph in the Kieckow church, with the faithful Pastor Reimer from

Naseband presiding and all the family members, villagers and friends within bicycle distance attending. Mieze is uneasy throughout the entire service. Afterward she confesses that she cannot call to mind Jürgen Christoph's face, but only that of his younger brother Hans Friedrich. Despite appearances to the contrary, this poor mother is overwhelmed by grief.

The day after the service, when the official notification arrives, the family is thrown into shock—it is Hans Friedrich, *not* Jürgen Christoph, who has been killed! Henning only heard the name "the young Kleist" and did not know Hans Jürgen and Mieze had three sons serving in General von Bock's army. There is also a letter from Hans Friedrich's commanding officer, a lieutenant, explaining the circumstances of the young soldier's death. His regiment was caught in a skirmish in which the Russian troops advanced and then retreated, and by the time his lieutenant found him on the battlefield, Hans Friedrich was dying. When the lieutenant asked how he was, the young soldier replied bravely, "Sir, it is all right with me." Grandmother Ruth is comforted, for she is sure an angel was watching over him in those last hours of his life.

AUGUST. On August 6, a telegram arrives at Kieckow from the Russian front: "Yesterday, August 5, Lieutenant Jürgen Christoph von Kleist-Retzow gave his life for the Fatherland." In the villages it is whispered that Jürgen Christoph died because his death was already mourned. Up at the manor house, such talk is dismissed as the superstition of the ignorant.

Once again Mieze rides her bicycle to Klein Krössin to report to her mother-in-law the death of a son, then returns to her own home as the grandmother retreats to her room. Once again the Schleicher children marvel that no one is crying.

On August 7, there is a service for Jürgen Christoph and Hans Friedrich in the Kieckow church, attended by family, by villagers and by neighborhood friends. Once again Pastor Reimer from Naseband presides, this time taking his message from Dietrich Bonhoeffer's sermon on the occasion of Hans Friedrich's confirmation. The grandmother finds comfort in this recollection.

Hans Friedrich's burial in the Russian countryside was presided over by a chaplain who took as his Scripture reading,

"My time stands in Your hands." Ruth can only marvel at the strange and wonderful ways in which the Lord works, for along the edge of the roof at her Klein Krössin home, in old German letters, is inscribed the house motto she selected years ago: "My time stands in Your hands."

The final message from Jürgen Christoph arrives after the Kieckow memorial service, in a letter he wrote on August 5, the last day of his life. It is a tribute to his fallen brother and a statement of faith to comfort his parents.

In his office at Center Army Group headquarters on the Russian front, Henning von Tresckow realizes the terrible mistake he made when he unofficially informed the Kieckow parents of their son's death. He now feels doubly burdened, for of the three Kieckow sons serving at the front, only Konstantin survives. Henning arranges to have Konstantin transferred to the rear and telegraphs Hans Jürgen of the decision. Hans Jürgen immediately telegraphs back to Henning that Konstantin should not be treated differently from any other soldier. They are all in this together, and no Kleist would want to give less than the others!

Hans Jürgen's telegram arrives too late; Konstantin has already been pulled from battle by order of Center Army Group headquarters. Six hours later his battery comes under attack and his closest comrade is killed. Konstantin is overwhelmed with guilt that he was not there to comfort his friend nor to die at his side. But when he arrives at headquarters and learns that both his brothers are dead, he is consumed by one thought alone—he must go home to his parents.

On August 24, Ruth writes to Eberhard:

> . . . I live as if in a dream world. I have not yet grasped the enormity of our bereavement here. We live between heaven and earth. Noble and lighthearted moments become interchangeable with gloom and despair, interweaving their images into our souls. Almost daily now we are told of a death at the front. Each report tears open the wounds of the earlier deaths. Dietrich alluded to this in his recent letter: "War, death and then the future."
>
> There is growing in me a new sense of belonging to these terrible events. Through my nephew Tresckow, we

learned that Konstantin is to be pulled from the front.
My son has telegraphed to Tresckow that he is not in
agreement with this transfer of Konstantin. No one
should be excluded from the fate and the guilt that is
upon us.

I feel compelled to tell you that for the first time I am
unsure of your and Dietrich's course in these times.
Aren't we all involved in this together? Shouldn't we put
all our spiritual strength out there where they are fighting it out, and not turn aside? . . . I don't know whether
you can really understand what has taken hold of me.
Probably Dietrich would entirely reject such thoughts.

All of this perhaps has come as a result of the many
letters I am reading from the friends and the superiors of
the two boys and also through my own inability to come
to terms with their deaths. I hear how bravely our children died and how it was not only their spiritual strength
but also the instinct of self-control that sustained them.
Out of all this I do not mean to come up with some false
doctrine, just because it seems that way to me. In your
case, I know I can trust that you will not make more out
of these words than is meant.

There is something else also that tears me apart. When
our news reports speak of the "unimaginable" destruction we are inflicting on the enemy, I feel it as a stab in
my soul. . . .

I have so much I want to say to you, but there is not
enough time. I enclose a copy of Alla's letter. You will
enjoy it because you know how close he is to me. He is
now in great danger. God can protect him if it is His will.
It becomes ever clearer to me that we live under God's
keeping. . . .

Now it is quiet here, and this too is good for a while.
My garden blooms and this revives me. How little is
required to quiet my heart. And now I grow closer to my
children. . . .

Here at home I had a memorial service for the entire
[Klein Krössin] village. One of our workers' sons fell in
battle and I drew in my own two so that it was a service

for all three. We had a very large gathering. . . .

Take care and once again thank you for the dear letter
from Hamburg. In all faithfulness, your Ruth.

P.S. Dietrich was going to write me from Munich. It
depresses me when I must wait so long [to hear from
him] . . .

Two days after sending off this letter, Ruth is so overcome with
regret that she writes Eberhard again:

My dear Eberhard, I have such a bad conscience thinking
I might have put doubt into your path. How can I know
what your commitment is? Forgive me for offering an
opinion that in truth was no opinion, but rather an
impulsive feeling. . . . It is the temptation of our time . . .

Konstantin is now home. . . . It seems to me that the
front-line soldier is of a different substance than we at
home—more confident, less aggressive and more duty-
bound. . . . Where is Dietrich? . . . Perhaps you can
inquire of his brother Klaus? With all my heart, your
Ruth

SEPTEMBER. By the time Ruth's letters reach Eberhard, Dietrich
is once again in Switzerland on his threefold mission, outwardly
gathering support for his church while at the same time gathering intelligence for Germany as to the stance of the world
church community regarding Germany's ambitions, and finally
carrying the conspirators' messages, ultimately destined for
England and the Vatican.

OCTOBER. Dietrich is in Berlin at his parents' home, ill with
pneumonia. Ruth travels to the capital, expecting to visit her sick
friend, but he is too ill to see anyone. Even the pleasant experience of staying next door with the Schleicher family and renew-
ing her friendship with the Schleicher daughters in no way
compensates for this huge disappointment.

All Jews are now required to wear a six-pointed yellow star
securely sewn to their outer garments. Those living in buildings
owned by Aryans have been evicted from their homes and forced
to report to temporary relocation centers in synagogues, if they

are not already on trains being transported east. The "Final Solution," a euphemism for the systematic destruction of European Jewry, is on its well-ordered way.

Little to Celebrate

1941: DECEMBER. The number of casualties on the eastern front continues to grow. While relatives of the fighting men wonder to themselves where the slaughter will end, the government announces a victory of sorts. On December 2, German troops reach the suburbs of Moscow, bringing them within striking distance of the Soviet capital. What the government does not announce is that the entire winter supply of fuel for these forces was needed to bring the armies this far through the mud of the Russian landscape. Nor does it announce that the troops outside the Soviet capital are not equipped with winter clothing.

On the eighth of December, the United States enters the war on the side of Germany's enemies. It is an event that is hardly unexpected, yet across the Pomeranian landscape memories of the World War are kindled anew. The thought of that giant industrial machine across the Atlantic turning out planes and tanks and every kind of weapon needed to wage war is a sobering one for both friends and foes of the government. For those who still hope to rid Germany of Hitler and make an honorable peace, the situation has worsened considerably.

On the nineteenth of December, Adolf Hitler dismisses General von Brauchitsch as Supreme Commander of the German army and appoints himself successor. Simultaneously, General von Bock resigns his command on the eastern front, citing his opposition to continuing the Russian invasion. Yet he refuses to have anything to do with a plot to overthrow the government, despite pressure from his adjutant, Henning von Tresckow. Bock's successor is General von Kluge, and Henning's task begins anew—to draw this field marshal into the conspirators' circle.

Dietrich is still in Berlin, but has almost fully recovered from his bout with pneumonia. Ruth is at her flat in Stettin, intent on influencing the affairs of the Confessing Church even though the Council of Brethren office in Stettin has been closed. A few of the faithful still remain, and the little discussion group Ruth organized in better times continues to meet. Ruth feels a sense of ownership when it comes to Dietrich's *The Cost of Discipleship*, which her group continues to read chapter by chapter. She fairly bursts with pride when in the course of discussion she can also make reference to points from Dietrich's new manuscript, which is slowly taking shape under her roof at Klein Krössin.

In the wee hours of a Friday morning, Ruth writes to her friend:

> Dear Dietrich, I have set aside for you five hundred sheets of typing paper, two hundred sheets of white scratch paper and one hundred envelopes—the kind I use when writing to you. What should I do with these? Should I send the package to Berlin or will you come and make use of it at Kieckow? . . . The death of my Rohr nephew is another terrible blow to our family . . . He was my sister's only son and I can well imagine her pain. What will come next in all this?
>
> I want to tell you how great a joy it is for me when our group reads aloud from your *The Cost of Discipleship*. Most recently we analyzed two sections—the one on "The Enemy—the 'Extraordinary'" and the other on "The Hidden Righteousness." The discussions were long and fruitful. The hours together do us such good in these times when our nerves are so overstrained. . . .
>
> I believe that this book is not simply to be read through. Rather one must read into it. Perhaps that is its greatest value. I often have the impression that much of what you put forth is not developed to its conclusion—if I may use better words, that links have been omitted. Surely you will develop these further. Are you planning to do this in your new manuscript or have you not gotten to it? I greet you from my heart. Your RKR

Even in wartime, the postal service in Germany continues to function in all its efficiency. Ruth's letter reaches Dietrich in Berlin on Saturday, and on Sunday morning he boards the train for Kieckow, to spend a few days with Mieze and Hans Jürgen and their children.

Sunday night Ruth is informed by telephone of Dietrich's arrival, and on Monday morning she too is bound for Kieckow, where the manor house is now almost overflowing with family and guests. Mieze insists that both Dietrich and Ruth remain in their home, not only for their physical comfort but also to conserve fuel. In such times as these, one less building to heat will benefit the entire estate community.

During this Advent season, Dietrich presides at both the morning and evening devotions in the large dining hall of the manor house. His congregation regularly numbers some forty people—the entire household staff, the parents and children, Grandmother Ruth, and two distant cousins who have found shelter under the Kieckow roof. More often than not, Hans Jürgen is absent from morning devotions as he continues to suffer from the symptoms of his gall bladder condition. Thanks to Dietrich's father, arrangements have been made for him to be operated on in Berlin.

Cousin Ewald from Schmenzin comes almost daily for evening devotions, on horseback as he once did in his childhood. This free-thinking Kleist has given up on the conspiracy that was supposed to free Germany from Hitler. In Ewald's opinion, Brauchitsch's dismissal is the final blow, dashing any hope of a military coup. Personally, Ewald feels betrayed and left out, maintaining that every chance for a coup has been passed up. He has serious doubts about the courage of those in high places, privately criticizing them for being too cautious. He speaks of the invasion of Russia as the death knell for Germany and scoffs at the "good news" of German troops being within striking distance of Moscow.

Disillusioned, Ewald has retreated into his family life. His world hardly goes beyond the manor house and the six children who are at home—Anning's three daughters and son, and now Alice's small son and daughter. His two older sons, by Anning, are at the front—Ewald Heinrich with the Center Army Group in Russia and Hermann in Italy. Ewald's trusted Pastor Reimer from Naseband is often at the Schmenzin dinner table. He lives almost underground with his little parish in the woods, protected only by his patron at Schmenzin and the closed mouths of the Naseband villagers. And every night Ewald sits in his library with

Alice, often with Mieze and the ailing Hans Jürgen alongside, listening to radio transmissions from the BBC (British Broadcasting Company). Never mind that any discovery of a short-wave radio by the authorities can lead to serious punishment. Such possibilities disturb these Kleists not one bit.

Ewald's automobile sits in its shed unused, yet its tank is kept filled with gasoline, ready for the dash to Berlin should the coup ever take place. He is slated to be a member of the provisional government that will take over the nation and seek peace with Germany's enemies. He has little confidence that the coup will ever happen, and he has no tolerance at all for the generals who failed to act while there was still a chance.

Hans Jürgen's son Konstantin, pulled from the front by Henning von Tresckow over Hans Jürgen's objections, is now at home. After Christmas this oldest son will report to a training base out of harm's way. Just as Ewald is drawn to Dietrich Bonhoeffer, so is Konstantin. He has seen unimaginable suffering in his short lifetime, both at the front and in conquered lands. With Dietrich, one can discuss such things freely, gaining insights that allow one to go forward in life. At Kieckow, at Klein Krössin, and at Schmenzin, each one questions and each one despairs, but not always for the same reasons nor in the same way. Dietrich alone can console and counsel. Truly his presence this Advent season is God's response to their prayers for his intercession; so says the grandmother from Klein Krössin.

Just before Christmas, Dietrich returns to Berlin and the visiting cousins return to their families. The Kleists of Kieckow are alone with one another, their first Christmas without the two fallen sons. A few days later, Mieze and Hans Jürgen also leave for Berlin, where Hans Jürgen will undergo his scheduled operation. Grandmother Ruth is left to supervise the children and the manor house that once was hers. Late at night and far into the wee hours of the morning she writes to her friend in Berlin:

> My dear good Dietrich, I simply cannot let the old year pass without sending you a special greeting and my thanks. Although I am not without worry over my son's operation, it is a great relief for me to know that you will be near him. Certainly it is a sacrifice on my part not to

Ewald von Kleist of Schmenzin

be with him during these days. Even though I long ago
gave up my rights to him, still he is my child. He will
always be that child who long ago was completely dependent on me. Possibly these thoughts strike you as strange;
but they were brought to the surface again while I was
reading the book that you gave me. (I am not yet finished with it because my eyes refuse to cooperate; they
demand that I use them sparingly.) . . .

I thank you especially for the kind words that accompanied your gift. Do you know that in this message you
granted me a privilege? The privilege is that with you I
do not need to measure my words; for if some private
word slips by, it will not be weighed on your scale. I
promise not to misuse this privilege; if I do, you may certainly withdraw it. On the other side, you have also
granted me spiritual tasks, this in spite of your youth and
my age. When one is nearing the end of life, it is very

important to know that there is a friend whom one can go to for guidance. We should both thank God that he brought about our meeting and we should make the most of it while we are here.

On the morning of New Year's Eve, Ewald rides to the Kieckow manor house to call on the grandmother and to inquire about Hans Jürgen's condition in Berlin. He also brings news from the BBC broadcast of the previous night. The Russians have mounted a fierce offensive along the full flank of the eastern front. The fighting is intense and casualties are mounting. Ruth thinks of her own far-flung family—her grandsons Alla and Maximilian, Ruthchen's husband Hans, Luitgarde's husband Fabian and Ruth Alice's husband Klaus. There are also the Tresckow nephews, Henning and Gerd, sons of the dear dead Anni. Each is out there somewhere on the eastern front—all except Gerd, who is reasonably safe in Italy. And always there is the unspoken fear for Henning and Fabian, and also for Dietrich—that they will all be discovered and end up in a Gestapo prison.

On German radio, the only news from the eastern front comes in the form of human interest stories—front-line soldiers of the Fatherland gathering in little groups to sing the familiar carols before a candlelit Christmas tree—all to comfort those at home. Ruth is disbelieving and she writes again to Dietrich:

> December 31
>
> How uncanny is the stillness that follows the storm. What is happening? What lies ahead? Last evening Konstantin and I visited the "hermit in the forest" [Pastor Reimer]. He knew nothing more than we know, but he was very disturbed. May God stay by us. Today I held a New Year's Eve devotion at Kieckow and one at Klein Krössin also. Both carried the theme: Fear not—just have faith! Perhaps these paltry words of mine yet carried a light beam from God. I would not venture to open my mouth were I not convinced that I am only the tool that God has chosen, according to his will.
>
> On the third [of January] I will drive with the children to Lasbeck. There I will spend two days and on the fifth I

will land in Stettin. Did you receive your laundry package
undamaged? It was mailed before Christmas. Yes, it gives
me a kind of maternal joy when I can do something to
take care of you. How good it is that your entire family is
watching over my son! I would appreciate it very much if
you could write down your impressions of his condition.
Tonight I will inquire again. . . . Naturally I am happy
that I can be among the children and among our people.
I am learning to know the children so much better than
before. They appear to me to have come a long way in
life.

Please greet your parents and especially all the
Schleichers, who are so dear in their thoughtfulness
toward me. I will write them as soon as I am able to. It
bothers me greatly that their flower bouquet never
reached me. It apparently was left at my closed door,
whence it disappeared.

May God keep us in the New Year with all its cares and
all its troubles. . . . Oh, our poor soldiers. What will
become of them? In all faithfulness, Your RK

1942: JANUARY. Hans Jürgen recovers completely from his
surgery and returns to Kieckow less one gall bladder. The physician marvels at the stamina of this fifty-five-year-old man.

FEBRUARY. Emotionally, it is a time of few peaks and many
valleys—not only the constant anxieties about those loved ones at
the front, but also the even less comfortable anxieties about
Dietrich and the shadowy circle into which he steps ever deeper.
Still he remembers Ruth on her seventy-fifth birthday, and by
and by she replies:

> My dear Dietrich, Your dear letter was a real birthday joy.
> Your statement on a solution that will be comfortable for
> us both was particularly helpful to me. Indeed one needs
> only to be faithful in serving God, rather than striving for
> great things, since even these are simply gifts from God.
> So we must part from one another—I because of my
> advanced age and you by reason of lowering your visibil-

ity. It really does not matter so much as you may think. If only I could speak with you once more in quietness, rather than always trying to make the most out of every moment. But that possibility seems to lie far in the distance. Is it possible that you can spend Easter at Klein Krössin? I will certainly be there. And after that the doctor wants me at the Karolus Hospital [in Stettin] for about four weeks, possibly less, on account of an irregular heartbeat. He says it is nothing serious but still should be looked into. It is a bitter pill for me, to which I don't really feel equal. I would much rather be in Berlin, where there are other activities. This new year of my life starts out by pointing up my limitations. . . . The eightieth birthday that you promise me is a very uncertain eventuality. As an alternative, why not celebrate my seventy-sixth birthday together [a year hence]? Or is that anniversary not festive enough? Nowadays one can hardly plan for tomorrow. Granted that in life one can never plan with certainty, still formerly one's plans and wishes had a reasonable chance for fulfillment. . . .

Recently my son-in-law B. [Herbert von Bismarck] wrote to me: "If everything in my life went as happily and as successfully as our marriage, then I would certainly be among the greats in the history of the world." Thirty years ago, in February, he came to me to ask for my daughter's [Maria's] hand. Now each year since then he thanks me for my trust in him at that earlier time. His message is always a joy to receive.

How different are the paths in which God leads his own. One is inclined to want to help him, but I believe that one can do nothing better than leave the reins in his hands. . . .

From Alla [Stahlberg] I have heard nothing since the twelfth. Through Ruthchen at Pätzig I heard that he wrote from Paris on the eighteenth. I fear he is again in danger. It is the same with Klaus [Bismarck, Ruth Alice's husband], who flew this morning to join his battalion. How difficult it all is.

And I still haven't thanked you for the wonderful azaleas, which your sister brought me—oh no, I mean

Eberhard's sister. Please thank him on my behalf. How will I ever thank for the almost one hundred messages that I received on my birthday? It is remarkable how much undeserved good can be worked up on such an occasion in one's lifetime. Let me once again thank you for your friendship and wish you well from all my heart. Your faithful RKR

A few days later Ruth writes to Eberhard:

My dear Eberhard, Slowly I am working through the mountain of good wishes that poured into my house on the fourth. Your dear letter ought to have been answered long ago. It was one of the dearest. You have a great gift in that you are able to speak from your warm heart. I am so thankful for your friendship and for Dietrich's, which light the evening of my life. At the moment it seems very much like "evening." I live to see more clearly the road to eternal life and yet I find my distress greater than ever before. How little we are receptive to the promise of the gift of the Holy Spirit. And how empty it all is without this gift.

I want so to speak either with you or with Dietrich in quietness. Instead, Dietrich will be at Kieckow just at the time when I can't possibly be there. Until Easter I am bound to Stettin, for health reasons and also due to household responsibilities. [Three house guests are staying in Ruth's Stettin flat.] . . . I could leave the flat for just a week, but now the doctor says my heart problem will not allow that. I am waiting until a room at the Karolus Hospital is free; then I will undergo treatments there. Please tell Dietrich that I cannot take his cousin into my home because from Palm Sunday through the summer I hope to be at Klein Krössin. In April I hope to be at Klein Krössin unless it is too cold, in which case I will return here so as not to waste fuel. I would be so happy if you could visit me at that time so that we might speak about the questions that weigh on me. . . .

At the moment I am reading a book that has touched me as no other. It was a gift from Raba [Stahlberg]—The Quest for Russia[37] by Andrei Russinov. I will try to get another copy. It would be perfect for Dietrich's family. Because the print is so good, I am able to read many pages at one sitting. Probably the book will not be available much longer; there is such a dearth of books now.

Finally now I thank you for the wonderful azaleas that your sister brought me. I carefully tend them so that they will last me even longer. She is really a treasure and spoke so faithfully the words of greeting from you and from Dietrich, while I stood so undeservedly at the birthday table.

How are things now with you? . . . I wish you well and greet you from my heart. Your Ruth

P.S. Alla is once again in danger—in the infantry at Wolchov. It sounds just terrible there. Oh, I don't even like to talk about it.

MARCH. According to plan, Ruth enters the hospital at Stettin, her spirits buoyed by the hope of a homecoming reunion with both Eberhard and Dietrich. This hope dims considerably, however, when the doctor insists her confinement be extended. What a nuisance are the twin burdens of old age and ill health.

A Meeting at Klein Krössin

1942: APRIL. Trapped in the Karolus Hospital at Stettin, Grandmother Ruth is beside herself with frustration. Surely she will not be at Kieckow for Easter when both Dietrich and Eberhard have promised to visit. She asks herself why the visit couldn't have been postponed just one week so that she might see them both, and she begins to wonder: Are Dietrich and Eberhard avoiding her? Then why do they visit Kieckow at all?

Ruth of course cannot know the truth—that Dietrich is at Kieckow not only to continue his writing but also to speak with Hans Jürgen and Ewald about a proposed journey to Switzerland. With him is Eberhard, who assists and advises while ostensibly pursuing the missionary aims of the Confessing Church in the rural lands.

Dietrich's time is no longer his own, for within the Abwehr conspiracy there is renewed urgency. If the military is to act at all, the generals must move now. And when the generals move, communication with the leadership of Germany's western enemies, principally England and America, must be clear and swift. To ensure this communication and trust is Dietrich's awesome responsibility.

Alone in her hospital room on Good Friday, Ruth ponders this world and the world beyond. She writes to Eberhard at Kieckow:

> . . . During this Holy Week I have been wrestling with such difficult questions. Christ's Resurrection! Certainly without it this world would lie in total darkness. Here we need the living Christ at every moment. But there? It is impossible to picture eternal life—either materially or spiritually. At best everything is speculative and unreal. Then what is left? Even Judgment Day and the long sleep that is to precede it do not offer any hope. "We will be with the Lord forever"—with no tasks and no future? So many of my dearest kin and friends are already there. Will it be a reunion with these loved ones or will each one of us be separate? This I would dread above all else. Are these matters harder for an old person? I dare not speak of it with younger people—at least not beyond you two theologians who are closest to me.
>
> May God keep you. It is a bitter pill for me to swallow, not to be at Klein Krössin these days. I greet you and Dietrich from my heart. Your Ruth

Early on Easter morning, Dietrich conducts family devotions in the dining hall of the Kieckow manor house. Later, while the German Christian pastor at Kieckow expounds on Nazi "Christian" themes, the entire Kleist household is on its way to Naseband, riding in two horse-drawn vehicles. They are welcomed by Pastor Reimer and the Schmenzin Kleists, Ewald and Alice, who enter the patron's pew with their children, leaving just enough space for Eberhard and Dietrich. The Kleists of Kieckow sit among the villagers, Hans Jürgen and his son Heinrich on the right side, and Mieze with Ruthi and Elisabeth on the left. At Naseband, as at Kieckow, this separation of sexes, which dates from Old Testament times, is still the custom.

Toward evening four men gather in the Kieckow library to go over names and to discuss Dietrich's pending journey to Switzerland. They are promptly interrupted by a phone call from

Berlin. Hans von Dohnanyi, Dietrich's brother-in-law and also his superior in the Abwehr, wants him to leave immediately for Norway. The outward purpose of the trip is to ascertain why the Norwegian Church is so obstinate in its resistance to the *nazifica-tion* of that country. Its true purpose is to gain the release of Norwegian Bishop Berggrav, who has been imprisoned for his refusal to cooperate with Norway's conquerors. The urgency of Dietrich's mission is to obtain the bishop's release before he is ever brought to trial. In Norway as in Germany, once one is brought to trial in a Nazi court, there is little opportunity for clogging the wheels of injustice. Thus the Pomeranian visit that might otherwise have lasted until Ruth's homecoming is promptly concluded. Dietrich and Eberhard board the evening train bound for Berlin. (Bonhoeffer's mission will succeed. Bishop Berggrav will be released and exiled to a forest chalet.)

Ruth is doubly vexed. Not only is she kept from home while Dietrich is visiting Kieckow, but she is also kept from attending the graduation of her granddaughter Maria von Wedemeyer, Ruthchen's lively child who captured her grandmother's heart during their Stettin years together. At that time Maria was always considered too young, whether it was to attend concerts or to prepare for confirmation. Still the child always wanted to be taken seriously and to be a part of things, as even Pastor Bonhoeffer must have realized that long ago day when he turned around to find her mimicking his every motion. Ruth still smiles at the memory of that harmless occasion, never daring to ask Dietrich whether he also remembers.

Since those Stettin days in Grandmother's flat, Maria has grown and she has blossomed. Ruth wonders how many young men now have an eye for her and are perhaps waiting until these terrible times have passed before approaching the young lady's parents. There are already rumors afloat in Pomerania and the Neumark that this or that landowner's son is writing Maria in earnest from the front lines, but reluctant to promise anything for fear that he might never return.

Maria has completed her gymnasium education at the Wie-blingen Castle School[38] in western Germany, and on the twenti-eth of March she graduates. It is hard to believe that the child who once came under Dietrich Bonhoeffer's stern gaze for disturbing the peace is graduating near the head of her class from a school that demands the very best from all its students.

The Wieblingen Castle School is a remarkable institution—at least it was until last year when the government dismissed its founder and director and placed it under supervision of the Nazi SS. The school's founder is Elisabeth von Thadden of Trieglaff, whom Grandmother Ruth knew in the 1920s when the youthful Fraulein von Thadden both inspired and was the benefactor of the Trieglaff Conferences. This Thadden daughter, who was far ahead of her time, observed the despair of a defeated nation and a failed monarchy. She determined to bring depth and stability to Germany's infant republic by raising the social consciousness of her peers—the landed aristocracy of Pomerania. At the annual Trieglaff Conferences she invited political and social scientists from all over the land to speak on the problems of contemporary society. As long as Fraulein von Thadden was at Trieglaff, these gatherings were successful beyond all expectations.

But Elisabeth von Thadden of Trieglaff also had another dream—to establish a school where all of the academic opportunities available to upper-class boys would likewise be available to girls. In 1927 she brought this dream to life, using her inheritance to purchase the Wieblingen Castle, just outside Heidelberg, and founding her school. Over the years she set a standard for excellence that attracted the brightest and the best of the daughters from the great estates of Germany as well as from Heidelberg's middle class.

And so it was that after their oldest daughter Ruth Alice graduated from the gymnasium at Stettin, the Wedemeyers decided to withdraw their other two children from the public schools. Max was sent away to Templin, and Maria was enrolled in the school owned by Elisabeth von Thadden. Maria has been at Wieblingen for more than two years now, and in that short time she has matured immensely, yet she has remained a totally independent spirit.

During her last year at Wieblingen, Maria taught the mathematics classes after the regular teacher became ill and left.

Clearly Maria excels academically. In the family of Ruth von Kleist, however, to excel is only what is expected; thus at home Maria's scholastic achievements are not considered exceptional. But her siblings, her cousins, her parents, and most of all her grandmother, acknowledge that Maria is different from them in other ways, somehow more original. She has an unbounded love for life, and she seizes each moment as if it were the first and the last. One might say she is a child of the earth, without affectation and with a life-giving energy that can be felt by all who come into her presence. For Maria's mother Ruthchen, raising this daughter has not been easy. It was always Hans, the father, who could handle such a child, and it is the father to whom the child-woman, not quite eighteen years old, still looks for approval.

Ruthchen has come alone to Wieblingen for the graduation exercises. Hans is somewhere on the eastern front, and Grandmother Ruth is in the hospital. It is a time for mother and daughter to share only with each other, a time to speak of the past as well as the future. Conversations invariably turn to the absent father, who taught Maria all about life on the broad Prussian landscape, who taught her the ways of the forest, of the animals and of the fields, and who trained her in the business of the estate as an added insurance should anything ever happen to him.

One is tempted not to speak of the present, for after the SS took control of the Wieblingen Castle School, Elisabeth von Thadden was denounced and dismissed. She will eventually be arrested, imprisoned and interrogated by the Gestapo. Then she will be tried and convicted by a People's Court as a traitor to the Fatherland. Finally she will be beheaded, all for the protection of the Third Reich.

The institution whose religious and academic standards Elisabeth von Thadden so carefully nurtured is gradually being brought into line with the Nazi SS view of education for young women of the Fatherland.

For this and other reasons, graduation is uncomfortably differ-ent from earlier school festivals. First of all, there is hardly a student who does not have a father or a brother, or both, some-where in a position of danger. And whereas at one time all school events opened with an invocation to the Father in heaven, this graduation opens with a tribute to the führer in Berlin. Above all, the closing words of the ceremonies remind one that Wieblingen has come a long way from the spirit of "Thadden" (as the director was known to her students). Instead of a bene-diction spoken by the pastor, the graduates in unison recite the Nazi pledge: "We declare our unconditional devotion to the fate of the State and the People."

Grandmother Ruth is finally released from her hospital prison. Hans Jürgen goes by train to Stettin to fetch her and then puts her on the train for Pätzig, where she is to recuperate with Ruthchen and the children. Hans Jürgen is not sure this is such a good idea since Pätzig is known for its liveliness and the Wedemeyer children for their unexpected antics. The lovely manor house is a place of joy, but not the best place for relax-ation. Grandmother is well aware of this, however, and has declared that right now she is more in need of joy than of rest.

With Maria at home, Grandmother Ruth is surrounded by five of her seven Wedemeyer grandchildren. The only ones missing are Ruth Alice and Max, both so loved from the Stettin days. Ruth Alice, now mistress of Kniephof, has just given birth to her first child. Max, like his father, is somewhere on the eastern front. Father is in relative safety, stationed at staff headquarters. The same cannot be said for Max.

At Pätzig, Maria sees to it that life goes on as if Father were there, each day planning some activity for her younger siblings. One afternoon she insists that Hans Werner, now thirteen years old, learn to dance. When the war is over, there will be ball seasons again, just as in the old days, and Hans Werner must not be found wanting. Together she and Hans roll up the oriental carpet that covers the floor of the great hall, and Maria turns on the phonograph. To the music of Johann Strauss, she leads her hesitant brother from one end of the room to the other and back in a round of Viennese waltzes, while Grandmother Ruth sits and watches with amusement.

Ruth is enjoying her convalescence with this lively family, yet a corner of her consciousness is always occupied by thoughts of the two young theologians she counts among her dearest friends.

Maria von Wedemeyer, home at Pätzig

On April 24, she writes from Pätzig:

> Dear Dietrich, Your letter of the twenty-first just arrived
> today. . . . I hope finally on the fifteenth of May to be at
> Klein Krössin. You know how welcome you are there. But
> I have about given up when it comes to any plans involv-
> ing you and Eberhard. In all honesty I must say that it
> would be much pleasanter at [Klein] Krössin if you were
> a little more serious about planning ahead for your visits.
> But then who can know ahead of time any more?
>
> How happy it would be for me, as you well know, if you
> and Eberhard could spare a little time for me while I am
> still here [at Pätzig]. But I won't be a beggar. . . .
> Faithfully your RKR

This letter is the first hint that the grandmother has something
new on her mind—something that has to do with the Wedemeyers of Pätzig.

MAY. Ruth is back at Klein Krössin, and her garden is in the full
bloom of early summer. In other years this garden provided her
with serenity and peace, no matter what the world might offer;
but this year the flowers seem to have lost their power. This
grandmother, to whom reading and ideas are as necessary as
food and drink, is rapidly losing her eyesight, and along with it
her independence. Bored and restless, her mind turns to her
friend Dietrich. If only he would write or phone from Berlin, or
best of all just turn up on the doorstep without doing either.
"Where is he?" she asks impatiently.

If this grandmother only knew. Dietrich is nowhere near Berlin
these days. For the first half of the month he is in Switzerland,
quietly attending an international gathering of Protestant
church leaders in the hope of cultivating further conduits for
future political negotiations. He had expected to see the British
cleric, Dr. George Bell, Bishop of Chichester, whom he considers
the most valuable person for passing information to the British
government. He is disappointed to find that Bishop Bell is not
present, but rather is on a trip to Sweden. Dietrich cuts short his
Swiss visit, returns to Berlin, and flies immediately to Stockholm.

JUNE. At a church academy in Sigtuna outside Stockholm, Dietrich Bonhoeffer calls on the visiting Bishop Bell and turns over to him seven names—the three generals who will unleash a *Putsch* at the front and dispose of Adolf Hitler and the four principals who will form the government to negotiate peace with the British and their allies. The bishop promises to deliver these names to British Foreign Minister Anthony Eden, who is expected to pass them along to the prime minister.

Long after the war is over, Fabian von Schlabrendorff will visit Winston Churchill and will inquire about the many messages transmitted to him through Bonhoeffer and others by way of Switzerland and Sweden. Churchill will reply that he never heard of any such messages. Much later they will all be found among Eden's effects—filed away in his private papers without ever reaching the Foreign Office, let alone Prime Minister Churchill.

At Klein Krössin, Ruth makes her own assessment of the situation. She now surmises that Dietrich is indeed out of the country. She senses further that his journeys abroad in the midst of war have to do with other than church matters, and that he will certainly be wanting to visit with Cousin Ewald, if not with her, as soon as he returns. His arrival cannot be that far away. Thus she sends an urgent letter to Pätzig, asking Maria to come immediately under the pretext of needing this granddaughter to read aloud and help with her correspondence. In truth, she wants to discuss with Maria the young woman's future plans. University studies are out of the question for the duration of the war. Unless Maria prepares for some kind of health care profession, she will be required to report immediately for factory work. However, Grandmother Ruth is less interested in Maria's immediate plans than in her future aspirations. She senses that this granddaughter is meant for something other than becoming a landowner's wife and estate mistress. If Ruth has learned anything from Dietrich Bonhoeffer, it is that places like Kieckow and Pätzig are to be loved and to be treasured as ephemeral objects, but that they will not endure.

Not unexpectedly, Dietrich arrives the day before Maria is scheduled to leave. His Swedish journey has gone well from all aspects; if only their plans for Germany could be carried through so smoothly! Best of all, Bishop Bell brought written messages and personal greetings from his sister Sabine and her family. Dietrich worries constantly about the London bombings, and Sabine likewise worries about her family in Berlin. The bombing of German cities increases week by week.

In recent years Dietrich has become rather dour. The times are hardly conducive to lightheartedness, and the strain of living a kind of double life has taken its toll. But there is a noticeable softening of his demeanor when he arrives at Klein Krössin to find Maria von Wedemeyer, the somewhat unruly child he remembers from Stettin, now fully grown and immensely attractive.

On the first evening of his visit, Dietrich announces that he will walk to Kieckow to report on his trip to Sweden. Almost shyly, he asks Ruth if Maria might join him. "Why, of course!" she replies. She intends to retire early, and Maria must say her good-byes at Kieckow anyway.

Together Dietrich and Maria make their way along the cobble-stone road, Maria talking cheerfully most of the time—not about herself, but rather her observations of the world. At first Dietrich is surprised by the directness and clarity of his companion's dis-course, so unlike the convoluted dialogue that often passes for conversation in Berlin circles. Occasionally he interrupts to correct some error of fact or judgment. Maria listens and accepts. Dietrich begins to compare and contrast the grand-mother and the granddaughter, both of whom hold such firm convictions, yet neither of whom is averse to changing an opinion given new facts or perspective. If there is a difference, it is not principally one of age. Rather it lies in their view of the future—the grandmother having almost given up hope for this world and the granddaughter a veritable well of optimism as far as what the future might hold. The walk to Kieckow is like a fresh breeze, yet to be so stirred by an eighteen-year-old girl is disturb-ing to this thirty-six-year-old pastor turned intelligence agent. He barely knows how to conduct himself.

At Kieckow, Maria bids a quick farewell to Tante Mieze, Uncle Hans Jürgen and the cousins. She will leave for Pätzig on the morning train, and would Uncle Hans Jürgen please send a wagon for her at Klein Krössin? For Dietrich there is a hearty handshake and a reminder that she will see him again at breakfast. Then Maria is gone, and the visitor turns to the discussion of more serious matters.

On the twenty-fifth of June, Dietrich is on his way to Rome with Hans von Dohnanyi, their destination the Vatican. The Abwehr conspirators are making peace overtures, though they have little reason to believe that the military will stand behind them. The train ride from Berlin is a long one, and Dietrich writes to Eberhard:

> . . . I have not written to Maria. As things stand, it is impossible now. Even if we never meet again, the delightful thought of those few minutes of high tension will undoubtedly melt once again into the realm of my unfulfilled fantasies, a realm that in any case is already adequately populated. . . .

After years of bachelorhood, and at a time when his own future is more precarious than ever before, Dietrich Bonhoeffer is falling in love!

The Engagement

1942: AUGUST. On the eastern front, two separate German armies are closing in on Stalingrad, the key to Russia's Caucasian oil fields. Major Hans von Wedemeyer has just been reassigned from the Southern Army Group's staff headquarters to command of an infantry regiment, and for the first time he will be in the front line of the fighting. Hans's file states that this change in status was made at his own request. In staff headquarters, there are those who maintain that Major von Wedemeyer asked for the reassignment in protest over staff decisions regarding the treatment of enemy civilians and captured enemy soldiers.

On the twenty-second of August, Hans von Wedemeyer is killed in the battle raging outside Stalingrad. His family is notified immediately. On the twenty-fifth, from the Abwehr office in Munich, Dietrich writes to the widow Ruth von Wedemeyer:

> Dear Madam, It was about seven years ago that your husband sat in my room at Finkenwalde, where we talked about the instruction that Max was to receive as a candi-

date for confirmation. I have never forgotten that meeting. The thought of it remained with me during the entire period of instruction. I knew that Max was receiving at home what was most vital; and it was also clear to me how important it is these days for a boy to have a devout father who lives a full and active life.

As the years went by, I came to know nearly all of your children. Clearly they are living proof that it is an immense blessing to have a truly Christian father. I have had this same impression in meeting and knowing other members of your family—your mother and your brother and sisters. The blessing is not something purely spiritual, but rather something that goes deep down and affects one's entire earthly life. . . . The picture of your husband that still stands in my mind's eye is of one who lived under such a blessing and who passed it on with a sense of ultimate responsibility. . . .

The spirit in which he lived will continue to abide with you and your children. The same earnestness with which he spoke to me years ago about his son's Christian upbringing will now sustain you as you help your children to a Christian mourning for their father. . . . The spirit he exemplified of sacrifice and obedience to the will of God will also help you in accepting quietly and thankfully what God has sent you. . . .

My thoughts go out especially to Max. How he must miss his father now. I am confident that he will neither forget nor lose what he received from his father and that he is as safe in God as his father was and is.

God help you, dear Madam, through his Word and Sacrament, to be comforted and to comfort others. With kind regards to you and to all your people. Yours respectfully and sincerely, Dietrich Bonhoeffer

SEPTEMBER. The widow at Pätzig is not the only one to receive letters of condolence. At Klein Krössin Grandmother Ruth receives her share, for she too was warmed by the radiance of Hans von Wedemeyer—a kind of Christian joy that she has rarely found among the men in her life. Ruth has difficulty in preserv-

ing Hans's positive outlook, though, as she responds to each
message. To Dietrich's mother, she writes:

> My dear Frau Bonhoeffer, You wrote so kindly on the
> death of my son-in-law. I believe it was a worse blow than
> the deaths of my three young grandsons. In his case, the
> head of the family is gone. Sometimes I think my daugh-
> ter does not yet realize this, with all the other problems
> that beset her. She is so unbelievably brave and com-
> posed and she goes about her duties without complaint.
> But she must bear exactly the same grief that I once had
> to fight through and she has many more crucial deci-
> sions to make—regarding the children and the proper-
> ties—than I ever had. But God will help her. May God
> protect my son [Hans Jürgen] and my son-in-law
> [Herbert von Bismarck]. . . .

Shortly after Hans's death, Dietrich makes his way to
Pomerania to call on his friend and benefactor and express his
condolences in person. It is a brief visit—so brief that there are
misunderstandings between Ruth and Dietrich which have not
been totally resolved. Dietrich has hinted for the first time of a
romantic interest in Maria, presenting Ruth with a new dynamic
with which to wrestle. There is simply too much to deal with all at
once. Following Dietrich's departure, Ruth turns to their mutual
friend:

> My dear Eberhard, What must you have thought when I
> did not write on your birthday. Probably Dietrich told
> you already that I am so overwhelmed these days I have
> forgotten dates and anniversaries. But subsequently I did
> remember your birthday and I asked God for his blessing
> on you. . . .
>
> In hindsight I have real regrets about Dietrich's visit
> here. It is as if I said too much and, even without words,
> made judgments on what ought or ought not to be. May
> God forgive me if I conducted myself badly. I hope
> Dietrich will not be influenced by my behavior. With you,
> there is not so much at stake because you are less compli-
> cated than he.

So many questions have turned up and they all need to be answered. How happy I would be if you could resolve them with me. Even if a happy marriage is cut asunder too soon [by death], still one is rewarded for an entire lifetime. Marriage is a mystery. Not every marriage is entered into as God would have it. I am too inclined to take my own marriage as the standard.

I thank you for the dear words at the time of my son-in-law's death. It is so hard for me to realize that my daughter must tread the same road that I once traveled; I know the way too well. But she is older and much more mature than I was. Still the overwhelming sense of loss will be the same. No doubt she has a foreboding as to what this broken tie means though she is only at the beginning of it.

I talked much too much with Dietrich about this; I told him everything that weighed upon me. . . . May God keep you. Faithfully, Your RvK

OCTOBER. It is Ruth's turn now to go to Berlin for surgery. Dietrich's father has made all the arrangements, just as he did for Hans Jürgen, and Dietrich declares that he will stay in Berlin during the entire hospitalization. Ruth will have a cataract removed in the hope of improving her vision. Cataract surgery is always risky, and since it involves days and weeks of lying perfectly still in bed, she has asked Ruthchen if Maria might be spared from Pätzig to be with her in Berlin. It is a sacrifice for the newly widowed mistress of Pätzig, but Ruthchen gladly obliges.

Maria will stay with Tante Spes while she is in Berlin. Spes, who is increasingly busy with full-time volunteer work for the German Red Cross, welcomes this niece to her empty apartment. Alla and Hans Conrad are now both on the eastern front, and Raba, married to a physician in Breslau, is flirting dangerously with elements of the left-wing conspiracy against Hitler. This visit from Maria brings a bit of much-needed sunshine to Spes's Berlin flat.

Grandmother Ruth is a very demanding patient. She insists that Maria be with her every afternoon and that Dietrich make his daily visit at the same time. Often when both Dietrich and

Maria are at her side, she becomes restless and calls for a nurse. Her bodily functions must be attended to, or she needs to be turned in her bed, or the flowers and cards must be rearranged—there is no end to the services this patient demands from the nursing staff, which of course must be administered in complete privacy. When these excuses have been exhausted, Grandmother insists that she must sleep and not be awakened for at least three-quarters of an hour. Dutifully the two visitors leave the room to wait on a bench in the corridor and keep each other company. If Maria has not yet realized the purpose of her grandmother's ploys, Dietrich certainly has. It is up to him to decide how to make use of these opportunities, and he suggests that they might have enough time to drink a cup of coffee together in the restaurant across from the hospital. Dietrich cautions his companion on one thing, however. The restaurant is owned by Adolf Hitler's brother, and though one must always be careful when speaking in public places these days, in this case, it is doubly true. Maria is delighted to move from the hospital corridor to a more comfortable restaurant table, and the fact that one Herr Hitler owns the place simply makes the prospect more enticing.

By the time Ruth is sufficiently recovered to leave the hospital, Dietrich Bonhoeffer and Maria von Wedemeyer have made a firm commitment to each other. However, Dietrich must go to Munich on an Abwehr assignment, and Maria returns to Klein Krössin with her grandmother. She says nothing of what has transpired, nor does her grandmother inquire. Propriety still demands that Dietrich approach Maria's mother first of all, and this is not the time to burden Ruthchen with such a decision.

OCTOBER. At Munich, the Abwehr office to which Dietrich is connected is now under surveillance. Hans von Dohnanyi is being watched by the Gestapo. Everything is done under a cloak of secrecy, but both Dohnanyi and Dietrich know that their telephones are being tapped, for they have received warning from counterespionage agents at Gestapo headquarters.

In Russia, winter has closed in early. German troops failed to capture Stalingrad while the weather held, and now this is no longer possible. Russian troops are on the offensive all along the eastern front. On the twenty-sixth of October, Maximilian von Wedemeyer is killed in battle.

NOVEMBER. On the eighth of November there is a memorial service for Max at the Pätzig church. Afterward, Maria finally tells her mother of the feelings that exist between herself and Dietrich and of the commitment they have made to each other. Ruthchen is not surprised, for the two have exchanged a number of letters since Maria's stay in Berlin. She is worried, though, and she asks Dietrich to come to Pätzig and discuss the matter.

Two weeks later Dietrich is seated with Frau von Wedemeyer in the Pätzig study. They face one another on opposite sides of the oversized work desk that once belonged to Hans's father and more recently to Hans. Its writing surface is obscured by piles of letters, each letter carefully preserved in its mailing envelope. They represent twenty-five years of correspondence between a husband and his wife—letters that Ruthchen is rereading, sorting and tying into bundles so that her children and her children's children will remember. High above the desk hang two large etchings depicting the hunt; these are flanked on both sides by a veritable crowd of deer antlers, all evidence of great Pätzig hunts over many decades. Dietrich ignores the letters, the pictures and the antlers. His attention is focused on the death mask of Friedrich the Great, which hangs directly above his hostess' head. The old king appears to sleep peacefully; the discussion can begin.

Ruthchen voices her concerns. She feels that Maria, who is just eighteen, is too young to be making decisions about marriage; she has been greatly affected by her father's death, and now by her brother's also; it may be that she is attracted to Dietrich, who is thirty-six years old, simply because she is looking for another father figure. In addition, the times are so uncertain—and what will become of Pastor Bonhoeffer? One hears daily of arrests and trials for little or no cause; what is to prevent a man as deeply involved in dangerous work as this pastor from suffering a similar fate? Furthermore there is Maria's guardian, her uncle Hans Jürgen von Kleist, to consider. He too is unsure whether this marriage would be a good idea.

Ruthchen lays out all of her doubts, and Dietrich does his best to counter them by taking each negative point and turning it to his own advantage. All in all, he presents a well-constructed defense of his marriage proposal, which is not surprising with his years of experience in theological debate. After both have had their say, Ruthchen makes her decision: "Wait—at least a year."

Three days later, back in Berlin, Dietrich writes of his frustrations in a letter to Eberhard:

> I think I could have my way if I wanted to; I can argue better than the others and I could probably convince her; but that would not be natural for me; it seems wrong . . . as if I were exploiting someone else's weakness. Frau von Wedemeyer is stronger because of the loss of her husband—that is, in her very weakness, she is stronger than she would have been if I were dealing with him also. I must not allow her to feel defenseless; that would be unkind. As it stands now, though, my situation is more difficult.

A few days later he writes Eberhard again:

> I have been wondering whether you could at this time—without my knowing anything about it—very gently and very nicely write to Frau von Wedemeyer, just as a friend. Or it could be later on as well; perhaps that would be even better.

DECEMBER. From Pätzig to Klein Krössin to Kieckow, and back to Pätzig again, the letters and phone calls are exchanged. At the center of it all is Maria, who insists that she knows well her own mind. Isn't an early marriage even more important in these uncertain times? Her most potent argument is the reminder to Mother that Father proposed in the very midst of a revolution. It was 1918, in the wake of Germany's World War defeat, when he wrote his intended: "If you and I are to hang, at least it must be from the same tree."

1943: JANUARY. Just after the New Year, Ruth is in Berlin for a party to announce the engagement of Renate Schleicher, Dietrich's niece, to Eberhard Bethge, his closest friend and confidant.

The road to this engagement has not been smooth. Renate, not yet eighteen years old, has barely finished the gymnasium, and Eberhard, his studies long completed, seems to travel in a kind of shadow world, though he continues to fulfill his pastoral functions. Originally Renate's parents objected, citing her youth, the uncertain times, and Eberhard's precarious position. But all that is past, and on this January afternoon a joyful mood prevails in both the Schleicher and Bonhoeffer homes, which are next door to each other in the Grunewald section of the city. If there is any undercurrent of tension or sadness, it lies mostly with Dietrich, who leaves the party early and retreats to one of the upstairs rooms. Ruth is the first to notice, and she guesses the reason. She resolves to go directly from Berlin to Pätzig for a serious talk with Ruthchen.

Two weeks later, at Pätzig in the Neumark, Ruth von Wedemeyer and Hans Jürgen von Kleist formally agree to the engagement of Dietrich Bonhoeffer and Maria von Wedemeyer. Dietrich personally assures them that there will be no public announcement until sometime in the future and that the marriage will not take place for at least a year.

FEBRUARY. On February fourth Ruth and Dietrich Bonhoeffer each celebrate a birthday, Ruth at Lasbeck with her daughter Maria von Bismarck and Dietrich in Berlin with his parents. It is the day on which he informs them that he is now engaged to Maria von Wedemeyer.

On the following morning Ruth writes from Lasbeck:

> My dear Dietrich, I thank you for your dear birthday letter, and even more for your evening phone call. I am especially thankful that I am now freed from the agonizing uncertainty. In this regard, this [marriage decision] is probably the greatest act of your life. Do you understand what I mean? I wrestle so with my own will—to remain silent, even when I am not in full accord. How much I would have liked to send you the letter from Maria for it brought me so much happiness. However, since there has been so much mix-up in this affair, I dare not. You know how it all stands, so the letter holds nothing new for you.
>
> Now my heart is so full of things I want to tell you. And

still I do not know enough to be permitted to discuss it all. What you have said is sufficient for me: "I am happy and I am grateful." I repeat that to myself many times each day and I pray to God that it all turns out not just good, but very good. That I will accept you as a son when the time comes—certainly you know this without my saying it. I gather that it is by principle that Maria's mother and Hans Jürgen insist on the long waiting period. Perhaps it is necessary for Maria so that she is clear in her mind. But certainly if it appears too long a time for you and for her, there are ways and means to shorten it.

What does time mean nowadays? Will you really visit me in March? Believe me, it would be so good. God protect you and all of us. Konstantin [Hans Jürgen's son] is in Tunis [North Africa]. But the hand of God is there with him.

In Stettin I am always up at dawn or earlier in case there is anything you want to phone me about. Oh, how I rejoice. Grandmother

MARCH. Grandmother Ruth is ill again and in the hospital. After each illness she loses something of her vitality, and now her eyesight has become even worse. Hans Jürgen decides it is time to give up the Stettin flat entirely. If it is too uncomfortable at Klein Krössin in winter, Grandmother can easily be brought over to Kieckow.

Maria von Wedemeyer has been drafted to work in a munitions factory at Hannover.

Failed Plans

1943. For years, Henning von Tresckow, career officer in the German army, has been trying to convince his peers and his superiors to cooperate in the overthrow of Adolf Hitler. He has kept a dossier on every general in the army, sounding out dozens he thought might agree with his point of view and talking repeatedly with the handful that presumably can be counted upon to support a coup d'état. At first General Bock held the top rank in the military opposition; now General von Kluge is the senior officer to be counted upon when the time is ripe. But there are dozens of others, from General von Manstein and General Rommel on down, who have agreed at least to stand aside should the Nazi government be overthrown. In addition, the esprit de corps within the German army is such that even those officers who insist they will remain loyal to the führer and to the Nazis can be counted on not to betray Tresckow and his fellow conspirators.

Henning has hopes of involving General von Manstein more deeply in his plans and has arranged to have his cousin's son, Alexander Stahlberg, assigned to Manstein's staff as a friendly conduit. Through Alla, Henning hopes to encourage greater commitment from the general, but so far Manstein has not budged.

Henning von Tresckow has now come around to the point of view Ewald von Kleist has held for years: One cannot bring down the German government without first killing Adolf Hitler. Even the most supportive of the generals insist upon this, but who will volunteer to commit the deed? A number of trusted confederates have been approached but have been dropped from consideration for one reason or another—a large family, a wife, elderly parents, a key military position, lands to be managed—there are more than enough reasons to excuse all potential volunteers.

Of the six men who will lay hands on one of the bombs intended to dispose of Adolf Hitler, three will be from among the leftover vassals of the old Prussian kings—Colonel Henning von Tresckow, Lieutenant Fabian von Schlabrendorff and Lieutenant Ewald Heinrich von Kleist of Schmenzin. Henning has a wife and four children; Fabian has a wife and two children; only Ewald Heinrich, the heir to Schmenzin, is single.

MARCH. The time appears to be optimum. The defeat at Stalingrad is nothing less than cataclysmic. The führer insisted that the German armies fight to the last man, when in fact they could have retreated in good order. As a result, tens of thousands have perished, and news of such a disaster is difficult to keep from the home front. Nor is the war going much better in North Africa; it is only a matter of time until the British and Americans make a clean sweep of that continent. The best one can hope for is to evacuate the men and salvage at least some of the vehicles.

Henning is serving as staff officer to General von Kluge at Center Army Group headquarters near Smolensk, in Russia, and Fabian, his cousin by marriage, is his adjutant.

Fabian has flown to Berlin, where he is apprised of the latest plans by Dohnanyi and Oster, the two Abwehr men who have been his trusted colleagues since before the war. Adolf Hitler is to be killed this month at Smolensk, one of the scheduled stops on his visit to the eastern front. It took a great amount of persuasion on the part of Kluge to get Hitler to include this stop in his itinerary, as if the führer has qualms about Kluge's headquarters. And justifiably so, for a special cavalry regiment has been created to escort his party from the Smolensk airfield to staff headquarters, and with Kluge's blessing, the deed will be carried out en route.

The visit is scheduled for March 13, but the plans are beginning to unravel. General von Kluge now shies away from any assassination attempt being carried out under his command, and Henning's most ardent pleas are of no avail. Without Kluge's support, the cavalry escort is useless. Furthermore, on the day preceding the führer's arrival, several planeloads of men and supplies are delivered to the airfield—a company of well-armed SS bodyguards, an armored limousine, Hitler's personal physician and his personal chef, eating utensils and dishes, and every ingredient for the meal the führer will consume in the company of Kluge's staff.

Given the increased difficulty of shooting Hitler while he is en route to staff headquarters, Henning and Fabian have devised an alternate plan involving explosives. The plan cannot be carried out while Hitler is meeting with Kluge's staff, however. A simple calculation reveals that at least a dozen of those who will be in attendance are men who must be counted on to take part in the coup.

For days Fabian and Henning have been experimenting with captured British fuses and plastic explosives, which are far more compact and effective than the materials normally used by the German army. Confident that these explosives are right for their purposes, Fabian has constructed a time bomb with a thirty-

Lieutenant Fabian von Schlabrendorff, 1943

minute fuse and Henning has fashioned a container to look like a package containing two bottles of Cointreau, the only brandy that comes in square bottles.

On the morning of March 13, Fabian takes the package with him to group headquarters and telephones Oster's agent at the Abwehr: "Operation Flash is in effect." This message is the signal that Hitler is about to be assassinated, putting the entire coup protocol, from one end of Germany to the other, on active status. All that is needed now is word that Adolf Hitler is dead.

Henning accompanies General von Kluge to the airport, and the two are at the front of the welcoming group as the führer's plane touches down at noon. The stairway is lowered from the aircraft, and two bodyguards exit first. Behind them the führer

steps out, gives his characteristic salute and descends the stairs.
General von Kluge and Colonel von Tresckow click their heals
and salute their führer, visible assurance that they are his loyal
subordinates. As expected, every precaution is taken to isolate
the führer from Kluge and his staff. Hitler is immediately
escorted to his limousine, surrounded by an SS guard. On the
short drive to Center Army Group headquarters, the vehicle is
flanked by four SS staff cars—one in front, one in back and one
on either side.

Hitler is once again accompanied by SS officers as he exits his
limousine and enters the crowded conference room for the
meeting with Kluge and his staff. At lunch, he is served by his
own chef, after each item has been tasted by his physician, and
he declines the offer of wine or brandy. Immediately after the
meal he leaves for the airfield, again closely guarded by his staff
and his SS guard. This time Fabian joins Henning and the others
in the drive to the airfield. Fabian is carrying a gift package
under his arm, and as the last of Hitler's party boards the plane,
he surreptitiously presses the fuse that protrudes unnoticeably
from its side. At the last minute, he asks one of the führer's aides,
a Colonel Brandt, to deliver the package to a mutual friend at
Hitler's East Prussian headquarters. The colonel is more than
happy to carry out this errand for Lieutenant von Schlabrendorff.

Fabian returns to headquarters to make another phone call to
Berlin, reporting that the führer's plane has just taken off and
that it is expected to crash within the quarter hour. Huddled
together over a field radio, he and Henning—both kin to the
Bismarcks, the Zedlitzes and the Kleists—wait for word of the
plane's fate. It is news that never comes, for the package had
been placed in the unheated baggage compartment. There the
temperature had dropped significantly in flight, rendering the
temperature-sensitive fuse completely harmless.

Fabian makes a third call to Berlin with the coded message
that the assassination attempt has failed. Then it is Henning's
turn to place a call—to Hitler's next stop at Rastenburg in East
Prussia, where the plane has just landed. Henning gets Colonel
Brandt on the line and asks him to hold the package, explaining
that a mistake was made and it is the wrong liqueur. Fabian

immediately boards a courier flight to Rastenburg and exchanges two fresh bottles of Cointreau for the unopened package. The conspirators can breathe more easily.

Within a few days, another opportunity presents itself. Fabian hears from Dohnanyi that on Sunday, March 21, the führer will open an exhibition of war trophies in Berlin. Fabian goes immediately to Berlin, where he learns that Baron Rudolph von Gersdorff, an army major who is attached to the Abwehr and fully committed to the conspiracy, will accompany Hitler to the exhibition. The next day Henning too makes his way to Berlin carrying a briefcase of explosives and immediately goes to see Gersdorff. The major agrees to commit the deed without hesitation.

In the meantime, word of the failed attempt and the new opportunity is communicated to Ewald von Kleist at Schmenzin. It is clear that vacillating generals like Kluge need added persuasion—a dose of the moral certainty that is still present in abundance on these Kleist lands. In the few remaining days before the Berlin exhibition, Ewald has been handed the task of incorporating a restored monarchy into the proposed provisional government.

On March 17 Hans Jürgen and Ewald meet quietly at Schmenzin. Hans Jürgen's mother Ruth is in the hospital and quite unaware of the plans that are in motion. Still she is part of it all, for without her the link between the eastern front conspiracy and the Bonhoeffer clan would never have been forged. From Ewald's library Hans Jürgen makes a phone call to the Bonhoeffer home in Berlin; the following morning Ewald is on a train bound for the capital.

On Friday afternoon, March 19, in the home of Dietrich's brother Klaus, Ewald von Kleist meets with Klaus, Dietrich, and Louis Ferdinand of Hohenzollern, prince of Prussia. Louis Ferdinand is the oldest living son of Crown Prince Wilhelm and the grandson of the late Prussian king and former kaiser, Wilhelm II. Ten years ago, in 1933, the crown prince stood before the tomb of Friedrich the Great and, along with a large company of Prussia's aristocracy, pledged his allegiance to Adolf Hitler. He now proudly wears the swastika on his sleeve. Louis Ferdinand, however, is made of other stuff. Brought into the con-

spiracy through Ewald's urging, he is committed to the plot to
remove Hitler. He is informed of the imminent assassination
attempt, and he agrees to go on national radio the moment he
hears that Hitler is dead. He will call for a general strike throughout the nation. Beginning at noon on Sunday the twenty-first, he
will situate himself within five minutes of the broadcasting headquarters.

On Sunday morning, Fabian meets Gersdorff at the Hotel
Eden and turns over to him a small bomb with a quarter-hour
fuse. This time there should be no temperature problems. The
major conceals the compact device in his pocket.

That afternoon, next door to the Bonhoeffer home in suburban Grunewald, Professor Bonhoeffer's children and grandchildren are gathered in the Schleicher music room to practice a
cantata based on the well-known hymn, "Lobe den Herren," in
preparation for the seventy-fifth birthday of the Bonhoeffer
patriarch. Eberhard Bethge is directing the ensemble—Dietrich
at the piano and Klaus playing the cello, Rüdiger Schleicher
playing violin, and Hans von Dohnanyi singing with the children's choir. Dohnanyi is also watching the clock. His automobile waits outside. The men know what is about to happen, as
does Christine von Dohnanyi; the other women and the children
do not.

The führer and his party have just arrived at the Berlin exhibition hall. Hitler breezes into the hall, makes a brisk tour of a few
exhibits—mainly captured Russian tanks and weapons—and
leaves within five minutes. His scheduled speech is never given,
nor does he accept the well-orchestrated accolades from the
invited guests, all of which was to take at least a half hour. It is an
immense disappointment to those present, particularly to Major
von Gersdorff. Fortunately he still has time to reach the lavatory
and deactivate the fuse next to his body. At the national broadcasting center and at the Schleicher home in Berlin, at Center
Army Group headquarters in Smolensk, at Schmenzin and at
Kieckow in the Belgard District, and at other points throughout
the land the expected phone call is never received.

On Wednesday afternoon, the thirty-first of March, Professor
Karl Bonhoeffer celebrates his birthday at home with his three

sons and three of his daughters and their families. Also present is
Eberhard Bethge, always a close friend and now almost family
since his engagement to Renate Schleicher. Missing is the professor's daughter Sabine, who lives in exile with her husband and
children.

Also missing is Dietrich's fiancée, Maria von Wedemeyer. After
some discussion, the Bonhoeffers decided it would be better to
wait until their son's engagement is publicly announced and
accepted by Maria's family before extending social invitations to
the young lady. Perhaps it would be different if her grandmother
were able to attend, but Ruth von Kleist is not well and presently
confined to a hospital. Maria is working in Hannover and uses
her few free weekends to visit her grandmother. If Dietrich does
not agree with his parents' view, he has decided not to force the
issue. Right now there is more at stake than a single birthday
party.

Even with close friends and family members absent, the party
is large and festive. The well-rehearsed hymn is performed with a
professionalism that is remarkable, after which Klaus Bonhoeffer,
the oldest son, makes a magnificent toast, thanking his father for
the principles he instilled in his children. There are letters of
congratulation from colleagues, family and friends throughout
Europe, even from those in enemy lands, sent through contacts
in neutral Switzerland. And from the führer himself there is a
hand-written message, presented with a medal from the
Fatherland:

> In the name of the German people I bestow on Professor
> Emeritus Dr. Karl Bonhoeffer the Goethe medal for art
> and science, instituted by the late Reich President von
> Hindenburg. The Führer Adolf Hitler

APRIL. A week after the party, on Monday the fifth of April,
Dietrich is still in Berlin. There is a scandal brewing at the
Munich Abwehr office, and Dohnanyi encourages his brother-in-
law to remain at home a while longer. At noon, when Dietrich
phones his sister Christine, an unknown man's voice informs
him that Frau von Dohnanyi is not available. Clearly Christine

has been arrested and her house is being searched. Dietrich goes next door to the Schleicher residence, where Eberhard is staying. Together he and Eberhard and his sister Ursula go to Rüdiger's study to search through his papers for any incriminating evidence. Satisfied that Rüdiger is safe, at least to the extent that they can help him, the three sit down together over coffee to await whatever may come.

At 4:00 P.M., Professor Bonhoeffer comes through the garden that separates the two homes to deliver an ominous message: "Dietrich, there are two men wanting to speak to you upstairs in your room." Dietrich returns home, and a few minutes later he is driven away by the two men, one a military judge and the other a Gestapo official. Dietrich Bonhoeffer is under arrest.

At Tegel prison in Berlin, Dietrich is placed in solitary confinement. Likewise at the Lehrterstrasse prison, Hans von Dohnanyi is in solitary confinement. Hans's wife Christine, Dietrich's sister, is under interrogation at the women's prison in Charlottenburg. All three are in an exceedingly unenviable position. The crux of Christine's interrogations has to do with slips of paper, found in Hans's desk. With courage and shrewdness, she manages to last through two weeks of questioning without giving anything away. When her interrogators take her to confront her husband and brother, she can assure them by glance and by hint that they have not been exposed.

MAY. Christine von Dohnanyi is released from prison, and the Bonhoeffer family is optimistic that freedom will soon follow for Dietrich. He continues to be interrogated by the Gestapo, however, for Christine's husband Hans von Dohnanyi is suspected of being the key figure in a treasonous conspiracy spawned in the Abwehr's Munich office, and Dietrich is thought to have knowledge of the plot. The Gestapo is dangerously close to the truth, but Dietrich continues to lie with aplomb.

With so much of the family now under siege, Dietrich's mother reaches out to her imprisoned son's fiancée. She sends a letter to Maria in Hannover, inviting her to stay at their home so that she might take advantage of any visiting privileges at Tegel. In the meantime, Ruth von Wedemeyer's efforts to have her daughter released from the factory in Hannover have borne fruit. Maria is granted permission to return home and prepare for a nursing position; instead she goes directly to Berlin. Maria does not visit Dietrich, however; no one visits him during this period, for the Gestapo and the courts are jointly preparing to try Hans von Dohnanyi, and Dietrich is continually under interrogation. The Tegel prison commandant promises a loosening of the rules once the Gestapo has all the information it needs.

After many weeks of waiting, Maria finally gives up and returns to Pätzig, where she is better able to come to grips with the situation. In Berlin, Maria felt she had to keep her thoughts and emotions to herself, sensing that among the Bonhoeffers one says very little of one's inner feelings. Raised in an atmosphere that was far more open, she is used to speaking freely of what is in her heart.

From Pätzig Maria finds it easier to communicate with Dietrich's mother than she did in Berlin. To her future mother-in-law she writes:

> Dear Mama, Whenever I think about the hours with you [in Berlin] I am happy and deeply thankful. Even without my saying it, you must believe that I am well aware of the gift of your friendship. Every moment with you helps me to carry on now—leaving me with deep happiness and great humility. I would like so much to tell you what is in my heart, but I simply don't find the right words. Still, I know that you understand what I feel. In great thanksgiving and veneration, I kiss your hand. Your Maria

Since returning home, Maria has found her own mother to be inordinately distraught over Dietrich's imprisonment—not so much the fact of the arrest (for she is a Prussian who knows that a true patriot will live in danger and must be prepared to suffer), but rather over her own reticence with respect to the engagement. Ruthchen has already written to Dietrich at the Tegel prison and has laid out her regrets in this regard. She informs him that she will make a public announcement of the engagement and that the selection of a marriage date is entirely in the young couple's hands.

In between sleepless nights and exhausting interrogations,

Dietrich is comforted by Ruthchen's emotion-filled letter. To Eberhard he writes:

> I can hardly tell you how very much my [future] mother-in-law's letter moved me. Since the first day of my detention I have been haunted by the knowledge that I caused her such an added burden, after all the anguish of her past year. And here she has taken our common distress as the occasion to shorten the period of waiting. It makes me so happy.
>
> Now I want to assure you that I have not for a moment regretted coming back in 1939—nor any of its consequences. I knew quite well what I was doing and I acted with a clear conscience. I have no wish to cross out of my life anything that has happened since....

Letters and Gifts

1943: JUNE. On the twenty-fourth of June, two and a half months after Dietrich's arrest, Maria is permitted to see him for the first time. Dietrich has not been forewarned, and when Maria is brought into his presence, he is visibly shaken. At first he says nothing. They sit silently together on a bench, Dietrich holding Maria's hand, while a guard sits across from them. The only sign of emotion that comes through to Maria is the varying pressure of Dietrich's hand on hers. She tells him that her mother announced their engagement this morning and that tomorrow she herself will go to Pomerania and give the news to Grandmother.

After fifteen minutes, the guard informs them that their time is up. Dietrich returns to his cell, still showing no sign of emotion. That night he writes:

> . . . I have just come back from seeing Maria—an indescribable surprise and joy! I heard about it only a minute before. It is still like a dream—it is really an almost incomprehensible situation—how we shall think back to it later! Whatever one says at such a moment is so irrelevant, but that is not the main thing. It was so brave of her

to come; I should never have dared to ask it of her, for it
is much harder for her than it is for me. I know what I
am doing, but for her it is all unimaginable, bewildering,
terrible. What a prospect when this terrible nightmare is
over!

Grandmother Ruth is out of the hospital and back at Klein
Krössin. She has become uncharacteristically frail and is now
prone to depression. The complications that plagued Maria and
Dietrich's engagement have already taken their toll on this
grandmother. With Dietrich's arrest and isolation, her cup of
misgivings overflows. Even Maria's letters, each one a well of
optimism even in the worst of circumstances, do little to cheer
the matriarch of Kieckow.

Then on June 25 Maria arrives at Gross Tychow by train. She is
met by Uncle Hans Jürgen and his driver, with a horse and
wagon, and taken to grandmother's house at Klein Krössin. On
the way Maria shares with her uncle the happy news that yesterday she visited Dietrich in the Tegel prison, while Mother publicly announced their engagement from Pätzig.

As soon as the wagon reaches Klein Krössin, Maria jumps from
the seat without waiting for the driver to help her down.
Grandmother Ruth is standing in her garden, one hand on her
cane and the other outstretched to embrace her granddaughter.
Their greeting is long and emotional, the bond between them
much stronger because of their mutual affection for Dietrich.
Maria seats Grandmother beside her and waves her uncle away.
She wastes few words in telling Grandmother about her visit with
Dietrich yesterday afternoon, and the public announcement of
their engagement. She proclaims that Dietrich is well and that he
sends his deepest love.

Now it is the grandmother's turn to speak, time to tell Maria
what it is in Dietrich that changed her own life so dramatically.
Call it *freedom*—an inner freedom that prompts one to act not
only responsibly, but even courageously. In these times when the
power of evil is so evident, one's traditional devotion to duty is
no longer sufficient. It is Dietrich who has led her to a new
plateau—a place under God that demands risk in this world.
How empty, how full of despair life would be now without this

new knowledge of God's intent and God's command. The grand-mother concludes: "Maria, if I had known earlier in my life what I know now, my life would have surely gone a different way."

The granddaughter leans across the chair and throws her arms about the old woman, unwilling to let this moment of regret go unchallenged: "But Grandmama, it wouldn't have been nearly as interesting!"

With Maria, one cannot be serious for long. Ruth rises from her chair and excuses herself; she must look for a gift to send the bridegroom. She leaves the garden and goes into the house. From her bookcase she selects the biography of her father-in-law, Hans Hugo von Kleist. The book was written long ago by a distant relative, and Ruth has always considered herself its midwife. She sits down at her desk and inscribes this copy to Dietrich, dating it to coincide with the engagement announce-ment:

> Dietrich Bonhoeffer from Ruth von Kleist-Retzow née Countess of Zedlitz and Trützschler: It makes me so happy, my dear Dietrich, that on this day I may express my thanks to you for the most important event of my entire life, by presenting this book to you. The man whose story it tells left behind a blessed legacy, in which you also are now included. Klein Krössin (Kieckow), the twenty-fourth of June 1943.

Grandmother Ruth vows that she feels better today than she has in many weeks!

AUGUST. Dietrich Bonhoeffer and Hans von Dohnanyi are still in prison. Dohnanyi is ill and has been taken to the prison clinic. Efforts have been made to have the case against him dropped, but they have not been successful. Dietrich, on the other hand, is in good health. Maria is in Berlin now, staying indefinitely with his parents. Professor Bonhoeffer has requisitioned her to help in his psychiatry office, to be available for prison visits whenever permission is granted. Dietrich recognizes that the Bonhoeffers and the Wedemeyers represent two different lifestyles, and he anticipates that adjustments will have to be made. To Maria he writes:

It happens to be the case that certain things remain
unsaid in my family while they are expressed in yours.
There is no point discussing what is the "right" way. It
involves different people who act as they inwardly must. I
can imagine that at first it will be hard for you because
many things, especially in religious matters, remain unex-
pressed at home. But I will be very glad if you can adjust
to the ways of my parents as I have tried through your
grandmother to adjust to the ways of your family. . . .

Maria is permitted to deliver one package to Tegel each
week—books, paper, pencils, cigarettes, razor blades and whatever else Dietrich requests, plus clean laundry and food. This last
consists mostly of delicacies from Pätzig, for Berlin is now under
siege—from shortages in everything to nightly bombing attacks.

Renate Schleicher and Eberhard Bethge are married, but
neither Ruth nor Dietrich can be present at the wedding. In his
prison cell Dietrich writes a sermon for the occasion, but it does
not arrive in time.

Dietrich is writing most of the time, working on a novel that
started out as a stage drama. Besides the principal character and
protagonist—Dietrich himself—there is a young girl from the
South African veldt, undoubtedly Maria; the girl's father, who
reminds one of Hans von Wedemeyer; a grandmother, perhaps a
mixture of Dietrich's grandmother and Ruth von Kleist; a friend
(Eberhard?); and the principal character's sister. The novel
opens with a picnic in the countryside—the protagonist with his
brother, his sister and his friend. They talk and they swim, and
during the afternoon they accidentally trespass on the estate of
the South African family. Somehow it sounds much like a picnic
at Kieckow in the summer of 1941.

The novel is never completed, for as the weeks drag on
Dietrich turns more and more to theological writings. Fifteen-
minute visits are permitted once each month, and Maria is always
there. Then there are letters to answer. At first they are sent
through normal channels, which means censorship and delays;
later they are smuggled in and out of Dietrich's cell by a friendly
guard.

After one long-awaited visit from Maria, Dietrich puts on paper
all the words he could not say in the presence of the guard:

You cannot imagine what it means in my present situation to have you. I am certain of God's special guidance here. The way in which we found each other and the time, so shortly before my imprisonment, are a clear sign for this. . . . Everyday I am overcome anew at how I received this happiness, which I did not deserve. And everyday I am deeply moved at what a hard school God has led you through in this past year. And now it appears to be his will that I have to bring you sorrow and suffering. . . . When I also think about the situation of the world, the complete darkness over our personal fate and my present imprisonment, then I believe that our union can only be a sign of God's grace and kindness, which calls us to faith. . . . Our marriage shall be a yes to God's earth; it shall strengthen our courage to act and accomplish something on the earth. . . .

NOVEMBER. Dietrich is still in prison; he has been charged with antiwar activity, mainly avoidance of military service through the intervention of Abwehr officials. This means that he will be brought to trial after all. The Gestapo does not yet know about the conspiracy linking Dietrich and the Abwehr to important segments of the military. Dietrich writes to Eberhard in a state of high optimism:

My marriage plans: If I am free and not called up for at least a few months, I shall get married. If I have only two to three weeks before I am called up, I shall wait until the end of the war. What an engagement we are having!

From Klein Krössin, Dietrich's friend and future "grandmother" writes to Dita Koch:

My dear Dita, . . . Fortunately we don't suffer from air raids, but the nearness of the eastern front, where most of our relatives are fighting, is unsettling. . . . In addition there are the worries about Dietrich and these affect me very much. Recently we have been given hope that in the not too distant future we will see him again.

How wonderful were those days when I took my grand-

Maria von Wedemeyer

children to Finkenwalde and we were all led to a rich spiritual life. All four grandsons who were with me at Stettin [Finkenwalde] have fallen [in battle]. Sometimes the pain simply overwhelms me. But they have overcome death and are now in God's hands. . . .

Unfortunately my eyes have failed me considerably. I can still write even if the lines are somewhat uneven, but reading is difficult and straining. Take care, dear Dita, and keep me in your love. God protect you. . . . My heartfelt greetings to Werner. From my heart, Your RKR

DECEMBER. In his cell at Tegel Dietrich is busy with pencil and paper. To Maria, he writes in a spiritual vein:

In a prison cell one waits and hopes; one does various unessential things and is completely dependent on the fact that the door to freedom must be opened from the outside. It is not a bad picture of Advent.

311

To Eberhard, he vents his frustrations:

> We have been engaged now for nearly a year and have never been alone together for one hour? Isn't it absurd . . . we have to talk and write about things that are not most important ones for us both; once a month we sit beside each other, like good children at school, and then we are torn apart. We know practically nothing about each other; we have no common experiences. Even these months we are going through separately. Maria thinks I am a model of virtue, an exemplary Christian. In order to satisfy her, I have to write letters like an early martyr and her image of me becomes more and more false. Isn't that an impossible situation for her? And yet she goes through everything with a marvelous naturalness.

At Kieckow and Klein Krössin, Christmas preparations are under way. Grandmother Ruth and Mieze have compiled their lists of villagers, by sex and by age. This year all of the gifts will be homemade. For the men it will be something created in the leather shop, still in operation under the skilled hand of a very old man. The gifts for the women will be fashioned from cotton fabrics stored in the manor house attic. The seamstress is already busy sewing pinafore aprons with the help of Mieze's daughters, Ruthi and Elisabeth.

In the absence of the Kieckow men, fifty Russian prisoners of war are working the estate lands. They live in a converted stable and are guarded at all times by a German soldier. At Klein Krössin there are a like number of captured Frenchmen, also guarded by German soldiers. The guards are not so bad, but they are supervised by Nazi group leaders from Gross Tychow—civilians totally committed to enforcing the government strictures regarding the treatment of prisoners of war. According to these strictures, each prisoner may be given only a single straw cover and each prisoner's ration of food must be limited to the bare minimum needed for survival. Yet these men are expected to do heavy manual labor each day on the estate. The malevolence of the Nazi government is there for all to see.

From the beginning, Hans Jürgen has insisted that every prisoner be provided with two straw mats—one to lie on and one to use as a blanket. Clearly there is no other way to survive a Pomeranian winter. He has also insisted that the prisoners receive the same rations as the village workers. In the village these rations are always supplemented by fruits and vegetables from the villagers' gardens; Hans Jürgen therefore sees to it that the prisoners receive an extra portion from the manor house larder. It makes good sense, he tells the complaining Nazi official; one must have healthy workers to run an estate.

In the two years that there have been prisoners on Hans Jürgen's lands, he has operated in this manner. Invariably when a new group leader arrives at Gross Tychow there is a fresh confrontation at Kieckow. Hans Jürgen has been warned repeatedly about violations in his treatment of prisoners on his property, but he persists. It gives him immense satisfaction to know that in Pomerania, the landowner still counts for something!

But what can be done for the prisoners at Christmastime? There is a fine line to be drawn, and it is Mieze who finds the solution. The French are probably all Catholics, and the Russians as well, though of the Eastern Orthodox variety. Mieze, like other Prussian Protestants, perceives Catholic Christians to be different from her people in many ways, particularly when it comes to the veneration of Jesus's mother Mary. She and her daughters therefore scour every town in the Belgard District trying to find Christmas cards that carry a portrait of the Virgin Mary. The rest of each prisoner's gift will come from the estate itself.

At Pätzig, similar decisions must be made. Ruthchen has taken a violent dislike to the group of German soldiers that guards the Russian prisoners on her land. Hans Werner, just fourteen years old, observes his helpless mother tolerating these bullies over whom she has no control. The future master of Pätzig acts out his mother's frustration in his own way. From behind an attic window in the manor house, one can look down on the soldiers when they stand guard in the courtyard. From time to time Hans Werner mounts the attic stairs and spits at the soldiers through the open window, always retreating from view before the spittle strikes their metal helmets or the dirt at their feet. Over the weeks he improves his aim, until he is finally discovered—not by the soldiers, but by his mother. A stern lecture follows. Whatever one thinks of the man who wears the uniform of the Fatherland, one must never dishonor it!

For those at Pätzig, there is a special prisoner to be remembered this Advent season—Dietrich, still behind bars at Tegel. In the kitchen, the cook has baked an extra batch of holiday cookies, and Maria packs a box of them to take with her to Berlin for her monthly visit with Dietrich. In the forest, she and Hans Werner cut a small tree, which she will also take by train to Berlin.

A few days before Christmas, Maria arrives at Tegel with her Christmas tree and packages. In the visitors' cell there is outright laughter. Even the guards cannot keep from smiling, for Maria's tree is far too large for Dietrich's cell, which she has never seen. Later Dietrich will write: "Isn't it so that even when we are laughing, we are a bit sad."

On Christmas Eve in Berlin, Dietrich is invited into the Tegel prison guards' room to sit before Maria's tree. On Christmas Eve at Kieckow and Klein Krössin, Mieze and her daughters deliver one hundred Christmas gifts to the French and Russian prisoner barracks. Each gift consists of an apple, a candle, and a card bearing the likeness of the Virgin Mary. Late that night, the inhabitants of the Kieckow village and manor house are awakened by the deep sounds of a men's choir coming from the prisoner barracks. Leaving their beds and throwing coats about themselves, they go outside. Through the windows of the converted stables, the glow from fifty burning candles lights the snowy landscape, at first brilliantly, then gradually fading as the minutes pass. The Russian prisoners are singing the haunting songs of their homeland, harmonizing beautifully in many voices. One wonders if the brave men from Kieckow are also singing somewhere on the snowy Russian landscape.

Eventually the candlelight dies down and the music also ends; in the cold Pomeranian night at least one inhabitant asks, "Will Kieckow die too?"

On New Year's Eve—Sylvester Night—Lieutenant Ewald Heinrich von Kleist is with his father in the library of the Schmenzin manor house. He has arrived by train from his post in Potsdam, just outside Berlin, without announcement. He will leave early in the morning. The double doors that separate the library from the great hall are closed; father and son are speaking privately.

Ewald Heinrich is now deeply involved with Colonel von Tresckow and Colonel von Stauffenberg, the acknowledged leaders of the military conspiracy to overthrow the führer. He has come to discuss an unusual opportunity that has presented itself—to kill Adolf Hitler right in Berlin—but it will mean Ewald Heinrich must die also.

Ewald von Kleist says nothing, but rather walks around his desk to the window and gazes out upon the snow-covered expanse of the estate, lands that will belong to this oldest son one day. After some minutes, he returns from the window to stand before his son: "Yes, you must do it; if you should refuse such an opportunity, you would never again find happiness in your life."

VII

THE LAST MATRIARCH

1944-1945

The Führer Lives!

JANUARY. Clearly Germany is on the way to defeat. North Africa is lost, and with it went an inordinate number of German soldiers, either killed or captured. Italy, Germany's former ally, is now its enemy, for Mussolini's fascist government has fallen. American, British, French and Polish troops are slowly making their way up the boot of that nation; German forces resist at every turn and casualties mount. On the eastern front, Russian troops have crossed into Poland from the east. There is no doubt now that Germany itself will be invaded unless those who are brave enough can bring an end to Hitler and negotiate peace with Germany's enemies.

In Berlin, First Lieutenant Ewald Heinrich von Kleist of Schmenzin reports to Colonel Claus von Stauffenberg, chief of staff to the army reserve commander: The lieutenant is ready to dispose of Adolf Hitler. He will be joined in the attempt by his friend Captain Axel von dem Bussche. Ewald Heinrich has no problem with mixed loyalties, growing up at Schmenzin where contempt for the führer is endemic. For Axel, however, animosity toward the führer is a new experience and the result of something he witnessed on the eastern front more than a year ago. While fighting in the Latvian campaign, Axel was flying a small plane over the city of Borisov early one morning. There he happened to see several thousand people standing naked in the cold air, digging trenches. They were working under the apparent supervision of armed SS troops, who were standing guard. Bussche reported the incident to General von Bock of the

317

Center Army Group, and within a few hours the whole affair came out. These naked people were Jews who had been made to undress, then were given shovels with which to dig their own mass graves. Afterward they were lined up beside the trenches and shot, layer upon layer. In this way five thousand Latvian Jews were disposed of in a single day.

The Jews of Borisov had been forewarned of the SS's intentions and had appealed to the army commander of Borisov for protection, but none was forthcoming. The commander was later ordered to appear before General von Bock at Center Army Group headquarters, but on the way there he committed suicide, and that was the end of the incident. Not so for Axel von dem Bussche. He immediately pledged himself to work with Colonel Henning von Tresckow in conspiring against the government. Henning arranged for Axel to be transferred to Potsdam outside of Berlin, where he now reports to Colonel von Stauffenberg.

In Tegel prison, the lot of Dietrich Bonhoeffer is somewhat improved. His chief interrogator has been dismissed and the harsh interrogations have ceased for the time being.

FEBRUARY. On the third of February, in Berlin, Dietrich's niece Renate Bethge gives birth to a baby boy. Eberhard cannot be present, for he is now in uniform, somewhere on the Italian front. The child is given the name Dietrich after his godfather and great-uncle Dietrich Bonhoeffer! Grandmother Ruth of Klein Krössin rejoices, and from her home in Pomerania, she writes to the father:

> My dear Eberhard, What a priceless gift from God's hand! How it must disturb you not to have been present [at the birth]; perhaps it will not be long until you can take the young mother—your dear Renate—into your arms again. . . . Now you are all really a family and, as I know you, this new feeling of responsibility will take vigorous hold of you. God's blessing be with you daily, even hourly. . . .
>
> Oh, if only we could have celebrated this joyous occasion with Dietrich. Instead, Renate's mother writes me that it may still take months. I was quite undone [by the news]. But that is not the right word. I am so convinced

that it is God—not we humans—who makes these decisions and that our part consists of waiting patiently for
the moment. It occurs to me that one ought to rejoice!
God's way is often so very amazing and mysterious.

I often raise the idle question as to whether it was good
that Maria came into his life—whether it sweetens his situation or makes it more difficult. Both are possible. I
would also consider another question—whether I pushed
my own wish into the foreground and therefore expe-
dited something that had not yet matured. But Eberhard,
this I say only to you and it is better that these thoughts
do not go any further. In fact it is incredible that I even
think such thoughts. If only I did not have this feeling of
guilt. As old as I am [now seventy-seven], I still never
have learned the great art of waiting.

You should not make so many praise-filled compli-
ments about me as you did in your letter of January 16. If
you only knew how imperfect everything in me is. . . .

In the meantime you probably heard that on New
Year's Day we received news of Konstantin—missing in
action near Ortona [Italy], where he was a forward
observer. We had three and a half weeks of uncertainty
after that. Then on the twenty-fourth of January we
received a printed document, reporting that he was alive
and well in captivity. It was signed with his signature and
addressed with his own hand. . . . "He was dead and he
has risen again." You can imagine our happiness! . . .
Now if God will also help him through his captivity. He
[Konstantin] lives from God.

Jürgen Bismarck [son of Maria and Herbert] is leading
a battalion in the same area. . . . Do I understand that
you are not yet in combat? Oh, may God spare your life.
. . . Your Tante Ruth

In Berlin, Admiral Canaris, chief of the Abwehr, has been dismissed and is under investigation. The entire Abwehr is under
suspicion and has been incorporated into the Reich Security
Head Office. There are too many irregularities and allegations
associated with this organization.

At Potsdam Army Reserve headquarters, the time for action is at hand. New uniforms are being designed for the German officer corps, and Colonel von Stauffenberg has arranged for two of his dedicated young officers, Lieutenant von Kleist and Captain von dem Bussche, to model them for the führer. Samples of the uniforms have been shipped to Berlin on a cargo plane, and an appointment has been scheduled with Hitler in his headquarters. Ewald Heinrich and Axel will each wear a different version of the new uniform. Under their tunics, each will have strapped to his inside pocket one of Henning von Tresckow's powerful plastic explosives.

Two days before the scheduled appointment, it is canceled. A British bombing of Berlin's Tempelhof airfield has destroyed the cargo plane that carried the uniforms. Luck continues to stand on the side of the führer.

MARCH. In her Pomeranian home, Grandmother Ruth receives a letter from Eberhard, who is at the front in Italy. She responds immediately:

> Dear Eberhard, Today I received your dear letter and I thank you with all my heart. . . . I also received very dear letters from Renate and your mother-in-law. You write so charmingly of your young marriage. Thank God that it is so. It will still be a while before you see your son. What a hardship!
>
> I am especially happy over what you write about Dietrich's fate. Maria will have to endure it and he must carry his own cross in being so isolated. But I believe that their love will grow on both sides and that such a period of purification is necessary for both of them, in order to grow together. I had imagined that it would be easier than it has turned out to be.
>
> I thank you for the message from Dietrich that you sent: "I am too proud ever to be unhappy." This thought fits exactly in my memoirs, which I am working on now. Dietrich has repeatedly urged me to continue writing. If [these memoirs] should ever be completed, you will find them very disappointing. . .
>
> Konstantin has now been transferred to American captivity and the beginning of February he was preparing for

a sea voyage. We have received several cheerful letters from him. Now there will be a longer interval. Jürgen [Bismarck] was in the worst of the fighting at Nettuno [Italy]. Yesterday we received news that he is in a hospital at Rieti, slightly wounded with shrapnel in his calf. We thank God for this breathing space, which perhaps—perhaps—will mean a leave for rest and recuperation.

May God keep you from all danger, my dear Eberhard. Thinking of you in faithful love, Your Tante R.

Maria von Wedemeyer writes also:

Dear Eberhard, . . . I must tell you how much I rejoice with you both over your little boy. It was a great gift for me that I could be present for the event. He is the dearest little fellow. To admire him in his crib brings nothing but joy and thanksgiving. Each time it is a great new wonder that such a little being has come into the world. Especially in wartime when all thoughts are burdened with destruction, suffering and death and when one knows not where it will all lead, what a comfort to stand at the bed of such a tiny infant. I have never before experienced this with such force. After the long ride diagonally across Berlin—totally destroyed—I came upon the little cottage. And Renate looked so peaceful as she lay modestly and quietly in her bed. One could read the joy in her expression.

It was something very special for me, to be the one to bring Dietrich the report of the birth. Yet after I told him about it, I thought it was not right for me to be sitting so close to him. You should have been there to hear his joy. . . .

I say thank you for your letter. Parts of it I read aloud to Dietrich during our visiting period and he rejoiced no less than I. That was a dear thought of yours, to write me on Dietrich's birthday. Actually I rejoice in all the dear things that you write me. . . .

Your leave should begin at the end of May or first of June. Be sure that you include on your travel permit Bad Schönfliess—the railroad station for Pätzig. What do you think of that? . . .

Dietrich will be reassigned* the end of May and he is working hard. But recently he commented that he is short of creative thoughts and that a "vacation" would do him good. He declined the deck of solitaire cards that Christl [von Dohnanyi] gave him for his birthday. He has no time to play solitaire! I am really so proud of him!!!

Don't feel obligated to answer this letter. I know just how difficult it is for soldiers to write letters. Do you have a package label that you can send me? I would be so pleased to send you a package as I know this is not so easy for Renate. May all go well with you. Greetings from your Maria

At Potsdam, Colonel von Stauffenberg has made fresh arrangements for the modeling of the new officer corps uniforms. Replacements for those lost in the bombing raid are now in Berlin, and a new appointment has been scheduled at the führer's headquarters.

Lieutenant Ewald Heinrich von Kleist and Captain Axel von dem Bussche stand in the waiting room of Hitler's headquarters, looking as erect and proud as any German officer has ever looked, and why not? Very few lieutenants or captains in the German army are granted an audience with the führer. No one would suspect that strapped to their bodies are powerful plastic explosives with thirty-minute fuses. A quarter hour has passed and the führer still has not arrived. The two officers become nervous, but they do not panic. Five minutes later the phone rings. The führer has changed his plans; he will not appear at headquarters this morning. The two men rush to the lavatory, tearing off their shirts and deactivating the explosives—just in time! Fate has again intervened on behalf of Adolf Hitler.

At Schmenzin, Ewald von Kleist has been informed that Hitler may die today. Although he knows that the assassination may require the life of his son, still he waits impatiently for the phone call and the news that the deed is done. If the plan is successful, he will immediately fly to Sweden to make contact with certain British and American agents. When the phone call finally comes, it is from his son. The führer lives!

*Dietrich has knowledge that the charges against him may be dropped.

APRIL. Mieze and Hans Jürgen retire early each evening. An hour after midnight they rise again and quietly go to the salon of the manor house, where they uncover the short-wave radio. It is always tuned to the BBC broadcasts from London. The drapes are drawn and the couple sits quietly in the dark, listening to meaningless static and waiting for the sound of the first four notes of Beethoven's Fifth Symphony: " · · · — ." These four notes are the Morse code for the letter "V," for "victory," and they announce the BBC's nightly news broadcast—the only one that gives any inkling as to the state of the war and the location of the front. It is clear that Italy will soon be lost and that there will be an invasion along the English Channel. But it is the eastern front that is most disturbing to those who live on the ancient Kleist lands—how far are the Russian armies from Kieckow and how long does one have? These unspoken questions are constantly in the minds of the parents, the grandmother, and the children.

The manor house is overflowing with guests—friends, relatives and sometimes even strangers from the cities of western Germany who are awaiting an end to the incessant bombings. The end never comes, but eventually they leave and others take their places. There is constant tension in the household since one cannot always trust these visitors. Although the children have been cautioned to be careful in what they say, Mieze is shocked one day when she hears them singing aloud the four familiar notes that begin Beethoven's famous symphony—and the BBC broadcasts. Clearly they have been eavesdropping late at night, and yet another warning must be given.

Even in wartime, Hans Jürgen and Mieze insist on keeping the age-old Easter traditions. Early on Easter morning the old Kieckow carriage is dispatched to bring Grandmother Ruth to the manor house portico, where with Hans Jürgen's family she awaits the Easter greeting of the village children. It is barely sunrise when the children are spotted in procession, turning up the manor house road. All are dressed in their Easter finest, the girls with long ribbons in their hair. All are carrying in their arms budding birch twigs—cut before Lent and brought indoors to be forced into bloom. The children form a semicircle below the manor house portico, in front of Hans Jürgen, and cry out in unison: "The Lord is risen!" Hans Jürgen replies: "Yes, he has risen, indeed." This exchange of greetings dates back farther than anyone can remember. Then each of the children hands over to the master his or her birch twig and recites a Bible verse or a poem. Each is rewarded with a colored hard-cooked egg and a small coin.

MAY. Dietrich is still in the Tegel prison, but all charges against him have been dropped. For him the future looks hopeful. Things are not nearly as hopeful for his brother-in-law Hans von Dohnanyi. He is still at the Lehrterstrasse prison, suspected of being much more involved with Canaris and the machinations of the Abwehr.

JUNE. On the sixth of June the long-feared western invasion finally begins—at Normandy Beach in France. Then Rome falls and so does most of Italy. Worst of all, Russian troops break through all along the eastern front, making their way deep into Poland. In a matter of three weeks they destroy twenty-seven German divisions.

Here and there in Pomerania and the Neumark, families talk of sending their children west for safety, but there is yet no thought of abandoning the lands. The refugees from Berlin, from Hamburg, from Cologne and other bombed-out cities still come seeking shelter at the estates of this "safe" eastern countryside.

In the military, certain army officers still talk of a coup d'état, even though their Abwehr contacts have been paralyzed. Others see no point in a coup now that the Atlantic invasion is under way and there is no longer hope for a negotiated peace with Germany's western enemies.

Colonel von Stauffenberg continues to be the rallying point of the military conspiracy in Berlin. He sends a messenger to General von Tresckow on the eastern front seeking Tresckow's opinion under the current circumstances. Henning relays an oral reply through this same messenger:

> The assassination [of Hitler] must be attempted at all costs. Even if it should not succeed, an attempt to seize power in Berlin must be undertaken. What matters now is no longer the practical purpose of the coup but rather

a proof for the world and for the records of history that the men of the resistance movement dared to take the decisive step. Compared to this objective nothing else is of consequence.[39]

JULY. Adolf Hitler has scheduled a meeting of his staff for July 20 at his headquarters in East Prussia. From here he operates as commander in chief of the entire German armed forces. East Prussia is a long way from anywhere except Germany's northeastern battlefront, yet even with Russian troops dangerously close, the führer feels safer here than in Berlin or at Berchtesgaden, his Bavarian mountain retreat.

Three security zones surround the führer's East Prussian headquarters. Each zone requires a separate pass, difficult to acquire. However, this presents no problem for Colonel von Stauffenberg, who flew in early this morning from Berlin to attend the meeting. Even though he was not personally invited, he is entitled to certain privileges as chief of staff to the commander of Germany's entire reserve army. Upon his arrival, Stauffenberg is slightly disappointed—first upon learning that neither Heinrich Himmler nor Hermann Göring will be in attendance, and second upon learning that the meeting is to take place in a wooden teahouse rather than in the headquarters' concrete bunker.

The meeting room has a heavy wooden map table at its center with chairs along the wall. Hitler is standing at the table, leaning over an outspread map and commanding the attention of everyone else in the room. Stauffenberg has placed his briefcase against a table leg, near the führer. It contains a bomb with a timed fuse. While the führer lectures on military strategy, Stauffenberg excuses himself and leaves the teahouse.

Minutes later there is a mighty explosion. From a safe distance, Stauffenberg observes that the entire wall of the teahouse has collapsed. Bodies are lying about and there is blood everywhere. In the resulting panic he escapes to his plane and takes off for Berlin, certain that Adolf Hitler is dead.

From his plane Stauffenberg radios the signal for the coup to Berlin. General Beck, one of the conspirators, races to the War Ministry and telephones the commanders in chief of all German army groups, informing them that they are now under his command. He issues an order to the commander of the North Army Group to evacuate the Baltic territories and withdraw to East Prussia. He also urges General von Kluge—now commander in chief on the western front—to prepare to evacuate France and Belgium.

Early in the afternoon, General Fromm of the Army Home Office, also one of the conspirators, telephones one of Hitler's loyal generals, General Keitel, to inform him that Hitler is dead and that a coup has taken place. Keitel challenges the report, for he was with the führer when the bomb exploded and in fact helped him to his feet afterward. Astounded by Keitel's claim, General Fromm withholds his orders involving internal Germany.

By the time Stauffenberg returns to his office in Berlin, the entire story is known. In the explosion, Hitler was thrown clear of the room and was only slightly burned and bruised. The führer is alive and well. His wounds have been treated at a military hospital near his East Prussian headquarters. At the moment he is making the rounds of the hospital wards, greeting the wounded soldiers.

Unfortunately four men were killed by the blast, including Colonel Heinz Brandt of the führer's staff—the same colonel who a year ago unwittingly transported the two bombs disguised as bottles of Cointreau. Once again the führer has escaped!

A Hero's Death

1944: JULY *(continued)*. At Center Army Group headquarters, now moved westward to Ostrow in Poland, General Henning von Tresckow is listening to the latest military radio broadcast. With him is his colleague and cousin by marriage, Fabian von Schlabrendorff. Both men are puzzled. On the open radio frequency there is an official news bulletin describing an assassination attempt on the führer, from which he has miraculously escaped; yet orders coming through on military frequencies report that Hitler is dead and that all orders from Berlin should be ignored. Which is rumor and which is fact? Henning chooses to believe that Hitler is dead and waits for further orders; they fail to arrive.

At midnight the führer himself broadcasts nationwide. Expressing his grief for the four men who were killed by the bomb meant for him, he promises the nation that the perpetrators of this crime will be hunted down with all means available. Henning and Fabian realize that it is all over for them.

JULY 21. The rest of the night is spent in intense argument— Henning insisting that he will kill himself in the morning and Fabian attempting to dissuade him. As dawn breaks, Henning no longer talks about the danger of discovery and implication or the practicality of self-inflicted death. He has turned philosophical:

> Fabian, I know that they will attack us now and they will heap abuse upon us. But I am convinced, now more than ever, that we have done the right thing. Hitler is the arch-enemy, not only of Germany but indeed of the entire world. In a few hours' time, I shall stand before God and answer both for my actions and for my omissions. With a clear conscience I can stand by everything I have done in this battle against Hitler. God once promised Abraham that He would spare Sodom if only ten just men could be found in the city. I too have reason to hope that, for our sake, He will not destroy Germany. None of us can complain about death, for whoever joined our ranks put on the poisoned shirt of Nessus. A man's moral worth is established only at the point that he is prepared to give his life for his convictions.[40]

It is clear to Fabian that Henning knows his own mind. The two men shake hands, embrace, and part for the last time.

General von Tresckow makes an early morning call on his first staff officer, a major, and insists that they make a tour of the front together. As they approach the area that separates the Russian forces from the Germans, the major becomes uneasy, fearing that they may already be in no man's land. But the general orders their chauffeur to drive on through the front line. At the edge of a wooded area, he orders his vehicle to halt, then steps out and instructs his companions to stay back while he walks into the forest. There is a sudden exchange of fire, as if the general has been ambushed. This is followed by a grenade explo-

Major General Henning von Tresckow,
shortly before his death

sion, and finally there is silence. The major rushes into the forest
in the direction of the sounds. There he discovers the general's
body, his head blown off by a hand grenade. His pistol has been
emptied, but there appear to be no bullet wounds.

The major and the chauffeur return to headquarters with
Henning's body. The major files an official report: "This
morning Lieutenant General Henning von Tresckow died in
combat, having been ambushed by Soviet troops."

While Fabian and Henning argued through the night at
Ostrow, their Kleist cousins slept quietly at Kieckow—at least
until dawn.

Hans Jürgen's secretary, who sleeps on the main level of the
manor house behind the Kieckow office, was awakened at 5:00

A.M. this morning by the sound of pebbles hitting against her window. She was out of bed in an instant and at her window, where in the early dawn light she could see the police superintendent from Gross Tychow with a handful of pebbles ready to throw again. After signaling him that she was awake, the young woman threw on her robe and went to the front door of the manor house. She unbolted the door and stepped outside to find a police vehicle parked on the ramp with two officers pacing alongside. Alone in the back seat was the master of Schmenzin, Ewald von Kleist. The police superintendent hurried from the back of the manor house, greeting the secretary with apologies: "Madam, please rouse Herr von Kleist immediately; have him dress and come to the car. He is under arrest."

Within five minutes Hans Jürgen was dressed and in the automobile, seated next to Ewald—his kinsman, his colleague and his trusted friend from childhood. Neither man looked at the other, nor were any words exchanged. At Gestapo headquarters, the two were left alone long enough for Ewald to whisper a farewell to his cousin: "You will probably be free one day. I shall not, but that doesn't matter so much. It may sound strange, but I feel exulted that it has come this far." By noon each man is alone in his cell at the Köslin jail.

Later in the day Gestapo officers arrive at Kieckow to search desks and closets for incriminating evidence. By now the names of some of the conspirators have been made public, including that of Colonel von Stauffenberg. The Gestapo are looking for the other collaborators.

At Kieckow, there is little to uncover except evidence of connections with the Confessing Church and family ties to men and women whose names are on suspect lists. At Schmenzin, it is otherwise. Among Ewald's papers, the Gestapo discover a document that will later earn one officer a commendation—a letter from Winston Churchill, the British prime minister and leader of Germany's enemies. It is handwritten by Churchill and dated August 17, 1938:

> I am as certain as I was at the end of July 1914 that England will march with France, and certainly the United States is now strongly anti-Nazi. It is difficult for democracies to make precise declarations, but the spectacle of an

armed attack by Germany upon a small neighbour and
the bloody fighting that will follow will rouse the whole
British Empire and compel the gravest decisions. Do not,
I pray you, be misled upon this point. Such a war, once
started, would be fought out like the last to the bitter
end, and one must consider not what might happen in
the first few months, but where we should all be at the
end of the third or fourth year.[41]

The letter that was not strong enough to motivate Germany's
generals in 1938 will be more than enough to convict Ewald in
1945.

JULY 24. The entire general staff of the Center Army Group at
Ostrow gathers for a memorial service to honor General von
Tresckow, who died a hero's death in defense of the Fatherland.
Immediately after the service, the casket with Henning's body is
lifted into a military vehicle for transport to Wartenberg in the
Neumark, the ancestral home of the Tresckow family. Lieutenant
von Schlabrendorff is selected to accompany the body, for the
general is his wife's kinsman.

JULY 27. There is a wave of arrests throughout the nation. The
government has been compiling lists for years, but there was
always a certain reluctance to close in, particularly when suspects
were known to have connections with influential military officers. In June, the discovery of treachery in the Abwehr opened
up a Pandora's box, with trails that led to both the Foreign
Office and the army. The perpetrators were never vigorously
pursued, but now that these traitors have acted so boldly,
Germany's entire judicial system is committed to tracking down
and bringing to justice each and every one of them. The Gestapo
is the instrument of pursuit and arrest, and the Reich Security
Office is responsible for gathering evidence and prosecuting the
crimes. In cases of treason, most of the evidence is extracted
from witnesses through interrogation. The interrogations routinely make use of various forms of torture, giving the Reich a
decided advantage in prosecuting such cases.

All of this is obvious to those who have flirted with the opposition—the women as well as the men. For the protection of those who are most in danger, one chooses to know as little as possible.

At Wartenberg, it is the day of Henning's funeral. His casket lies in the grand hall of the manor house between the large French doors that open out to the terrace. Beyond is the Wartenberg lake with its sky-blue water. The scene hardly differs from that of seventeen years ago, when the coffin of Henning's mother Anni von Tresckow lay in the same great hall. In other ways there is no comparison.

Henning's widow Erika welcomes the mourners in the entry hall. Many are from the village; others are neighbors who live within wagon distance. An inordinate number wear the uniform of the German army. General von Tresckow's rank and heroism call for full military honors.

Erika von Tresckow's appearance is remarkably dignified. Her dress is solid black, of an elegance and cut that one associates more with Berlin than with the rugged countryside, but it is right for the occasion. Standing with her are her young daughters. Two sons, aged sixteen and seventeen, are already in military service. Also standing in the entry hall are Henning's half-brother Jürgen von Tresckow, his wife Hete, and their fourteen-year-old son Rüdiger. Jürgen and Hete are master and mistress of Wartenberg.

The Wedemeyers of Pätzig have always been very close to Henning and Erika. The friendship has complex roots: the kinship of Ruthchen and Henning; the proximity of Pätzig to Wartenberg; the affinity of both Hans von Wedemeyer and Henning von Tresckow for the military, combined with their contempt for the Nazis; and now the two widows, Ruthchen and Erika, each of whose husbands has died at the front.

From Pätzig, two wagonloads of cousins have come across the back road that connects the two estates. Ruthchen leads the way with her son Hans Werner and her oldest daughter Ruth Alice von Bismarck from Kniephof. Ruthchen's second daughter Maria is in Berlin and chooses not to leave that city for any reason. Since the twentieth of the month, Maria's imprisoned fiancé is in danger as never before. The younger Wedemeyer children are home at Pätzig. In the second wagon are the Lasbeck Bismarcks, who have come south by train as far as Pätzig—Maria and Herbert with their daughter Luitgarde von Schlabrendorff. Luitgarde's presence is motivated not only out of respect for her mother's cousin, but also by the expectation that she will spend time alone with her husband Fabian.

Conspicuous by their absence are the Kleists of Kieckow and Klein Krössin. Hans Jürgen is in prison in Köslin; his wife and mother wait nearby.

With the impressive military presence, the funeral procession at Wartenberg is a spectacle to behold—first from the manor house to the church for the service, then from the church to the cemetery, all the while accompanied by a dirge played on three trumpets. At the cemetery, it becomes Fabian's privilege to present the highest German medal of bravery to the widow Erika. When his eyes meet hers, a flash of understanding passes between them. The ceremony ends with a twelve-gun salute and a "Heil Hitler." Erika is stunned by such words being spoken on ground consecrated to God, but the thought is only fleeting; she has much more serious things on her mind. Fabian has said only that he was with Henning throughout the night before he died. More than that he claims not to know. But his eyes have told her something different; Erika decides it is better not to pursue the matter.

The burial is followed by a dignified reception in the Wartenberg manor house. Afterward the Pätzig wagons return home across the primitive field road. The Bismarcks are to spend the night at the Wedemeyer estate. That evening a trio of women walks arm in arm through the Pätzig park—Ruthchen, Ruth Alice and Maria von Bismarck. Not one of them speaks, for each is reluctant to say the words that all three believe to be true.

AUGUST 5. Grandmother Ruth has not yet been told of this nephew's death. Too many questions remain unanswered, and it is better to wait and see if the truth is discovered. It is just as well, for Ruth has all she can handle with the arrest of her own son, Hans Jürgen. She writes to Dita Koch, whose friendship goes back to the Finkenwalde days. She carefully avoids mentioning

the name of Dita's husband Werner, for ever since his imprisonment he has been under continued Gestapo surveillance. At
present he is assigned to a work brigade that replaces fire
bombed roofs in Germany's cities.

> My dear Dita, In recent weeks I have had so many ques-
> tions about you. I have heard nothing from you or from
> your husband; I wanted so to write but I didn't get to it.
> . . . You are now dangerously near to the theater of war,
> just as we are. It takes a brave heart not to be uneasy.
> Here, the refugees from East Prussia are pouring in.
> They have lost everything. But that is not the worst. We
> ourselves need your prayers of supplication. Two weeks
> ago my son was arrested, along with many others, and he
> has not yet been released. There were no stated grounds
> for his arrest. His imprisonment is such that he is her-
> metically sealed from the outside—no communication at
> all. They call that "detention" [*Sperre*]. It is so terrible
> that he knows nothing of us and must suffer alone when
> he is innocent. My son lived here in peace, pursuing the
> demanding work [of the estate]. Now, just at harvest time
> he has been torn away. We wait daily for his return. But
> when so many thousands must suffer, we shouldn't com-
> plain that it has come upon us too. The sorrow that
> afflicts the whole world now is terrible. My daughter-in-
> law [Mieze] is heroic in her courage. Two of her sons
> have been killed in action and the oldest son is a pris-
> oner of war in America. The entire business operation
> rests on her, whose troubles eat at my heart. I am so
> thankful that our faith has not been shaken. On the con-
> trary, it grows in proportion to our tribulations. . . .
>
> It is worse and worse with my eyes. I almost cannot see
> at all. But still I write, better on some days than on
> others. And what lies ahead? Eberhard is at the front in
> Italy. . . . My oldest grandson [Alla Stahlberg] is also in
> Italy in a forward position. May life be good to you! . . .
> Greet your husband. I will never forget either of you.
> From my heart, Your RKR

AUGUST 7. At Wartenberg, 160 kilometers south of Klein Krössin, the suspense is broken. An SS squad drives through the Wartenberg village to the cemetery, and someone runs to the manor house to notify the master, who rushes to intercept the SS delegation. The leader is curt at best, informing him that Henning Tresckow has been implicated in a plot against the führer and the Fatherland. He has been stripped of his officer's rank and his honors, and he has been dismissed from the German army posthumously; in line with government protocol, his body is to be destroyed.

Of all the accouterments of a Prussian estate, the church and cemetery alone have remained under control of the master, but no more! While Jürgen looks on in shocked silence, the SS soldiers open the grave with pick and shovel. They remove Henning's casket and load it into their truck. When they are gone, Jürgen instructs two of his workers to fill the empty grave.

At nearby Pätzig, there is a knock at the manor house door. Ruthchen is told by a servant that there is a Gestapo car parked in front of the house. Rushing into the entry hall, she takes the family guest book from its table and throws it behind the drape. Then she opens the door to the police officers. "It is just a formality," one of them says. Will Frau von Wedemeyer please accompany them into the study?

After six hours of interrogation behind closed doors, the officers leave. It turns out that Ruthchen knows very little; she tells even less. That night after the children are asleep, Ruthchen reads through the names in the Pätzig guest book for the last time: a large assortment of family and friends, including those brave men who these days are called traitors. When she is finished, she lights a match to the pages and throws the burning book into the fireplace.

AUGUST 8. The list of traitors is growing, and German radio broadcasts the names repeatedly. No longer are front-line soldiers spared the news of what is happening at home. They too must be told that treachery permeates the highest echelons of the military.

On a hilltop somewhere in northern Italy, Colonel Gerd von Tresckow relaxes in front of his tent and listens to German radio.

Gerd is brother to Henning and nephew to Ruth von Kleist. As a child, Gerd's serious nature confounded his Tante Ruth, and later she often spoke of a visit the Tresckow brothers made to her children's pension at Stettin. It was before the first war when the family came for the marriage of Maria and Herbert von Bismarck. The Tresckow children were very young. While Henning and his Kleist cousins romped in the garden, eight-year-old Gerd paced back and forth in Ruth's sitting room, his hands clasped tightly behind his back. In answer to Ruth's question as to what was troubling the boy, Gerd replied: "I am thinking about Germany."

On this day of rest, Gerd cannot help but think about Germany, hearing for the first time the radio announcement of his brother's treason and death. He promptly goes into his tent and puts on a fresh uniform. Then, reporting to his commander's headquarters, he confronts his superior: "Sir, I am one with the deeds of my brother." His commander, a general, is incredulous. He too has heard the news about General von Tresckow, but he cautions the colonel to keep silent. Recognizing that Gerd is distraught, he assures him that he has heard nothing and orders him to pull himself together. The general even offers to reassign Colonel von Tresckow to a rest location. When the colonel declines, the general excuses him from his responsibilities for the day and orders him to return to his own quarters to rest.

AUGUST 9. Before breakfast, Colonel von Tresckow again appears at the tent of his commander: "Sir, I am one with the deeds of my brother." This time the general is not alone. With witnesses present, he has no choice but to issue the order for the colonel's arrest. By the end of the day, Gerd von Tresckow is on his way to Berlin for "interrogation."

A month later, in a Berlin prison, Gerd von Tresckow will decide that his torture has been too much. He will take his own life by cutting his wrists with a razor.

AUGUST 15. Luitgarde bids farewell to Lasbeck and to her parents. Pregnant with her third child, she boards a train for the west, taking along not only her own two small children but also her young brothers Gottfried and Fritz Christoph von Bismarck. Their destination is the home of Fabian's relatives in Bavaria.

The Prinz Albrechtstrasse Prison

AUGUST 15. The widow and two daughters of Henning von Tresckow have left Wartenberg. It was an emotional farewell, for without it being said aloud, they all suspected this to be the final farewell to Henning's grave, to the lake, the manor house, the fields, the forests and the lifestyle that Wartenberg represented over the centuries.

Erika von Tresckow and the girls are staying in Berlin with Erika's mother, the widow of General Erich von Falkenhayn, who during the World War was chief of Germany's General Staff. Not very long ago Frau von Falkenhayn was the grande dame of Berlin. Today there is a knock on the door of the Falkenhayn flat; two Gestapo officers have come for Erika and her children. Erika protests, "Why the children?" The oldest girl is just thirteen and the younger barely five. "Orders!" That is all these officers know.

At Gestapo headquarters, Erika is immediately separated from her daughters. For the first time since the twentieth of July she gives way to her emotions. The Gestapo chief comforts her by promising that her children will have "a good home."

Erika is being held in the Prinz Albrechtstrasse prison, a fortresslike structure in the heart of the city. For the next seven weeks she will be under interrogation by Gestapo Commissioner Habecker, a specialist in the activities of the group that plotted the July 20 bombing. Fortunately Erika knows nothing of the group and very little of her husband's activities. She is not in a position to betray any of his colleagues.

On October 2 Habecker will order the prisoner released. Her interrogation will have been an exercise in futility. Erika will be reunited with her daughters and she will learn that her seventeen-year-old son has been killed in combat.

AUGUST 17. At Center Army Group headquarters in Poland, Lieutenant Fabian von Schlabrendorff is roused from his bed before dawn. For him too the ruse is over. He is escorted under military guard—a lieutenant and two sergeants—first by auto to a railroad station in East Prussia, then by train to Berlin.

AUGUST 18. Late in the evening Fabian is delivered to the notorious Gestapo prison on the Prinz Albrechtstrasse in Berlin. Here he is turned over to the Gestapo and handcuffed for the first time. His interrogation will begin in two days, under the supervision of Commissioner Habecker.

On this same evening at another Berlin prison—Moabit—two other Kleist kinsman are brought together. Ewald von Kleist has just been delivered from the jail in Köslin with his hands manacled behind his back. Ewald Heinrich von Kleist has been brought by military police direct from the front, also in handcuffs. Father and son are placed next to each other, facing the wall. The older man whispers an admonition to the younger one: "Do not lose your self-control whatever happens." Ewald is still father to his son.

AUGUST 25. Fabian von Schlabrendorff is taken from his prison cell and driven by car to the Sachsenhausen concentration camp just outside Berlin. There he is confronted with the casket of his kinsman and confidant, Henning von Tresckow. The Reich Security Office intends to extract a confession from Fabian by presenting him with evidence of Henning's duplicity. It has been discovered that General von Tresckow evaded Hitler's orders on a number of occasions by ordering retreat when he saw that anything else would be futile. The theory is that Tresckow went over to the Russian side and that his casket contains the body of a Russian soldier. Fabian vehemently denies this; the prosecutors hope to gain a full confession of his own duplicity by confronting him with the evidence. The casket is opened in his presence, and the sack encasing Henning's body is torn apart. A brief glance at the contents convinces the officials of their error. While Fabian looks on, they torch and incinerate the body.

SEPTEMBER. Fabian has been interrogated repeatedly under less than comfortable conditions. He has been kept awake at night, he has been placed in overheated rooms, and he has been denied visitors and mail; but he has not confessed to any part of a conspiracy against the Reich, nor has he implicated any others in such a conspiracy. Fabian Schlabrendorff (no longer "lieutenant," for he has been dishonorably discharged from the officer corps) is not cooperating with the Reich Security Office, which is responsible for ferreting out the truth in these matters.

Commissioner Habecker decides to put more pressure on the prisoner. Fabian will survive the ordeal, and later he will describe the procedures in detail:

> This torture was executed in four stages. First, my hands were chained behind my back, and a device which gripped all the fingers separately was fastened to my hands. The inner side of this mechanism was studded with pins whose points pressed against my fingertips. The turning of a screw caused the instrument to contract, thus forcing the pinpoints into my fingers.
>
> When that did not achieve the desired confession, the second stage followed. I was strapped, face down, on a frame resembling a bedstead, and my head was covered with a blanket. Then cylinders resembling stovepipes studded with nails on the inner surface were shoved over my bare legs. Here, too, a screw mechanism was used to contract these tubes so that the nails pierced my legs from ankle to thigh.
>
> For the third state of torture, the "bedstead" itself was the main instrument. I was strapped down as described above, again with a blanket over my head. With the help of a special mechanism this medieval torture rack was then expanded—either in sudden jerks, or gradually— each time stretching my shackled body.
>
> In the fourth and final stage I was tied in a bent position which did not allow me to move even slightly backwards or sideways. Then the police commissioner [Habecker] and the police sergeant together descended on me from behind, beating me with heavy clubs. Each blow caused me to fall forward, and because my hands were chained behind my back, I crashed with full force on my face.[42]

During this fourth stage, Fabian loses consciousness. He is returned to his cell, where he is treated by the prison doctor.

When he has recovered a bit and the open wounds have begun to heal, he is taken back for another round—stage one, stage two, stage three and stage four. So it goes at the prison on Prinz Albrechtstrasse.

OCTOBER. The Prinz Albrechtstrasse prison is headquarters for Reich Security Office efforts to uncover all aspects of the conspiracy that led to the July 20 event. The authorities have linked the army's counterintelligence agency—the Abwehr—to a group of high-ranking officers and to a clique of officials in the Foreign Office. These suspects have all been brought together at the prison. The list reads like a Kleist family reunion—Fabian von Schlabrendorff, his wife's uncle Hans Jürgen von Kleist, Hans Jürgen's cousin Ewald von Kleist of Schmenzin, Ewald's son Ewald Heinrich, and Dietrich Bonhoeffer, soon to be related to all of them through his pending marriage to Maria von Wedemeyer. Amazingly, this group of prisoners comprises most of the adult males in the closely knit family circle of Ruth von Kleist, the matriarch of Kieckow who lives in Pomerania.

Nearby is the Lehrterstrasse prison where Dietrich's brother Klaus Bonhoeffer and his brother-in-law Rüdiger Schleicher are incarcerated. Soon they will be joined by Schleicher's son-in-law, Eberhard Bethge. The men are brought from Lehrterstrasse to the main interrogation chambers as their cases require.

Of course these men are not the only prisoners in the main prison and its nearby annex. Admiral Canaris and General Oster, both of the Abwehr, and a host of others—conspirators and innocents alike—are imprisoned here and subjected to treatment that ranges from malevolent neglect to repeated torture. Such is the capriciousness of the Nazi judicial system.

At Klein Krössin, Ruth is plagued outwardly by her failing eyesight and inwardly by worries over loved ones at the front and in prison. She writes again to Dita Koch, who lives directly in the path of the American army's advance:

> My dear Dita, Is it possible that this letter will reach you or are you now beyond reach. Recently things have not gone well for me. I wanted to write you a detailed letter and to thank you for your dear letter that was written so long ago—the sixteenth of August. Since then you have

probably left your home or are so under siege that postal communications have broken down. Oh how I think about the grief that you must be going through. And here I am writing you now though it is possible that the letter will never reach you. When I read newspapers and follow the reports from the west, my thoughts are so much with you. I imagine that I would be determined to glue myself firmly to the land and not leave my home. But who can say what one ought to do and what one can do in your situation. We do not know whether it will be sooner or later that we are in a similar situation from the other side. In that case it will be more problematical. Yet it has never been so clear to me as now that this world offers no security and that we must give ourselves over to God's care.

I thank you so much for the valuable essay that your husband [Werner] sent me. Would you believe that it was read aloud to me for the first time just a week ago? Earlier it was not possible. It fit, so well, the correspondence I recently received from Dietrich through Eberhard. It calls out deep theological issues. There is so little opportunity now to speak of such questions. Everyone is so preoccupied with the present that there is no energy left to dig into such [theological] problems. If only I could speak about these things with your husband. How I miss such friends! We are all torn from one another and can no longer share our thoughts.

You write so affectionately. Yes, you are one of those who long ago tasted the troubles that we are now going through [the Nazi imprisonment of a loved one]. I often recall that my first contact with this kind of suffering was through you. You presume correctly that nothing has changed as yet. Now as before, we have no idea when it will end. But each one is careful to say nothing. Life is not as it used to be—when an important decision was where to play tennis at Wiesbaden. May I keep [Werner's] essay or should I send it back? When you write your husband, greet him cordially from me. I can only say, may God keep you both and also your dear mother. In faithful affection, Your RKR

NOVEMBER. Maria von Wedemeyer continues to stay with Dietrich's parents in the Grunewald suburb of Berlin. The neighborhood is not immune to British and American bombs, but the destruction is nothing like that in the central city of Berlin. The Bonhoeffer and Schleicher homes are relatively intact. Still, the family is under constant pressure, both from the bombings and from worry over the two sons and two sons-in-law in prison. Were it not for the men in prison, Frau Bonhoeffer and her daughters would have left the city long ago.

Maria delivers packages to the prison every Wednesday. She is not permitted to see Dietrich or her various relatives, but she has established a kind of rapport with the prison director. She specifies that this package be delivered here and that one there—some to the main prison and others to the annex—all quite contrary to prison rules. Thus all of those dear to her in prison benefit from the slim rations of the Bonhoeffer household and the abundance of the Pätzig lands.

Mieze von Kleist comes from Kieckow and Alice von Kleist from Schmenzin to spend days at a time in Berlin, away from their lands and their children, in the faint hope of being with their husbands for a quarter of an hour. More often than not, they are disappointed. Luitgarde too is in Berlin now for days at a time, on the chance of seeing Fabian. She has left her children and her younger brothers with a nursemaid in Bavaria.

DECEMBER. During the first week of Advent, Ewald Heinrich von Kleist is released from prison by personal order of the führer. Some say that Ewald Heinrich and his friend Axel* have been the bravest of them all, for by agreeing to carry the activated bombs against their bodies, each intended to die with his victim. Hitler has seen Ewald Heinrich's name on the list of prisoners, a list he personally peruses from time to time, and he has erroneously presumed this Kleist to be the son of General Ewald von Kleist. (General von Kleist is a distant relative of Ewald von Kleist of Schmenzin.) Why not a Christmas surprise for a general who can still be trusted? So reasons Germany's führer.

Ewald Heinrich is ordered to report immediately to his frontline unit, but he chooses to disobey these orders and instead

*Axel von dem Bussche was never arrested.

goes underground in Berlin. A day later Alice von Kleist is finally granted a visit with her husband. It will be the last. Afterward Ewald writes:

> Yesterday I finally saw you and spoke with you. That was my final great wish. I had been so uneasy that something would prevent my seeing you. Such a joy this last meeting was for me, for which I thank God. And that God sheltered you from the terrible air raid. You have made me so happy through the short half-hour [we were together]. No doubt I shall not see you again in this lifetime. Our farewell was so difficult for me. I was amazed how you held yourself together and how you did not let me see your pain. God has given you so much strength. This is a great comfort for me.
>
> I thank God also that Ewald Heinrich walks free again. By mortal reckoning I shall never see you again—never. And yet: God's will be done.[43]

Hans Jürgen continues to be questioned by Commissioner Habecker, who is preparing the case against him. However, Habecker is not so much interested in Hans Jürgen's deeds as he is in his knowledge of others' deeds. When Hans Jürgen refuses to give names, Habecker repeatedly threatens torture. Hans Jürgen is prepared for this eventuality, which he is convinced will result in his betraying others. He recently stole a razor blade from the prison barbershop and has slipped it into a bar of soap for safekeeping. He also has a steel nail carefully hidden away in his cell.

Early in the morning on the second Sunday of Advent, the prisoner offers up a prayer. Without a special sign from God, he will take his own life that night. For the sake of others, there is no alternative. At noon the guard delivers to his cell a package from Mieze—a change of clothing and a tiny Christmas tree on which a little wooden angel is perched. Hans Jürgen sees the angel as the sign for which he has prayed. He sets the tree on his stool and slips the angel into his pocket.

On the days that follow, Hans Jürgen is interrogated unmercifully. During sleepless nights he often reaches for the angel in his pocket. The threatened tortures never take place.

Dietrich Bonhoeffer is rarely taken from his basement cell. He is always isolated, sometimes tormented, but almost never questioned anymore. He has confounded his interrogators by admitting to all of the connections the investigators have uncovered— the links to Sweden, to Switzerland, and hence to England. Dietrich denies nothing. Yet he has succeeded in withholding the damaging information—the messages he carried from the Abwehr conspirators to their agents abroad. He can still thank God for the damage he has not inflicted on others. On the nineteenth of December he writes a Christmas letter to Maria, the last communication she will ever receive from him:

> These will be quiet days in our homes. But I have had the experience over and over again that the quieter it is around me, the clearer do I feel the connection to you. It is as though in solitude the soul develops senses which we hardly know in everyday life. Therefore I have not felt lonely or abandoned for one moment. You, our parents, all of you, the friends and students of mine at the front, all are constantly present to me. Your prayers and good thoughts, words from the Bible, discussions long past, pieces of music, and books—all these gain life and reality as never before.
>
> It is a great invisible sphere in which one lives and in whose reality there is no doubt. If it says in the old children's song about the angels: "Two to cover me, two to wake me," so is this guardianship by good invisible powers in the morning and at night something which grownups need today no less than children. Therefore you must not think that I am unhappy. What is happiness and unhappiness? It depends so little on the circumstances; it depends really only on that which happens inside a person. I am grateful every day that I have you and that makes me happy.[44]

On December 22 Luitgarde is permitted a fifteen-minute visit with Fabian. It is a conversation more with the eyes than with words. A few hours later she goes into labor and delivers her third child, a boy. Two weeks later, still in Berlin, the child is christened in a simple ceremony. His great-grandmother Ruth

von Kleist is named godmother in absentia. Luitgarde is granted
one more visit with her imprisoned husband, this time with his
infant son in her arms. After that she leaves for Bavaria to join
the other children.

Wind of Fire

1945. For six months the Russians have been building up their
communications and supply systems east of the Vistula River in
Poland. The Red Army now has solid numerical superiority over
the Germans—in tanks and trucks, and especially in manpower.
Hitler's decision to mount a last desperate counteroffensive in
the west, later to be known as the Battle of the Bulge, has exacer-
bated the situation by taking even more forces from the battered
eastern front.

JANUARY 12. On this day the Russian army begins an offensive
that will go down in history. In a matter of two weeks the Red
Army will capture Krakow, encircle Warsaw, reach the Baltic Sea
at Danzig, and drive deep into Silesia and the Neumark, as far as
the Oder River.

JANUARY 21. In a medium-sized town near the city of Breslau,
where Great-grandfather Robert, the count of Zedlitz and
Trützschler, once held forth as governor-general of Silesia, Hans
Conrad Stahlberg is marrying Maria von Loesch. She too is
descended from a branch of the Zedlitz family. The affair comes
close to being a Zedlitz family reunion. Hans Conrad's mother
Spes has come from Berlin amidst all kinds of difficulties. No
one comes to Silesia these days; one only goes away from this
land, for it has become a battlefield. But not Spes Stahlberg! Not
only is she present at this marriage, she has written a humorous
poem to commemorate it. Stefan and Lene, the count and
countess of Zedlitz and Trützschler, have come from their nearby
estate. Hans Conrad's great-uncle Stefan is Grandmother Ruth's
brother. If anyone is particularly missed today, it is Grandmother
Ruth herself.

Hans Conrad's sister Raba lives with her husband near Breslau,
and they are both present, as is their brother Alla. He is adjutant

to General Erich von Manstein, who is also among the guests. The general is an old friend of the Zedlitz clan. Best of all, eighteen-year-old Ruthi von Kleist, Hans Conrad's cousin from Kieckow, has come with a friend, all the way from Pomerania.

In front of the church an entire collection of horse-drawn wagons is assembled to accommodate all of the guests. Among the wagons stands a single military automobile, for General von Manstein and his adjutant Alla Stahlberg. After the religious ceremony, all of the participants proceed to the Loesch family castle. There they celebrate the marriage and the rejoining of an ancient family, all within earshot of thundering artillery. Ruthi reads Tante Spes's poem, purported to be advice from the Baron of Vernezobre, a common ancestor of both bride and groom. Then Uncle Stefan gives a moving tribute to his nephew Hans Jürgen von Kleist, imprisoned in Berlin and not expected to survive.

Just at that moment a German soldier bursts into the banquet hall, announcing that the Russians have reached the outskirts of the town. All civilians are advised to leave immediately. Abandoning the banquet table, the wedding guests climb into the wagons and make for the nearest railroad station, while the general and his adjutant race back to their posts.

Panic and confusion reign on the railroad platform, where a train has stopped to take on passengers. Although it is already full, people still push their way aboard, trying desperately to reach the west. Ruthi and her friend have taken Tante Lene and Uncle Stefan under their care. They go from car to car, looking in vain for a place for them to climb aboard. Then Ruthi has an idea. While the old couple stands out of view of the engineer's cab, the two comely girls walk up to the cab and ask the engineer whether he could take two passengers with him. He answers their broad smiles with one of his own and beckons them to come aboard. Quickly they run to get Tante Lene and Uncle Stefan and help them climb the ladder into the cab. The engineer's friendly smile has disappeared.

Fully loaded, the train pulls away from the station to continue its journey west over the Neisse River. Thus Stefan and Lene, the count and countess of Zedlitz and Trützschler, escape the terrible vengeance of the conquerors from the east.

Ruthi and her friend are left alone on the station platform, but they are in luck. Fearing that some of his relatives might not find a seat on this last train, Alla Stahlberg has commandeered a military transport and returned to the platform. The girls jump into the truck and Alla drives them across the countryside to another town, where he knows one more train is still expected. He drops them off and returns to his post, confident that they are on their way to safety. He will later be severely reprimanded for his absence and for his misuse of a military vehicle.

While the young women wait on the platform for a train to the west, another train—virtually empty—halts on its way in the opposite direction. Ruthi's friend suddenly has the urge to return east and rescue her mother. Foolishly, Ruthi agrees to go along, and the two board the train and are off. Within minutes, they realize they have made a mistake. The train is surrounded by Russian troops and they are forced to make their escape. As they jump to the ground, they are shot at, but they prostrate themselves in the brush and remain hidden until the soldiers leave. When no one is in sight they move on, hoping they can elude any Russian soldiers. They manage to avoid capture for a day or so, but they are soon caught and subsequently subjected to the sexual violations that will forever after brand the Red Army invasion of Germany. Within a week they are put to work in a Russian military horse stable.

JANUARY 26. There is a crisis at Pätzig in the Neumark. Herr Döpke, the bailiff, was notified last night that he must report for military service immediately, and Ruthchen von Wedemeyer is incredulous. Ever since her husband Hans went away to war, it has been Herr Döpke who has kept the three-thousand-acre agricultural enterprise running—at first with the Pätzig workers, virtually all of whom are now at the front or already dead, and more recently with prisoners of war and other workers from captured lands.

One can hear the roar of the big guns to the south and east, so close that sometimes the manor house windows rattle. Ruthchen orders a horse-drawn sleigh be made ready to take her to the railroad station south of Pätzig. It is a cold morning, minus twelve degrees Celsius, and the roads are covered with ice and snow. At the station she has no problem finding space on a train headed south, for those who flee the Red Army are all traveling in the opposite direction. Ruthchen intends to visit the recruiting office at Frankfurt an der Oder, where her bailiff's call-up order was issued.

Along the way, at Küstrin, Ruthchen observes masses of refugees gathered at the riverbank hoping to cross the Oder River ahead of the Red Army. It is a stark revelation for this estate mistress, but still she continues on to Frankfurt. There she confronts the official who issued the call-up order and inquires whether he is aware that the war is already lost. Wouldn't it be far better for an able-bodied man like Döpke to be in a position to prevent complete chaos rather than be put in uniform at this late date. Ruthchen's logic is persuasive, and Herr Döpke's call-up order is rescinded.

On the way home, Ruthchen's mind is made up. The children and two frail house guests, both older women from Berlin whose homes have been destroyed in the bombing, will leave this very night. Thank God Maria is home from Berlin for a visit; she will lead the caravan, and Ruthchen will follow later with the entire village.

That night a wagon and three horses are made ready. One of the Polish workers is selected to be its driver. A framework is quickly assembled over the open wagon, and a large oriental rug from the manor house is spread over it to provide warmth; a waterproof tarpaulin is placed over this. There will be ten passengers in the wagon—the four children still at home (Maria, Christine, Werburg and Peter Christian), Frau Döpke and her child and foster child, the two elderly ladies and the driver. Ruthchen has given orders—only one suitcase per person. The wagon is filled mostly with food—for the travelers and, even more important, for the horses.

The two Berlin ladies seem unable to comprehend the nature of the journey. Both have two large suitcases standing ready, one of which is more like a trunk. It contains valuable art books the visitor earlier saved from her Berlin flat, and it is immensely heavy. Ruthchen is annoyed, but she remains silent. This is not the time to encourage an outbreak of emotion.

The journey, which would take less than a day by automobile, is expected to last two weeks. Each of the Pätzig children has selected an item or two that will be his or her memory of a lifetime at Pätzig. For Maria, it is Dietrich's letters. She has tied them with ribbon, all in order of date received, and she tucks them lovingly between her warmest clothes. Then on impulse she runs back into the manor house one last time, going straight to the dumbwaiter above the kitchen where the washed silver lies. Taking the entire tray of flatware outside, she dumps it onto the floor of the wagon.

Much later, these pieces—several knives, a few forks and some spoons—will be carefully parceled among her siblings, a treasured memory of a distant time and place.

Ruthchen insists that the wagons leave before dawn. She calmly goes over a road map with Maria and the driver, advising them to travel north into Pomerania, then across the Oder River, circling to the north of Berlin, and finally making their way to Celle near Hannover. It is a long and indirect way to the west, but more certain to evade the Russians.

With a heavy heart, Ruthchen embraces each of her children. As the wagon begins to move out of the courtyard, Ruthchen climbs into the sleigh. Herr Döpke is at the reins; for him too life's future depends on the success of the wagon's journey. He and Ruthchen follow the wagon past the lake and the village, along the snow-covered fields, and finally through the forest. There they wave a last farewell and return to the estate, where even greater decisions must still be made.

JANUARY 27. Not long after sunrise, the road becomes extremely slippery and the wagon has difficulty making it up the steep grades. Maria calls a halt and orders everyone out. Taking stock of the load, she begins to dump item after item, in particular the heavy suitcases of the two Berlin ladies. They make no protest, for they realize they are in no position to complain.

For their first night out, Mother has phoned ahead to the estate of distant Wedemeyer relatives, and their manor house is made ready for nine visitors and a driver. Maria sends the children directly inside, and after helping the elderly women from the wagon, she and the driver take the horses to the barn for shelter. The driver will sleep in the barn; Maria has decided to sleep in the wagon, and all the pleading of her companions and the mistress of the manor house cannot dissuade her. With coat after coat piled on top of her, she sleeps well, knowing that her vehicle will not be stolen by those more desperate than she.

JANUARY 28. An interesting phenomenon is occurring. The farther the wagon travels, the more crowded the highway becomes. It is as if the Oder River to the east of Berlin is the center of a great wheel, being fed by a semicircle of spokes. The road is clogged with wagons, horses, bicycles, baby carriages, children's wagons and immense numbers of people—from as far to the northeast as East Prussia and as far to the southeast as Silesia, and all points in between. Some are heavily laden with bundles, and others are empty-handed. Here and there the government has set up food centers and makeshift shelters, but they are totally inadequate. Who would have dreamed that such a migration would develop in a matter of a few days. From time to time, orders are shouted through megaphones: "Clear the highway; motor convoy coming through." People and horses tumble over each other to get off the road so that Germany's armies can pass. The worst of it is that the convoys also seem to be in retreat. The travelers cannot help but feel that there is less and less protection between them and the enemy forces.

Maria decides that her wagon will avoid the Oder bridges entirely. She has seen other refugees being turned back, and many of them have been treated roughly by the SS patrols. She will take her wagon into the countryside, always moving north, and they will cross where the ice looks solid. On the Oder the ice never looks especially good, but Maria determines it will have to do. At last she finds a spot that appears to be sound, and the wagon is emptied of its human cargo. One by one, each person crosses the ice on foot. Then it is the wagon's turn, with the driver leading the horses on foot and ready to leap clear. The ice sags and it creaks, but it holds; Maria is the last to come across. The little band has made it safely across the Oder, and they are elated!

Late at night in the Pätzig manor house, by the light of a kerosene lamp, Ruthchen writes to the mother of Dietrich Bonhoeffer:

Dear Frau Bonhoeffer, I have had to do something very unkind. Please forgive me. In twelve degrees of frost and an icy east wind I sent Maria with my three [youngest] children, Frau Döpke and her two children, Fraulein Rath, who was sick with a fever, and the very delicate Fraulein Dienel in a covered wagon to the west, towards Celle, where Döpke's relatives live in a village.

I needed her help now desperately. It is a task far beyond her strength. Her driver is a Pole, and she has the best three farm horses. Pray with me that she will be equal to this hard task.

If all goes well, the journey will take fourteen days. But there has been a lot of snow and the winds are very strong.

People have advised me strongly against Berlin. We are deeply grateful for your offer to take the children. Herr Döpke wanted at all costs to get his family to the west to his parents. I couldn't let them go away in two wagons because there were not enough of the necessary spare parts and we would have needed another driver. We couldn't have afforded it.

Perhaps we shall soon get the order here for general evacuation. We have prepared everything in secret. I hope that I can help to save human lives and prevent panic. When she has delivered the children, Maria hopes to be able to reach you again. But it will take a long time.

May God have mercy and protect you and yours and spare you from suffering too long. Whether we shall see each other in this life or the next rests with him. In any case we can look forward to that with great happiness.

Thank you so much for all the motherly and fatherly love you have shown and are showing my child. Yours, Ruth Wedemeyer[45]

JANUARY 29. Today Wartenberg in the Neumark is seized by the Red Army. The master of the estate, Jürgen von Tresckow, died a week ago from blood poisoning following a hunting accident. His widow Hete stands alone in the entry hall, ready to meet the enemy. As three soldiers rush the door, Hete prepares to offer them whatever the manor house contains. For the moment, they are interested only in her. One of the soldiers grabs Hete and, forcing her to the floor, begins to tear off her clothes. From behind the manor house, fourteen-year-old Rüdiger hears his mother's screams and runs to her defense. A second soldier pulls his gun, and in an instant both mother and son are dead. An hour later, after the conquerors have taken what interests them most, they set fire to the manor house. So it ends for the Tresckows of Wartenberg.

North and west of Wartenberg, at Pätzig, the sounds of large artillery fire come ever closer. Ruthchen learns that the Russians are just fifty kilometers away, as the crow flies, and that the last train will leave Schönfliess this afternoon. She still has a houseful of Berlin refugees, and she informs them that they must leave Pätzig immediately. Two wagons stand waiting in the courtyard to take them to the station. She then orders all of the household and estate workers who want to leave to assemble a caravan by nightfall. Under her calm direction, bags are packed and food-stuffs loaded into the wagons, all within an hour or two.

Unfortunately the mistress of Pätzig has no control over what is reported to the authorities, and suddenly she is confronted by the Nazi group leader from Schönfliess. "Flight is forbidden now," he maintains. The Pätzig inhabitants will only clog the road even more, making it impossible to bring reinforcements from the front. Ruthchen does not hide her contempt: "What reinforcements? What front?" The artillery fire that drives them to distraction is Russian, not German. The armies of the Father-land are in full retreat in the Neumark; the only ones left are civilians and government officials.

The group leader can only repeat the party line: To abandon the land is to betray the Fatherland, and those who do so will be made to answer for it. He tells the mistress that at the nearby Oder River crossing, men have been publicly hanged for leading their wagons across the bridge. Ruthchen is sufficiently intimi-dated to cancel the plans. The supplies and belongings are unloaded from the wagons and the horses are returned to their stalls.

JANUARY 31. Ruthchen has every quilt and pillow in the manor house brought to the main floor hall, as well as every item of men's underwear. Her five household servants bring all the food they can carry from the larder and the storeroom downstairs. It is rumored that the Russian soldiers have almost no warm clothing or bedding, and Ruthchen intends to share what she has willingly rather than have them wreak havoc on the manor house.

Around two o'clock in the afternoon, her work is interrupted by a hysterical woman from the village. A refugee camping in the area caught a glimpse of some Russian tanks at the north edge of the village. Panic stricken, the woman cut the wrists of her mother and daughter, and finally her own as well. All three are slowly bleeding to death in the courtyard. Grabbing a sheet and pillowcase from the pile in the entry hall, Ruthchen rushes outside. She tears the linen into strips and manages to bind the wounds of the two women and the child.

In the meantime, a column of more than a hundred Russian tanks moves diagonally across the estate lands, along with an equal number of personnel transports. The vehicles move slowly, and here and there a few soldiers jump off to plunder something from the buildings and then return to their formation. The Nazi village spokesman is identified and summarily executed on the spot. So far they have paid no attention to the manor house.

At five o'clock, Herr Döpke, the faithful bailiff, is still going about his afternoon chores. Ruthchen intercepts him and advises him to leave at once. Döpke refuses, insisting that he will organize the village caravan after the Russian troops have moved on.

At six o'clock, the Pätzig forester appears at the back door of the manor house, still wearing the gray-green uniform foresters have worn for centuries on German lands. He is afraid to stay on the estate any longer and asks the mistress if he might take the sleigh and a horse to make his getaway. "Of course," she replies. The man never even reaches the barn. Two soldiers overpower him, and within minutes he is dead.

A half hour later, Döpke comes to the house and begs his employer to leave with him immediately. A Russian tank is now standing before the main entrance, and he fears that the manor house will be demolished with them inside. Ruthchen orders the women of the house to leave through the back terrace doors and go to the gardener's cottage. She will follow. But first she must stop at her husband's desk to gather up money and other papers. On Hans's desk she spies the pile of letters, so carefully arranged and lovingly tied in bundles. Sadly, she must leave them; they are much too cumbersome to take along.

Quickly she makes her way out the terrace doors and across the kitchen courtyard, only stopping long enough to untie the dogs and give them their freedom. At that moment, there is a thunderous explosion in the front courtyard; the Russian tank is bombarding the manor house.

One by one the household servants, the estate secretary, and the mistress reach the gardener's cottage, where they join the pastor's wife, the gardener and Herr Döpke. Ruthchen prevails on Döpke to leave without delay; he has his family and her children to consider. Meanwhile the others discuss what to do. Döpke speculates that the other women have a chance to survive if they stay in the village; on the other hand, if they run and are caught, they will certainly be killed. However, he fears that the mistress will be killed in any case, and he urges Frau von Wedemeyer to leave with him. Ruthchen's heart is torn; she bows to the bailiff's logic but insists that he go ahead. Then she begins to assemble a backpack with whatever is available in the cottage. Whoever wishes to join her is welcome to go along. Of all the women in the cottage, only the secretary chooses to cast her lot with Frau von Wedemeyer.

At midnight, the two women crawl through a break in the fence behind the gardener's cottage, each carrying a backpack. It is a fortunate choice, for the entire perimeter of the estate has been sealed with sentries at every gate. The Russians are no longer just passing through; on this night they have occupied Pätzig.

The moon is almost full, and its light is reflected brilliantly off the snow. The women walk cautiously, their heads down. It occurs to Ruthchen that no one milked the cows this evening, and for a moment she is overcome by a painful sense of loss. The two women are well beyond the Pätzig lands when a fresh flash of mortar fire sprays the night sky. They turn to see clouds of smoke rising from the house. As they watch, a wind of fire sweeps across the chimneys. Less than a minute later, the entire manor house is engulfed in a sea of flames. At that moment, the weight of leaving Pätzig is lifted from Ruthchen's shoulders. She holds her head high and begins to walk at a brisker pace, thinking now only of her children. Have they made it across the Oder? Are they now safe somewhere in the west?

Journey to the West

1945: FEBRUARY 3. Shortly before ten o'clock in the morning, Ewald Kleist-Schmenzin and Fabian Schlabrendorff are brought over from their prison cells to the courthouse on Bellevuestrasse with hands and feet manacled. They are seated together in one of the courtrooms, on a bench reserved for defendants, and their chains are removed.

Precisely at 10:00 A.M., Roland Freisler, justice of the People's Court of the Third Reich, enters the courtroom. The robe he wears is so long that it trails behind him on the floor. The defendants rise and stand at attention, as does everyone else. Besides the accused, there are the witnesses, the guards, and the various bureaucrats whose presence is required at every such trial.

In a nation where monstrous excesses have become commonplace, it can still be said of Roland Freisler that he is the most monstrous of all the People's Court justices. His harangues, his humiliation of prisoners, his capricious decisions and his brutal sentences epitomize his unmitigated evil.

Yesterday, in this same courtroom, Freisler sentenced to death Klaus Bonhoeffer and Rüdiger Schleicher, the brother and brother-in-law of Dietrich Bonhoeffer. Today Freisler will deal with the family of Dietrich's fiancée, Maria von Wedemeyer. Both men on the prisoners' bench are cousins of Maria; both are charged with high treason against the nation. A single prosecutor will present the state's charges against the defendants, each of whom is represented by a defense attorney. But if the trials proceed as others have, these defense attorneys will soon join the prosecution in assailing the defendants. Such is the state of justice in the Third Reich.

Freisler opens the session with the same tirade he has used against every man, and woman, who has been accused of complicity in the July 20 plot to kill the führer. Then it is the prosecutor's turn on stage. Ewald Kleist-Schmenzin takes his place in the prisoner's dock, and the prosecutor reads the grave accusations against him that are to be proved in Freisler's court. When the charges have been read, Freisler asks whether the defendant has anything to say. Ewald Kleist-Schmenzin has something to say indeed:

> Yes, I have carried on high treason since the thirtieth of January 1933, continually and with all means available to me. I have never concealed my fight against Hitler and National Socialism. I believe this fight to be a commandment ordered by God. God alone will be my judge.[46]

Freisler is not used to such audacity in his courtroom. He is sufficiently taken aback that he dismisses this defendant for the moment and calls for the case of Schlabrendorff. Just at that moment the air raid sirens go off. Freisler sends the sergeant at arms out to assess the situation, and a few minutes later he returns with the news that a massive formation of American bombers is approaching the city. The prisoners are quickly manacled and led to the bomb shelter beneath the building—to sit with the attorneys and other bureaucrats, the witnesses, the guards and the judge while the largest daytime bombing raid ever inflicted on Berlin demolishes most of what is left of the city. Above them a direct hit on the Bellevuestrasse courthouse causes an entire wall to collapse. A steel beam topples with such force that it plunges through the ceiling of the air raid shelter, and great chunks of concrete tumble down through the opening. The room fills with smoke and dust, and it becomes difficult to see and even to breathe. There are murmurs that someone is injured, and while some go to his aid, others go to open the entry door.

For Ewald and Fabian, this air raid will take on Old Testament proportions—like a bolt of lightning direct from the hand of God. When the dust has cleared, it is discovered that Roland Freisler is dead, his skull fractured by the steel beam that penetrated the shelter. No one else has been injured. It is equally providential that the fire raging in the courtroom above has destroyed the files—the carefully prepared cases against these Kleist cousins from Pomerania.

After the all-clear sirens sound, Fabian and Ewald are returned to their cells. The prison on Prinz Albrechtstrasse has also sustained a direct hit. The upper floors of the prison have been destroyed, but the basement cells are still intact and the prisoners are led inside. There they will sit until the prosecution rebuilds each of the cases. The world may be crumbling down on every side, but the Nazi system of justice grinds on.

FEBRUARY 7. Twenty prisoners from the Prinz Albrechtstrasse prison are ordered to pack their belongings, for there is to be a transfer. All twenty prisoners selected have international reputations, and at first glance, one might surmise that they are to be used in some sort of trade with the enemy. Dietrich Bonhoeffer is among them. So are Admiral Canaris and General Oster, the chiefs of the Abwehr, and Gottfried, count of Bismarck, a cousin to both Herbert and Klaus von Bismarck. There is some confusion as to who should be assigned to which van, since one of them is destined for the Buchenwald concentration camp and the other for Flossenbürg, a concentration camp that specializes in executions. As it turns out, Dietrich will go to Buchenwald, Canaris and Oster to Flossenbürg.

February 12. The Reich Security Office, for whatever reason, has decided not to reconstruct the case against Hans Jürgen von Kleist.* He is summarily released from prison, under three stipulations: one, that he refrain from political activities; two, that he do nothing in opposition to the Nazi state; and three, that he speak to no one about his interrogations.

Hans Jürgen has but one thought in mind—to return to Kieckow and lead his family and his villagers in a migration to the west. His fear is that he will be too late; he has heard that south of Pomerania, the Red Army has already seized all of the land east of the Oder River. Unfortunately he is forced to remain in Berlin another two days; he must report to the Prinz Albrechtstrasse prison one more time to obtain all the required documents.

*His file was destroyed, along with others, in the bombing raid that killed Roland Freisler.

FEBRUARY 13. Hans Jürgen spends his first two nights of freedom in the flat of his sister, Spes Stahlberg, which has been severely damaged by bombs. Much of the roof is gone and the windows are virtually all blown out, but it is still habitable. Spes continues her work in Berlin, wherever she can help most, all under the auspices of the German Red Cross. From there Hans Jürgen writes to his family, not sure which members he will ever see again:

> ... Even in these times our God can perform genuine miracles and he does perform them. This has been my experience in the last half year, a hundred, a thousand times. I would not have traded this experience for anything, not even for a peaceful and comfortable life. Even if we should never again see one another in this world, still we can look forward to the priceless reunion with all our loved ones who have gone ahead to our Heavenly Father and who we know are so well taken care of there. . . .
>
> Let our daily prayer be from Matthew 6:10: "Thy kingdom come, Thy will be done, on earth as it is in heaven." Let us also learn to sing and to pray the last verse of "A Mighty Fortress is our God." . . . God be with us all! Hans Jürgen von Kleist-Retzow

This same day, the Pätzig wagon, having surmounted all kinds of obstacles, reaches its destination, a village near Celle, west of Berlin. The wagon's arrival precipitates an emotional Döpke family reunion, for Herr Döpke is already there. Even the two elderly women from Berlin are in good spirits, despite the dumping of their extra trunks along the way. The Wedemeyer children can hardly contain themselves in their eagerness to report on their adventure.

At first the journey wasn't so difficult, as long as they were in Brandenburg, where ancient family ties opened wide the doors of castles and manor houses. After that things were much more uncertain. Some nights Maria was able to parcel out everyone— one or two to a house—in some tiny village. Always she found a barn or a shed for the horses, but never did she sleep anywhere but in the wagon on top of the provisions. When there were no friendly houses, they all slept in the wagon or in some abandoned building. Some days they were forced to travel on the highway, where there was often the danger of strafing from Allied aircraft. American airplanes were particularly effective at this. On more than one occasion, they all had to leap from the wagon into the ditches along the road, or if there was no time, to crawl under the wagon for the minimal protection it provided. When the highway was clogged, they removed themselves to the back roads, where there was little traffic and also more opportunity for shelter at night. Where possible, Maria purchased provisions to conserve what they had, and after two weeks on the road, there is still food in the wagon, for the horses as well as the passengers.

Although the Polish driver and Maria are both exhausted, they are also restless. The driver is anxious to go back to Poland. Maria wants to leave immediately for Berlin. Dietrich is on her mind continuously, and tomorrow is the day on which she is permitted to deliver a parcel to him.

Mother is somewhere between Pätzig and Celle, making her way through front lines and rear lines amid columns of retreating German soldiers and migrating refugees. She travels in turn on foot, in a wagon of friendly strangers, by railroad, even in an SS automobile, and then on foot again. She sleeps in refugee barracks, in a barn still inhabited by cows, on a bench in a railroad station, and on straw in an empty shed.

At Celle, no one has any fear that Ruthchen will not reach her children, least of all Maria. She prevails upon the driver not to leave until Frau von Wedemeyer arrives, for she must go to Berlin immediately.

FEBRUARY 14. Late last night Maria arrived at the Bonhoeffer home after making her way in total darkness from a suburban station. Much of Berlin is now without electricity, and in any case there is a total blackout throughout the city each night. From Dietrich's parents Maria learns that both Klaus Bonhoeffer and Rüdiger Schleicher have been sentenced to death and that Hans von Dohnanyi has been transferred to Prinz Albrechtstrasse, where the others are interned. Hans is now paralyzed from the waist down, the result of ingesting diphtheria germs furnished by Christine, his wife, in the hope of postponing his trial.

Early in the morning, Maria prepares her package for Dietrich—food, cigars, fresh laundry, paper, pencils and a new book to read. At the prison office, she again meets up with her old acquaintance, the prison director. There is bad news, he informs her. A week ago Bonhoeffer was moved from the prison, along with nineteen other prominent prisoners. There were transported in two vans. He doesn't know where they went— maybe Buchenwald, maybe Flossenbürg. There is no way to know.

Worried but undaunted, Maria decides to start with Buchenwald. Fortunately, outside the large cities the railroads are still running relatively undisturbed throughout central and western Germany. She boards a train for the station nearest the camp and arrives before nightfall. It is a long walk to the village of Buchenwald and to the concentration camp beyond, especially with Dietrich's package under her arm.

Managing concentration camps is one of the major responsibilities of the SS, and like all other concentration camps, Buchenwald is run entirely by this military organization. Maria is aware that she wants information and privileges normally not granted, yet she gathers every bit of self-assurance still left in her and enters the Buchenwald camp office with somewhat of a flourish. With disarming grace and confidence, she demands information about her fiancé. Self-assurance is something that comes quite naturally to the Junkers of Old Prussia, and the SS clerk is inclined not to refuse. He brings forth the camp ledger and searches the list of prisoners, whose names are carefully recorded in ink, by date and time of arrival. There is no name that even resembles Dietrich's or any of the others mentioned by the prison director in Berlin.

(One must surmise that the names of the special prisoners brought from Berlin a week earlier were never entered into the camp ledger, for Dietrich was indeed at Buchenwald on the day Maria visited the camp.)

Now the clerk produces a second book—listing those who have died in one way or another, also by date. Together Maria and the clerk check the deaths for the past week. Dietrich's name is not there. Abandoning her decorous behavior, Maria bolts from the camp office and races back toward the railway station, covering the long distance at a half run, only to discover that the last train has left. Totally exhausted, she begs the station superintendent for shelter and spends the night in his tiny hut.

The following day, again by train, she makes her way to the camp at Flossenbürg, and again she prevails upon the SS bureaucrat to review the ledger of prisoners, both living and dead. There is no record of Dietrich Bonhoeffer ever having been at Flossenbürg.

After such an exhausting effort, this disappointment is the last straw for Maria. Contrary to her nature, she gives up entirely—not only on Dietrich, but on life itself. It is all she can do to get on board a train for Berlin, where she can only sit and stare out the window. Presently an SS officer sits down next to her, and guessing that she has been to the Flossenbürg camp, he tries to generate some semblance of pleasant conversation; Maria does not respond. Before long there are planes overhead—bombers—and the train is under attack. "Everyone out," the conductor shouts. Maria does not move from her seat. The SS soldier urges her, even commands her, but Maria refuses to move. At last he picks her up bodily and carries her from the car, throwing her clear of the train. The next instant the car sustains a direct hit.

While Maria recovers from her abrupt collision with the ground and her brush with death, train crews detach the destroyed rail car and repair the damaged tracks. It takes little more than a half-hour since a repair crew complete with the necessary equipment now rides every train in Germany. Such is the efficiency of the German railroad even in these worst of times!

FEBRUARY 16. Hans Jürgen has made his way back to Kieckow. It took all his remaining energy and all the influence he could muster. Civilian rail service no longer exists in Pomerania, but Hans Jürgen somehow managed to find a series of military vehicles that delivered him as far as Gross Tychow. The ensuing reunion is one of highest joy, somehow beyond description.

FEBRUARY 17. An uneasy quiet reigns on the Kleist estate. Periodically one hears the sounds of large artillery fire in the distance. Occasionally planes fly over the landscape, and military trains still make their way across the Kleist lands. Always Hans

Jürgen is making plans. In the crypt of the Kieckow church, two caskets still stand unburied from the last century—Hans Hugo and his wife Charlotte. The decisions that were once so difficult to make now seem trivial. On Hans Jürgen's orders, two graves are dug and the caskets of his grandparents are interred in the Kieckow cemetery, near those of his father and brother.

FEBRUARY 20. Hans Jürgen begins to organize the flight west. All of the villagers from Kieckow and Klein Krössin will join the landowner's family. In this case, *family* means Hans Jürgen, Mieze, Grandmother Ruth, the children's governess and the governess' mother. None of the Kleist children are left at Kieckow; two sons are dead, one is in captivity, and the oldest daughter Ruthi is missing somewhere in Silesia. The two youngest, Elisabeth and Heinrich, are relatively safe in the west, staying with relatives in Mecklenburg.

A large caravan of wagons and horses is being prepared, with food staples and other provisions packaged and loaded. There will be no suitcases on this journey. Hans Jürgen orders that the preparations be made in secrecy, but just as at Pätzig, someone informs the Nazi leader at Gross Tychow of the plans. Now it is impossible; it has been reported that in some cases the caravan leader has been publicly hanged and the vehicles and provisions confiscated. It might be better to cast one's lot with the invaders!

FEBRUARY 26. Ruth von Kleist is rapidly losing her eyesight. Although the letters she receives must be read aloud to her, she continues to answer them with her own pen, aware that they may be intercepted and read by unfriendly eyes. Today she writes to Dita Koch and alludes to their predicament:

> My dear, good Dita, . . . I have thought so often of you and your husband [Werner]. Will my letter ever reach you? We live in a mousetrap here. Behind us and on one side of us are the Russians; on the other side is the [Baltic] sea. My house and the village are full of refugees, and sometimes it is difficult to provide food for everyone. But we have had the greatest joy in that my son recently returned home after seven months, as quietly as your

husband returned in that earlier time. Our thanksgiving is beyond description. At the same time we are in great despair over his oldest daughter—nineteen years old. She was visiting in Silesia when the Russians suddenly broke through. We only know that she was with her friend and they intended to bring out the friend's mother. It has been five and a half weeks and we still have no word.

How God puts us to the test! Four of my relatives, all landowners in the Neumark, have been murdered by the Russians. If we await the same fate, we will take it from God's hand. I am so happy that you have not yet been molested by the enemy. Perhaps the English do not take such severe measures as the Russians. God, however, can build walls around us. In recent times we have experienced so much protective care that would have been unthinkable if we did not put our faith in him.

You have written so dearly, Dita. Sometimes I think about your husband's sermons on Elijah and the ravens and the widow of Zarephath. Yes, we must ask for our faith.

Greet Werner from me. With Dietrich it is worse than ever. Also with his entire family. But that we can speak about only in person. And Eberhard [Bethge] has gone the same way, but it is not supposed to be as dangerous for him. I know nothing new of Martin [Niemöller]. His son is missing in action and his sixteen-year-old daughter died of diphtheria. My youngest daughter escaped at night, on foot, through the Russian lines. They destroyed the manor house and the buildings in the courtyard— her home.

God keep you and Werner and the little one and your mother. In faithful affection, Your R. v. Kl. R.

FEBRUARY 27. At Celle in western Germany, the Wedemeyer clan has increased from three to seven with the recent arrival of the oldest Wedemeyer daughter, Ruth Alice von Bismarck, and her wagonload of refugees. This young mother left Kniephof in Pomerania the same night her mother slipped out from Pätzig.

Ruth Alice's wagonload consists of a driver and five passengers—an elderly friend, Ruth Alice's two small children, their nursemaid, and Ruth Alice herself, pregnant with her third child. They came out of Pomerania north of Stettin, island-hopping across the Oder over little-known bridges. It was Ruth Alice's husband Klaus who arranged it all, even though he is deep in battle on the East Prussian front. His phone call to Lazbo lifted the prohibition against travel, given his wife's condition, and his careful directions to Ruth Alice brought them safely across bridges that were not on the official map. The Kniephof refugees rested a few days with relatives in Mecklenburg, then completed the final lap to Celle. In the meantime, Maria too has arrived back at Celle by way of Berlin after her fruitless journey. There is still no word of Dietrich.

On this day, late in the afternoon, the mother of them all—Ruthchen von Wedemeyer—arrives in Celle in amazingly good spirits after the trials of her month-long journey from Pätzig.

FEBRUARY 28. After breakfast Ruthchen and her family bid farewell to the kindhearted Döpkes—the Pätzig bailiff, his wife, the children and his parents, who have cared for them so tenderly these past days. In a caravan of two wagons, six horses, and fifteen people they head for the home of relatives in Westphalia. There is a hint of spring in the air, and the travelers share a profound sense of thanksgiving. After several hours on the road, the procession comes upon a rural church, and Ruthchen orders the wagons to halt. The entire group disembarks and enters the empty sanctuary. At the altar, Ruthchen offers a short prayer, and they all join in singing an old Lutheran hymn of praise. Never before has any of them sung this hymn with more conviction!

By the Devil Possessed

1945: MARCH 2. Belgard has fallen and Gross Tychow is under siege. At Kieckow the sound of artillery is deafening, and the air is heavy with smoke from the burning buildings of nearby estates. The wagons are once again being made ready, under cover of darkness.

Kieckow and Klein Krössin are to be abandoned. The French prisoners have begged to be taken along. Hans Jürgen concurs. The soldier guarding them has already disappeared.

After the entire caravan is made ready to leave, the inhabitants of the two villages gather in the Kieckow church. Hans Jürgen stands before them and speaks words that have their origin in the Old Testament: "Go out of the land of your forefathers and out of your father's house and away from your circle of kinship into a land that I [God] will show to you."[47]

After the benediction, there is a quiet hustle as the refugees board the wagons, as if every minute is of value. The drivers call out to the horses the commands that have been spoken to horses on these lands for almost six hundred years; by ten o'clock the last wagon rolls out of Kieckow. Only the Russian prisoners, their guard, and the animals remain. In a few hours the guard will disappear and the prisoners will be free.

By 10:30 A.M. the caravan has cleared Klein Krössin, with all of the French prisoners on board.

Grandmother Ruth is in the forward wagon, behind Mieze and next to the mother of the children's governess. This proud matriarch continues to think of herself as the one who must set the example; she must not falter, and she certainly must not look back. In a literal sense this would be difficult, for her eyes have now deteriorated to the point where she can see almost nothing, and perhaps it is just as well.

MARCH 3. It is evening, and Hans Jürgen's caravan, which has traveled thirty kilometers from Kieckow, has been forced to halt. The road ahead is blocked, and for the moment they are an island surrounded by enemy forces. They can do nothing but seek cover in the forest and wait until the advancing columns have passed.

For six days and nights the Kieckow wagons remain in the forest while a thousand tanks and even more personnel and supply transports pass by along the highway. Tens of thousands of men, whole divisions of the Red Army, are moving as fast as the tanks can travel, with nothing whatsoever to stop them. This deadly horde of men and machines is inexorably drawn to Berlin, bent on conquering the capital city of Germany. No one notices the caravan of defenseless wagons hidden among the trees.

MARCH 5. In the dead of night a single horse-drawn wagon moves away from the Lasbeck estate, toward the Oder River and out of Pomerania. Among the passengers are Herbert and Maria von Bismarck and Herbert's mother, Hedwig von Bismarck. Fifty years ago this aged widow held the Bismarck lands together and passed them on intact to her sons Herbert and Gottfried, to be kept for Bismarcks of generations to come. Maria has always had a special bond with her mother-in-law, for it was Hedwig who long ago lent her support to Maria's own mother at Kieckow, encouraging the young widow to hold together the Kleist lands for her son and his descendants.

Behind the wagon the sky is brilliantly lit though the sun will not rise for another two hours. The relentless pounding of artillery fire can be heard from every direction. As Maria looks back toward the light, she can make out seven distinct pillars of flame rising from the Lasbeck courtyard—the manor house, the stalls, the sheds and the granary. Hedwig impulsively throws her arms about her daughter-in-law: "If we should ever come through this, then we have you to thank for it." As dawn breaks, their terror is lessened, and Maria begins to sing the hymn they always sang as children in the Kieckow manor house, at night when the thunder and lightning raged about them:

> Light us to those heavenly spheres,
> Sun of grace, in glory shrouded;
> Lead us through this vale of tears
> To the land where days unclouded,
> Purest joy, and perfect peace
> Never cease.[7]

Gradually the others join in, and soon the entire wagonload is singing this hymn, which has been sung in Pomerania for more than two hundred years. The last Bismarcks from Pomerania will most certainly come through!

MARCH 9. It is finally quiet on the highway near the forest where the Kieckow refugees have sat nearly motionless for six days.

Hans Jürgen decides it is safe for the caravan to return to Kieckow. They have nowhere else to go now, and they will be fortunate to make it back before their provisions are confiscated. As they make their way out to the highway they are immediately intercepted. Hans Jürgen, his wife and his mother are taken into custody by Russian troops. The others are ordered to return home, and on the way they are accosted by another group of Russian soldiers, who appropriate their food and their horses. It is a bedraggled group that at last reaches Kieckow on foot, dragging the wagons behind.

Hans Jürgen and Mieze and Grandmother Ruth are taken to a peasant hut, where they are to be held for the time being. Within hours a Russian general, a division commander no less, arrives to interview Hans Jürgen. He speaks fluent German, and it soon becomes obvious why such a high-ranking interrogator was warranted. The Russians suspect that Hans Jürgen might be General von Kleist. No, that Kleist is no near relative, he assures the general, then goes on to explain that he has just been released after seven months in a Nazi prison, proof that he is an antifascist. The general is sympathetic, but still the three captives must stay put. He orders a guard posted outside the hut, for the protection of those inside, and assures them that for the time being they are safer here than at Kieckow. In this he is probably correct.

MARCH 23. It has been two weeks since Hans Jürgen, Mieze and Grandmother Ruth were interned in the peasant hut somewhere in the Pomeranian countryside. They have been well fed and have not been ill-treated in any way. The presumption is that they are waiting for some key person to arrive, and today this must have happened. Hans Jürgen is taken off to another building and questioned further about his activities. The Russians do not entirely believe his story and suspect that he might be a spy; they decide that he should be sent to Moscow, where the matter will be settled by higher authorities. Hans Jürgen is not even permitted to bid his wife and mother farewell. A Russian major informs them that their husband and son is on his way to Moscow and assures them that he will be well treated.

Mieze and her mother-in-law are now free to go. Slowly they

make their way back to Kieckow, unsure whether life or death awaits them there.

By the end of March, American and British troops have crossed the Rhine River and, like the Russians, have pushed deep into the Fatherland. Still the trials and executions continue in Berlin as if nothing else mattered. Ewald von Kleist of Schmenzin is tried, convicted and sentenced to death. Although Fabian von Schlabrendorff is tried and acquitted, he is not released from prison. Someone higher up, probably Hitler's deputy Heinrich Himmler, wants him executed anyway.

APRIL. The remaining prisoners in the Prinz Albrechtstrasse cellar have all been transferred to the Flossenbürg concentration camp. On April 8 the special prisoner from Buchenwald— Dietrich Bonhoeffer—arrives in a wood-gas-powered Adler automobile. Late that evening, a summary court is conducted within the camp walls. Admiral Canaris, General Oster and Dietrich Bonhoeffer are sentenced to death.

Early in the morning of the ninth, Canaris, Oster and Bonhoeffer are led from their cells by SS guards. Dietrich takes nothing with him, leaving behind the last of his meager possessions—a volume of Plutarch's works and a Bible.

The three condemned men are led to the scaffold and hanged, each in turn. The SS guards who carry out the execution are given an extra ration of liquor for their efforts.

On that same morning, at the Sachsenhausen concentration camp, Dietrich's paralyzed brother-in-law Hans von Dohnanyi is carried to the scaffold and hanged without ever being brought to trial.

In Berlin, Ewald von Kleist is taken from his cell in the prison annex. The guard seems to be in no hurry, and as he is led past Eberhard Bethge's cell, Ewald pauses for a moment to speak to his fellow conspirator: "If you should come out of all this and ever meet my wife and family, tell them that I have made peace with my God. Tell them also that I leave this world in full faith and in peace." A quarter-hour later Ewald indeed leaves this world, by way of the guillotine.

American troops are now closing in on the Flossenbürg camp, and the remaining prisoners must be moved to the concentration camp at Dachau, outside Munich. Upon their arrival, it is discovered that a mistake must have been made. Fabian's name had already been crossed off the list at Flossenbürg, along with those of the three men who were hanged. Was he meant to have been the fourth?

The group of special prisoners is now augmented by a number of well-known men who have spent several years at Dachau, among them Grandmother Ruth's old friend, Pastor Martin Niemöller. They are not at Dachau long before orders arrive from Berlin and the prisoners are on the move again, south to an improvised camp in the foothills of the Alps. With each transfer, their numbers increase as more prisoners and SS guards are added to the caravan. It is rumored that if the Third Reich should fall, Hitler and the remnants of his followers intend to rebuild the regime from a hidden fortress in the mountains; the prisoners wonder among themselves if such a place is perhaps their final destination. But they are not without hope; all along the way they can hear the constant firing of large artillery. The end cannot be far off.

Two hundred kilometers to the north of the caravan, American troops have pushed through to the Czechoslovakian border, east of which all territory is in Russian hands; from the other side, the Red Army has crossed the Oder River and entered the suburbs of Berlin. Just hours before the Russians close in, Klaus Bonhoeffer, Rüdiger Schleicher and several other condemned prisoners are removed from the Lehrterstrasse prison annex and shot to death by the SS. Eberhard Bethge is released.

MAY 4. On this late spring morning, the SS sergeant in charge of the makeshift camp somewhere in the Alps enters the prison barracks smiling unctuously. Removing his cap, he politely wishes the prisoners a good morning. Behind him is another SS sergeant with pencil and paper. They would like a statement from the prisoners to the effect that they have been well treated while in SS custody. The prisoners refuse, and the SS soldiers do not press further; they are in a hurry to leave. When they are gone, the prisoners make their way outside to discover that they are the only ones left in the camp. Fabian von Schlabrendorff and his fellow captives are free! Within a few hours, American troops arrive at the camp. An American general informs the prisoners that they are now under the protection of Allied forces. Fabian can only marvel at the general's clean, pressed uniform— a sharp contrast to his shabby striped convict's garb. After eight months of Nazi incarceration, he has forgotten what it feels like to be so well groomed.

MAY 7. Adolf Hitler is dead, having committed suicide in his Berlin bunker just as the Red Army moved in. His designated successor, Admiral Karl Dönitz, surrenders unconditionally on behalf of Germany and assures the victors that all German forces will be notified of the ceasefire within twenty-four hours.

MAY 8. At midnight the war is over.

JUNE. Fabian von Schlabrendorff has seen a great deal of Italy in the last month. He and his fellow prisoners have been transported by jeep and by air, first to Verona, then to Naples, and finally to Capri. They have been provided with new clothing and plenty of cigarettes, they have been quartered at fine hotels, and they have eaten well; but it turns out they are still not quite free—not until the Americans have fully documented each prisoner. At last it is Fabian's turn to be released and to go back to Germany, with a military escort as far as Wiesbaden. From there he sets out in a borrowed American auto to find his wife and children, who are presumably safe somewhere in the countryside. Driving along a narrow country road a few days later, he slows to make room for a young woman on a bicycle approaching from the other direction. When he is parallel with the rider, he discovers she is Luitgarde, his wife!

All of the lands east of the Oder and Neisse rivers are occupied by the Red Army—East Prussia, Pomerania, the Neumark and Silesia. Grandmother Ruth and Mieze, her faithful daughter-in-law, are living in the Kieckow forester's house with the forester's widow. The forester was seized by the invading troops, no doubt mistaken for a German soldier because he wore a uniform. He died en route to a prison camp in Russia. The Kieckow village is fully inhabited by the villagers who tried to flee and failed, and

Germany, 1945-1990

1 Grossenborau
2 Wartenberg
3 Pätzig
4 Schmenzin
5 Klein Krössin
  and Kieckow
6 Lasbeck and
  Kniephof

by refugees from places as far away as East Prussia and as near as
Schmenzin. They are mostly women and children and old
men—but one by one the younger men return, released from
prisons or work camps somewhere in these conquered lands.
Always Ruth inquires whether any of the returning villagers has
met up with Herbert, her Bismarck son-in-law, or has any knowledge of his whereabouts.

Ruth and Mieze have no idea who is alive and who is dead.
Ruth cannot help but believe that Ruthi, her Kieckow granddaughter, is in heaven. She has not been heard of since
February, when she was caught by the Red Army in Silesia; the
grandmother has seen her in a dream, with the wings of an
angel. Hans Jürgen is supposed to be in Moscow. The Russian
officer assured his wife and mother that he would be well
treated, but with the Russians one can never tell. And what about
Klaus, Ruth Alice's husband, whose unit was encircled in East

Prussia? For those who bear the name Bismarck, it is best not to fall into Russian or Polish hands!

The Kieckow manor house has been stripped of its furnishings, its ancestral paintings, its telephone, its bathtub and toilet and wash basins, its water spigots and whatever else the conquerors felt might be useful back in their own devastated land. The building itself is now a dairy, used for separating the cream, churning the butter and pasteurizing the milk. The upstairs bedrooms are occupied by the commandant, three of his fellow Russians, and a Pole.

Ruth's own house at Klein Krössin is uninhabitable. She has given up the last of her personal treasures to the victors—her wedding ring, her spectacles, and her two ink pens. Still she and all the inhabitants of Kieckow are left in relative peace. The women of Kieckow have not been molested or degraded, and except for the forester, none of the men have been killed. For whatever reason, Kieckow and Klein Krössin stand as the single exception to the reign of terror the Red Army unleashed on German civilians in these eastern lands.

Six hundred cattle, gathered from here and there in the countryside, are now grazing at Kieckow, and they have eaten the meadows and the horse paddocks clean. Only a small plot of land has been planted with crops, but the flowers—especially the roses—are blooming more magnificently than at any time in recent memory.

The few inhabitants not directly involved with the dairy operation, male and female alike, are assigned to work brigades in the vicinity of Gross Tychow and Belgard, where there has been almost total destruction. As a result, the children are without supervision, and although lame and nearly blind, Ruth is teaching a kindergarten and Bible classes in the schoolhouse. With scraps of lumber from here and there, one of the workers has put together makeshift furnishings at night, and from the cellar at Klein Krössin, Ruth has rescued a treasure in which the conquerors showed no interest—the quantities of paper she husbanded for Dietrich's use all through the war years. Just handling the sheets stirs fond memories of better times. And always she wonders, Where is Dietrich? Is he with his Maria or with God?

Four days each week this great-grandmother gathers the children about her in the schoolhouse. She tells them Bible stories, then has them write about them and draw pictures of the Biblical scenes, all with a handful of shared pencils. Yet Great-grandmother Ruth is easily distracted each time a newcomer or an unfamiliar vehicle enters the village. She longs for news of any of her loved ones, and still there is no news at all.

Writing to her daughter Maria at Lasbeck, she pours out her hunger for some sign of life, unaware that Maria and Herbert left Lasbeck over three months ago in the wake of the Russian invasion:

> My Maria, My heart is constantly reaching out to you and I must write again. Nine days ago I wrote you for the first time, but how long does it take a letter to reach its destination? Some people are said to have received letters, but none has yet come here. Our men are gradually returning covered with grime from the work camp at Schneidemühl. Each arrival makes for an entire day of joy. Some have met Jürgen Woedtke [the anti-Nazi colleague of Hans Jürgen and Ewald]. . . . Of Herbert [Bismarck] they know nothing and they have forgotten other names. Thus I hope that your dear husband is at home. Oh, how one longs for some bit of news. . . .
>
> Many of our dear ones we will only see again in Eternity. Without my saying it, you know how I long for all your dear ones, my children, my grandchildren, my great-grandchildren. We have no word from any of them. I grieve over the unproven rumors that are circulating; they tear at my heart. So far we have been mercifully protected from so many dangers that our trust increases. Especially regarding Hans Jürgen. But God alone knows whether he will be preserved. Oh, what has become of Fabian? His fate stings my heart and his beloved wife [Luitgarde] and the children—my godchild Fabian, and the little girls! The anguish over them often affects my whole body. "Quiet, quiet, oh my soul."
>
> I would so like to hear you sing, my Maria. Greet those at Jarchlin and Kniephof [Bismarck estates] a thousand times. Where are Ruth Alice and her three children?

[The number includes the child that should have been born in the meantime.] Klaus must be interned in East Prussia. I heard that he was alive at the ceasefire. And what about Jürgen [Bismarck]? Is he in Germany?

Oh, where is my Ruthchen; where are her children? How does it look at Pätzig? It was in a sector of fierce fighting as was Pyritz. Those who have come through that region paint such a sad picture, but nothing is known of Pätzig.

Spes must have stayed with her work [at the Red Cross in Berlin]. At least that is one quieting thought. But where are her children and her grandchildren [Raba's children]? If only the letters would go through. I would be so thankful for any scrap of news. . . .

Adolf Hitler! Oh how the devil possessed you! Oh how we suffered over these past years because of you and always we knew it would come to an evil end!! And now it is we who must suffer for the delusions of those who hung onto you. God is our only assurance in the great wretchedness of these times. "Thou art with me."

Physically, I am remarkably well. It is only my sight that is worse and I have lost all my spectacles. Recently a woman found a pair on the ground at Klein Krössin and she gave them to me. They help a little. It is a miracle. . . .

I greet you with so much affection, my dear beloved children. Your old Mother

This is the last letter received by anyone from Ruth von Kleist, the last matriarch of Kieckow, written on the last of the Kleist lands in Pomerania.

A Distant Call

1945: SEPTEMBER. In a village near the Thuringian mountains, Ruthchen von Wedemeyer is working as a horticultural apprentice. With her are four of her six surviving children as well as her son-in-law Klaus von Bismarck. One day in July he simply appeared at the door of the place they now call home. Klaus and Ruth Alice's family has grown to three, their latest child, a boy, born shortly after Klaus's return. Ruthchen's daughter Maria is already at Göttingen University, where she will study mathematics. She and other would-be students are working to clean up the war damage and refurbish some of the buildings so that classes can begin again. Only Hans Werner has not yet returned. He was captured in April, but he scribbled a note as he was being transported to a prison camp and threw it from the truck as it passed through the town of Minden. A stranger picked up the message and delivered it by hand to Ruthchen. Each morning she awakens hoping that this will be the day of her son's return.

As for the Bismarcks of Lasbeck—Herbert and Maria, Luitgarde and Fabian, Jürgen, Spes, Gottfried and Fritz Christoph—they are all together and safe in the west, all except Hans Otto, who was killed early in the war.

Spes Stahlberg, her daughter Raba, and Raba's children are safe and well. So are Spes's son Hans Conrad and his bride, whose marriage banquet was interrupted when the Red Army broke through in Silesia. Alla too is no longer in danger; in fact, he is to be married this month!

Even the long-missing Ruthi von Kleist of Kieckow has been released from Russian captivity. She has been reunited with Elisabeth and Heinrich, her younger siblings, and is recovering from her ordeal at the hands of the Red Army. They expect to hear from their brother Konstantin any day, for he was to have sailed from America two weeks ago, in a shipload of German prisoners of war. These four are all that remain of Hans Jürgen's and Mieze's seven children.

Despite the almost universal destruction of Germany and the absence of all but the most basic provisions, a spirit of hope is beginning to spring anew in the daughters of the matriarch of Kieckow. Each time a loved one returns, or there is news that someone dear is still alive, there is great joy and thanksgiving. Yet there are so many who will never return, and there is still total silence when it comes to the whereabouts of their Kieckow brother Hans Jürgen, his wife Mieze, and their mother. While they still pray for the safety of Hans Jürgen and his wife, they cannot help but think that their mother—Grandmother Ruth—must be dead.

SEPTEMBER 8. But Grandmother Ruth is not dead. On this autumn afternoon she is just about to walk to the schoolhouse, where the village children are gathered. Although slowed by advanced age and near blindness, Ruth still feels responsible for teaching these children about God. As she leaves the forester's cottage, however, she stumbles and falls from the stone step; she tries to get up, but the pain is excruciating. The four women in the cottage rush to her side; three of them carry her inside and lift her onto a bed, while the fourth runs to the manor house. One must have the commandant's permission to summon a physician.

Hours later the German physician from Belgard pedals over on his bicycle. He determines that the leg is badly broken; however, he has no supplies or medicines. He immobilizes the leg with a temporary splint and recommends that she be taken to the hospital at Bublitz. Mieze obtains a permit from the Russian commandant, and they are allowed to use a horse and wagon to transport the injured woman to the hospital.

In the American-occupied zone of Germany, Ruth von Wedemeyer, the former mistress of Pätzig, is on her hands and knees gathering vegetables from her garden. She is thankful that she is able to feed her own children and hopeful that her horticultural training will eventually earn her some money. The future looks brighter, and Ruthchen is content.

As she goes about her task, she is suddenly gripped by a feeling of uneasiness. It is as if someone is calling for help, but there is no voice, for she is alone in the garden. Yet clearly it is a call—a distant call—from somewhere in the Russian-occupied lands to the east; but who is calling? Her first thought is of Gerd von Tresckow's fatherless children; or could it be the Pätzig villagers, whose fate still bothers her conscience? She rises from her knees, knowing that she must heed this distant call and go back across the Oder River.

These days no one willingly goes back into the hands of the Russians—and now of the Poles. The eastern third of Poland has been given over to the Soviet Union, along with the three Baltic nations—Lithuania, Latvia and Estonia—and Germany's East Prussia. To compensate for its loss of territory, Poland has received a smaller amount of German land on the west—everything east of the Oder-Neisse line is now part of that nation. Even before the war ended, it was all agreed upon by the leaders of Russia, England and America, at a place called Yalta in the Soviet Crimea. Tens of thousands of Poles who do not wish to live in Russia have been allowed to leave. They have already been transported from the east to the west, and those Germans east of the Oder and Neisse rivers who did not flee when the Red Army invaded are now forced to leave, completely dispossessed. Such is the revenge against the hapless remnants of the nation that inflicted such terror on the conquered Slavs!

Ruthchen's loved ones are in a state of disbelief that she should even think of returning. They are concerned for her safety and fear that she may even be killed; they urge her to consider her children, who will most certainly be orphaned! But Ruthchen has thought it all over. Whoever is calling needs her desperately, otherwise she would not be so distressed by the call.

Berlin is still a capital city of sorts, though it is occupied jointly by the United States, Russia, England and France. Likewise all of Germany is now divided into four zones, each occupied by one of the four victorious powers. There is a Polish Consulate in Berlin where one can obtain a permit to travel into Poland, but for a German to reach Berlin from the west is nearly impossible, for it lies in the middle of the Russian zone. To prevent mass migration to the west, the Russians have sealed their zone; no one is supposed to go in and no one is supposed to come out.

Ruthchen was not deterred from crossing the Russian lines in wartime, nor will she be deterred in this time of so-called peace. Dressed in castoff German army trousers and a light windbreaker, she embarks on her journey with a backpack full of provisions and messages to be delivered if she ever reaches her destination.

SEPTEMBER 17. Traveling by train, Ruthchen makes her way to Hannover, and then to Göttingen, always in the direction of Berlin. She continues to hear the call for help, now louder and more insistent, yet she cannot recognize the source.

SEPTEMBER 19. Overnight Ruthchen has lost her backpack—stolen while she slept with other travelers in a hay shed. She has arrived at the border of the British zone, beyond which the rail-road does not operate. The road is blocked by a large wooden barrier; English soldiers guard this side, and Russians the other. Ruthchen wanders into fields that appear to straddle the border. With nothing to carry, she has an easy time mingling with some peasant workers who are digging potatoes. Joining in their work, she begins to converse with these laborers and learns they are mostly members of a single peasant family who have come across the border from the Russian zone to harvest potatoes on their land, now occupied by the British army. They dare not take any back with them, for the British forbid it.

Throughout the day, Ruthchen digs potatoes and shares her story—the loss of her provisions and her hopes of reaching Berlin. Hearing that she has not eaten since yesterday, the peasant woman opens her bag and cuts off a slice of bread, spreading it with lard and liver sausage. Never has anything tasted quite so good. When evening comes, Ruthchen encour-ages the workers to take along two sacks of potatoes for them-selves; she finds it hard to believe that the British would shoot them for keeping the crops of their own land. At last she con-vinces the women to try, and when the peasants load two of the sacks onto the wagon, she grabs an empty sack and begs them to let her climb on board and crawl inside of it. They are very uneasy, but they agree. Slowly the wagon makes its way back across the border. On the far side, Russian sentries count the pas-sengers and wave them on.

Once again Ruth von Wedemeyer has crossed through Russian lines. Even in her distress over being without provisions, she feels rather proud of herself. Thanking her peasant companions, she heads along the road to the next station, where she finds a train to Nordhausen. She knows that her husband Hans's favorite sister Anne and Anne's husband have taken refuge there. Their reunion is both wonderful and filled with sadness. Anne still mourns her oldest grandson, who was lost before they even left their estate; the boy ran back to the courtyard to feed his cow; the Russians spotted him and shot him down.

SEPTEMBER 23. Ruthchen is making her way ever closer to Berlin, but the trains are now filled to capacity. Obviously many others want to reach the city, for it is the only way out of the Russian zone. Unable to find space in any of the crowded cars, she climbs to the roof of one of them and joins others who are seated there. Before the train leaves, they are all hustled to the ground, but as the cars begin to move, Ruthchen breaks into a run and grabs one of the ladders where the railroad personnel used to ride. Locking her foot and arm behind the metal steps, she manages to hang on until the train reaches the next station, careful to jump off before she is discovered. From station to station, this forty-eight-year-old matron rides in this fashion, each time improving her technique.

At the Gräfenhainichen station, she inquires of an old friend and finds that she is still in the vicinity, though of course not in her castle. Ruthchen decides to rest for a day, and once again there is a reunion, both joyful and sad. Her friend's husband and son are both dead. After a good night's sleep, Ruthchen is off for the final segment of her journey to Berlin. Her friend has provided a backpack, a blanket and a warm jacket to wear under the windbreaker. No traveler ever felt better clothed than this one!

SEPTEMBER 24. Ruthchen at last arrives in Berlin and makes her way on foot to the Bonhoeffer home. The city is like a desert, but Dietrich's parents are still there. They seem far older now, and so much sadder—two sons and two sons-in-law killed by the Nazis so close to the end of the war. In spite of all the old professor's efforts through his many important contacts, not one of them could be saved!

SEPTEMBER 26. For two days Ruthchen has gone from one makeshift office to another in Berlin's bombed-out government buildings, searching through whatever records remain. Everywhere she looks for some trace of the Pätzig villagers and some clue to her Tresckow cousins—the orphaned children of Gerd von Tresckow—that brooding German officer who insisted on declaring loyalty to his dead brother Henning, for which he was so brutally tortured. She cannot escape the calling in her head, which is now so insistent it wouldn't surprise her if some lost loved one suddenly appeared from behind the wall next to her. Still she cannot recognize the caller.

As she makes her way to yet another office at the far end of the corridor, she cannot believe her eyes. Coming toward her is Eberhard Bethge, that dear friend to both Dietrich and Grandmother Ruth. Eberhard looks at Ruthchen as if he has seen a ghost. He has just come from the post office, where he has received a letter from his sister in Köslin, once a major city of Pomerania. It is the first sign of life from her in seven months. But that is not all. The letter also contains the information that Ruth von Kleist is still alive! She has broken her leg and is in the hospital at Bublitz. Ruthchen is overcome with tears of joy and relief, for it is clear to her now who was calling to her. She had truly counted her mother among the dead, and perhaps that is why she was unable to recognize the voice.

SEPTEMBER 28. At 4:00 o'clock in the morning Ruth von Wedemeyer is standing on the station platform in Berlin in the company of one Pan Sukalski, once a Polish landowner and for the past six years a captive worker in Germany. Sukalski is returning to Poland, hoping to reclaim his German-confiscated lands. The two travelers have met through a mutual Berlin friend. Ruthchen's only possessions are her jacket, her backpack, a small amount of German currency and a sturdy carrying belt. If her mother is still alive, she will carry her west out of Poland on her back if necessary.

They board the train to Stettin, which is crowded with Polish civilians—those who chose to return to a Communist Poland after years of imprisonment and forced labor in Germany. The day is cold, and there is no glass in the windows. When the train stops, Ruthchen and her traveling companion find shelter in the stationmaster's house.

SEPTEMBER 29. After another cold, day-long ride, they have almost reached Stettin. When they stop for the night, the Russian soldiers who guard the train tear down the wooden fence surrounding the station and build a giant bonfire on the platform. When they have warmed up a bit, Sukalski and Ruthchen leave the group and find an empty pigsty nearby. Climbing over the manure into the straw, they sleep fitfully until morning.

SEPTEMBER 30. The weary pair finally reaches Stettin. They are in Poland now and they have agreed they will no longer speak German. Sukalski inquires about a train through Pomerania and takes care of buying the tickets. By evening they reach Stargard, so near the Bismarck estates. It is now a control point monitored by Poles, and the signs in the train proclaim, "No Germans allowed." Sukalski manages to pass Ruthchen off as a Pole, but at the next stop they are not as lucky. Ruthchen is recognized as a German and promptly evicted from the train. She is left standing alone in the rain, unable even to thank Pan Sukalski for bringing her so far.

Ruthchen tries to board another car, but is pushed from the door. Desperately she tries again, this time climbing into a freight car, where she comes upon two stretchers in the darkness. The people lying on them are either gravely ill or they are already dead. Ruthchen moves deep into the car, away from the open doors, and at last the train is in motion. Presently there is a light in the freight car, and from a straw bed in the opposite corner, a Pole crawls over to Ruthchen and shines a lantern in her face. She lets out a sudden stream of English words; satisfied that she is not a German, the Pole returns to his bed.

Ruthchen leaves the train at Belgard, the city where she was born and where her father presided as Landrat. It is almost midnight, and she must find a place to sleep. There are still plenty of people on the street, but they speak only Polish. Ruthchen goes from one to another, asking whether there is a pastor's home in the city, but they do not understand. Reaching the residential section, she stops to listen wherever there is a light in the window, but nowhere does she hear a word of German being spoken.

With no place to stay, Ruthchen continues along the highway toward Bublitz. The sky, which was so bright earlier in the evening, has now clouded over, but Ruthchen is confident she is going in the right direction. After nearly an hour, she sees a light in a cottage. Again she creeps to the window and listens, and again she hears only Polish. On to the next village, always toward Bublitz, with its hospital and hopefully Mother Ruth. Just after dawn she finds a cottage with an open window, and to her relief, a woman is speaking German. Ruthchen knocks and asks how far it is to Bublitz. "To Bublitz?" Pointing in the opposite direction, the woman tells her, "You must go through Gross Tychow and circle back." Gross Tychow! Ruthchen is dumbfounded. In her confusion—the cloud-covered sky and her total exhaustion—she has walked not toward the hospital in Bublitz, but rather home toward Kieckow!

The village is Grüssow, home to the sister of Hete von Tresckow, that dear mistress of Wartenberg who was so cruelly killed by the invaders. Ruthchen inquires about this old family friend and is directed to a hut behind the village. Making her way between the houses, through the gardens and across the stream, Ruthchen comes upon a hut with two doors—probably two apartments. As she stands in the gray light of early morning, debating which door to try, one of them swings open and out steps her friend. As Ruthchen rushes to embrace her, the woman claps her hand over her mouth, signaling her to keep silent, and pushes Ruthchen into the house. They hug each other joyously, but then there is sadness as Ruthchen, speaking in whispers, conveys the news that Hete and Jürgen and their son Rüdiger are all dead. Until now, the sister had not known.

Ruthchen is urged to lie down and sleep in her friend's bed, but not before she learns that her error was in fact a blessing—Mother is home at Kieckow! The hospital could do nothing for her; they did not even have plaster for a cast.

OCTOBER 1. At 9:00 A.M., after only a short rest, Ruthchen is impatient to be off. She still has thirty kilometers to go before she has her mother in her arms. Fortified with a hearty breakfast prepared by her hostess, she is on her way again—past Gross Tychow and into Klein Krössin. After months of living amidst utter destruction, which most of Germany has sustained, Ruthchen is amazed at what she finds; the village houses at Klein Krössin are completely undisturbed, a herd of a hundred and fifty young cattle is grazing peacefully in the meadow, and beside it is a field planted with potatoes. She meets with a worker, who informs her that Herr von Kleist is in Russia and that the Frau Landrat—her mother—is at Kieckow, living with her daughter-in-law in the forester's cottage.

On the final stretch to Kieckow, just past the little monument to Ferdinande and the familiar forest, Ruthchen meets a stranger on a bicycle—a nurse from Gross Tychow. The old Frau von Kleist has pneumonia; it is very serious. Without a word of thanks, Ruthchen breaks into a run—past the cattle barns, past the road to the manor house—she even passes the old family coachman with only a wave of her hand. Without slowing, this Kieckow daughter makes straight for the forester's cottage.

There is boundless joy mixed with astonishment as Ruthchen and Mieze embrace one another. "Is it really you? . . . Mother is dying." Hearing these words from her sister-in-law, Ruthchen nearly faints with relief that she is not too late.

Mother has been in and out of a coma for more than two days, but as Ruthchen kneels at her bedside and gently takes her hands, the old woman's head slowly turns to face her. She opens her eyes and gazes at her daughter, but with no sign of recognition. Ruthchen speaks the words which Mieze says will move this grandmother most: "Mother, Fabian is alive."

Grandmother moves her lips to form the words—"is alive." There is a fleeting smile, and the daughter is encouraged.

"Klaus is with us and he is well!" Again there is the hint of a smile. She continues the roll call.

"Ruth Alice has a healthy baby boy; Maria and Herbert are in the west."

Now the dying matriarch actually speaks aloud, softly: "I don't seem to remember anymore; it is all so far away."

Ruthchen does not move nor does she speak; Mieze and the other women also stand motionless. Grandmother Ruth has not spoken so clearly since returning from the hospital. The mother's eyes are fixed on her daughter, and once again she speaks: "And Dietrich, is he alive?"

It is her final question. On hearing the answer, the dying woman's face betrays no pain, nor even sadness. She closes her eyes for the last time, seemingly content that she will soon see him in heaven.

EPILOGUE

Ruth von Kleist was buried in the Kieckow cemetery between her husband Jürgen and her son Konstantin. The Kieckow workers were granted an afternoon off to attend the funeral because, in the words of the Russian commandant, "the Frau Kleist was a great lady." It was the first day of no work in seven months of Russian occupation. Ruthchen begged her sister-in-law Mieze to come along to the west with her and join her own children. Mieze refused; she must not leave without taking along the villagers.

Ruthchen von Wedemeyer made the return trip alone. It took more than two weeks, for she was jailed by the Poles and put to work cleaning and mending the jailers' clothing. But she soon escaped, and by the end of October she was reunited with her children.

In January of 1946, Hans Werner von Wedemeyer was rejoined with his mother. In April Mieze von Kleist was forced to leave Kieckow on a Red Cross train. All the villagers followed soon thereafter. A few weeks after Mieze settled in the west, her son Konstantin arrived from America, where he had been detained all these months. A year later, in January, Mieze received a telegram from Frankfurt an der Oder, a city in what was then East Germany. It contained the following message: "In a few days, with you, Psalm 126."*

A week later Hans Jürgen appeared at the door of Mieze's little cottage, frostbitten and thin, but otherwise well after almost two years in Russian captivity. He had undergone three months of interrogation in Moscow's infamous Lubyanka prison and nineteen months of forced labor in Siberia. But he felt very fortunate; of all the German prisoners he had seen, he was one of the few who were set free.

---

*Psalm 126: ". . . Turn again our captivity, O Jehovah, as the streams in the south. They that sow in tears shall reap in joy."

With the return of Hans Jürgen von Kleist, this family saga comes to an end.

MORE THAN a half century later, all the children of Ruth von Kleist are gone, each having contributed in one way or another to the rebuilding of Germany. Along the way, Hans Jürgen, Maria, and Ruthchen all left fragment memoirs for their children. They wrote of their feudal childhood, the Nazi times, the war, and the final denouement. Hans Jürgen also wrote a loving memoir of his faithful friend and cousin, Ewald of Schmenzin. This memoir later became the major source material for the Bodo Scheurig biography of Ewald entitled *Ewald von Kleist-Schmenzin*.

The last survivor of that generation is Ruth's nephew and godson Friedrich Carl, the count of Zedlitz and Trützschler, who abandoned Grossenborau and Germany before the Second World War. He is long retired in Argentina and has recently begun to write his own memoirs.

Of Ruth's grandchildren who survived the war, four have died in the meantime. Maria von Wedemeyer Weller died in 1977 following a short bout with cancer. After completing her university studies at Göttingen, this granddaughter emigrated to America, where she had an illustrious career, both technically and managerially, in the computer division of Honeywell Inc. In her lifetime she was the highest ranking woman in the corporation. Throughout her life, Maria treasured the few possessions that survived from her earlier life. The oriental rug that graced her Boston home had once protected the parquet floor in the Pätzig manor house, and later covered the Pätzig wagon on its journey west. The few pieces of silver Maria impulsively threw into the wagon also claimed a place of honor in her home. The letters from Dietrich Bonhoeffer were carefully stowed away, and before she died, Maria gave them to the Houghton Library at Harvard University, with the stipulation that they not be opened until the year 2002.

She had also given copies of the letters to her sister Ruth Alice. Recently, these letters, along with a number of surviving letters written by Maria to her fiancé in prison, have been published. They appear in a volume entitled *Love Letters from Cell Ninety-two*.[48] The availability of this correspondence only deepens the reader's insight into the relationship between the increasingly despondent Dietrich and his ever optimistic fiancée Maria.

Maria's sister Christine von Wedemeyer Beshar also emigrated to America, and today she lives in New York. All the other Wedemeyer children are living in Germany—Ruth Alice von Bismarck, Hans Werner, Werburg Doerr and Peter Christian.

Of the many weddings of the children of the Wedemeyer siblings that have taken place in recent years, one is to be noted here. In 1986, the daughter of Werburg Doerr married the grandson of Ursula Bonhoeffer Schleicher. The groom's uncle, Professor Emeritus Eberhard Bethge, performed the ceremony at this marriage of Dietrich Bonhoeffer's grandnephew to the great-granddaughter of Ruth von Kleist.

The recent death of Ruth's oldest granddaughter, Ruth Roberta Stahlberg Ripke-Heckscher, brings to a close a generation of Stahlberg siblings. Raba lived most of her last years in Jerusalem, having converted to Judaism and taken the family name of her Jewish forbears. As a young mother in Nazi Germany, Raba had entered into a brief correspondence with Dietrich Bonhoeffer,[49] and during her last years she maintained that she felt closer to Bonhoeffer in Jerusalem than she had in Germany. Nevertheless, shortly before her death, Raba returned to her homeland and is buried there. Raba's brothers, Alexander and Hans Conrad, both had successful business careers in Germany. Alexander—the handsome Alla, who always claimed to be his grandmother's favorite—wrote his own memoir, which has been published in both German and English.[50]

Ruthi von Kleist, now Ruth de Pourtales, is retired from her position with the World Council of Churches in Geneva, Switzerland. She and her husband live and garden on his ancestral estate in Tannay, Switzerland. After Mieze's death, Hans Jürgen gave to this daughter the black gold-rimmed Stolberg cross, once known to the Kieckow villagers as the kaiser's magic cross. She treasures this family heirloom even as she remembers with sadness that it was never worn by Grandmother Ruth. Ruthi's younger sister Elisabeth Sittig resides in Bremen. Their older brother Konstantin, who would have inherited Kieckow if Hitler had never come to power, also lives in Germany, after spending fourteen years as a Lutheran missionary and pastor in

the black townships of South Africa. Heinrich, the youngest of
the Kieckow Kleists, has recently retired as director of a large
German manufacturing firm, successor to that of old Merton the
Jew. Now, as director of philanthropy for the ancient Order of St.
John, Heinrich travels frequently to Pomorze, Poland. In the
towns and villages that he and his St. John colleagues once called
home, they have established and continue to support a series of
community health clinics.

Luitgarde von Schlabrendorff, the oldest child of Maria and
Herbert von Bismarck, is living in Wiesbaden. Her husband
Fabian died several years ago after an illustrious career as justice
in the Supreme Court of the Federal Republic of Germany. He
also authored two books on the German conspiracy against
Hitler, an effort in which Luitgarde played a major role. Jürgen,
the oldest Bismarck son, returned safely from the war. Spes,
whom Dietrich Bonhoeffer confirmed at Kieckow, married one
of Dietrich's Finkenwalde seminarians, Hans Dietrich Pompe.
Jürgen, Spes and Fritz Christoph all live near Bonn; Gottfried
resides in Switzerland.

And what of the Kleists of Schmenzin? Ewald's widow Alice
and all eight of his children survived the war and reside in
Germany and Switzerland. Ewald's brother and sister-in-law did
not fare as well; both were killed by Russian soldiers when the
Red Army seized their estate. Ewald's aged mother, the Countess
Lili of Kleist, still wearing the somber gray gown of an estate mistress, was killed a few weeks later.

Ewald's daughter Reinhild von Kleist Hausherr lives in Switzerland, not far from Hans Jürgen's daughter Ruth de Pourtales.
These two cousins carry on the deep commitment to each other
that so characterized their fathers' friendship in that earlier,
more dangerous time.

In southeast Poland, in the province of Slansk, lies Borowielke,
once upon a time Grossenborau, the childhood home of Ruth
von Kleist. The stone church and the sturdy brick and stucco
dwellings that once defined the village at Grossenborau have
changed very little over the years, but the manor house is sorely
in need of repair. The stone steps leading from the carriage
stoop to the main entrance have collapsed, and the little family
chapel is in shambles. In the grand entry hall there is nothing

Germany, 1991

1 Grossenborau
2 Wartenberg
3 Pätzig
4 Schmenzin
5 Klein Krössin
  and Kieckow
6 Lasbeck and
  Kniephof

left but the remains of the marble fireplace. The building is no longer occupied. Yet this graceful edifice still dominates the landscape—a lifeless survivor from a time long past.

Far to the north, in Polish Pomorze, lie the old Kleist lands and the village called Kikowo, formerly Kieckow. Unlike most of Poland, it changed very little in the last half century. The old stone roads lined with linden and chestnut and oak and maple trees still carry the traffic through the Byalogard District. The monument to the child Ferdinande, a stone cross along the roadside, stands as it has since 1924.

The Kieckow manor house now has a tin roof, rather than the red tiles of old. The edifice was restuccoed some years ago when Kikowo was a somewhat thriving State Farm under Communism. The manor house once contained clubrooms for the workers, a shop for sundries, a nursery school, and offices for administration. In those years, the large Kikowo agricultural enterprise employed a hundred workers, breadwinners for an entire village. The fall of Communism in Poland, however, meant the end of state control, state subsidies, and a guaranteed market in the East bloc. After several years of a collapsed economy, the area is picking up. An industrialist from south Poland has leased the Kikowo lands from the government and has hired an administrator who understands free market economics. The enterprise operates efficiently with twenty-four employees. Yet there are many mouths to feed in the village. Some of the young men find work in Germany and elsewhere in Poland. Very slowly a modicum of prosperity grows across the land. The manor house is for sale by the Polish government, as are dozens of old German manor houses in the region. As yet there are few buyers.

The old Kleist church was never harmed. The cross above the altar, the only existing replica of the long-gone cross in the kaiser's Charlottenburg crypt, hangs just as it did a hundred years ago in the days of old Hans Hugo von Kleist. And as in earlier times, the priest from Tychowo comes weekly for Mass in this small mission church. The church has been repaired after years of physical neglect, thanks to funds contributed by Heinrich von Kleist. In recognition of the Kleist heritage, a bronze plaque with the Kleist family crest was designed by a local Polish artist and now hangs in the church. It reads: "In memoriam Familie von Kleist-Retzow."

Until recently, the cemetery behind the church was in shambles, having been wantonly destroyed in the early decades after the war. The newer Polish cemetery lies elsewhere. The passion and the pride of Heinrich is the restoration of this old cemetery, an effort that was completed in 1997. A large wooden cross has been erected and is surrounded by a stone wall containing four grave markers unearthed during the construction. One of the surviving markers commemorates the life of Ruth von Kleist's husband Jürgen, who died in 1897. Another is the marker of Ruth's oldest son Konstantin, killed in the First World War: ". . . mit Flügeln wie Adler." The other two markers recall the lives of two villagers out of the hundreds who were buried in the cemetery over a span of two centuries. On a recent spring visit, Heinrich and his son found a bed of his grandmother's favorite blue cilia in bloom.

IN THE FALL of 1997, Mayor Lukiewski of Tychowo, Poland, and Heinrich von Kleist of Germany jointly planted ten young oak trees in the memorial grove that was once dedicated to Uncle Konstantin and the other fourteen young men of Kieckow and Klein Krössin who died in the First World War. Once again, there are fifteen oaks in the memorial circle. The original commemorative stone, still at rest in the overgrown forest, was once again placed at the center of the grove:

"1914–1918, Mit Gott für König und Vaterland"

A memorial plaque was likewise put alongside the stone. Inscribed both in German and in Polish, the plaque reads: "In the year 1920, this grove of centuries-old oak trees was dedicated as the symbolic resting place for those from Kieckow and Klein Krössin who fell at the front in the First World War. In the year 1997, thanks to Polish and German cooperation, the inhabitants of the Tychowo Township have restored the grove as evidence of peace and reconciliation between Poles and Germans."

GUIDE TO RUTH'S FAMILY

The Zedlitz and Trützschler Family
1100-1885

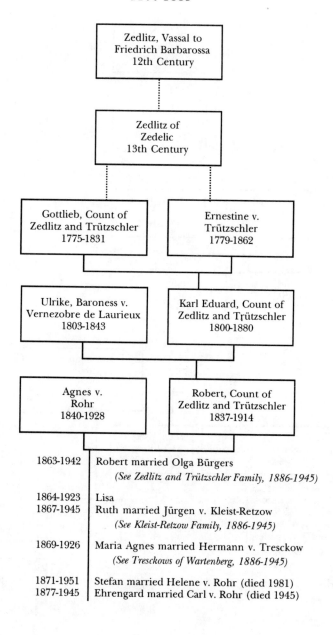

Zedlitz, Vassal to
Friedrich Barbarossa
12th Century

Zedlitz of
Zedelic
13th Century

Gottlieb, Count of
Zedlitz and Trützschler
1775-1831

Ernestine v.
Trützschler
1779-1862

Ulrike, Baroness v.
Vernezobre de Laurieux
1803-1843

Karl Eduard, Count of
Zedlitz and Trützschler
1800-1880

Agnes v.
Rohr
1840-1928

Robert, Count of
Zedlitz and Trützschler
1837-1914

1863-1942	Robert married Olga Bürgers
	(See Zedlitz and Trützschler Family, 1886-1945)
1864-1923	Lisa
1867-1945	Ruth married Jürgen v. Kleist-Retzow
	(See Kleist-Retzow Family, 1886-1945)
1869-1926	Maria Agnes married Hermann v. Tresckow
	(See Tresckows of Wartenberg, 1886-1945)
1871-1951	Stefan married Helene v. Rohr (died 1981)
1877-1945	Ehrengard married Carl v. Rohr (died 1945)

The Kleist Family
1200-1885

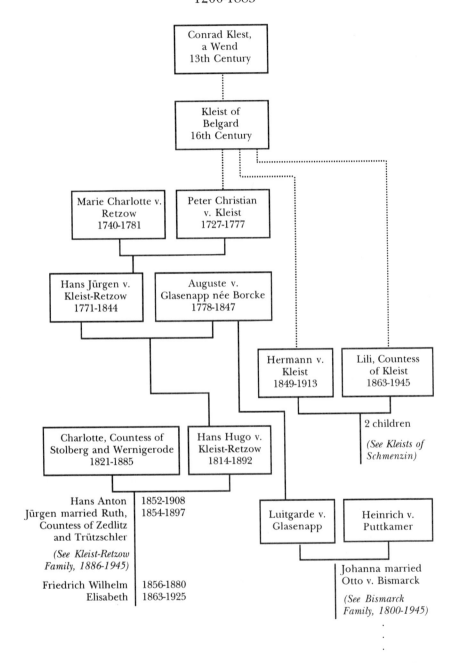

Conrad Klest,
a Wend
13th Century

Kleist of
Belgard
16th Century

Marie Charlotte v.
Retzow
1740-1781

Peter Christian
v. Kleist
1727-1777

Hans Jürgen v.
Kleist-Retzow
1771-1844

Auguste v.
Glasenapp née Borcke
1778-1847

Hermann v.
Kleist
1849-1913

Lili, Countess
of Kleist
1863-1945

2 children

(See Kleists of Schmenzin)

Charlotte, Countess of
Stolberg and Wernigerode
1821-1885

Hans Hugo v.
Kleist-Retzow
1814-1892

Hans Anton
Jürgen married Ruth,
Countess of Zedlitz
and Trützschler

(See Kleist-Retzow Family, 1886-1945)

1852-1908
1854-1897

Luitgarde v.
Glasenapp

Heinrich v.
Puttkamer

Johanna married
Otto v. Bismarck

(See Bismarck Family, 1800-1945)

Friedrich Wilhelm
Elisabeth

1856-1880
1863-1925

The Bismarck Family
1800-1945

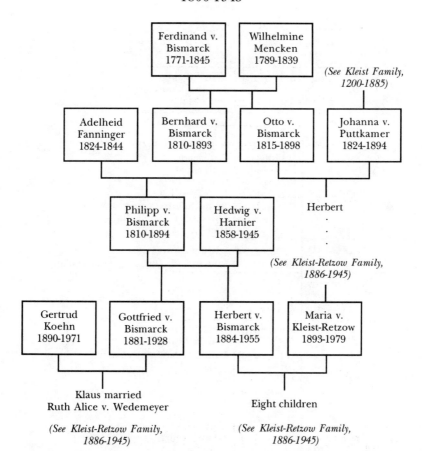

The Kleist-Retzow Family
1886-1945

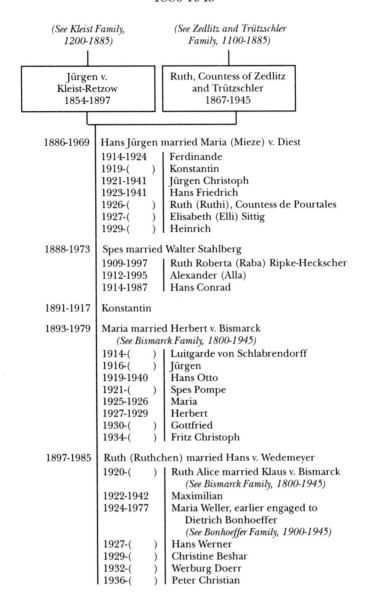

(See Kleist Family, 1200-1885)

(See Zedlitz and Trützschler Family, 1100-1885)

Jürgen v.
Kleist-Retzow
1854-1897

Ruth, Countess of Zedlitz
and Trützschler
1867-1945

1886-1969 | Hans Jürgen married Maria (Mieze) v. Diest

1914-1924	Ferdinande
1919-( )	Konstantin
1921-1941	Jürgen Christoph
1923-1941	Hans Friedrich
1926-( )	Ruth (Ruthi), Countess de Pourtales
1927-( )	Elisabeth (Elli) Sittig
1929-( )	Heinrich

1888-1973 | Spes married Walter Stahlberg

1909-1997	Ruth Roberta (Raba) Ripke-Heckscher
1912-1995	Alexander (Alla)
1914-1987	Hans Conrad

1891-1917 | Konstantin

1893-1979 | Maria married Herbert v. Bismarck
(See Bismarck Family, 1800-1945)

1914-( )	Luitgarde von Schlabrendorff
1916-( )	Jürgen
1919-1940	Hans Otto
1921-( )	Spes Pompe
1925-1926	Maria
1927-1929	Herbert
1930-( )	Gottfried
1934-( )	Fritz Christoph

1897-1985 | Ruth (Ruthchen) married Hans v. Wedemeyer

1920-( )	Ruth Alice married Klaus v. Bismarck
	(See Bismarck Family, 1800-1945)
1922-1942	Maximilian
1924-1977	Maria Weller, earlier engaged to
	Dietrich Bonhoeffer
	(See Bonhoeffer Family, 1900-1945)
1927-( )	Hans Werner
1929-( )	Christine Beshar
1932-( )	Werburg Doerr
1936-( )	Peter Christian

The Kleists of Schmenzin
1886-1945

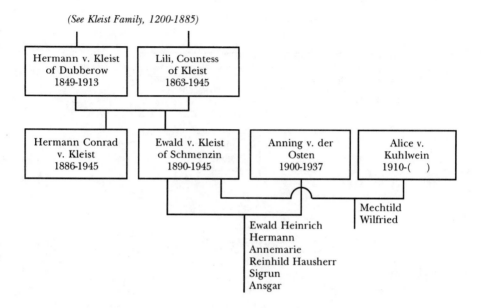

(See Kleist Family, 1200-1885)

Hermann v. Kleist of Dubberow 1849-1913

Lili, Countess of Kleist 1863-1945

Hermann Conrad v. Kleist 1886-1945

Ewald v. Kleist of Schmenzin 1890-1945

Anning v. der Osten 1900-1937

Alice v. Kuhlwein 1910-( )

Ewald Heinrich
Hermann
Annemarie
Reinhild Hausherr
Sigrun
Ansgar

Mechtild
Wilfried

The Tresckows of Wartenberg
1886-1945

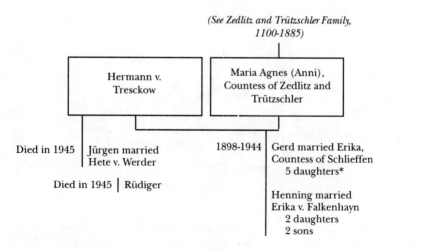

(See Zedlitz and Trützschler Family, 1100-1885)

Hermann v. Tresckow

Maria Agnes (Anni), Countess of Zedlitz and Trützschler

Died in 1945 | Jürgen married Hete v. Werder

Died in 1945 | Rüdiger

1898-1944 | Gerd married Erika, Countess of Schlieffen 5 daughters*

Henning married Erika v. Falkenhayn 2 daughters 2 sons

*Two daughters from Gerd's previous marriage.

The Zedlitz and Trützschler Family
1886-1945

(See Zedlitz and Trützschler Family,
1100-1945)

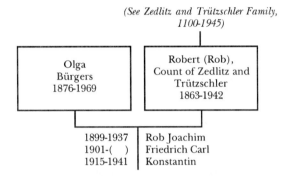

1899-1937	Rob Joachim
1901-( )	Friedrich Carl
1915-1941	Konstantin

The Bonhoeffer Family
1900-1945

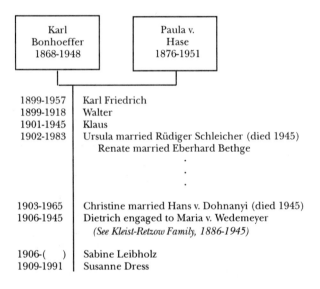

1899-1957	Karl Friedrich
1899-1918	Walter
1901-1945	Klaus
1902-1983	Ursula married Rüdiger Schleicher (died 1945)
	Renate married Eberhard Bethge
	.
	.
	.
1903-1965	Christine married Hans v. Dohnanyi (died 1945)
1906-1945	Dietrich engaged to Maria v. Wedemeyer
	(See Kleist-Retzow Family, 1886-1945)
1906-( )	Sabine Leibholz
1909-1991	Susanne Dress

NOTES

1. Since 1945, the Humboldt University.
2. *Kürassiere.*
3. The estate, or *Gut*, was known as *Niedergrossenborau*. For ease of reading, the *Nieder* ("lower") has been dropped.
4. *Regierungspräsident.*
5. More formally, "Herr *Konsistorialrat* Geisler."
6. *"Reichsfeinde,"* Gall, Lothar, *Bismarck, Der weisse Revolutionär,* Ullstein Sachbuch Edition, pp. 537 and 590. The issue was the sovereignty of Prussia vis-à-vis the German Reich.
7. *"Morgenglanz der Ewigkeit,"* translated: "Come, Thou Bright and Morning Star."
8. *"Nun danket alle Gott/Mit Herzen, Mund und Händen . . ."*
9. *"Treue bis zum Tod."*
10. *"Der alte Barbarossa"* by Friedrich Rückert, freely translated.
11. *Ein Krautjunker.*
12. *"Sturm und Drang."*
13. *Mutterchen.*
14. Robert Graf v. Zedlitz-Trützschler, *Zwölf Jahre am Deutschen Kaiserhof.*
15. Carl Schweitzer und Ruth v. Kleist-Retzow, *Die Soziale Krisis und die Verantwortung des Gutsbesitzes.*
16. Adolf Hitler, *Mein Kampf*, p. 152.
17. Ibid., p. 118.
18. Ibid., p. 180.
19. Ibid., p. 185.
20. Ibid., p. 302.
21. Ibid., p. 303.
22. Ibid., p. 306.
23. Ibid., p. 113.
24. Ibid., pp. 246-247.
25. Stefan and Helene (von Rohr), count and countess of Zedlitz and Trützschler.
26. Ehrengard (von Zedlitz-Trützschler) and Carl von Rohr.
27. Freely translated from *"Wenn das Judenblut vom Messer spritzt, dann geht es nochmal so gut."*
28. Interview with Ruth Stahlberg Heckscher, *Jerusalem Post,* June 8, 1989.
29. Ewald v. Kleist-Schmenzin, *Selbsterlebte wichtige Begebenheiten aus den Jahren 1933 und 1934*, written in 1934.
30. In German, *Hitlerjugend* and *Bund deutscher Mädchen*, or *BDM*.
31. Eberhard Bethge, *Dietrich Bonhoeffer*, p. 193.

32. *Bruderrat.*

33. Dietrich Bonhoeffer, *Gesammelte Schriften,* Vol. 4.

34. *"Lobe den Herren."*

35. Eberhard Bethge, *Dietrich Bonhoeffer,* p. 549.

36. Ibid., pp. 556-560.

37. Andrei Russinov, *Auf der Suche Nach Russland.*

38. *Landerziehungsheim.*

39. Fabian von Schlabrendorff, *The Secret War Against Hitler,* p. 277.

40. Ibid, pp. 294-5.

41. Anthony Brown, *Bodyguard of Lies,* p. 168.

42. Fabian von Schlabrendorff, *The Secret War Against Hitler,* pp. 312-3.

43. Bodo Scheurig, *Ewald von Kleist-Schmenzin,* p. 284.

44. Translated by Maria von Wedemeyer-Weller, *The Other Letters from Prison.*

45. Eberhard Bethge, *Dietrich Bonhoeffer,* p. 814.

46. Bodo Scheurig, *Ewald von Kleist-Schmenzin,* p. 195.

47. Genesis XII:1.

48. *Love Letters from Cell Ninety-two: The Correspondence Between Dietrich Bonhoeffer and Maria von Wedemeyer, 1943–45.* Edited by Ruth Alice von Bismarck and Ulrich Kabitz, published in 1995 by Abingdon Press, Nashville.

49. Jane Pejsa, "Dietrich Bonhoeffer's Letter to an Unknown Woman."

50. Alexander Stahlberg, *Die verdammte Pflicht, Erinnerungen 1932 bis 1945,* published in 1987 by Ullstein, Berlin; *Bounden Duty: The Memoirs of a German Officer, 1932-45,* published in 1990 by Maxwell, London.

BIBLIOGRAPHY

PUBLISHED SOURCES

The following sources were used either to gain general background information or to extract significant details that were then incorporated into the story of Ruth von Kleist-Retzow.

Berneuchener Konferenz. *Das Berneuchener Buch.* Schwerin im Mecklenburg, Germany: Verlag Friedrich Bahn, 1926.

Bethge, Eberhard. *Costly Grace, An Illustrated Introduction to Dietrich Bonhoeffer.* New York: Harper & Row, 1979.

Bethge, Eberhard and Renate, and Gremmels, Christian. *Dietrich Bonhoeffer: A Life in Pictures.* Translated by John Bowden. Philadelphia: Fortress Press, 1986.

Bethge, Eberhard. *Dietrich Bonhoeffer, Man of Vision - Man of Courage.* Translation editor, Edwin Robertson. New York: Harper & Row, 1970.

Bonhoeffer, Dietrich. *Fiction From Prison.* Edited by Renate and Eberhard Bethge, translated by Ursula Hoffmann. Philadelphia: Fortress Press, 1981.

Bonhoeffer, Dietrich. *Gesammelte Schriften,* Vols. 2 and 4. Edited by Eberhard Bethge. Munich: Chr. Kaiser Verlag, 1961.

Bonhoeffer, Dietrich. *Letters and Papers From Prison.* Edited by Eberhard Bethge. London: SCM Press, 1967.

Brown, Anthony Cave. *Bodyguard of Lies.* New York: Harper & Row, 1975.

Colvin, Ian. *Master Spy.* New York: McGraw-Hill, 1952.

Cronau, Curt. *Hinter-Pommern.* Stettin, Germany: Verlag M.Bauchwitz, 1929.

Deutsch, Harold C. *Hitler and His Generals; The Hidden Crisis January-June 1938.* Minneapolis: University of Minnesota Press, 1974.

Deutsch, Harold C. *The Conspiracy Against Hitler in the Twilight War.* Minneapolis: University of Minnesota Press, 1968.

de Diesbach, Ghislain. *Secrets of the Gotha.* London: Chapman and Hall Ltd., 1967.

Eichendorff, Josef Freiherr von. *Erzählungen: Der Adel und die Revolution.* Zurich: Manesse Verlag, 1955.

Encyclopaedia Brittanica, various volumes. Chicago: William Benton, 1970.

Eyck, Erich. *Bismarck,* Vol. 1. Zurich: Eugen Rentsch Verlag, Erlenbach-Zurich, 1941.

Gall, Lothar. *Bismarck der weisse Revolutionär.* Frankfurt am Main, Germany: Propylaeen, 1980.

Görlitz, Walter. *Die Junker: Adel und Bauer im deutschen Osten.* Glücksburg am Ostsee, Germany: Verlag Starke, 1956.

Hitler, Adolf. *Mein Kampf.* Verlag Frz. Eher Nachf. GmbH., 1925 and 1927; translated by Ralph Manheim. Boston: Houghton Mifflin Company, 1971.

Kaps, Johannes. *The Tragedy of Silesia 1945-46.* Translated by Gladys H. Hartinger. Munich: Verlag Christ Unterwegs, 1952.

Kleist-Retzow, Ruth von. *Konstantin von Kleist-Retzow: Ein Lebensbild.* Bielefeld, Germany: Anstalt Bethel, 1935.

Koch, Werner. *Sollen wir K. weiter beobachten?* Stuttgart, Germany: Im Radius-Verlag, 1982.

Kramarz, Joachim. *Stauffenberg.* Translated from the German by R.H. Barry. New York: The Macmillan Company, 1967.

Krockow, Christian Graf von. *Die Reise nach Pommern, Bericht aus einem verschwiegenen Land.* Stuttgart, Germany: Deutsche Verlags-Anstalt GmbH, 1985.

Lehndorff, Hans von. *East Prussian Diary.* London: Oswald Wolff, 1963.

Lühe, Irmgard von der. *Elisabeth von Thadden ein Schicksal unserer Zeit.* Düsseldorf, Germany: Eugen Diederichs Verlag, 1966.

Meyer, Arnold Oskar. "Hans von Kleist-Retzow." Source and date not available.

Michaelis, Georg. *Für Staat und Volk, ein Lebensgeschichte.* Berlin: Furche-Verlag, 1922.

Muncy, Lysbeth Walker. *The Junker in the Prussian Administration Under William II, 1888-1914.* Providence, Rhode Island: Brown University, 1944.

Muralt, Leonhard von. *Bismarcks Verantwortlichkeit.* Frankfurt: Musterschmidt Göttingen, 1955.

Nichols, J. Alden. *Germany After Bismarck, The Caprivi Era 1890-1894.* Cambridge, Massachusetts: Harvard University Press, 1958.

Niekisch, Ernst. *Erinnerungen eines deutschen Revolutionärs.* Köln, Germany: Kiepeheuer & Witsch, 1958-1974.

Paine, Lauran. *German Military Intelligence in World War II.* New York: Stein and Day, 1984.

Papen, Franz von. *Memoirs.* Translated by Brian Connell. New York: E.P. Dutton & Company, Inc., 1953.

Petersdorff, Herman von. *Kleist-Retzow: Ein Lebensbild.* Stuttgart und Berlin, Germany: I.G. Cotta Buchhandlung Nachfolger, 1907.

Rad, Ursula von, ed. *Elisabeth-von-Thadden-Schule Heidelberg-Wieblingen, Annäherung an eine 60-Jährige Schul-Geschichte.* Heidelberg, Germany: Wieblingen, 1987.

Ramm, Agatha. *Germany 1789-1919, A Political History.* London: Methuen & Co Ltd., 1967.

Ryder, A.J. *Twentieth-Century Germany: From Bismarck to Brandt.* New York: Columbia University Press, 1973.

Scheurig, Bodo. *Ewald von Kleist-Schmenzin ein Konservativer gegen Hitler.* Hamburg, Germany: Gerhard Stalling Verlag, 1968.

Scheurig, Bodo. *Henning von Tresckow eine Biographie.* Oldenburg, Germany: Gerhard Stalling Verlag, 1973.

Schimmelpfennig, M. *Robert Graf von Zedlitz und Trützschler.* Breslau, Germany: R. Nischkowsky, 1922.

Schlabrendorff, Fabian von. *Begegnungen in fünf Jahrzehnten.* Tübingen, Germany: Verlag Hermann Leins GmbH. & Co., 1979.

Schlabrendorff, Fabian von. *The Secret War Against Hitler.* London: Hodder and Stoughton, 1966.

Schlabrendorff, Fabian von. *They Almost Killed Hitler.* New York: The Macmillan Co., 1947.

Scholz, Albert A. *Silesia Yesterday & Today.* The Hague, Netherlands: Martinus Nijhoff, 1964.

Schweitzer, Carl, und Kleist-Retzow, Ruth von. *Die Soziale Krisis und die Verantwortung des Gutsbesitzes.* Mecklenburg, Germany: Lehmann & Bernhard Verlagsbuch-druckerei, Schönberg, 1925.

Spruth, Herbert. *Bibliographie für Pommern.* Drucke und Handschriften, Band 2. Neustadt an der Aisch, Germany: Verlag Degener & Co., 1965.

Wedemeyer-Weller, Maria von. "The Other Letters from Prison," *Union Seminary Quarterly Review,* Vol. XXIII, No.1, pp. 23-29. New York: Fall 1967.

Zedlitz-Trützschler, Robert Graf von. *Zwölf Jahre am Deutschen Kaiserhof.* Stuttgart, Germany: Deutsche Verlags-Anstalt, 1924.

Zedlitz-Trützschler, Count Robert von. *Twelve Years at the Imperial German Court.* Translation of the book cited above by Alfred Kalisch. New York: George H. Doran Company, 1924.

Zimmermann, Wolf Dieter, and Smith, Ronald Gregor, eds. *I Knew Dietrich Bonhoeffer.* Translated from the German by Käthe Gregor Smith. London: Collins, 1966.

Zucker, Stanley. *Ludwig Bamberger, German Liberal Politician and Social Critic 1899-1923.* Pittsburgh: University of Pittsburgh Press, 1975.

UNPUBLISHED SOURCES

Personal Interviews

Bethge, Eberhard, and Renate née Schleicher, August 29, 1986, in Wachtberg-Villiprott, Germany.

Bismarck, Ruth Alice née Wedemeyer, and Klaus von, September 23, 1985, May 29 and 30, 1986, in Munich, Germany.

Hausherr, Reinhild née Kleist-Schmenzin, May 25, 1987, in Bern, Switzerland.

Heckscher, Ruth Roberta née Stahlberg, August 31, 1986, in Hannover, Germany.

Kleist-Retzow, Heinrich von, May 23, 1987, in Cologne, Germany.

Kleist-Retzow, Konstantin von, August 31, 1986, in Rinteln, Germany.

Pompe, Spes née Bismarck, May 28 and September 8, 1986, in Wiesbaden, Germany.

de Pourtales, Countess Ruth née Kleist-Retzow, May 24 and 25, 1987, in Tannay, Switzerland.

Schlabrendorff, Luitgarde née Bismarck von, May 28 and September 8, 1986, in Wiesbaden, Germany.

Stahlberg, Alexander, September 1, 1986, in Berlin, Germany.

Wedemeyer, Hans Werner von, June 1, 1986, in Baden-Baden, Germany.

Wedemeyer-Weller, Maria von, transcription of an interview with Mary Glazener in 1976 at Lincoln, Massachusetts.

Zedlitz-Trützschler, Count Friedrich Carl von, May 2, 1987, by telephone from New York, and May 2, 1989, at luncheon in Rochester, Minnesota.

Zimmermann, Wolf Dieter, August 26, 1986, in St. Paul, Minnesota.

Copies of Original Letters

Herbert von Bismarck to Dietrich Bonhoeffer, dated June 24, 1940.

Spes von Bismarck (Pompe) to Dietrich Bonhoeffer, dated February 2, 1939.

Dietrich Bonhoeffer to Ruth von Wedemeyer née Kleist-Retzow, dated August 25, 1942, and April 10, 1944.

Hans Friedrich von Kleist-Retzow to Dietrich Bonhoeffer, dated February 2, 1939.

Hans Jürgen von Kleist-Retzow to:
> Ruth von Wedemeyer née Kleist-Retzow, dated February 27, 1945;
> Children and siblings, dated February 13, 1945.

Maria von Kleist-Retzow née Diest to:
> Dietrich Bonhoeffer, dated January 12, 1939;
> Frau Schlicht, dated March 12, 1947.

Ruth von Kleist-Retzow to:
> Eberhard Bethge, dated December 12, 1937; May 21, June 8, August 21 and September 14, 1938; February 7, 1939; June 13, July 16 and August 23, 1940; August 24 and 26, 1941; February 17, April 8 and September 6, 1942.
> Maria von Bismarck née Kleist-Retzow (her daughter), dated June 19, 1945.
> Dietrich Bonhoeffer, dated January 7, 1938; May 31, 1939; June 23, 1940; February 15, October 30, December 12 and December 30, 1941; February 13 and April 24, 1942; January 21 and February 5, 1943.

Paula Bonhoeffer, Dietrich's mother, dated September 17, 1942.

Frau Häger, dated June 7, 1945.

Anna von Harnier, dated March 24, 1913.

Dita Koch née Stockmann, dated November 20, November 27 and December 28, 1936; February 24, March 3, April 17, May 20, July 7, August 19, September 11 and November 8, 1937; January 2, February 22, February 25, March 4, March 19, March 29, and December 11, 1938; May 17, 1940; June 3 and November 4, 1943; August 5 and October 11, 1944.

Werner Koch, dated December 19, 1936, and December 8, 1938.

Pastor Onnasch, dated January 2, 1938.

Renate Schleicher (Bethge), dated February 24, 1943, and February 7, 1944.

Ursula Schleicher (Renate's mother and Dietrich's sister), dated January 16, 1943.

Grandchildren, relatives and friends, dated May 28, 1940.

Renate Schleicher (Bethge) to Ursula and Rüdiger Schleicher, her parents, dated July 18 and August 25, 1941.

Maria von Wedemeyer (Weller) to:
  Eberhard Bethge, dated March 19, 1944;
  Dietrich Bonhoeffer, dated March 26, 1943;
  Paula Bonhoeffer, dated May 24, July 23 and August 4, 1943, February 7, 1944, and March 27, 1945.
Max von Wedemeyer to Dietrich Bonhoeffer, dated February 2, 1939.

Other Unpublished Papers

Bismarck, Maria née Kleist-Retzow von, memoirs, undated.
Bismarck, Maria née Kleist-Retzow von, "Morgenglanz der Ewigkeit," undated.
Kleist-Retzow, Hans Jürgen von, "Erinnerungen an Hans von Wedemeyer, Freund und Schwager," undated.
Kleist-Retzow, Konstantin von, "Meine Mutter, aus meiner Erinnerung: Maria von Kleist-Retzow geb. von Diest," 1987.
Kleist-Retzow, Ruth von, "Warum soll ich in der Bibel lesen? Ein Wort an meine lieben Enkel, alle Patenkinder und an die Urenkel," 1938.
Kleist-Retzow, Ruth von, "Meine Ehe," undated.
Kleist-Retzow, Ruth von, "Karl Eduard Graf von Zedlitz-Trützschler," undated.
Stolberg-Wernigerode, Konstantin Graf zu, "Eindrücke und Erfahrungen aus meinem amtlichen Leben," undated.
Wedemeyer, Hans Werner von, "Preussen—ist tot?" speech given January 3, 1983, in Baden-Baden, Germany.
Wedemeyer, Ruth née Kleist-Retzow von, "Bericht über Pätzigs Untergang und Flucht Januar 1945," Drölitz, Germany, February 1945.
Wedemeyer, Ruth née Kleist-Retzow von, "Bericht über meine Reise nach Kieckow Kreis Belgard Pommern vom 18.9.1945 bis 27.10.1945," December 1970.
Wedemeyer, Ruth née Kleist-Retzow von, "Hans von Wedemeyer: Erinnerungen aus seinem Leben," Gernsbach, Germany, 1965.
Zedlitz-Trützschler, Helene Gräfin von, "Das Leben meines Grossvaters: Robert Graf Zedlitz-Trützschler," Schweidnitz, Germany, 1934.
Zedlitz-Trützschler, Helene Gräfin von, family tree, undated.

INDEX

Note: For Ruth von Kleist and her immediate family—husband, children, and their spouses—only first and last pages of citations are recorded here.

OTHER BOOKS BY JANE PEJSA

Available through Kenwood Publishing

• *The Molineux Affair*	Soft cover, 240 pages	$12.95
• *Matriarch of Conspiracy: Ruth von Kleist 1867–1945*	German-language hard cover	$32.00
• *To Pomerania in Search of Dietrich Bonhoeffer: A Traveler's Companion and Guide,* Second Expanded Edition	Soft cover, 70 pages	$7.50
• *Gratia Countryman: Her Life, Her Loves and Her Library*	Soft cover, 340 pages	$14.95
• *Romanoff, Prince of Rogues: The Life and Times of a Hollywood Icon*	Hard cover, 220 pages	$22.95

All books may be ordered through your bookstore or directly from Kenwood Publishing, 2120 Kenwood Parkway, Minneapolis, MN 55405-2326. Minnesota residents add 6.5% sales tax. Add $3.00 shipping for a single book; add $1.00 for each subsequent book in the order. Your personal check payable to Kenwood Publishing is welcome. By E-mail: Pejsa@sprintmail.com. We accept the following credit cards: American Express, Discover/Novus, Mastercard, VISA. Specify credit card number and expiration date.